The Power of Imagination:
The Neville Goddard Treasury

Neville Goddard

GRAPEVINE INDIA

Published by

GRAPEVINE INDIA PUBLISHERS PVT LTD

www.grapevineindia.com
Delhi | Mumbai
email: grapevineindiapublishers@gmail.com

Ordering Information:
Quantity sales: Special discounts are available on quantity
purchases by corporations, associations, and others.
For details, reach out to the publisher.

First published by Grapevine India 2022
Copyright © Grapevine 2022
All rights reserved

CONTENTS

AWAKENED IMAGINATION

THE SEARCH

FEELING IS THE SECRET

FREEDOM FOR ALL

OUT OF THIS WORLD

POWER OF AWARENESS

YOUR FAITH IS YOUR FORTUNE

AT YOUR COMMAND

SEEDTIME AND HARVEST

PRAYER: THE ART OF BELIEVING

Awakened Imagination

CHAPTER ONE
WHO IS YOUR IMAGINATION?

I rest not from my great task To open the Eternal Worlds, to open the immortal Eyes Of Man inwards into the Worlds of Thought: into Eternity Ever expanding in the Bosom of God, the Human Imagination. - Blake, Jerusalem 5:18-20

CERTAIN WORDS in the course of long use gather so many strange connotations that they almost cease to mean anything at all. Such a word is imagination. This word is made to serve all manner of ideas, some of them directly opposed to one another. Fancy, thought, hallucination, suspicion: indeed, so wide is its use and so varied its meanings, the word imagination has no status nor fixed significance.

For example, we ask a man to "use his imagination", meaning that his present outlook is too restricted and therefore not equal to the task. In the next breath, we tell him that his ideas are "pure imagination", thereby implying that his ideas are unsound. We speak of a jealous or suspicious person as a "victim of his own imagination", meaning that his thoughts are untrue. A minute later we pay a man the highest tribute by describing him as a "man of imagination".

Thus the word imagination has no definite meaning. Even the dictionary gives us no help. It defines imagination as (1) the picturing power or act of the mind, the constructive or creative principle; (2) a phantasm; (3) an irrational notion or belief; (4) planning, plotting or scheming as involving mental construction.

I identify the central figure of the Gospels with human imagination, the power which makes the forgiveness of sins, the achievement of our goals, inevitable.

All things were made by Him; and without Him was not anything made that was made. [John 1:3]

There is only one thing in the world, Imagination, and all our deformations of it.

He is despised and rejected of men; a man of sorrows, and acquainted with grief. [Isaiah 53:3]

Imagination is the very gateway of reality.

"Man", said Blake, "is either the ark of God or a phantom of the earth and of the water". "Naturally he is only a natural organ subject to Sense". "The Eternal Body of Man is The Imagination: that is God himself, The Divine Body. [yod, shin, ayin; from right to the left]: Jesus: we are His Members".

I know of no greater and truer definition of the Imagination than that of Blake. By imagination we have the power to be anything we desire to be.

Through imagination, we disarm and transform the violence of the world. Our most intimate as well as our most casual relationships become imaginative, as we awaken to "the mystery hid from the ages" [Colossians 1:26], that Christ in us is our imagination.

We then realize that only as we live by imagination can we truly be said to live at all.

I want this book to be the simplest, clearest, frankest work I have the power to make it, that I may encourage you to function imaginatively, that you may open your "Immortal Eyes inwards into the Worlds of Thought" [William Blake], where you behold every desire of your heart as ripe grain "white already to harvest" [John 4:35].

I am come that they might have life, and that they might have it more abundantly. [John 10:10]

The abundant life that Christ promised us is ours to experience now, but not until we have the sense of Christ as our imagination can we experience it.

The mystery hid from the ages… Christ in you, the hope of glory, [Colossians 1:26,27,] is your imagination.

This is the mystery which I am ever striving to realize more keenly myself and to urge upon others.

Imagination is our redeemer, "the Lord from Heaven" born of man but not begotten of man [The Nicene-Constantinopolitan Creed or the Symbol of Faith, 325/381 A.D.].

Every man is Mary and birth to Christ must give.

If the story of the immaculate conception and birth of Christ appears irrational to man, it is only because it is misread as biography, history, and cosmology, and the modern explorers of the imagination do not help by calling It the unconscious or subconscious mind.

Imagination's birth and growth is the gradual transition from a God of tradition to a God of experience. If the birth of Christ in man seems slow, it is only because man is unwilling to let go the comfortable but false anchorage of tradition.

When imagination is discovered as the first principle of religion, the stone of literal understanding will have felt the rod of Moses and, like the rock of Zion [Isaiah 28:16; Romans 9:33], issue forth the water of psychological meaning to quench the thirst of humanity; and all who take the proffered cup and live a life according to this truth will transform the water of psychological meaning into the wine of forgiveness. Then, like the good Samaritan [Luke 10:33-35], they will pour it on the wounds of all.

The Son of God is not to be found in history, nor in any external form. He can only be found as the imagination of him in whom His presence becomes manifest.

O, would thy heart but be a manger for His birth! God would once more become a child on earth. [Angelus Silesius, a 17th century poet]

Man is the garden in which this only-begotten Son of God sleeps. He awakens this Son by lifting his imagination up to heaven and clothing men in godlike stature. We must go on imagining better than the best we know.

Man in the moment of his awakening to the imaginative life must meet the test of Sonship.

"Father, reveal Thy Son in me" [James Montgomery] and "It pleased God to reveal His Son in me".

[Galatians 1:15,16]

The supreme test of Sonship is the forgiveness of sin. The test that your imagination is Christ Jesus, the Son of God, is your ability to forgive sin. Sin means missing one's mark in life, falling short of one's ideal, failing to achieve one's aim. Forgiveness means identification of man with his ideal or aim in life. This is the work of awakened imagination, the supreme work, for it tests man's ability to enter into and partake of the nature of his opposite.

Let the weak man say, I am strong. [Joel 3:10]

Reasonably, this is impossible. Only awakened imagination can enter into and partake of the nature of its opposite.

This conception of Christ Jesus as human imagination raises these fundamental questions: Is imagination a power sufficient, not merely to enable me to assume that I am strong, but is it also of itself capable of executing the idea?

Suppose that I desire to be in some other place or situation. Could I, by imagining myself into such a state and place, bring about their physical realization? Suppose I could not afford the journey and suppose my present social and financial status oppose the idea that I want to realize. Would imagination be sufficient of itself to incarnate these desires? Does imagination comprehend reason? By reason, I mean deductions from the observations of the senses.

Does it recognize the external world of facts? In the practical way of everyday life is imagination a complete guide to behaviour?

Suppose I am capable of acting with continuous imagination, that is, suppose I am capable of sustaining the feeling of my wish fulfilled, will my assumption harden into fact?

And, if it does harden into fact, shall I on reflection find that my actions through the period of incubation have been reasonable? Is my imagination a power sufficient, not merely to assume the feeling of the wish fulfilled, but is it also of itself capable of incarnating the idea?

After assuming that I am already what I want to be, must I continually guide myself by reasonable ideas and actions in order to bring about the fulfillment of my assumption?

Experience has convinced me that an assumption, though false, if persisted in, will harden into fact, that continuous imagination is sufficient for all things, and all my reasonable plans and actions will never make up for my lack of continuous imagination.

Is it not true that the teachings of the Gospels can only be received in terms of faith and that the Son of God is constantly looking for signs of faith in people – that is, faith in their own imagination?

Is not the promise Believe that ye receive and ye shall receive, [Mark 11:24,] the same as "Imagine that you are and you shall be"? Was it not an imaginary state in which Moses

"Endured, as seeing Him who is invisible" [Hebrews 11:27]? Was it not by the power of his own imagination that he endured?

Truth depends upon the intensity of the imagination, not upon external facts. Facts are the fruit bearing witness of the use or misuse of the imagination.

Man becomes what he imagines. He has a self-determined history. Imagination is the way, the truth, the life revealed.

We cannot get hold of truth with the logical mind. Where the natural man of sense sees a bud, imagination sees a rose full-blown.

Truth cannot be encompassed by facts.

As we awaken to the imaginative life, we discover that to imagine a thing is to make it so, that a true judgment need not conform to the external reality to which it relates.

The imaginative man does not deny the reality of the sensuous outer world of Becoming, but he knows that it is the inner world of continuous Imagination that is the force by which the sensuous outer world of Becoming is brought to pass. He sees the outer world and all its happenings as projections of the inner world of Imagination.

To him, everything is a manifestation of the mental activity which goes on in man's imagination, without the sensuous reasonable man being aware of it.

But he realizes that every man must become conscious of this inner activity and see the relationship between the inner causal world of imagination and the sensuous outer world of effects.

It is a marvelous thing to find that you can imagine yourself into the state of your fulfilled desire and escape from the jails which ignorance built.

The Real Man is a Magnificent Imagination.

It is this self that must be awakened.

Awake thou that sleepest, and arise from the dead, and Christ shall give thee light. [Ephesians 5:14]

The moment man discovers that his imagination is Christ, he accomplishes acts which on this level can only be called miraculous.

But until man has the sense of Christ as his imagination, "You did not choose me, I have chosen you", John 15:16, he will see everything in pure objectivity without any subjective relationship.

Not realizing that all that he encounters is part of himself, he rebels at the thought that he has chosen the conditions of his life, that they are related by affinity to his own mental activity.

Man must firmly come to believe that reality lies within him and not without.

Although others have bodies, a life of their own, their reality is rooted in you, ends in you, as yours ends in God.

CHAPTER TWO
SEALED INSTRUCTIONS

The first power that meets us at the threshold of the soul's domain is the power of imagination. Dr. Franz Hartmann

I WAS FIRST made conscious of the power, nature, and redemptive function of imagination through the teachings of my friend Abdullah; and through subsequent experiences, I learned that Jesus was a symbol of the coming of imagination to man, that the test of His birth in man was the individual's ability to forgive sin; that is, his ability to identify himself or another with his aim in life.

Without the identification of man with his aim, the forgiveness of sin is an impossibility, and only the Son of God can forgive sin.

Therefore, man's ability to identify himself with his aim, though reason and his senses deny it, is proof of the birth of Christ in him.

To passively surrender to appearances and bow before the evidence of facts is to confess that Christ is not yet born in you.

Although this teaching shocked and repelled me at first – for I was a convinced and earnest Christian, and did not then know that Christianity could not be inherited by the mere accident of birth but must be consciously adopted as a way of life – it stole later on, through visions, mystical revelations, and practical experiences, into my understanding and found its interpretation in a deeper mood. But I must confess that it is a trying time when those things are shaken which one has always taken for granted.

Seest thou these great buildings? There shall not be left one stone upon another that shall not be thrown down. Mark 13:2 Not one stone of literal understanding will be left after one drinks the water of psychological meaning.

All that has been built up by natural religion is cast into the flames of mental fire. Yet, what better way is there to understand Christ Jesus than to identify the central character of the Gospels with human imagination – knowing that, every time you exercise your imagination lovingly on behalf of another, you are literally mediating God to man and thereby feeding and clothing Christ Jesus and that, whenever you imagine evil against another, you are literally beating and crucifying Christ Jesus?

Every imagination of man is either the cup of cold water or the sponge

[11] THE POWER OF IMAGINATION: THE NEVILLE GODDARD TREASURY

of vinegar to the parched lips of Christ.

Let none of you imagine evil in your hearts against his neighbor, warned the prophet Zechariah [8:17].

When man heeds this advice, he will awake from the imposed sleep of Adam into the full consciousness of the Son of God. He is in the world, and the world is made by Him, and the world knows Him not [Approx., John 1:10]: Human Imagination.

I asked myself many times, "If my imagination is Christ Jesus and all things are possible to Christ Jesus, are all things possible to me?"

Through experience, I have come to know that, when I identify myself with my aim in life, then Christ is awake in me.

Christ is sufficient for all things. ["For in Him dwelleth all the fullness of the Godhead bodily, And ye are complete in Him, which is the head of all principality and power", Colossians 2:9,10; "My grace is sufficient for thee", 2Corinthians 12:9]

I lay down My life that I might take it again. No man taketh it from Me, but I lay it down of Myself. John 10:17,18 What a comfort it is to know that all that I experience is the result of my own standard of beliefs; that I am the center of my own web of circumstances and that as I change, so must my outer world!

The world presents different appearances according as our states of consciousness differ.

What we see when we are identified with a state cannot be seen when we are no longer fused with it.

By state is meant all that man believes and consents to as true.

No idea presented to the mind can realize itself unless the mind accepts it.

It depends on the acceptance, the state with which we are identified, how things present themselves. In the fusion of imagination and states is to be found the shaping of the world as it seems. The world is a revelation of the states with which imagination is fused. It is the state from which we think that determines the objective world in which we live. The rich man, the poor man, the good man, the thief are what they are by virtue of the states from which they view the world. On the distinction between these states depends the distinction between the worlds of these men.

Individually so different is this same world. It is not the actions and behaviour of the good man that should be matched but his point of

[12] NEVILLE GODDARD

view.

Outer reforms are useless if the inner state is not changed.

Success is gained not by imitating the outer actions of the successful but by right inner actions and inner talking.

If we detach ourselves from a state, and we may at any moment, the conditions and circumstances to which that union gave being vanish.

It was in the fall of 1933 in New York City that I approached Abdullah with a problem. He asked me one simple question, "What do you want?"

I told him that I would like to spend the winter in Barbados, but that I was broke. I literally did not have a nickel.

"If you will imagine yourself to be in Barbados", said he, "thinking and viewing the world from that state of consciousness instead of thinking of Barbados, you will spend the winter there.

You must not concern yourself with the ways and means of getting there, for the state of consciousness of already being in Barbados, if occupied by your imagination, will devise the means best suited to realize itself."

Man lives by committing himself to invisible states, by fusing his imagination with what he knows to be other than himself, and in this union he experiences the results of that fusion. No one can lose what he has, save by detachment from the state where the things experienced have their natural life.

"You must imagine yourself right into the state of your fulfilled desire", Abdullah told me, "and fall asleep viewing the world from Barbados."

The world which we describe from observation must be as we describe it relative to ourselves.

Our imagination connects us with the state desired.

But we must use imagination masterfully, not as an onlooker thinking of the end, but as a partaker thinking from the end.

We must actually be there in imagination.

If we do this, our subjective experience will be realized objectively. "This is not mere fancy", said he, "but a truth you can prove by experience."

His appeal to enter into the wish fulfilled was the secret of thinking from the end. Every state is already there as "mere possibility" as long as you think of it, but is overpoweringly real when you think from it. Thinking from the end is the way of Christ.

I began right there and then, fixing my thoughts beyond the limits of sense, beyond that aspect to which my present state gave being, towards the feeling of already being in Barbados and viewing the world from that standpoint.

He emphasized the importance of the state from which man views the world as he falls asleep. All prophets claim that the voice of God is chiefly heard by man in dreams In a dream, in a vision of the night, when deep sleep falleth upon men, in slumbering upon the bed; then he openeth the ears of men, and sealeth their instruction. [Job 33:15,16]

That night and for several nights thereafter, I fell asleep in the assumption that I was in my father's house in Barbados. Within a month, I received a letter from my brother, saying that he had a strong desire to have the family together at Christmas and asking me to use the enclosed steamship ticket for Barbados. I sailed two days after I received my brother's letter and spent a wonderful winter in Barbados.

This experience has convinced me that man can be anything he pleases if he will make the conception habitual and think from the end.

It has also shown me that I can no longer excuse myself by placing the blame on the world of external things – that my good and my evil have no dependency except from myself – that it depends on the state from which I view the world how things present themselves.

Man, who is free in his choice, acts from conceptions which he freely, though not always wisely, chooses. All conceivable states are awaiting our choice and occupancy, but no amount of rationalizing will of itself yield us the state of consciousness which is the only thing worth having.

The imaginative image is the only thing to seek.

The ultimate purpose of imagination is to create in us "the spirit of Jesus", which is continual forgiveness of sin, continual identification of man with his ideal.

Only by identifying ourselves with our aim can we forgive ourselves for having missed it. All else is labor in vain. On this path, to whatever place or state we convey our imagination, to that place or state we will gravitate physically also.

In My Father's house are many mansions; if it were not so, I would have told you. I go to prepare a place for you. And if I go and prepare a place for you, I will come again, and receive you unto Myself; that where I am, there ye may be also. [John 14:2,3]

By sleeping in my father's house in my imagination as though I slept there in the flesh, I fused my imagination with that state and was compelled to experience that state in the flesh also.

So vivid was this state to me, I could have been seen in my father's house had any sensitive entered the room where in imagination I was sleeping. A man can be seen where in imagination he is, for a man must be where his imagination is, for his imagination is himself. This I know from experience, for I have been seen by a few to whom I desired to be seen, when physically I was hundreds of miles away.

I, by the intensity of my imagination and feeling, imagining and feeling myself to be in Barbados instead of merely thinking of Barbados, had spanned the vast Atlantic to influence my brother into desiring my presence to complete the family circle at Christmas.

Thinking from the end, from the feeling of my wish fulfilled, was the source of everything that happened as outer cause, such as my brother's impulse to send me a steamship ticket; and it was also the cause of everything that appeared as results.

In Ideas of Good and Evil, W. B. Yeats, having described a few experiences similar to this experience of mine, writes:

If all who have described events like this have not dreamed, we should rewrite our histories, for all men, certainly all imaginative men, must be forever casting forth enchantments, glamour, illusions; and all men, especially tranquil men who have no powerful egotistic life, must be continually passing under their power.

Determined imagination, thinking from the end, is the beginning of all miracles.

I would like to give you an immense belief in miracles, but a miracle is only the name given by those who have no knowledge of the power and function of imagination to the works of imagination.

Imagining oneself into the feeling of the wish fulfilled is the means by which a new state is entered. This gives the state the quality of is-ness.

Hermes tells us:

That which is, is manifested; that which has been or shall be, is unmanifested, but not dead; for Soul, the eternal activity of God, animates all things.

The future must become the present in the imagination of the one who would wisely and consciously create circumstances.

We must translate vision into Being, thinking of into thinking from. Imagination must center itself in some state and view the world from that state. Thinking from the end is an intense perception of the world of fulfilled desire.

Thinking from the state desired is creative living. Ignorance of this ability to think from the end is bondage.

It is the root of all bondage with which man is bound. To passively surrender to the evidence of the senses underestimates the capacities of the Inner Self.Once man accepts thinking from the end as a creative principle in which he can cooperate, then he is redeemed from the absurdity of ever attempting to achieve his objective by merely thinking of it.

Construct all ends according to the pattern of fulfilled desire.

The whole of life is just the appeasement of hunger, and the infinite states of consciousness from which a man can view the world are purely a means of satisfying that hunger.

The principle upon which each state is organized is some form of hunger to lift the passion for self-gratification to ever higher and higher levels of experience.

Desire is the mainspring of the mental machinery. It is a blessed thing. It is a right and natural craving which has a state of consciousness as its right and natural satisfaction.

But one thing I do, forgetting the things which are behind, and stretching forward to the things which are before, I press on toward the goal. [Philippians 3:13,14]

It is necessary to have an aim in life. Without an aim, we drift. "What wantest thou of Me?" [What wilt thou that I shall do unto thee? Luke 18:41] is the implied question asked most often by the central figure of the Gospels. In defining your aim, you must want it.

As the hart panteth after the water brooks, so panteth my soul after Thee, O, God. [Psalms 42:1]

It is lack of this passionate direction to life that makes man fail of accomplishment.

The spanning of the bridge between desire – thinking of – and satisfaction – thinking from – is all-important.

We must move mentally from thinking of the end to thinking from the end.

This, reason could never do. By its nature, it is restricted to the evidence of the senses; but imagination, having no such limitation, can.

Desire exists to be gratified in the activity of imagination.

Through imagination, man escapes from the limitation of the senses and the bondage of reason.

There is no stopping the man who can think from the end. Nothing can stop him. He creates the means and grows his way out of limitation into ever greater and greater mansions of the Lord.

It does not matter what he has been or what he is. All that matters is "what does he want?"

He knows that the world is a manifestation of the mental activity which goes on within himself, so he strives to determine and control the ends from which he thinks.

In his imagination he dwells in the end, confident that he shall dwell there in the flesh also He puts his whole trust in the feeling of the wish fulfilled and lives by committing himself to that state, for the art of fortune is to tempt him so to do.

Like the man at the pool of Bethesda, he is ready for the moving of the waters of imagination.

Knowing that every desire is ripe grain to him who knows how to think from the end, he is indifferent to mere reasonable probability and confident that through continuous imagination his assumptions will harden into fact.

But how to persuade men everywhere that thinking from the end is the only living, how to foster it in every activity of man, how to reveal it as the plenitude of life and not the compensation of the disappointed: that is the problem.

Life is a controllable thing. You can experience what you please once you realize that you are His Son, and that you are what you are by virtue of the state of consciousness from which you think and view the world, Son, Thou art ever with Me, and all that I have is Thine.

[Luke 15:31]

CHAPTER THREE
HIGHWAYS OF THE INNER WORLD

And the children struggled within her... and the Lord said unto her, two nations are in thy womb, and two manner of people shall be separated from thy bowels; and the one people shall be stronger than the other people; and the elder shall serve the younger. [Genesis 25:22,23]

DUALITY IS an inherent condition of life. Everything that exists is double. Man is a dual creature with contrary principles embedded in his nature. They war within him and present attitudes to life which are antagonistic. This conflict is the eternal enterprise, the war in heaven, the never-ending struggle of the younger or inner man of imagination to assert His supremacy over the elder or outer man of sense.

The first shall be last and the last shall be first. [Matthew 19:30]

He it is, Who coming after me is preferred before me. [John 1:27]

The second Man is the Lord from heaven. [1Corinthians 15:47]

Man begins to awake to the imaginative life the moment he feels the presence of another being in himself.

In your limbs lie nations twain, rival races from their birth; one the mastery shall gain, the younger o'er the elder reign.

There are two distinct centers of thought or outlooks on the world possessed by every man. The Bible speaks of these two outlooks as natural and spiritual.

The natural man receiveth not the things of the Spirit of God: for they are foolishness unto him: neither can he know them, because they are spiritually discerned. [1Corinthians 2:14]

Man's inner body is as real in the world of subjective experience as his outer physical body is real in the world of external realities, but the inner body expresses a more fundamental part of reality.

This existing inner body of man must be consciously exercised and directed.

The inner world of thought and feeling to which the inner body is attuned has its real structure and exists in its own higher space.

There are two kinds of movement, one that is according to the inner body and another that is according to the outer body. The movement which is according to the inner body is causal, but the outer movement is under compulsion. The inner movement determines the outer which is joined to it, bringing into the outer a movement that is similar to the actions of the inner body. Inner movement is the force by which all events are brought to pass. Outer movement is subject to the compulsion applied to it by the movement of the inner body.

Whenever the actions of the inner body match the actions which the outer must take to appease desire, that desire will be realized.

Construct mentally a drama which implies that your desire is realized and make it one which involves movement of self. Immobilize your outer physical self. Act precisely as though you were going to take a nap, and start the predetermined action in imagination.

A vivid representation of the action is the beginning of that action. Then, as you are falling asleep, consciously imagine yourself into the scene. The length of the sleep is not important, a short nap is sufficient, but carrying the action into sleep thickens fancy into fact.

At first your thoughts may be like rambling sheep that have no shepherd. Don't despair. Should your attention stray seventy times seven, bring it back seventy times seven to its predetermined course until from sheer exhaustion it follows the appointed path. The inner journey must never be without direction. When you take to the inner road, it is to do what you did mentally before you started. You go for the prize you have already seen and accepted.

In The Road to Xanadu, Professor John Livingston Lowes says:

But I have long had the feeling, which this study had matured to a conviction, that Fancy and Imagination are not two powers at all, but one. The valid distinction which exists between them lies, not in the materials with which they operate, but in the degree of intensity of the operant power itself. Working at high tension, the imaginative energy assimilates and transmutes; keyed low, the same energy aggregates and yokes together those images which at its highest pitch, it merges indissolubly into one.

Fancy assembles, imagination fuses.

Here is a practical application of this theory. A year ago, a blind girl living in the city of San Francisco found herself confronted with a transportation problem. A rerouting of buses forced her to make three transfers between her home and her office. This lengthened her trip from fifteen minutes to two hours and fifteen minutes. She thought seriously about this problem and came to the decision that a car was the solution. She knew that she could not drive a car but felt that she could be driven in one. Putting this theory to the test that "whenever the actions of the inner self correspond to the actions which the outer, physical self must take to appease desire, that desire will be realized", she said to herself, "I will sit here and imagine that I am being driven to my office."

Sitting in her living room, she began to imagine herself seated in a car. She felt the rhythm of the motor. She imagined that she smelled the odor of gasoline, felt the motion of the car, touched the sleeve of the driver and felt that the driver was a man. She felt the car stop, and turning to her companion, said, "Thank you very much, sir."

To which he replied, "The pleasure is all mine."

Then she stepped from the car and heard the door snap shut as she closed it.

She told me that she centered her imagination on being in a car and, although blind, viewed the city from her imaginary ride. She did not think of the ride. She thought from the ride and all that it implied. This controlled and subjectively directed purposive ride raised her imagination to its full potency. She kept her purpose ever before her, knowing there was cohesion in purposive inner movement. In these mental journeys an emotional continuity must be sustained – the emotion of fulfilled desire. Expectancy and desire were so intensely joined that they passed at once from a mental state into a physical act.

The inner self moves along the predetermined course best when the emotions collaborate. The inner self must be fired, and it is best fired by the thought of great deeds and personal gain. We must take pleasure in our actions.

On two successive days, the blind girl took her imaginary ride, giving it all the joy and sensory vividness of reality. A few hours after her second imaginary ride, a friend told her of a story in the evening paper. It was a story of a man who was interested in the blind. The blind girl phoned him and stated her problem. The very next day, on his way home, he stopped in at a bar and while there had the urge to tell the story of the blind girl to his friend the proprietor. A total stranger, on hearing the story, volunteered to drive the blind girl home every day. The man who told the story then said, "If you will take her home, I will take her to work."

This was over a year ago, and since that day, this blind girl has been driven to and from her office by these two gentlemen. Now, instead of spending two hours and fifteen minutes on three buses, she is at her office in less than fifteen minutes. And on that first ride to her office, she turned to her good Samaritan and said,

"Thank you very much, sir"; and he replied, "The pleasure is all mine."

Thus, the objects of her imagination were to her the realities of which the physical manifestation was only the witness.

The determinative animating principle was the imaginative ride. Her triumph could be a surprise only to those who did not know of her inner ride. She mentally viewed the world from this imaginative ride with such a clearness of vision that every aspect of the city attained identity.

These inner movements not only produce corresponding outer movements: this is the law which operates beneath all physical appearances.

He who practices these exercises of bilocation will develop unusual powers of concentration and quiescence and will inevitably achieve waking consciousness on the inner and dimensionally larger world.

Actualizing strongly, she fulfilled her desire, for, viewing the city from the feeling of her wish fulfilled, she matched the state desired and granted that to herself which sleeping men ask of God.

To realize your desire, an action must start in your imagination, apart from the evidence of the senses, involving movement of self and implying fulfillment of your desire. Whenever it is the action which the outer self takes to appease desire, that desire will be realized.

The movement of every visible object is caused not by things outside the body, but by things within it, which operate from within outward.

The journey is in yourself. You travel along the highways of the inner world. Without inner movement, it is impossible to bring forth anything. Inner action is introverted sensation. If you will construct mentally a drama which implies that you have realized your objective, then close your eyes and drop your thoughts inward, centering your imagination all the while in the predetermined action and partake in that action, you will become a self-determined being.

Inner action orders all things according to the nature of itself.

Try it and see whether a desirable ideal once formulated is possible, for only by this process of experiment can you realize your potentialities.

It is thus that this creative principle is being realized. So the clue to purposive living is to center your imagination in the action and feeling of fulfilled desire with such awareness, such sensitiveness, that you initiate and experience movement upon the inner world.

Ideas only act if they are felt, if they awaken inner movement. Inner movement is conditioned by self-motivation, outer movement by compulsion.

Wherever the sole of your foot shall tread, the same give I unto you. [Joshua 1:3] and remember, The Lord thy God in the midst of thee is mighty. [Zephaniah 3:17]

CHAPTER FOUR
THE PRUNING SHEARS OF REVISION

The second Man is the Lord from Heaven. [1Corinthians 15:47]

Never will he say caterpillars. He'll say, "There's a lot of butterflies-as-is-to-be on our cabbages, Pure." He won't say, "It's winter." He'll say, "Summer's sleeping."

And there's no bud little enough nor sad-coloured enough for Kester not to callen it the beginnings of the blow.

Mary Webb, Precious Bane THE VERY first act of correction or cure is always "revise". One must start with oneself. It is one's attitude that must be changed. What we are, that only can we see. Emerson

It is a most healthy and productive exercise to daily relive the day as you wish you had lived it, revising the scenes to make them conform to your ideals.

For instance, suppose today's mail brought disappointing news. Revise the letter. Mentally rewrite it and make it conform to the news you wish you had received. Then, in imagination, read the revised letter over and over again. This is the essence of revision, and revision results in repeal.

The one requisite is to arouse your attention in a way and to such intensity that you become wholly absorbed in the revised action. You will experience an expansion and refinement of the senses by this imaginative exercise and eventually achieve vision.

But always remember that the ultimate purpose of this exercise is to create in you "the Spirit of Jesus", which is continual forgiveness of sin.

Revision is of greatest importance when the motive is to change oneself, when there is a sincere desire to be something different, when the longing is to awaken the ideal active spirit of forgiveness.

Without imagination, man remains a being of sin.

Man either goes forward to imagination or remains imprisoned in his senses. To go forward to imagination is to forgive. Forgiveness is the life of the imagination. The art of living is the art of forgiving

Forgiveness is, in fact, experiencing in imagination the revised version of the day, experiencing in imagination what you wish you had experienced in the flesh.

Every time one really forgives – that is, every time one relives the event as it should have been lived – one is born again.

"Father, forgive them" is not the plea that comes once a year but the opportunity that comes every day. The idea of forgiving is a daily possibility, and, if it is sincerely done, it will lift man to higher and higher levels of being. He will experience a daily Easter, and Easter is the idea of rising transformed.

And that should be almost a continuous process. Freedom and forgiveness are indissolubly linked.

Not to forgive is to be at war with ourselves, for we are freed according to our capacity to forgive.

Forgive, and you shall be forgiven. [Luke 6:37]

Forgive, not merely from a sense of duty or service; forgive because you want to.

Thy ways are ways of pleasantness and all thy paths are peace.

[Proverbs 3:17]

You must take pleasure in revision. You can forgive others effectively only when you have a sincere desire to identify them with their ideal. Duty has no momentum.

Forgiveness is a matter of deliberately withdrawing attention from the unrevised day and giving it full strength, and joyously, to the revised day. If a man begins to revise even a little of the vexations and troubles of the day, then he begins to work practically on himself. Every revision is a victory over himself and therefore a victory over his enemy.

A man's foes are those of his own household, [Matthew 10:36,] and his household is his state of mind. He changes his future as he revises his day.

When a man practices the art of forgiveness, of revision, however factual the scene on which sight then rests, he revises it with his imagination and gazes on one never before witnessed. The magnitude of the change which any act of revision involves makes such change appear wholly improbable to the realist – the unimaginative man; but the radical changes in the fortunes of the Prodigal [Luke 15:11-32] were all produced by a "change of heart".

The battle man fights is fought out in his own imagination. The man who does not revise the day has lost the vision of that life, into the likeness of which it is the true labour of the "Spirit of Jesus" to transform this life.

All things whatsoever ye would that men should do to you, even so do ye to them: for this is the law.

[Matthew 7:12]

Here is the way an artist friend forgave herself and was set free from pain, annoyance and unfriendliness. Knowing that nothing but forgetfulness and forgiveness will bring us to new values, she cast herself upon her imagination and escaped from the prison of her senses.

She writes

: "Thursday, I taught all day in the art school. Only one small thing marred the day. Coming into my afternoon classroom, I discovered the janitor had left all the chairs on top of the desks after cleaning the floor. As I lifted a chair down, it slipped from my grasp and struck me a sharp blow on the instep of my right foot. I immediately examined my thoughts and found that I had criticized the man for not doing his job properly. Since he had lost his helper, I realized he probably felt he had done more than enough and it was an unwanted gift that had bounced and hit me on the foot. Looking down at my foot, I saw both my skin and nylons were intact, so forgot the whole thing.

"That night, after I had been working intensely for about three hours on a drawing, I decided to make myself a cup of coffee. To my utter amazement, I couldn't manage my right foot at all and it was giving out great bumps of pain. I hopped over to a chair and took off my slipper to look at it. The entire foot was a strange purplish pink, swollen out of shape and red hot. I tried walking on it and found that it just flapped. I had no control over it whatsoever. It looked like one of two things: either I had cracked a bone when I dropped the chair on it or something could be dislocated.

" 'No use speculating what it is. Better get rid of it right away.'

So I became quiet, all ready to melt myself into light. To my complete bewilderment, my imagination refused to cooperate. It just said 'No.'

This sort of thing often happens when I am painting. I just started to argue 'Why not?'

It just kept saying 'No.'

Finally, I gave up and said, 'You know I am in pain. I am trying hard not to be frightened, but you are the

boss. What do you want to do?'

The answer: 'Go to bed and review the day's events.'

So I said 'All right. But let me tell you if my foot isn't perfect by tomorrow morning, you have only yourself to blame.'

"After arranging the bed clothes so they didn't touch my foot, I started to review the day. It was slow going as I had difficulty keeping my attention away from my foot. I went through the whole day, saw nothing to add to the chair incident. But when I reached the early evening, I found myself coming face to face with a man who for the past year has made a point of not speaking. The first time this happened, I thought he had grown deaf. I had known him since school days, but we had never done more than say 'hello' and comment on the weather. Mutual friends assured me I had done nothing, that he had said he never liked me and finally decided it was not worthwhile speaking. I had said 'Hi!'

He hadn't answered. I found that I thought 'Poor guy – what a horrid state to be in. I shall do something about

this ridiculous state of affairs.'

So, in my imagination, I stopped right there and re-did the scene. I said 'Hi!' He answered 'Hi!' and smiled. I now thought 'Good old Ed.'

I ran the scene over a couple of times and went on to the next incident and finished up the day.

"'Now what – do we do my foot or the concert?'

I had been melting and wrapping up a wonderful present of courage and success for a friend who was to make her debut the following day and I had been looking forward to giving it to her tonight. My imagination sounded a little bit solemn as it said 'Let us do the concert. It will be more fun.' 'But first couldn't we just take my perfectly good imagination foot out of this physical one before we start?' I pleaded. 'By all means.'

"That done, I had a lovely time at the concert and my friend got a tremendous ovation.

"By now I was very, very sleepy and fell asleep doing my project. The next morning, as I was putting on my slipper, I suddenly had a quick memory picture of withdrawing a discolored and swollen foot from the same slipper. I took my foot out and looked at it. It was perfectly normal in every respect. There was a tiny pink spot on the instep where I remembered I had hit it with the chair.

'What a vivid dream that was!' I thought and dressed. While waiting for my coffee, I wandered over to my drafting table and saw that all my brushes were lying helter-skelter and unwashed. 'Whatever possessed you to leave your brushes like that?

'Don't you remember? It was because of your foot.'

So it hadn't been a dream after all, but a beautiful healing."

She had won by the art of revision what she would never have won by force.

In Heaven, the only Art of Living Is Forgetting & Forgiving. Especially to the Female. – Blake

We should take our life, not as it appears to be, but from the vision of this artist, from the vision of the world made perfect that is buried under all minds – buried and waiting for us to revise the day.

We are led to believe a lie when we see with, not through the eye. Blake

A revision of the day, and what she held to be so stubbornly real was no longer so to her and, like a dream, had quietly faded away.

You can revise the day to please yourself and by experiencing in imagination the revised speech and actions not only modify the trend of your life story but turn all its discords into harmonies.

The one who discovers the secret of revision cannot do otherwise than let himself be guided by love.

Your effectiveness will increase with practice. Revision is the way by which right can find its appropriate might.

"Resist not evil" [Matthew 5:39], for all passionate conflicts result in an interchange of characteristics.

To him that knoweth to do good, and doeth it not, to him it is sin. [James 4:17]

To know the truth, you must live the truth, and to live the truth, your inner actions must match the actions of your fulfilled desire.

Expectancy and desire must become one.

Your outer world is only actualized inner movement.

Through ignorance of the law of revision, those who take to warfare

are perpetually defeated.

Only concepts that idealize depict the truth.

Your ideal of man is his truest self. It is because I firmly believe that whatever is most profoundly imaginative is, in reality, most directly practical that I ask you to live imaginatively and to think into, and to personally appropriate the transcendent saying "Christ in you, the hope of glory." [Colossians 1:27] Don't blame; only resolve.

It is not man and the earth at their loveliest, but you practicing the art of revision make paradise.

The evidence of this truth can lie only in your own experience of it.

Try revising the day. It is to the pruning shears of revision that we owe our prime fruit.

CHAPTER FIVE
THE COIN OF HEAVEN

"Does a firm persuasion that a thing is so, make it so?"

And the prophet replied, "All poets believe that it does. And in ages of imagination, this firm persuasion

removed mountains: but many are not capable of a firm persuasion of anything."

Blake, Marriage of Heaven and Hell

Let every man be fully persuaded in his own mind. Romans 14:5

PERSUASION IS an inner effort of intense attention.

To listen attentively as though you heard is to evoke, to activate.

By listening, you can hear what you want to hear and persuade those beyond the range of the outer ear. Speak it inwardly in your imagination only.

Make your inner conversation match your fulfilled desire. What you desire to hear without, you must hear within.

Embrace the without within and become one who hears only that which implies the fulfillment of his desire, and all the external happenings in the world will become a bridge leading to the objective realization of your desire.

Your inner speech is perpetually written all around you in happenings.

Learn to relate these happenings to your inner speech and you will become self-taught.

By inner speech is meant those mental conversations which you carry on with yourself.

They may be inaudible when you are awake because of the noise and distractions of the outer world of becoming, but they are quite audible in deep meditation and dream.

But whether they be audible or inaudible, you are their author and fashion your world in their likeness.

There is a God in heaven [and heaven is within you] that revealeth secrets, and maketh known to the king Nebuchadnezzar what shall be in the latter days. Thy dream, and the visions of thy head upon thy bed, are these. [Daniel 2:28]

Inner speech from premises of fulfilled desire is the way to create an intelligible world for yourself.

Observe your inner speech for it is the cause of future action. Inner speech reveals the state of consciousness from which you view the world.

Make your inner speech match your fulfilled desire, for your inner speech is manifested all around you in happenings.

If any man offend not in word, the same is a perfect man and able also to bridle the whole body. Behold, we put bits in the horses' mouths, that they may obey us; and we turn about their whole body. Behold also the ships, which though they be so great, and are driven by fierce winds, yet are they turned about with a very small helm, whithersoever the governor listeth. Even so the tongue is a little member, and boasteth great things. Behold, how great a matter a little fire kindleth! [James 3:2-5]

The whole manifested world goes to show us what use we have made of the Word – Inner Speech.

An uncritical observation of our inner talking will reveal to us the ideas from which we view the world.

Inner talking mirrors our imagination, and our imagination mirrors the state with which it is fused. If the state with which we are fused is the cause of the phenomenon of our life, then we are relieved of the burden of wondering what to do, for we have no alternative but to identify ourselves with our aim, and inasmuch as the state with which we are identified mirrors itself in our inner speech, then to change the state with which we are fused, we must first change our inner talking.

It is our inner conversations which make tomorrow's facts.

Put off the former conversation, the old man, which is corrupt… and be renewed in the spirit of your mind… put on the new man, which is created in righteousness. [Ephesians 4:22-24]

Our minds, like our stomachs, are whetted by change of food. Quintilian Stop all of the old mechanical negative inner talking and start a new positive and constructive inner speech from premises of fulfilled desire. Inner talking is the beginning, the sowing of the seeds of future action. To determine the action, you must consciously initiate and control your inner talking.

Construct a sentence which implies the fulfillment of your aim, such as "I have a large, steady, dependable income, consistent with integrity and mutual benefit", or "I am happily married", "I am wanted", "I am contributing to the good of the world", and repeat such a sentence over and over until you are inwardly affected by it. Our inner speech represents in various ways the world we live in.

In the beginning was the Word. [John 1:1]

That which ye sow ye reap. See yonder fields! The sesamum was sesamum, the corn was corn. The Silence and the Darkness knew! So is a man's fate born. The Light of Asia [Edwin Arnold] Ends run true to origins.

Those that go searching for love only make manifest their own lovelessness. And the loveless never find love, only the loving find love, and they never have to seek for it. D. H. Lawrence Man attracts what he is. The art of life is to sustain the feeling of the wish fulfilled and let things come to you, not to go after them or think they flee away.

Observe your inner talking and remember your aim. Do they match?

Does your inner talking match what you would say audibly had you achieved your goal?

The individual's inner speech and actions attract the conditions of his life.

Through uncritical self-observation of your inner talking you find where you are in the inner world, and where you are in the inner world is what you are in the outer world.

You put on the new man whenever ideals and inner speech match. In this way alone can the new man be born.

Inner talking matures in the dark.

From the dark it issues into the light. The right inner speech is the speech that would be yours were you to realize your ideal. In other words, it is the speech of fulfilled desire.

"I am that." [Exodus 3:14].

There are two gifts which God has bestowed upon man alone, and on no other mortal creature. These two are mind and speech; and the gift of mind and speech is equivalent to that of immortality. If a man uses these two gifts rightly, he will differ in nothing from the immortals... and when he quits the body, mind and speech will be his guides, and by them he will be brought into the troop of the gods and the souls that have attained to bliss. Hermetica, Walter Scott's translation

The circumstances and conditions of life are outpictured inner talking, solidified sound. Inner speech calls events into existence. In every event is the creative sound that is its life and being.

All that a man believes and consents to as true reveals itself in his inner speech. It is his Word, his life.

Try to notice what you are saying in yourself at this moment, to what thoughts and feelings you are consenting. They will be perfectly woven into your tapestry of life. To change your life, you must change your inner talking, for "life", said Hermes, "is the union of Word and Mind".

When imagination matches your inner speech to fulfilled desire, there will then be a straight path in yourself from within out, and the without will instantly reflect the within for you, and you will know reality is only actualized inner talking.

Receive with meekness the inborn Word which is able to save your souls. [James 1:21]

Every stage of man's progress is made by the conscious exercise of his imagination matching his inner speech to his fulfilled desire.

Because man does not perfectly match them, the results are uncertain, while they might be perfectly certain. Persistent assumption of the wish fulfilled is the means of fulfilling the intention.

As we control our inner talking, matching it to our fulfilled desires, we can lay aside all other processes.

Then we simply act by clear imagination and intention.

We imagine the wish fulfilled and carry on mental conversations from that premise.

Through controlled inner talking from premises of fulfilled desire, seeming miracles are performed.

The future becomes the present and reveals itself in our inner speech.

To be held by the inner speech of fulfilled desire is to be safely anchored in life.

Our lives may seem to be broken by events, but they are never broken so long as we retain the inner speech of fulfilled desire.

All happiness depends on the active voluntary use of imagination to construct and inwardly affirm that we are what we want to be. We match ourselves to our ideals by constantly remembering our aim and identifying ourselves with it. We fuse with our aims by frequently occupying the feeling of our wish fulfilled.

It is the frequency, the habitual occupancy, that is the secret of success. The oftener we do it, the more natural it is. Fancy assembles. Continuous imagination fuses It is possible to resolve every situation by the proper use of imagination.

Our task is to get the right sentence, the one which implies that our desire is realized, and fire the imagination with it.

All this is intimately connected with the mystery of "the still small voice".

Inner talking reveals the activities of imagination, activities which are the causes of the circumstances of life.

As a rule, man is totally unaware of his inner talking and therefore sees himself not as the cause but the victim of circumstance.

To consciously create circumstance, man must consciously direct his inner speech, matching "the still small voice" to his fulfilled desires.

He calls things not seen as though they were. Romans 4:17 Right inner speech is essential. It is the greatest of the arts. It is the way out of limitation into freedom.

Ignorance of this art has made the world a battlefield and penitentiary where blood and sweat alone are expected, when it should be a place of marveling and wondering.Right inner talking is the first step to becoming what you want to be.

Speech is an image of mind, and mind is an image of God. Hermetica, Scott translation On the morning of April 12, 1953, my wife was awakened by the sound of a great voice of authority speaking within her and saying, "You must stop spending your thoughts, time, and money. Everything in life must be an investment.

" To spend is to waste, to squander, to layout without return. To invest is to layout for a purpose from which a profit is expected. This revelation of my wife is about the importance of the moment. It is about the transformation of the moment. What we desire does not lie in the future but in ourselves at this very moment.

At any moment in our lives, we are faced with an infinite choice:

"what we are and what we want to be".

And what we want to be is already existent, but to realize it we must match our inner speech and actions to it.

If two of you shall agree on earth as touching anything that they shall ask, it shall be done for them of My Father which is in heaven. [Matthew 18:19] It is only what is done now that counts.

The present moment does not recede into the past. It advances into the future to confront us, spent or invested.

Thought is the coin of heaven. Money is its earthly symbol.

Every moment must be invested, and our inner talking reveals whether we are spending or investing.

Be more interested in what you are inwardly "saying now" than what you "have said" by choosing wisely what you think and what you feel now.

Any time we feel misunderstood, misused, neglected, suspicious, afraid, we are spending our thoughts and wasting our time.

Whenever we assume the feeling of being what we want to be, we are investing.

We cannot abandon the moment to negative inner talking and expect to retain command of life.

Before us go the results of all that seemingly is behind. Not gone is the last moment – but oncoming.

My word shall not return unto Me void, but it shall accomplish that which I please, and it shall prosper in the thing whereto I sent it. [Isaiah 55:11]

The circumstances of life are the muffled utterances of the inner talking that made them – the word made visible.

"The Word", said Hermes, "is Son, and the Mind is Father of the Word. They are not separate one from the other; for life is the union of Word and Mind."

He willed us forth from Himself by the Word of Truth. [James 1:18]

Let us be imitators of God as dear children, [Ephesians 5:1,] and use our inner speech wisely to mould an outer world in harmony with our ideal. The Lord spake by me, and His Word was in my tongue. [2Samuel 23:2]

The mouth of God is the mind of man. Feed God only the best. Whatsoever things are of good report... think on these things. [Philippians 4:8]

The present moment is always precisely right for an investment, to inwardly speak the right word.

The word is very near to you, in your mouth, and in your heart, that you may do it. See, I have set before you this day life and good, death and evil, blessings and cursings. Choose life. [Deuteronomy 30:14,15,19]

You choose life and good and blessings by being that which you choose. Like is known to like alone.

Make your inner speech bless and give good reports.

Man's ignorance of the future is the result of his ignorance of his inner talking. His inner talking mirrors his imagination, and his imagination is a government in which the opposition never comes into power.

If the reader ask, "What if the inner speech remains subjective and is unable to find an object for its love?", the answer is: it will not remain subjective, for the very simple reason that inner speech is always objectifying itself.

What frustrates and festers and becomes the disease that afflicts humanity is man's ignorance of the art of matching inner words to fulfilled desire.

Inner speech mirrors imagination, and imagination is Christ.

Alter your inner speech, and your perceptual world changes. Whenever inner speech and desire are in conflict, inner speech invariably wins. Because inner speech objectifies itself, it is easy to see that if it matches desire, desire will be objectively realized. Were this not so, I would say with Blake,

Sooner murder an infant in its cradle than nurse unacted desires.

But I know from experience, The tongue… setteth on fire the course of nature. [James 3:

CHAPTER SIX
IT IS WITHIN

Rivers, Mountains, Cities, Villages, All are Human, & when you enter into their Bosoms you walk In Heavens & Earths, as in your own Bosom you bear your Heaven And Earth & all you behold; tho' it appears Without, it is Within, In your Imagination, of which this World of Mortality is but a Shadow. - Blake, Jerusalem THE INNER world was as real to Blake as the outer land of waking life. He looked upon his dreams and visions as the realities of the forms of nature. Blake reduced everything to the bedrock of his own consciousness.

The Kingdom of Heaven is within you. [Luke 17:21]

The Real Man, the Imaginative Man, has invested the outer world with all of its properties. The apparent reality of the outer world which is so hard to dissolve is only proof of the absolute reality of the inner world of his own imagination.

No man can come to me, except the Father which hath sent Me draw him… I and My Father are One. [John 6:44; 10:30]

The world which is described from observation is a manifestation of the mental activity of the observer.

When man discovers that his world is his own mental activity made visible, that no man can come unto him except he draws him, and that there is no one to change but himself, his own imaginative self, his first impulse is to reshape the world in the image of his ideal.

But his ideal is not so easily incarnated. In that moment when he ceases to conform to external discipline, he must impose upon himself a far more rigorous discipline, the self-discipline upon which the realization of his ideal depends.

Imagination is not entirely untrammeled and free to move at will without any rules to constrain it. In fact, the contrary is true. Imagination travels according to habit Imagination has choice, but it chooses according to habit. Awake or asleep, man's imagination is constrained to follow certain definite patterns. It is this benumbing influence of habit that man must change; if he does not, his dreams will fade under the paralysis of custom.

Imagination, which is Christ in man, is not subject to the necessity to produce only that which is perfect and good. It exercises its absolute freedom from necessity by endowing the outer physical self with free will to choose to follow good or evil, order or disorder.

Choose this day whom ye will serve. [Joshua 24:15]

But after the choice is made and accepted so that it forms the individual's habitual consciousness, then imagination manifests its infinite power and wisdom by moulding the outer sensuous world of becoming in the image of the habitual inner speech and actions of the individual.

To realize his ideal, man must first change the pattern which his imagination has followed.

Habitual thought is indicative of character.

The way to change the outer world is to make the inner speech and action match the outer speech and action of fulfilled desire.

Our ideals are waiting to be incarnated, but unless we ourselves match our inner speech and action to the speech and action of fulfilled desire, they are incapable of birth.

Inner speech and action are the channels of God's action. He cannot respond to our prayer unless these paths are offered.

The outer behaviour of man is mechanical. It is subject to the compulsion applied to it by the behaviour of the inner self, and old habits of the inner self hang on till replaced by new ones. It is a peculiar property of the second or inner man that he gives to the outer self something similar to his own reality of being. Any change in the behavior of the inner self will result in corresponding outer changes.

The mystic calls a change of consciousness "death". By death he means, not the destruction of imagination and the state with which it was fused, but the dissolution of their union.

Fusion is union rather than oneness. Thus the conditions to which that union gave vanished. "I die daily", said Paul to the Corinthians [1Corinthians

15:31]. Blake said to his friend Crabbe Robinson:

There is nothing like death. Death is the best thing that can happen in life; but most people die so late and take such an unmerciful time in dying. God knows, their neighbors never see them rise from the dead.

To the outer man of sense, who knows nothing of the inner man of Being, this is sheer nonsense. But Blake made the above quite clear when he wrote in the year before he died:

William Blake – one who is very much delighted with being in good company. Born 28 November 1757 in London and has died several times since.

When man has the sense of Christ as his imagination, he sees why Christ must die and rise again from the dead to save man – why he must detach his imagination from his present state and match it to a higher concept of himself if he would rise above his present limitations and thereby save himself.

Here is a lovely story of a mystical death which was witnessed by a "neighbor".

"Last week", writes the one "who rose from the dead", "a friend offered me her home in the mountains for the Christmas holidays as she thought she might go east. She said that she would let me know this week. We had a very pleasant conversation and I mentioned you and your teaching in connection with a discussion of Dunne's 'Experiment with Time' which she had been reading.

"Her letter arrived Monday. As I picked it up, I had a sudden sense of depression.

However, when I read it, she said I could have the house and told me where to get the keys. Instead of being cheerful, I grew still more depressed, so much so I decided there must have been something between the lines which I was getting intuitively. I unfolded the letter and read the first page through and as I turned to the second page, I noticed she had written a postscript on the back of the first sheet.

It consisted of an extremely blunt and heavy-handed description of an unlovely trait in my character which I had struggled for years to overcome, and for the past two years I thought I had succeeded.

Yet here it was again, described with clinical exactitude.

"I was stunned and desolated. I thought to myself, 'What is this letter trying to tell me? In the first place, she invited me to use her house, as I have been seeing myself in some lovely home during the holidays. In the second place, nothing comes to me except I draw it. And thirdly I have been hearing nothing but good news. So the obvious conclusion is that something in me corresponds to this letter and no matter what it looks like it is good news.' I reread the letter and as I did so, I asked, 'What is there here for me to see?'

And then I saw. It started out, 'After our conversation of last week, I feel I can tell you…' and the rest of the page was as studded with 'weres' and 'wases' as currants in a seed cake. A great feeling of elation swept over me.

It was all in the past. The thing I had labored so long to correct was done. I suddenly realized that my friend was a witness to my resurrection. I whirled around the studio, chanting, 'It's all in the past! It is done. Thank you, it is done!'

I gathered all my gratitude up in a big ball of light and shot it straight to you and if you saw a flash of lightning Monday evening shortly after six your time, that was it.

"Now, instead of writing a polite letter because it is the correct thing to do, I can write giving sincere thanks for her frankness and thanking her for the loan of her house.

Thank you so much for your teaching, which has made my beloved imagination truly my Saviour."

And now, if any man shall say unto her "Lo, here is Christ, or there" [Matthew 24:23], she will believe it not, for she knows that the Kingdom of God is within her and that she herself must assume full responsibility for the incarnation of her ideal and that nothing but death and resurrection will bring her to it.

She has found her Saviour, her beloved Imagination, forever expanding in the bosom of God.

There is only one reality, and that is Christ – Human Imagination, the inheritance and final achievement of the whole of Humanity,

That we… speaking the truth in love, may grow up into Him in all things, which is the head, even Christ.

[Ephesians 4:14,15]

CHAPTER SEVEN
CREATION IS FINISHED

I am the beginning and the end, there is nothing to come that has not been, and is. [Ecclesiastes 3:15 ERV]BLAKE SAW all possible human situations as"already-made" states. He saw every aspect, every plot and drama as already worked out as "mere possibilities" as long as we are not in them, but as overpowering realities when we are in them.

He described these states as "Sculptures of Los's Halls".

Distinguish therefore states from Individuals in those States. States change but Individual Identities never change nor cease... The Imagination is not a State. Said Blake,

It is the Human Existence itself. Affection or Love becomes a State when divided from imagination.

Just how important this is to remember is almost impossible to say, but the moment the individual realizes this for the first time is the most momentous in his life, and to be encouraged to feel this is the highest form of encouragement it is possible to give.

This truth is common to all men, but the consciousness of it – and much more, the self-consciousness of it – is another matter. The day I realized this great truth – that everything in my world is a manifestation of the mental activity which goes on within me, and that the conditions and circumstances of my life only reflect the state of consciousness with which I am fused – is the most momentous in my life.

But the experience that brought me to this certainty is so remote from ordinary existence, I have long hesitated to tell it, for my reason refused to admit the conclusions to which the experience impelled me. Nevertheless, this experience revealed to me that I am supreme within the circle of my own state of consciousness and that it is the state with which I am identified that determines what I experience.

Therefore it should be shared with all, for to know this is to become free from the world's greatest tyranny, the belief in a second cause.

Blessed are the pure in heart: for they shall see God. [Matthew 5:8]

Blessed are they whose imagination has been so purged of the beliefs in second causes they know that imagination is all, and all is imagination.

One day I quietly slipped from my apartment in New York City into some remote yesteryear's countryside. As I entered the dining room of a large inn, I became fully conscious. I knew that my physical body was immobilized on my bed back in New York.

Yet here I was as awake and as conscious as I have ever been. I intuitively knew that if I could stop the activity of my mind, everything before me would freeze. No sooner was the thought born than the urge to try it possessed me. I felt my head tighten, then thicken to a stillness. My attention concentrated into a crystal-clear focus, and the waitress walking, walked not. And I looked through the window and the leaves falling, fell not. And the family of four eating, ate not. And they lifting the food, lifted it not. Then my attention relaxed, the tightness eased, and of a sudden all moved onward in their course. The leaves fell, the waitress walked and the family ate. Then I understood Blake's vision of the "Sculptures of Los's Halls".

I sent you to reap that whereon ye bestowed no labor.

[John 4:38] Creation is finished.

I am the beginning and the end, there is nothing to come that has not been, and is. [Ecclesiastes 3:15, ERV]

The world of creation is finished and its original is within us. We saw it before we set forth, and have since been trying to remember it and to activate sections of it. There are infinite views of it. Our task is to get the right view and by determined direction of our attention make it pass in procession before the inner eye. If we assemble the right sequence and experience it in imagination until it has the tone of reality, then we consciously create circumstances.

This inner procession is the activity of imagination that must be consciously directed. We, by a series of mental transformations, become aware of increasing portions of that which already is, and by matching our own mental activity to that portion of creation which we desire to experience, we activate it, resurrect it, and give it life.

This experience of mine not only shows the world as a manifestation of the mental activity of the individual observer, but it also reveals our course of time as jumps of attention between eternal moments. An infinite abyss separates any two moments of ours.

We, by the movements of our attention, give life to the "Sculptures of Los's Halls".

Think of the world as containing an infinite number of states of consciousness from which it could be viewed. Think of these states as rooms or mansions in the House of God [John 14:2], and like the rooms of any house, they are fixed relative to one another.

But think of yourself, the Real Self, the Imaginative You, as the living, moving occupant of God's House.

Each room contains some of Los's Sculptures, with infinite plots and dramas and situations already worked out but not activated.

They are activated as soon as Human Imagination enters and fuses with them. Each represents certain mental and emotional activities. To enter a state, man must consent to the ideas and feelings which it represents.

These states represent an infinite number of possible mental transformations which man can experience. To move into another state or mansion necessitates a change of beliefs.

All that you could ever desire is already present and only waits to be matched by your beliefs.

But it must be matched, for that is the necessary condition by which alone it can be activated and objectified.

Matching the beliefs of a state is the seeking that finds, the knocking to which it is opened, the asking that receives [Matthew 7:8; Luke 11:10]. Go in and possess the land [Exodus 6:4;8].

The moment man matches the beliefs of any state, he fuses with it, and this union results in the activation and projection of its plots, plans, dramas, and situations.

It becomes the individual's home from which he views the world. It is his workshop, and, if he is observant, he will see outer reality shaping itself upon the model of his... Imagination.

It is for this purpose of training us in image-making that we were made subject to the limitations of the senses and clothed in bodies of flesh.

It is the awakening of the imagination, the returning of His Son, that our Father waits for.

The creature was made subject to vanity not willingly, but by reason of him who subjected it. [Romans 8:20]

But the victory of the Son, the return of the prodigal, assures us that the creature shall be delivered from the bondage of corruption into the glorious liberty of the Sons [children] of God. [Romans 8:21]

We were subjected to this biological experience because no one can know of imagination who has not been subjected to the vanities and limitations of the flesh, who has not taken his share of Sonship and gone prodigal, who has not experimented and tasted this cup of experience; and confusion will continue until man awakes and a fundamentally imaginative view of life has been reestablished and acknowledged as basic.

I should preach… the unsearchable riches of Christ and make all men see what is the fellowship of the mystery, which from the beginning of the world has been hid in God, Who created all things by Jesus Christ. [Ephesians 3:8,9]

Bear in mind that Christ in you is your imagination.

As the appearance of our world is determined by the particular state with which we are fused, so may we determine our fate as individuals by fusing our imaginations with ideals we seek to realize. On the distinction between our states of consciousness depends the distinction between the circumstances and conditions of our lives.

Man, who is free in his choice of state, often cries out to be saved from the state of his choice.

And ye shall cry out in that day, because of your king which ye shall have chosen you; and the Lord will not hear you in that day. Nevertheless, the people refused to obey the voice of Samuel; and they said, Nay; but we will have a king over us. [1Samuel 8:18,19]

Choose wisely the state that you will serve. All states are lifeless until imagination fuses with them.

All things when they are admitted are made manifest by the light: for everything that is made manifest is light, [Ephesians 5:13,] and Ye are the light of the world, [Matthew 5:14,] by which those ideas to which you have consented are made manifest.

Hold fast to your ideal. Nothing can take it from you but your imagination.

Don't think of your ideal, think from it. It is only the ideals from which you think that are ever realized.

Man lives not by bread alone, but by every word that proceeds out of the mouth of God, [Matthew 4:4,] and "the mouth of God" is the mind of man.

Become a drinker and an eater of the ideals you wish to realize. Have a set, definite aim or your mind will wander, and wandering it eats every negative suggestion.

If you live right mentally, everything else will be right.

By a change of mental diet, you can alter the course of observed events.

But unless there is a change of mental diet, your personal history remains the same.

You illuminate or darken your life by the ideas to which you consent.

Nothing is more important to you than the ideas on which you feed. And you feed on the ideas from which you think. If you find the world unchanged, it is a sure sign that you are wanting in fidelity to the new mental diet, which you neglect in order to condemn your environment. You are in need of a new and sustained attitude.

You can be anything you please if you will make the conception habitual, for any idea which excludes all others from the field of attention discharges in action.

The ideas and moods to which you constantly return define the state with which you are fused.

Therefore train yourself to occupy more frequently the feeling of your wish fulfilled. This is creative magic. It is the way to work toward fusion with the desired state.

If you would assume the feeling of your wish fulfilled more frequently, you would be master of your fate, but unfortunately you shut out your assumption for all but the occasional hour. Practice making real to yourself the feeling of the wish fulfilled.

After you have assumed the feeling of the wish fulfilled, do not close the experience as you would a book, but carry it around like a fragrant odor.

Instead of being completely forgotten, let it remain in the atmosphere communicating its influence automatically to your actions and reactions. A mood, often repeated, gains a momentum that is hard to break or check. So be careful of the feelings you entertain. Habitual moods reveal the state with which you are fused.

It is always possible to pass from thinking of the end you desire to realize, to thinking from the end.

But the crucial matter is thinking from the end, for thinking from means unification or fusion with the idea: whereas in thinking of the end, there is always subject and object – the thinking individual and the thing thought. You must imagine yourself into the state of your wish fulfilled, in your love for that state, and in so doing, live and think from it and no more of it. You pass from thinking of to thinking from by centering your imagination in the feeling of the wish fulfilled.

CHAPTER EIGHT
THE APPLE OF GOD'S EYE

What think ye of the Christ? Whose Son is He? [Matthew 22:42] WHEN THIS question is asked of you, let your answer be, "Christ is my imagination", and, though I See not yet all things put under him, [Hebrews 2:8,] yet I know that I am Mary from whom sooner or later He shall be born, and eventually Do all things through Christ [Philippians 4:13].

The birth of Christ is the awakening of the inner or Second man. It is becoming conscious of the mental activity within oneself, which activity continues whether we are conscious of it or not.

The birth of Christ does not bring any person from a distance, or make anything to be that was not there before. It is the unveiling of the Son of God in man. The Lord "cometh in clouds" [Mark 13:26, Luke 21:27] is the prophet's description of the pulsating rings of golden liquid light on the head of him in whom He awakes. The coming is from within and not from without, as Christ is in us [Romans 8:10; 2Corinthians 13:3; Galatians 2:20; Galatians 4:19; Colossians 1:27].

This great mystery God was manifest in the flesh [1Timothy 3:16] begins with Advent, and it is appropriate that the cleansing of the Temple, Which temple ye are, [1Corinthians 3:17,] stands in the forefront of the Christian mysteries:

The Kingdom of Heaven is within you. [Luke 17:21]

Advent is unveiling the mystery of your being. If you will practice the art of revision by a life lived according to the wise, imaginative use of your inner speech and inner actions, in confidence that by the conscious use of "the power that worketh in us" [Ephesians 3:20], Christ will awake in you; if you believe it, trust it, act upon it; Christ will awake in you. This is Advent.

Great is the mystery, God was manifest in the flesh. [1Timothy 3:16]

From Advent on, He that toucheth you toucheth the apple of God's eye. [Zechariah 2:8]

The Search

To Victoria:

the fulfillment of a dream.

ONCE IN an idle interval at sea, I meditated on "the perfect state", and wondered what I would be, were I of too pure eyes to behold iniquity, if to me all things were pure and were I without condemnation. As I became lost in this fiery brooding, I found myself lifted above the dark environment of the senses. So intense was the feeling, I felt myself a being of fire dwelling in a body of air. Voices as from a heavenly chorus, with the exaltation of those who had been conquerors in a conflict with death, were singing "He is risen – He is risen", and intuitively I knew they meant me.

Then I seemed to be walking in the night. I soon came upon a scene that might have been the ancient Pool of Bethesda, for in this place lay a great multitude of impotent folk – blind, halt, withered – waiting not for the moving of the water as of tradition, but waiting for me. As I came near, without thought or effort on my part they were, one after the other, molded as by the Magician of the Beautiful. Eyes, hands, feet – all missing members – were drawn from some invisible reservoir and molded in harmony with that perfection which I felt springing within me. When all were made perfect, the chorus exulted, "It is finished". Then the scene dissolved and I awoke.

I know this vision was the result of my intense meditation upon the idea of perfection, for my meditations invariably bring about union with the state contemplated. I had been so completely absorbed within the idea that for a while I had become what I contemplated, and the high purpose with which I had for that moment identified myself drew the companionship of high things and fashioned the vision in harmony with my inner nature. The ideal with which we are united works by association of ideas to awaken a thousand moods to create a drama in keeping with the central idea.

I first discovered this close relationship of moods to vision when I was aged about seven. I became aware of a mysterious life quickening within me like a stormy ocean of frightening might. I always knew when I would be united with this hidden identity, for my senses were expectant on the nights of these visitations and I knew beyond all doubt that before morning I would be alone with immensity. I so dreaded these visitations that I would lie awake until my eyes from sheer exhaustion closed. As my eyes closed in sleep, I was no longer solitary but smitten through and through with another being, and yet I knew it to be myself. It seemed older than life, yet nearer to me than my boyhood. If I tell what I discovered on these nights, I do so not to impose my ideas on others but that I may give hope to those who seek the law of life.

I discovered that my expectant mood worked as a magnet to unite me with this Greater Me, while my fears made It appear as a stormy sea. As a boy, I conceived of this mysterious self as might, and in my union with It I felt its majesty as a stormy sea which drenched me, then rolled and tossed me as a helpless wave.

As a man I conceived of It as love and myself the son of It, and in my union with It, now, what a love enfolds me! It is a mirror to all. Whatever we conceive It as being, that It is to us.

I believe It to be the center through which all the threads of the universe are drawn; therefore I have altered my values and changed my ideas so that they now depend upon and are in harmony with this sole cause of all that is. It is to me that changeless reality which fashions circumstances in harmony with our concepts of ourselves.

My mystical experiences have convinced me that there is no way to bring about the outer perfection we seek other than by the transformation of ourselves.

As soon as we succeed in transforming ourselves, the world will melt magically before our eyes and reshape itself in harmony with that which our transformation affirms.

Two other visions I will tell because they bear out the truth of my assertion that we, by intensity of love and hate, become what we contemplate.

Once, with closed eyes made radiant from brooding, I meditated on the eternal question, "Who Am I?" and felt myself gradually dissolve into a shoreless sea of vibrant light, imagination passing beyond all fear of death. In this state nothing existed but myself, a boundless ocean of liquid light. Never have I felt more intimate with Being.

How long this experience lasted I do not know, but my return to earth was accompanied by a distinct feeling of crystallizing again into human shape.

At another time, I lay on my bed and with my eyes shut as in sleep I brooded on the mystery of Buddha. In a little while, the dark caverns of my brain began to grow luminous.

I seemed to be surrounded by luminous clouds which emanated from my head as fiery, pulsating rings. I saw nothing but these luminous rings for a time. Then there appeared before my eyes a rock of quartz crystal. While I gazed upon it, the crystal broke into pieces which invisible hands quickly shaped into the living Buddha. As I looked

[49] THE POWER OF IMAGINATION: THE NEVILLE GODDARD TREASURY

on this meditative figure, I saw that it was myself. I was the living Buddha whom I contemplated. A light like the sun glowed from this living image of myself with increasing intensity until it exploded. Then the light gradually faded and once more I was back within the blackness of my room.

Out of what sphere or treasury of design came this being mightier than human, his garments, the crystal, the light? If I saw, heard and moved in a world of real beings when I seemed to myself to be walking in the night, when the lame, the halt, the blind were transformed in harmony with my inner nature, then I am justified in assuming that I have a more subtle body than the physical, a body that can be detached from the physical and used in other spheres; for to see, to hear, to move are functions of an organism however ethereal. If I brood over the alternative that my psychic experiences were self-begotten fantasy, no less am I moved to wonder at this mightier self who flashes on my mind a drama as real as those I experience when I am fully awake.

On these fiery meditations I have entered again and again, and I know beyond all doubt that both assumptions are true. Housed within this form of earth is a body attuned to a world of light, and I have, by intense meditation, lifted it as with a magnet through the skull of this dark house of flesh.

The first time I awoke the fires within me I thought my head would explode. There was intense vibration at the base of my skull, then sudden oblivion of all. Then I found myself clothed in a garment of light and attached by a silvery elastic cord to the slumbering body on the bed. So exalted were my feelings, I felt related to the stars. In this garment I roamed spheres more familiar than earth, but found that, as on earth, conditions were molded in harmony with my nature. "Self-begotten fantasy", I hear you say. No more so than the things of earth.

I am an immortal being conceiving myself as man and forming worlds in the likeness and image of my concept of self.

What we imagine, that we are. By our imagination, we have created this dream of life, and by our imagination we will re-enter that eternal world of light, becoming that which we were before we imagined the world.

In the divine economy nothing is lost. We cannot lose anything save by descent from the sphere where the thing has its natural life.

There is no transforming power in death and, whether we are here or there, we fashion the world that surrounds us by the intensity of our imagination and feeling, and we illuminate or darken our lives by the concepts we hold of ourselves. Nothing is more important to us than our conception of ourselves, and especially is this true of our concept of the deep, hidden One within us.

Those that help or hinder us, whether they know it or not, are the servants of that law which shapes outward circumstances in harmony with our inner nature.

It is our conception of ourselves which frees or constrains us, though it may use material agencies to achieve its purpose.

Because life molds the outer world to reflect the inner arrangement of our minds, there is no way of bringing about the outer perfection we seek other than by the transformation of ourselves.

No help cometh from without; the hills to which we lift our eyes are those of an inner range.

It is thus to our own consciousness that we must turn as to the only reality, the only foundation on which all phenomena can be explained. We can rely absolutely on the justice of this law to give us only that which is of the nature of ourselves.

To attempt to change the world before we change our concept of ourselves is to struggle against the nature of things. There can be no outer change until there is first an inner change. As within, so without. I am not advocating philosophical indifference when I suggest that we should imagine ourselves as already that which we want to be, living in a mental atmosphere of greatness, rather than using physical means and arguments to bring about the desired change.

Everything we do, unaccompanied by a change of consciousness, is but futile readjustment of surfaces. However we toil or struggle, we can receive no more than our subconscious assumptions affirm.

To protest against anything which happens to us is to protest against the law of our being and our rulership over our own destiny.

The circumstances of my life are too closely related to my conception of myself not to have been launched by my own spirit from some magical storehouse of my being.

If there is pain to me in these happenings, I should look within myself for the cause, for I am moved here and there and made to live in a world in harmony with my concept of myself.Intense meditation brings about a union with the state contemplated, and during this union we see visions, have experiences, and behave in keeping with our change of consciousness. This shows us that a transformation of consciousness will result in a change of environment and behavior.

However, our ordinary alterations of consciousness, as we pass from one state to another, are not transformations, because each of them is so rapidly succeeded by another in the reverse direction; but whenever one state grows so stable as to definitely expel its rivals, then that central habitual state defines the character and is a true transformation. To say that we are transformed means that ideas previously peripheral in our consciousness now take a central place and form the habitual center of our energy.

All wars prove that violent emotions are extremely potent in precipitating mental rearrangements. Every great conflict has been followed by an era of materialism and greed in which the ideals for which the conflict ostensibly was waged are submerged.

This is inevitable because war evokes hate, which impels a descent in consciousness from the plane of the ideal to the level where the conflict is waged.

If we would become as emotionally aroused over our ideals as we become over our dislikes, we would ascend to the plane of our ideals as easily as we now descend to the level of our hates.

Love and hate have a magical transforming power, and we grow through their exercise into the likeness of what we contemplate. By intensity of hatred we create in ourselves the character we imagine in our enemies. Qualities die for want of attention, so the unlovely states might best be rubbed out by imagining "beauty for ashes and joy for mourning" [Isaiah 61:3] rather than by direct attacks on the state from which we would be free.

"Whatsoever things are lovely and of good report, think on these things" [Philippians 4:8], for we become that with which we are en rapport.

There is nothing to change but our concept of self.

Humanity is a single being in spite of its many forms and faces, and there is in it only such seeming separation as we find in our own being when we are dreaming.

The pictures and circumstances we see in dreams are creations of our own imagination and have no existence save in ourselves. The same is true of the pictures and circumstances we see in this dream of life. They reveal our concepts of ourselves. As soon as we succeed in transforming self, our world will dissolve and reshape itself in harmony with that which our change affirms.

The universe which we study with such care is a dream, and we the dreamers of the dream, eternal dreamers dreaming non-eternal dreams. One day, like Nebuchadnezzar, we shall awaken from the dream, from the nightmare in which we fought with demons, to find that we really never left our eternal home; that we were never born and have never died save in our dream.

THE END.

Feeling Is the Secret

Foreword

THIS book is concerned with the art of realizing your desire. It gives you an account of the mechanism used in the production of the visible world. It is a small book but not slight. There is a treasure in it, a clearly defined road to the realization of your dreams.

Were it possible to carry conviction to another by means of reasoned arguments and detailed instances, this book would be many times its size. It is seldom possible, however, to do so by means of written statements or arguments since to the suspended judgment it always seems plausible to say that the author was dishonest or deluded, and, therefore, his evidence was tainted. Consequently, I have purposely omitted all arguments and testimonials, and simply challenge the open-minded reader to practice the law of consciousness as revealed in this book. Personal success will prove far more convincing than all the books that could be written on the subject. – NEVILLE

Chapter One – Law and Its Operation

THE world, and all within it, is man's conditioned consciousness objectified. Consciousness is the cause as well as the substance of the entire world.

So it is to consciousness that we must turn if we would discover the secret of creation.

Knowledge of the law of consciousness and the method of operating this law will enable you to accomplish all you desire in life.

Armed with a working knowledge of this law, you can build and maintain an ideal world.

Consciousness is the one and only reality, not figuratively but actually. This reality may for the sake of clarity be likened unto a stream which is divided into two parts, the conscious and the subconscious. In order to intelligently operate the law of consciousness, it is necessary to understand the relationship between the conscious and the subconscious.

The conscious is personal and selective; the subconscious is impersonal and non-selective. The conscious is the realm of effect; the subconscious is the realm of cause. These two aspects are the male and female divisions of consciousness. The conscious is male; the subconscious is female.

The conscious generates ideas and impresses these ideas on the subconscious; the subconscious receives ideas and gives form and expression to them.

By this law – first conceiving an idea and then impressing the idea conceived on the subconscious – all things evolve out of consciousness; and without this sequence, there is not anything made that is made.

The conscious impresses the subconscious, while the subconscious expresses all that is impressed upon it.

The subconscious does not originate ideas, but accepts as true those which the conscious mind feels to be true and, in a way known only to itself, objectifies the accepted ideas.

Therefore, through his power to imagine and feel and his freedom to choose the idea he will entertain, man has control over creation.

Control of the subconscious is accomplished through control of your ideas and feelings.

The mechanism of creation is hidden in the very depth of the subconscious, the female aspect or womb of creation.

The subconscious transcends reason and is independent of induction. It contemplates a feeling as a fact existing within itself and on this assumption proceeds to give expression to it. The creative process begins with an idea and its cycle runs its course as a feeling and ends in a volition to act.

Ideas are impressed on the subconscious through the medium of feeling.

No idea can be impressed on the subconscious until it is felt, but once felt – be it good, bad or indifferent – it must be expressed.

Feeling is the one and only medium through which ideas are conveyed to the subconscious.

Therefore, the man who does not control his feeling may easily impress the subconscious with undesirable states. By control of feeling is not meant restraint or suppression of your feeling, but rather the disciplining of self to imagine and entertain only such feeling as contributes to your happiness.

Control of your feeling is all important to a full and happy life.

Never entertain an undesirable feeling, nor think sympathetically about wrong in any shape or form. Do not dwell on the imperfection of yourself or others. To do so is to impress the subconscious with these limitations. What you do not want done unto you, do not feel that it is done unto you or another. This is the whole law of a full and happy life. Everything else is commentary.

Every feeling makes a subconscious impression and, unless it is counteracted by a more powerful feeling of an opposite nature, must be expressed.

The dominant of two feelings is the one expressed. I am healthy is a stronger feeling than I will be healthy. To feel I will be is to confess I am not; I am is stronger than I am not.

What you feel you are always dominates what you feel you would like to be; therefore, to be realized, the wish must be felt as a state that is rather than a state that is not

Sensation precedes manifestation and is the foundation upon which all manifestation rests. Be careful of your moods and feelings, for there is an unbroken connection between your feelings and your visible world. Your body is an emotional filter and bears the unmistakable marks of your prevalent emotions. Emotional disturbances, especially suppressed emotions, are the causes of all disease. To feel intensely about a wrong without voicing or expressing that feeling is the beginning of disease – dis-ease – in both body and environment. Do not entertain the feeling of regret or failure for frustration or detachment from your objective results in disease.

Think feelingly only of the state you desire to realize. Feeling the reality of the state sought and living and acting on that conviction is the way of all seeming miracles. All changes of expression are brought about through a change of feeling. A change of feeling is a change of destiny. All creation occurs in the domain of the subconscious. What you must acquire, then, is a reflective control of the operation of the subconscious, that is, control of your ideas and feelings.

Chance or accident is not responsible for the things that happen to you, nor is predestined fate the author of your fortune or misfortune. Your subconscious impressions determine the conditions of your world. The subconscious is not selective; it is impersonal and no respecter of persons [Acts 10:34; Romans 2:11]. The subconscious is not concerned with the truth or falsity of your feeling. It always accepts as true that which you feel to be true. Feeling is the assent of the subconscious to the truth of that which is declared to be true. Because of this quality of the subconscious there is nothing impossible to man. Whatever the mind of man can conceive and feel as true, the subconscious can and must objectify. Your feelings create the pattern from which your world is fashioned, and a change of feeling is a change of pattern.

The subconscious never fails to express that which has been impressed upon it.

The moment it receives an impression, it begins to work out the ways of its expression. It accepts the feeling impressed upon it, you're feeling, as a fact existing within itself and immediately sets about to produce in the outer or objective world the exact likeness of that feeling.

The subconscious never alters the accepted beliefs of man. It out-pictures them to the last detail whether or not they are beneficial.

To impress the subconscious with the desirable state, you must assume the feeling that would be yours had you already realized your wish. In defining your objective, you must be concerned only with the objective itself. The manner of expression or the difficulties involved are not to be considered by you. To think feelingly on any state impresses it on the subconscious. Therefore, if you dwell on difficulties, barriers or delay, the subconscious, by its very non-selective nature, accepts the feeling of difficulties and obstacles as your request and proceeds to produce them in your outer world.

The subconscious is the womb of creation. It receives the idea unto itself through the feelings of man. It never changes the idea received, but always gives it form. Hence the subconscious out-pictures the idea in the image and likeness of the feeling received. To feel a state as hopeless or impossible is to impress the subconscious with the idea of failure.

Although the subconscious faithfully serves man, it must not be inferred that the relation is that of a servant to a master as was anciently conceived. The ancient prophets called it the slave and servant of man. St. Paul personified it as a "woman" and said: "The woman should be subject to man in everything" [Ephesians

5:24; also, 1Corinthians 14:34, Ephesians 5:22, Colossians 3:18, 1Peter 3:1]. The subconscious does serve man and faithfully gives form to his feelings. However, the subconscious has a distinct distaste for compulsion and responds to persuasion rather than to command; consequently, it resembles the beloved wife more than the servant.

"The husband is head of the wife," Ephesians 5[:23], may not be true of man and woman in their earthly relationship, but it is true of the conscious and the subconscious, or the male and female aspects of consciousness. The mystery to which Paul referred when he wrote, "This is a great mystery [5:32] … He that loveth his wife loveth himself [5:28] … And they two shall be one flesh [5:31] ", is simply the mystery of consciousness. Consciousness is really one and undivided but for creation's sake it appears to be divided into two.

The conscious (objective) or male aspect truly is the head and dominates the subconscious (subjective) or female aspect.

However, this leadership is not that of the tyrant, but of the lover.

So, by assuming the feeling that would be yours were you already in possession of your objective, the subconscious is moved to build the exact likeness of your assumption.

Your desires are not subconsciously accepted until you assume the feeling of their reality, for only through feeling is an idea subconsciously accepted and only through this subconscious acceptance is it ever expressed.

It is easier to ascribe your feeling to events in the world than to admit that the conditions of the world reflect your feeling. However, it is eternally true that the outside mirrors the inside.

"As within, so without" ["As above, so below; as below, so above; as within, so without; as without, so within", "Correspondence", the second of The Seven Principles of Hermes Trismegistus].

"A man can receive nothing unless it is given him from heaven" [John 3:27] and "The kingdom of heaven is within you" [Luke 17:21]. Nothing comes from without; all things come from within – from the subconscious.

It is impossible for you to see other than the contents of your consciousness. Your world in its every detail is your consciousness objectified. Objective states bear witness of subconscious impressions. A change of impression results in a change of expression.

The subconscious accepts as true that which you feel as true, and because creation is the result of subconscious impressions, you, by your feeling, determine creation.

You are already that which you want to be, and your refusal to believe this is the only reason you do not see it.

To seek on the outside for that which you do not feel you are is to seek in vain, for we never find that which we want; we find only that which we are.

In short, you express and have only that which you are conscious of being or possessing. "To him that hath it is given" [Matthew 13:12; 25:29; Mark 4:25; Luke 8:18; 19:26]. Denying the evidence of the senses and appropriating the feeling of the wish fulfilled is the way to the realization of your desire.

Mastery of self-control of your thoughts and feelings is your highest achievement.

However, until perfect self-control is attained, so that, in spite of appearances, you feel all that you want to feel, use sleep and prayer to aid you in realizing your desired states.

These are the two gateways into the subconscious.

Chapter Two – Sleep

SLEEP, the life that occupies one-third of our stay on earth, is the natural door into the subconscious.

So it is with sleep that we are now concerned. The conscious two-thirds of our life on earth is measured by the degree of attention we give sleep. Our understanding of and delight in what sleep has to bestow will cause us, night after night, to set out for it as though we were keeping an appointment with a lover.

"In a dream, in a vision of the night, when deep sleep fillet upon men, in slumbering upon the bed; then he opened the ears of men and stealth their instruction", Job 33.

It is in sleep and in prayer, a state akin to sleep, that man enters the subconscious to make his impressions and receive his instructions. In these states the conscious and subconscious are creatively joined. The male and female become one flesh. Sleep is the time when the male or conscious mind turns from the world of sense to seek its lover or subconscious self.

The subconscious – unlike the woman of the world who marries her husband to change him – has no desire to change the conscious, waking state, but loves it as it is and faithfully reproduces its likeness in the outer world of form.

The conditions and events of your life are your children formed from the molds of your subconscious impressions in sleep. They are made in the image and likeness of your innermost feeling that they may reveal you to yourself.

"As in heaven, so on earth" [Matthew 6:10; Luke 11:2]. As in the subconscious, so on earth.

Whatever you have in consciousness as you go to sleep is the measure of your expression in the waking two-thirds of your life on earth.

Nothing stops you from realizing your objective save your failure to feel that you are already that which you wish to be, or that you are already in possession of the thing sought. Your subconscious gives form to your desires only when you feel your wish fulfilled.

The unconsciousness of sleep is the normal state of the subconscious. Because all things come from within yourself, and your conception of yourself determines that which comes, you should always feel the wish fulfilled before you drop off to sleep.

You never draw out of the deep of yourself that which you want; you always draw that which you are, and you are that which you feel yourself to be as well as that which you feel as true of others.

To be realized, then, the wish must be resolved into the feeling of being or having or witnessing the state sought. This is accomplished by assuming the feeling of the wish fulfilled. The feeling which comes in response to the question "How would I feel were my wish realized?" is the feeling which should monopolize and immobilize your attention as you relax into sleep. You must be in the consciousness of being or having that which you want to be or to have before you drop off to sleep.

Once asleep, man has no freedom of choice. His entire slumber is dominated by his last waking concept of self.

It follows, therefore, that he should always assume the feeling of accomplishment and satisfaction before he retires in sleep, "Come before me with singing and thanksgiving" [Psalm 95:2], "Enter into his gates with thanksgiving and into his courts with praise" [Psalm 100:4]. Your mood prior to sleep defines your state of consciousness as you enter into the presence of your everlasting lover, the subconscious.

She sees you exactly as you feel yourself to be. If, as you prepare for sleep, you assume and maintain the consciousness of success by feeling "I am successful", you must be successful. Lie flat on your back with your head on a level with your body. Feel as you would were you in possession of your wish and quietly relax into unconsciousness.

"He that keepnet Israel shall neither slumber nor sleep" [Psalm 121:4]. Nevertheless "He giveth his beloved sleep" [Psalm 127:2].

The subconscious never sleeps. Sleep is the door through which the conscious, waking mind passes to be creatively joined to the subconscious.

Sleep conceals the creative act, while the objective world reveals it.

In sleep, man impresses the subconscious with his conception of himself.

What more beautiful description of this romance of the conscious and subconscious is there than that told in the "Song of Solomon": "By night on my bed I sought him whom my soul loveth [3:1] … I found him whom my soul loveth; I held him and I not let him go, until I had brought him into my mother's house, and into the chamber of her that conceived me" [3:4].

Preparing to sleep, you feel yourself into the state of the answered wish, and then relax into unconsciousness. Your realized wish is he whom you seek. By night, on your bed, you seek the feeling of the wish fulfilled that you may take it with you into the chamber of her that conceived you, into sleep or the subconscious which gave you form, that this wish also may be given expression.

This is the way to discover and conduct your wishes into the subconscious. Feel yourself in the state of the realized wish and quietly drop off to sleep.

Night after night, you should assume the feeling of being, having and witnessing that which you seek to be, possess and see manifested. Never go to sleep feeling discouraged or dissatisfied. Never sleep in the consciousness of failure.

Your subconscious, whose natural state is sleep, sees you as you believe yourself to be, and whether it be good, bad or indifferent, the subconscious will faithfully embody your belief.

As you feel so do you impress her; and she, the perfect lover, gives form to these impressions and out-pictures them as the children of her beloved.

"Thou art all fair, my love; there is no spot in thee" [Song of Solomon 4:7] is the attitude of mind to adopt before dropping off to sleep.

Disregard appearances and feel that things are as you wish them to be, for "He calleth things that are not seen as though they were, and the unseen becomes seen" [Approx., Romans 4:17]. To assume the feeling of satisfaction is to call conditions into being which will mirror satisfaction.

"Signs follow, they do not precede".

Proof that you are will follow the consciousness that you are; it will not precede it.

You are an eternal dreamer dreaming non-eternal dreams. Your dreams take form as you assume the feeling of their reality.

Do not limit yourself to the past.

Knowing that nothing is impossible to consciousness, begin to imagine states beyond the experiences of the past.

Whatever the mind of man can imagine, man can realize. All objective (visible) states were first subjective (invisible) states, and you called them into visible by assuming the feeling of their reality.

The creative process is first imagining and then believing the state imagined. Always imagine and expect the best.

The world cannot change until you change your conception of it. "As within, so without".

Nations, as well as people, are only what you believe them to be. No matter what the problem is, no matter where it is, no matter whom it concerns, you have no one to change but yourself, and you have neither opponent nor helper in bringing about the change within yourself. You have nothing to do but convince yourself of the truth of that which you desire to see manifested.

As soon as you succeed in convincing yourself of the reality of the state sought, results follow to confirm your fixed belief. You never suggest to another the state which you desire to see him express; instead, you convince yourself that he is already that which you desire him to be.

Realization of your wish is accomplished by assuming the feeling of the wish fulfilled. You cannot fail unless you fail to convince yourself of the reality of your wish. A change of belief is confirmed by a change of expression.

Every night, as you drop off to sleep, feel satisfied and spotless, for your subjective lover always forms the objective world in the image and likeness of your conception of it, the conception defined by your feeling.

The waking two-thirds of your life on earth ever corroborates or bears witness to your subconscious impressions. The actions and events of the day are effects; they are not causes. Free will is only freedom of choice.

"Choose ye this day whom ye shall serve" [Joshua 24:15] is your freedom to choose the kind of mood you assume; but the expression of the mood is the secret of the subconscious.

The subconscious receives impressions only through the feelings of man and, in a way known only to itself, gives these impressions form and expression.

The actions of man are determined by his subconscious impressions.

His illusion of free will, his belief in freedom of action, is but ignorance of the causes which make him act. He thinks himself free because he has forgotten the link between himself and the event.

Man awake is under compulsion to express his subconscious impressions. If in the past he unwisely impressed himself, then let him begin to change his thought and feeling, for only as he does so will he change his world. Do not waste one moment in regret, for to think feelingly of the mistakes of the past is to reinfect yourself. "Let the dead bury the dead" [Matthew 8:22; Luke 9:60]. Turn from appearances and assume the feeling that would be yours were you already the one you wish to be.

Feeling a state produces that state.

The part you play on the world's stage is determined by your conception of yourself.

By feeling your wish fulfilled and quietly relaxing into sleep, you cast yourself in a star role to be played on earth tomorrow, and, while asleep, you are rehearsed and instructed in your part.

The acceptance of the end automatically wills the means of realization. Make no mistake about this. If, as you prepare for sleep, you do not consciously feel yourself into the state of the answered wish, then you will take with you into the chamber of her who conceived you the sum total of the reactions and feelings of the waking day; and while asleep, you will be instructed in the manner in which they will be expressed tomorrow. You will rise believing that you are a free agent, not realizing that every action and event of the day is predetermined by your concept of self as you fell asleep. Your only freedom, then, is your freedom of reaction. You are free to choose how you feel and react to the day's drama, but the drama – the actions, events and circumstances of the day – have already been determined.

Unless you consciously and purposely define the attitude of mind with which you go to sleep, you unconsciously go to sleep in the composite attitude of mind made up of all feelings and reactions of the day. Every reaction makes a subconscious impression and, unless counteracted by an opposite and more dominant feeling, is the cause of future action.

Ideas enveloped in feeling are creative actions. Use your divine right wisely. Through your ability to think and feel, you have dominion over all creation.

While you are awake, you are a gardener selecting seed for your garden, but "Except a corn of wheat fall into the ground and die, it abided alone; but if it dies, it bringeth forth much fruit" [John 12:24].

Your conception of yourself as you fall asleep is the seed you drop into the ground of the subconscious. Dropping off to sleep feeling satisfied and happy compels conditions and events to appear in your world which confirm these attitudes of mind.

Sleep is the door into heaven. What you take in as a feeling you bring out as a condition, action, or object in space. So, sleep in the feeling of the wish fulfilled.

Chapter Three – Prayer

PRAYER, like sleep, is also an entrance into the subconscious.

"When you pray, enter into your closet, and when you have shut your door, pray to your Father which is in secret and your Father which is in secret shall reward you openly" [Matthew 6:6].

Prayer is an illusion of sleep which diminishes the impression of the outer world and renders the mind more receptive to suggestion from within. The mind in prayer is in a state of relaxation and receptivity akin to the feeling attained just before dropping off to sleep.

Prayer is not so much what you ask for, as how you prepare for its reception. "Whatsoever things ye desire, when ye pray believe that you have received them, and ye shall have them" [Mark 11:24].

The only condition required is that you believe that your prayers are already realized.

Your prayer must be answered if you assume the feeling that would be yours were you already in possession of your objective. The moment you accept the wish as an accomplished fact, the subconscious finds mean for its realization. To pray successfully then, you must yield to the wish, that is, feel the wish fulfilled.

The perfectly disciplined man is always in tune with the wish as an accomplished fact.

He knows that consciousness is the one and only reality, that ideas and feelings are facts of consciousness and are as real as objects in space; therefore, he never entertains a feeling which does not contribute to his happiness, for feelings are the causes of the actions and circumstances of his life.

On the other hand, the undisciplined man finds it difficult to believe that which is denied by the senses and usually accepts or rejects solely on appearances of the senses. Because of this tendency to rely on the evidence of the senses, it is necessary to shut them out before starting to pray, before attempting to feel that which they deny. Whenever you are in the state of mind "I should like to, but I cannot", the harder you try, the less you are able to yield to the wish. You never attract that which you want, but always attract that which you are conscious of being.

Prayer is the art of assuming the feeling of being and having that which you want.

When the senses confirm the absence of your wish, all conscious effort to counteract this suggestion is futile and tends to intensify the suggestion.

Prayer is the art of yielding to the wish and not the forcing of the wish. Whenever your feeling is in conflict with your wish, feeling will be the victor. The dominant feeling invariably expresses itself. Prayer must be without effort. In attempting to fix an attitude of mind which is denied by the senses, effort is fatal.

To yield successfully to the wish as an accomplished fact, you must create a passive state, a kind of reverie or meditative reflection similar to the feeling which precedes sleep. In such a relaxed state, the mind is turned from the objective world and easily senses the reality of a subjective state. It is a state in which you are conscious and quite able to move or open your eyes but have no desire to do so. An easy way to create this passive state is to relax in a comfortable chair or on a bed. If on a bed, lie flat on your back with your head on a level with your body, close the eyes and imagine that you are sleepy. Feel – I am sleepy, so sleepy, so very sleepy.

In a little while, a faraway feeling accompanied by a general lassitude and loss of all desire to move envelops you. You feel a pleasant, comfortable rest and not inclined to alter your position, although under other circumstances you would not be at all comfortable. When this passive state is reached, imagine that you have realized your wish – not how it was realized, but simply the wish fulfilled. Imagine in picture form what you desire to achieve in life; then feel yourself as having already achieved it. Thoughts produce tiny little speech movements which may be heard in the passive state of prayer as pronouncements from without. However, this degree of passivity is not essential to the realization of your prayers. All that is necessary is to create a passive state and feel the wish fulfilled.

All you can possibly need or desire is already yours. You need no helper to give it to you; it is yours now. Call your desires into being by imagining and feeling your wish fulfilled. As the end is accepted, you become totally indifferent as to possible failure, for acceptance of the end wills the means to that end. When you emerge from the moment of prayer, it is as though you were shown the happy and successful end of a play although you were not shown how that end was achieved. However, having witnessed the end, regardless of any anticlimactic sequence, you remain calm and secure in the knowledge that the end has been perfectly defined.

Chapter Four – Feeling

"NOT by might, nor by power, but by my spirit, saith the Lord of hosts" [Zechariah 4:6]. Get into the spirit of the state desired by assuming the feeling that would be yours were you already the one you want to be. As you capture the feeling of the state sought, you are relieved of all effort to make it so, for it is already so. There is a definite feeling associated with every idea in the mind of man. Capture the feeling associated with your realized wish by assuming the feeling that would be yours were you already in possession of the thing you desire, and your wish will objectify itself.

Faith is feeling, "According to your faith (feeling) be it unto you" [Matthew 9:29]. You never attract that which you want, but always that which you are. As a man is, so does he see. "To him that hath it shall be given and to him that hath not it shall be taken away…" [Matthew 13:12; 25:29; Mark 4:25; Luke 8:18; 19:26]. That which you feel yourself to be, you are, and you are given that which you are. So, assume the feeling that would be yours were you already in possession of your wish, and your wish must be realized.

"So, God created man in his own image, in the image of God created he him" [Genesis 1:27]. "Let this mind be in you which was also in Christ Jesus, who being in the form of God, thought it not robbery to be equal with God" [Philippians 2:5,6]. You are that which you believe yourself to be.

Instead of believing in God or in Jesus – believe you are God or you are Jesus. "He that believeth on Me, the works that I do shall he do also" [John 14:12] should be "He that believes as I believe the works that I do he shall do also". Jesus found it not strange to do the works of God, because He believed Himself to be God. "I and My Father are one" [John 10:30]. It is natural to do the works of the one you believe yourself to be. So, live in the feeling of being the one you want to be and that you shall be.

When a man believes in the value of the advice given him and applies it, he establishes within himself the reality of success.

Freedom For All

Chapter One
THE ONENESS OF GOD

HEAR, O Israel: the Lord our God is one Lord. Hear, O Israel:

Hear, O man made of the very substance of God: You and God are one and undivided!

Man, the world and all within it are conditioned states of the unconditioned one, God. You are this one; you are God conditioned as man. All that you believe God to be, you are; but you will never know this to be true until you stop claiming it of another, and recognize this seeming other to be yourself. God and man, spirit and matter, the formless and the formed, the creator and the creation, the cause and the effect, your Father and you are one. This one, in whom all conditioned states live and move and have their being, is your I AM, your unconditioned consciousness.

Unconditioned consciousness is God, the one and only reality. By unconditioned consciousness is meant a sense of awareness; a sense of knowing that I AM apart from knowing who I AM; the consciousness of being, divorced from that which I am conscious of being.

I AM aware of being a man, but I need not be a man to be aware of being. Before I became aware of being someone, I, unconditioned awareness, was aware of being, and this awareness does not depend upon being someone. I AM self-existent, unconditioned consciousness; I became aware of being someone; and I shall become aware of being someone other than this that I am now aware of being; but I AM eternally aware of being whether I am unconditioned formlessness or I am conditioned form.

As the condition states, I (man)might forget who I am, or where I am, but I cannot forget that I AM. This knowing that I AM, this awareness of being, is the only reality.

This unconditioned consciousness, the I AM, is that knowing reality in whom all conditioned states – conceptions of myself – begin and end, but which ever remains the unknown knowing being when all the known ceases to be.

All that I have ever believed myself to be, all that I now believe myself to be, and all that I shall ever believe myself to be, are but attempts to know myself – the unknown, undefined reality.

This unknown knowing one, or unconditioned consciousness, is my true being, the one and only reality. I AM the unconditioned reality conditioned as that which I believe myself to be. I AM the believer limited by my beliefs, the knower defined by the known.

The world is my conditioned consciousness objectified.

That which I feel and believe to be true of myself is now projected in space as my world.

The world – my mirrored self – ever bears witness of the state of consciousness in which I live.

There is no chance or accident responsible for the things that happen to me or the environment in which I find myself. Nor is predestined fate the author of my fortunes or misfortunes. Innocence and guilt are mere words without meaning to the law of consciousness, except as they reflect the state of consciousness itself.

The consciousness of guilt calls forth condemnation. The consciousness of lack produces poverty.

Man everlastingly objectifies the state of consciousness in which he abides but he has somehow or other become confused in the interpretation of the law of cause and effect.

He has forgotten that it is the inner state which is the cause of the outer manifestation – "As within, so without" ["Correspondence", the second of The Seven Principles of Hermes Trismegistus] – and in his forgetfulness he believes that an outside God has his own peculiar reason for doing things, such reasons being beyond the comprehension of mere man; or he believes that people are suffering because of past mistakes which have been forgotten by the conscious mind; or, again, that blind chance alone plays the part of God.

One day man will realize that his own I AM-ness is the God he has been seeking throughout the ages, and that his own sense of awareness – his consciousness of being – is the one and only reality.

The most difficult thing for man to really grasp is this: That the "I AM-ness" in himself is God. It is his true being or Father state, the only state he can be sure of. The Son, his conception of himself, is an illusion. He always knows that he IS, but that which he is, is an illusion created by himself (the Father) in an attempt at self-definition.

This discovery reveals that all that I have believed God to be I AM.

"I AM the resurrection and the life" [John 11:25] is a statement of fact concerning my consciousness, for my consciousness resurrects or makes visibly alive that which I am conscious of being

"I AM the door [John 10:2, 10:7, 10:9]... all that ever came before me are thieves and robbers" [John 10:8] shows me that my consciousness is the one and only entrance into the world of expression; that by assuming the consciousness of being or possessing the thing which I desire to be or possess is the only way by which I can become it or possess it; that any attempt to express this desirable state in ways other than by assuming the consciousness of being or possessing it, is to be robbed of the joy of expression and possession.

"I AM the beginning and the end" [Revelation 1:8, 22:13] reveals my consciousness as the cause of the birth and death of all expression.

"I AM hath sent me" [Exodus 3:14] reveals my consciousness to be the Lord which sends me into the world in the image and likeness of that which I am conscious of being to live in a world composed of all that I am conscious of.

"I AM the Lord, and there is no God beside Me" [Isaiah 45:5] declares my consciousness to be the one and only Lord and beside my consciousness there is no God.

"BE still and know that I AM God" [Psalm 46:10] means that I should still the mind and know that consciousness is God.

"Thou shalt not take the Name of the Lord thy God in vain" [Exodus 20:7], "I AM the Lord: that is My Name" [Isaiah 42:8]. Now that you have discovered your I AM, your consciousness to be God, do not claim anything to be true of yourself that you would not claim to be true of God, for in defining yourself, you are defining God.

That which you are conscious of being is that which you have named God. God and man are one. You and your Father are one [John 10:30].

Your unconditioned consciousness, or I AM, and that which you are conscious of being, are one.

The conceiver and the conception are one. If your conception of yourself is less than that which you claim as true of God, you have robbed God [see Philippians 2:6], the Father, because you (the Son or conception) bear witness of the Father or conceiver. Do not take the magical Name of God, I AM, in vain for you will not be held guiltless; you must express all that you claim yourself to be.

Name God by consciously defining yourself as your highest ideal.

Chapter Two
THE NAME OF GOD

It cannot be stated too often that consciousness is the one and only reality, for this is the truth that sets man free.

This is the foundation upon which the whole structure of biblical literature rests. The stories of the Bible are all mystical revelations written in an Eastern symbolism which reveals to the intuitive the secret of creation and the formula of escape. The Bible is man's attempt to express in words the cause and manner of creation. Man discovered that his consciousness was the cause or creator of his world, so he proceeded to tell the story of creation in a series of symbolic stories known to us today as the Bible.

To understand this greatest of books you need a little intelligence and much intuition – intelligence enough to enable you to read the book, and intuition enough to interpret and understand what you read.

You may ask why the Bible was written symbolically. Why was it not written in a clear, simple style so that all who read it might understand it? To these questions I reply that all men speak symbolically to that part of the world which differs from their own.

The language of the West is clear to us of the West, but it is symbolic to the East; and vice versa. An example of this can be found in the Easterners instruction: "If thine hand offends thee, cut it off" [Mark 9:43]. He speaks of the hand, not as the hand of the body, but as any form of expression, and thereby he warns you to turn from that expression in your world which is offensive to you. At the same time the man of the West would unintentionally mislead the man of the East by saying: "This bank is on the rocks." For the expression "on the rocks" to the Westerner is equivalent to bankruptcy while a rock to an Easterner is a symbol of faith and security. "I will like him unto a wise man which built his house upon a rock; and the rain descended, and the floods came, and the winds blew and beat upon that house; and it fell not; for it was founded upon a rock" [Matthew 7:24,25].

To really understand the message of the Bible you must bear in mind that it was written by the Eastern mind and therefore cannot be taken literally by those of the West. Biologically, there is no difference between the East and the West. Love and hate are the same; hunger and thirst are the same; ambition and desire are the same; but the technique of expression is vastly different.

The first thing you must discover if you would unlock the secret of the Bible, is the meaning of the symbolic name of the creator which is known to all as Jehovah. This word "Jehovah" is composed of the four Hebrew letters – JOD HE VAU HE. The whole secret of creation is concealed within this name.

The first letter, JOD, represents the absolute state or consciousness unconditioned; the sense of undefined awareness; that all inclusiveness out of which all creation or conditioned states of consciousness come.

In the terminology of today JOD is I AM, or unconditioned consciousness.

The second letter, HE, represents the only begotten Son, a desire, an imaginary state. It symbolizes an idea; a defined subjective state or clarified mental picture.

The third letter, VAU, symbolizes the act of unifying or joining the conceiver (JOD), the consciousness desiring to the conception (HE), the state desired, so that the conceiver and the conception become one.

Fixing a mental state, consciously defining yourself as the state desired, impressing upon yourself the fact that you are now that which you imagined or conceived as your objective, is the function of VAU. It nails or joins the consciousness desiring to the thing desired. The cementing or joining process is accomplished subjectively by feeling the reality of that which is not yet objectified.

The fourth letter, HE, represents the objectifying of this subjective agreement. The JOD HE VAU makes man or the manifested world (HE), in the image and likeness of itself, the subjective conscious state. So the function of the final HE is to objectively bear witness to the subjective state JOD HE VAU.

Conditioned consciousness continually objectifies itself on the screen of space.

The world is the image and likeness of the subjective conscious state which created it.

The visible world of itself can do nothing; it only bears record of his creator, the subjective state. It is the visible Son (HE) bearing witness of the invisible Father, Son and Mother – JOD HE VAU – a Holy Trinity which can only be seen when made visible as man or manifestation.

Your unconditioned consciousness (JOD) is your I AM which visualizes or imagines a desirable state (HE), and then becomes conscious of being that state imagined by feeling and believing itself to be the imagined state. The conscious union between you who desire and that which you desire to be, is made possible through the VAU, or your capacity to feel and believe.

Believing is simply living in the feeling of actually being the state imagined – by assuming the consciousness of being the state desired. The subjective state symbolized as JOD HE VAU then objectifies itself as HE, thereby completing the mystery of the creator's name and nature, JOD HE VAU HE (Jehovah).

JOD is to be aware; HE is to be aware of something; VAU is to be aware as, or to be aware of being that which you were only aware of. The second HE is your visible objectified world which is made in the image and likeness of the JOD HE VAU, or that which you are aware of being.

"And God said, Let Us make man in Our image, after Our likeness" [Genesis 1:26]. Let us, JOD HE VAU make the objective manifestation (HE) in our image, the image of the subjective state.

The world is the objectified likeness of the subjective conscious

state in which consciousness abides.

This understanding that consciousness is the one and only reality is the foundation of the Bible.

The stories of the Bible are attempts to reveal in symbolic language the secret of creation as well as to show man the one formula to escape from all of his own creations.

This is the true meaning of the name of Jehovah, the name by which all things are made and without which there is nothing made that is made John 1:3].

First, you are aware; then you become aware of something; then you become aware of that which you were aware of; then you behold objectively that which you are aware of being.

Chapter Three
THE LAW OF CREATION

Let us take one of the stories of the Bible and see how the prophets and writers of old revealed the story of creation by this strange Eastern symbolism.

We all know the story of Noah and the Ark; that Noah was chosen to create a new world after the world was destroyed by the flood.

The Bible tells us that Noah had three sons, Shem, Ham and Japheth [Genesis 6:10].

The first son is called Shem, which means name. Ham, the second son, means warm, alive. The third son is called Japheth, which means extension. You will observe that Noah and his three sons Shem, Ham and Japheth contain the same formula of creation as does the divine name of JOD HE VAU HE.

Noah, the Father, the conceiver, the builder of a new world is equivalent to the JOD, or unconditioned consciousness, I AM. Shem is your desire; that which you are conscious of; that which you name and define as your objective, and is equivalent to the second letter in the divine name (HE). Ham is the warm, live state of feeling, which joins or binds together consciousness, desire and the thing desired, and is therefore equivalent to the third letter in the divine name, the VAU. The last son, Japheth, means extension, and is the extended or objectified state bearing witness of the subjective state and is equivalent to the last letter in the divine name, HE.

You are Noah, the knower, the creator.

The first thing you beget is an idea, an urge, a desire, the word, or your first son Shem (name).

Your second son Ham (warm, alive) is the secret of FEELING by which you are joined to your desire subjectively so that you, the consciousness desiring, become conscious of being or possessing the thing desired.

Your third son, Japheth, is the confirmation, the visible proof that you know the secret of creation.

He is the extended or objectified state bearing witness of the invisible or subjective state in which you abide.

In the story of Noah it is recorded that Ham saw the secrets of his

Father [Genesis 9:22], and, because of his discovery, he was made to serve his brothers, Shem and Japheth [9:25]. Ham, or feeling, is the secret of the Father, your I AM, for it is through feeling that the consciousness desiring is joined to the thing desired.

The conscious union or mystical marriage is made possible only through feeling.

It is the feeling which performs this heavenly union of Father and Son, Noah and Shem, unconditioned consciousness and conditioned consciousness. By performing this service, feeling automatically serves Japheth, the extended or expressed state, for there can be no objectified expression unless there is first a subjective impression.

To feel the presence of the thing desired, to subjectively actualize a state by impressing upon yourself, through feeling, a definite conscious state is the secret of creation.

Your present objectified world is Japheth which was made visible by Ham. Therefore Ham serves his brothers Shem and Japheth, for without feeling which is symbolized as Ham, the idea or thing desired (Shem) could not be made visible as Japheth.

The ability to feel the unseen, the ability to actualize and make real a definite subjective state through the sense of feeling is the secret of creation, the secret by which the word or unseen desire is made visible – is made flesh [John 1:14]. "And God calleth things that be not as though they were" [Romans 4:17].

Consciousness calls things that are not seen as though they were, and it does this by first defining itself as that which it desires to express, and second by remaining within the defined state until the invisible becomes visible.

Here is the perfect working of the law according to the story of Noah. This very moment you are aware of being. This awareness of being, this knowing that you are, is Noah, the creator.

Now with Noah's identity established as your own consciousness of being, name something that you would like to possess or express; define some objective (Shem), and with your desire clearly defined, close your eyes and feel that you have it or are expressing it.

Don't question how it can be done; simply feel that you have it.

Assume the attitude of mind that would be yours if you were already in possession of it so that you feel that it is done.

Feeling is the secret of creation.

Be as wise as Ham and make this discovery that you too may have the joy of serving your brothers Shem and Japheth; the joy of making the word or name flesh.

Chapter Four
THE SECRET OF FEELING

The secret of feeling or the calling of the invisible into visible states is beautifully told in the story of Isaac blessing his second son Jacob by the belief, based solely upon feeling, that he was blessing his first son Esau [Genesis 27:1-35].

It is recorded that Isaac, who was old and blind, felt that he was about to leave this world and wishing to bless his first son Esau before he died, sent Esau hunting for savory venison with the promise that upon his return from the hunt he would receive his father's blessing.

Now Jacob, who desired the birthright or right to be born through the blessing of his father, overheard his blind father's request for venison and his promise to Esau. So, as Esau went hunting for the venison, Jacob killed and dressed a kid of his father's flock.

Placing the skins upon his smooth body to give him the feel of his hairy and rough brother Esau, he brought the tastily prepared kid to his blind father Isaac. And Isaac who depended solely upon his sense of feel mistook his second son Jacob for his first son Esau, and pronounced his blessing on Jacob. Esau on his return from the hunt learned that his smooth-skinned brother Jacob had supplanted him so he appealed to his father for justice; but Isaac answered and said, "Thy brother came with subtlety and hath taken away thy blessing [27:35]. I have made him thy Lord, and all his brethren have I given to him for servants [27:37]."

Simple human decency should tell man that this story cannot be taken literally. There must be a message for man hidden somewhere in this treacherous and despicable act of Jacob! The hidden message, the formula of success buried in this story was intuitively revealed to the writer in this manner. Isaac, the blind father, is your consciousness; your awareness of being.

Esau, the hairy son, is your present objectified world – the rough or sensibly felt; the present moment; the present environment; your present conception of yourself; in short, the world you know by reason of your objective senses. Jacob, the smooth-skinned lad, the second son, is your desire or subjective state, an idea not yet embodied, a subjective state which is perceived and sensed but not objectively known or seen; a point in time and space removed from the present. In short, Jacob is your defined objective. The smooth-skinned Jacob

– or subjective state seeking embodiment or the right of birth – when

[80] NEVILLE GODDARD

properly felt or blessed by his father (when consciously felt and fixed as real), becomes objectified; and in so doing he supplants the rough, hairy Esau, or the former objectified state. Two things cannot occupy a given place at one and the same time, and so as the invisible is made visible, the former visible state vanishes.

Your consciousness is the cause of your world. The conscious state in which you abide determines the kind of world in which you live. Your present concept of yourself is now objectified as your environment, and this state is symbolized as Esau, the hairy, sensibly felt; the first son. That which you would like to be or possess is symbolized as your second son, Jacob, the smooth-skinned lad who is not yet seen but is subjectively senses and felt, and will, if properly touched, supplant his brother Esau, or your present world.

Always bear in mind the fact that Isaac, the father of these two sons, or states, is blind. He does not see his smooth-skinned son Jacob; he only feels him.

And through the sense of feeling he actually believes Jacob, the subjective, to be Esau, the real, the objectified.

You do not see your desire objectively; you simply sense it (feel it) subjectively.

You do not grope in space after a desirable state. Like Isaac, you sit still and send your first son hunting by removing your attention from your objective world.

Then in the absence of your first son, Esau, you invite the desirable state, your second son, Jacob, to come close so that you may feel it. "Come close, my son, so that I may feel you" [27:21]. First, you are aware of it in your immediate environment; then you draw it closer and closer and closer until you sense it and feel it in your immediate presence so that it is real and natural to you.

"If two of you shall agree on earth as touching on any point that they shall ask, it shall be done for them of My Father, Which is in heaven" [Matthew 18:19].

The two agree through the sense of feel; and the agreement is

established on earth – is objectified; is made real.

The two agreeing are Isaac and Jacob – you and that which you desire; and the agreement is made solely on the sense of feeling.

Esau symbolizes your present objectified world whether it be

pleasant or otherwise.

Jacob symbolizes any and every desire of your heart.

Isaac symbolizes your true self – with your eyes closed to the present world – in the act of sensing and feeling yourself to be or to possess that which you desire to be or to possess.

The secret of Isaac – the sensing, feeling state – is simply the act of mentally separating the sensibly felt (your present physical state) from the insensibly felt (that which you would like to be).

With the objective senses tightly shut Isaac made, and you can make the insensibly felt (the subjective state) seem real or sensibly known, for faith is knowledge.

Knowing the law of self-expression, the law by which the invisible is made visible, is not enough. It must be applied; and this is the method of application.

First: Send your first son Esau – your present objectified world or problem – hunting. This is accomplished simply by closing your eyes and taking your attention away from the objectified limitations. As your senses are removed from your objective world, it vanishes from your consciousness or goes hunting.

Second: With your eyes still closed and your attention removed from the world around you, consciously fix the natural time and place for the realization of your desire. With your objective senses closed to your present environment you can sense and feel the reality of any point in time or space, for both are psychological and can be created at will. It is vitally important that the natural time- space condition of Jacob, that is, the natural time and place for the realization of your desire be first fixed in your consciousness.

If Sunday is the day on which the thing desired is to be realized, then Sunday must be fixed in consciousness now.

Simply begin to feel that it is Sunday until the quietness and naturalness of Sunday is consciously established.

You have definite associations with the days, weeks, months and seasons of the year. You have said time and again "Today feels like Sunday, or Monday, or Saturday; or this feels like Spring, or summer, or Fall, or Winter." This should convince you that you have definite, conscious impressions that you associate with the days, weeks, and seasons of the year.

Then because of these associations you can select any desirable time, and by recalling the conscious impression associated with such time, you can make a subjective reality of that time now.

Do the same with space. If the room in which you are seated is not the room in which the thing desired would be naturally placed or realized, feel yourself seated in the room or place where it would be natural. Consciously fix this time space impression before you start the act of sensing and feeling the nearness, the reality, and the possession of the thing desired. It matters not whether the place desired be ten thousand miles away or only next door, you must fix in consciousness the fact that right where you are seated is the desired place.

You do not make a mental journey; you collapse space. Sit quietly where you are and make "there-ness" – "here-ness." Close your eyes and feel that the very place where you are is the place desired; feel and sense the reality of it until you are consciously impressed with this fact, for your knowledge of this fact is based solely on your subjective sensing.

Third: In the absence of Esau (the problem) and with the natural time-space established, you invite Jacob (the solution) to come and fill this space – to come and supplant his brother.

In your imagination see the thing desired. If you cannot visualize it, sense the general outline of it; contemplate it. Then mentally draw it close to you.

"Come close, my son, that I may feel you."

Feel the nearness of it; feel it to be in your immediate presence; feel the reality and solidity of it; feel it and see it naturally placed in the room in which you are seated; feel the thrill of actual accomplishment, and the joy of possession.

Now open your eyes. This brings you back to the objective world– the rough or sensibly felt world. Your hairy son Esau has returned from the hunt and by his very presence tells you that you have been betrayed by your smooth-skinned son Jacob – the subjective, psychologically felt.

But, like Isaac, whose confidence was based upon the knowledge of this changeless law, you too will say – "I have made him thy Lord and all his brethren have I given to him for servants".That is, even though your problems appears fixed and real, you have felt the subjective, psychological state to be real to the point of receiving the thrill of that reality; you have experienced the secret of creation for you have felt the reality of the subjective.

You have fixed a definite psychological state which in spite of all opposition or precedent will objectify itself, thereby fulfilling the name of Jacob – the supplanter.

Here are a few practical examples of this drama. First: The blessing or making a thing real.

Sit in your living room and name a piece of furniture, rug or lamp that you would like to have in this particular room. Look at that area of the room where you would place it if you had it. Close your eyes and let all that now occupies that area of the room vanish. In your imagination see this area as empty space – there is absolutely nothing there. Now begin to fill this space with the desired piece of furniture; sense and feel that you have it in this very area, imagine you are seeing that which you desired to see. Continue in this consciousness until you feel the thrill of possession.

Second. The blessing or the making of a place real.

You are now seated in your apartment in New York City, contemplating the joy that would be yours if you were on an ocean liner sailing across the great Atlantic. "I am going to prepare a place for you. And if I go and prepare a place for you, I will come again, and receive you unto myself; that where I am there ye may be also" [John 14:2- 3]. Your eyes are closed; you have consciously released the New York apartment and in its place you sense and feel that you are on an ocean liner. You are seated in a deck chair; there is nothing around you but the vast Atlantic.

Fix the reality of this ship and ocean so that in this state you can mentally recall the day when you were seated in your New York apartment dreaming of this day at sea. Recall the mental picture of yourself seated there in New York dreaming of this day. In your imagination see the memory picture of yourself back there in your New York apartment. If you succeed in looking back on your New York apartment without consciously returning there, then you have successfully prepared the reality of this voyage.

Remain in this conscious state feeling the reality of the ship and the ocean; feel the joy of this accomplishment – then open your eyes.

You have gone and prepared the place; you have fixed a definite psychological state and where you are in consciousness there you shall be in body also.

Third: The blessing or making real of a point in time.

You consciously let go of this day, month or year, as the case may be, and you imagine that it is now that day, month or year which you desire to experience. You sense and feel the reality of the desired time by impressing upon yourself the fact that it is now accomplished. As you sense the naturalness of this time, you begin to feel the thrill of having fully realized that which before you started this psychological journey in time you desired to experience at this time.

With the knowledge of your power to bless you can open the doors of any prison – the prison of illness or poverty or of a humdrum existence.

"The Spirit of the Lord God is upon me; because the Lord hath anointed me to preach good tidings unto the meek; he hath sent me to bind up the brokenhearted, to proclaim liberty to the captives, and the opening of the prison to them that are bound" [Isaiah 61:1, Luke 4:18].

Chapter Five
THE SABBATH

"Six days shall work be done, but on the seventh day there shall be to you an holy day, a Sabbath of rest to the Lord" [– Exodus 31:15, Leviticus 23:3]

These six days are not twenty-four-hour periods of time.

They symbolize the psychological moment a definite subjective state is fixed.

These six days of work are subjective experiences, and consequently cannot be measured by sidereal time, for the real work of fixing a definite psychological state is done in consciousness.

The time spent in consciously defining yourself as that which you desire to be is the measure of these six days.

A change of consciousness is the work done in these six creative days; a psychological adjustment, which is measured not by sidereal time but by actual (subjective) accomplishment. Just as a life in retrospect is measured not by years but by the content of those years, so too is this psychological interval measured – not by the time spent in making the adjustment, but by the accomplishment of that interval.

The true meaning of six days of work (creation) is revealed in the mystery of the VAU, which is the sixth letter in the Hebrew alphabet, and the third letter in the divine name – JOD HE VAU HE.

As previously explained in the mystery of the name of Jehovah, VAU means to nail or join.

The creator is joined to his creation through feeling; and the time that it takes you to fix a definite feeling is the true measure of these six days of creation.

Mentally separating yourself from the objective world and attaching yourself through the secret of feeling to the subjective state is the function of the sixth letter of the Hebrew alphabet, VAU, or the six days of work.

There is always an interval between the fixed impression, or subjective state, and the outward expression of that state. The interval is called the Sabbath.

The Sabbath is the mental rest which follows the fixed psychological state; it is the result of your six days of work.

"The Sabbath was made for man" [Mark 2:27]. This mental rest which follows a successful conscious impregnation is the period of mental pregnancy; a period which is made for the purpose of incubating the manifestation.

It was made for the manifestation; the manifestation was not made for it.

Automatically you keep the Sabbath a day of rest – a period of mental rest – if you succeed in accomplishing your six days of work.

There can be no Sabbath, no seventh day, no period of mental rest, until the six days are over – until the psychological adjustment is accomplished and the mental impression is fully made.

Man is warned that if he fails to keep the Sabbath, if he fails to enter into the rest of God he will also fail to receive the promise – he will fail to realize his desires.

The reason for this is simple and obvious. There can be no mental rest until a conscious impression is made.

If a man fails to fully impress upon himself the fact that he now has that which heretofore he desired to possess, he will continue to desire it, and therefore he will not be mentally at rest or satisfied.

If, on the other hand, he succeeds in making this conscious adjustment so that upon emerging from the period of silence or his subjective six days of work, he knows by his feeling that he has the thing desired, then he automatically enters the Sabbath or the period of mental rest.

Pregnancy follows impregnation. Man does not continue desiring that which he has already acquired. The Sabbath can be kept as a day of rest only after man succeeds in becoming conscious of being that which before entering the silence he desired to be.

The Sabbath is the result of the six days of work. The man who knows the true meaning of these six work days realizes that the observance of one day of the week as a day of physical quietness is not keeping the Sabbath.

The peace and the quiet of the Sabbath can be experienced only when man has succeeded in becoming conscious of being that which he desires to be. If he fails to make this conscious impression he has missed the mark; he has sinned, for to sin is to miss the mark – to fail to achieve one's objective; a state in which there is no peace of mind.

"If I had not come and spoken unto them, they had not had sin" [John

15:22]. If man had not been presented with an ideal state toward which to aim, a state to be desired and acquired, he would have been satisfied with his lot in life and would never have known sin.

Now that man knows that his capacities are infinite, knows that by working six days or by making a psychological adjustment he can realize his desires, he will not be satisfied until he achieves his every objective.

He will, with the true knowledge of these six workdays, define his objective and set about becoming conscious of being it.

When this conscious impression is made it is automatically followed by a period of mental rest, a period the mystic calls the Sabbath, an interval in which the conscious impression will be gestated and physically expressed.

The word will be made flesh. But that is not the end!

The Sabbath or rest which will be broken by the embodiment of the idea will sooner or later give way to another six days of work as man defines another objective and begins the act of defining himself as that which he desires to be.

Man has been stirred out of his sleep through the medium of desire, and can find no rest until he realizes his desire.

But before he can enter into the rest of God, or keep the Sabbath, before he can walk unafraid and at peace, he must become a good spiritual marksman and learn the secret of hitting the mark or working six days – the secret by which he lets go the objective state and adjusts himself to the subjective.

This secret was revealed in the divine name Jehovah, and again in the story of Isaac blessing his son Jacob. If man will apply the formula as it is revealed in these Bible dramas he will hit a spiritual bull's eye every time, for he will know that the mental rest or Sabbath is entered only as he succeeds in making a psychological adjustment.

The story of the crucifixion beautifully dramatizes these six days (psychological period) and the seventh day of rest.

It is recorded that it was the custom of the Jews to have someone released from prison at the feast of the Passover; and that they were given the choice of having released unto them either Barabbas the robber, or Jesus the savior. And they cried, "Release Barabbas" [John 18:40]. Whereupon Barabbas was released and Jesus was crucified.

It is further recorded that Jesus the Savior was crucified on the sixth day, entombed or buried on the seventh, and resurrected on the first day.

The savior in your case is that which would save you from that which you are not conscious of being, while Barabbas the thief is your present conception of yourself which robs you of that which you would like to be.

In defining your savior you define that which you would save you and not how you would be saved.

Your savior or desire has ways ye know not of; his ways are past finding out [Romans 11:33].

Every problem reveals its own solution. If you were imprisoned you would automatically desire to be free. Freedom, then, is the thing that would save you. It is your savior.

Having discovered your savior the next step in this great drama of the resurrection is to release Barabbas, the robber – your present concept of yourself – and to crucify your savior, or fix the consciousness of being or having that which would save you.

Barabbas represents your present problem. Your savior is that which would free you from this problem. You release Barabbas by taking your attention away from your problem – away from your sense of limitation – for it robs you of the freedom that you seek. And you crucify your savior by fixing a definite psychological state by feeling that you are free from the limitations of the past.

You deny the evidence of the senses and begin to feel subjectively the joy of being free. You feel this state of freedom to be so real that you too cry out, "I am free!" – "It is finished" [John 19:30].

The fixing of this subjective state – the crucifixion – takes place on the sixth day. Before the sun sets on this day you must have completed the fixation by feeling – "It is so" – "It is finished."

The subjective knowing is followed by the Sabbath or mental rest. You will be as one buried or entombed for you will know that no matter how mountainous the barriers, how impassable the walls appear to be, your crucified and buried savior (your present subjunctive fixation) will resurrect himself.

By keeping the Sabbath a period of mental rest, by assuming the attitude of mind that would be yours if you were already visibly expressing this freedom, you will receive the promise of the Lord, for the Word will be made flesh – the subjective fixation will embody itself. "And God did rest the seventh day from all His works"

[Hebrews 4:4].

Your consciousness is God resting in the knowledge that – "It is well" – "It is finished." And your objective senses shall confirm that it is so for the day shall reveal it.

Chapter Six
HEALING

The formula for the cure of leprosy as revealed in the fourteenth chapter of Leviticus is most illuminating when viewed through the eyes of a mystic. This formula can be prescribed as the positive cure of any disease in man's world, be it physical, mental, financial, social, moral – anything.

It matters not about the nature of the disease or its duration, for the formula can be successfully applied to any and all of them.

Here is the formula as it is recorded in the book of Leviticus. "Then shall the priest command to take for him that is to be cleansed two birds alive and clean… and the priest shall command that one of the birds be killed…..As for the living bird, he shall take it and shall dip it in the blood of the bird that was killed; and he shall sprinkle upon him that is to be cleansed from the leprosy seven times and shall pronounce him clean and shall let the living bird loose into the open field…. And he shall be clean" [14:4-8].

A literal application of this story would be stupid and fruitless, while on the other hand a psychological application of the formula is wise and fruitful.

A bird is a symbol of an idea. Every man who has a problem or who desires to express something other than that which he is now expressing can be said to have two birds. These two birds or conceptions can be defined as follows: the first bird is your present out-pictured conception of yourself; it is the description which you would give if you were asked to define yourself – your physical condition, your income, your obligations, your nationality, family, race and so on. Your sincere answer to these questions would necessarily be based solely upon the evidence of your senses and not upon any wishful thinking.

This true conception of yourself (based entirely upon the evidences of your senses) defines the first bird.

The second bird is defined by the answer you wish you might give in these questions of self-definition. In short, these two birds can be defined as that which you are conscious of being and that which you desire to be.

Another definition of the two birds would be, the first – your present problem regardless of its nature, and the second – the solution to that problem.

For example: if you were sick, good health would be the solution. If you were in debt, freedom from debt would be the solution. If you were hungry, food would be the solution. As you have noticed, the how, the manner of realizing the solution, is not considered.

Only the problem and the solution are considered.

Every problem reveals its own solution. For sickness it is health; for poverty it is riches; for weakness it is strength, for confinement it is freedom.

These two states then, your problem and its solution, are the two birds you bring to the priest. You are the priest who now performs the drama of the curing of the man of leprosy – you and your problem. You are the priest; and with the formula for the cure of leprosy you now free yourself from your problem.

First: Take one of the birds (your problem) and kill it by extracting the blood from it. Blood is man's consciousness. "He hath made of one blood all nations of men to dwell on all the face of the earth" [Acts 17:26].

Your consciousness is the one and only reality which animates and makes real that which you are conscious of being. So turning your attention away from the problem is equivalent to extracting the blood from the bird. Your consciousness is the one blood which makes all states living realities. By removing your attention from any given state you have drained the lifeblood from that state. You kill or eliminate the first bird (your problem) by removing your attention from it. Into this blood (your consciousness) you dip the live bird (the solution), or that which heretofore you desired to be or possess. This you do by freeing yourself to be the desirable state now.

The dipping of the live bird into the blood of the bird that was killed is similar to the blessing of Jacob by his blind father Isaac. As you recall, blind Isaac could not see his objective world, his son Esau. You, too, are blind to your problem – the first bird – for you have removed your attention from it and therefore you do not see it. Your attention (blood) is now placed upon the second bird (subjective state), and you feel and sense the reality of it.

Seven times you are told to sprinkle the one to be cleansed. This means you must dwell within the new conception of yourself until you mentally enter the seventh day (the Sabbath); until the mind is stilled or fixed in the belief that you are actually expressing or possessing that which you desire to be or to possess. At the seventh sprinkle you are instructed to loose the living bird and pronounce the man clean.

As you fully impress upon yourself the fact that you are that which you desire to be, you have symbolically sprinkled yourself seven times; then you are as free as the bird that is loosed. And like the bird in flight which must in a little while return to the earth, so must your subjective impressions or claim in a little while embody itself in your world.

This story and all the other stories of the Bible are psychological plays dramatized within the consciousness of man.

You are the high priest; you are the leper; you are the birds.

Your consciousness or I AM is the high priest; you, the man with the problem, are the leper. The problem, your present concept of yourself, is the bird that is killed; the solution of the problem, what you desire to be, is the living bird that is freed.

You re-enact this great drama within yourself by turning your attention away from your problem and placing it upon that which you desire to express.

You impress upon yourself the fact that you are that which you desire to be until your mind is stilled in the belief that it is so.

Living in this fixed attitude of mind, living in the consciousness that you are now that which you formerly desired to be, is the bird in flight, unfettered by the limitations of the past and moving toward the embodiment of your desire.

Chapter Seven
DESIRE, THE WORD OF GOD

"So shall My word be that goeth forth out of My mouth; it shall not return unto Me void, but it shall accomplish that which I please, and it shall prosper in the thing where unto I sent it." [– Isaiah 55:11]

God speaks to you through the medium of your basic desires. Your basic desires are words of promise or prophecies that contain within themselves the plan and power of expression.

By basic desire is meant your real objective. Secondary desires deal with the manner of realization. God, your I AM, speaks to you, the conditioned conscious state, through your basic desires. Secondary desires or ways of expression are the secrets of your I AM, the all wise Father. Your Father, I AM, reveals the first and last – "I am the beginning and the end" [Revelation 1:8, 22:13] – but never does He reveal the middle or secret of His ways; that is, the first is revealed as the word, your basic desire. The last is its fulfillment – the word made flesh. The second or middle (the plan of unfoldment) is never revealed to man but remains forever the Father's secret.

"For I testify unto every man that heareth the words of the prophecy of this book, if any man shall add unto those things, God shall add unto him the plagues that are written in this book; and if any man shall take away from the words of the book of this prophecy, God shall take away his part out of the book of life." [ibidem, 22:18-19]

The words of prophecy spoken of in the book of Revelation are your basic desires which must not be further conditioned. Man is constantly adding to and taking from these words. Not knowing that the basic desire contains the plan and power of expression man is always compromising and complicating his desire.

Here is an illustration of what man does to the word of prophecy – his desires.

Man desires freedom from his limitations or problems. The first thing he does after he defines his objective is to condition it upon something else.

He begins to speculate on the manner of acquiring it.

Not knowing that the thing desired has a way of expression all of its own he starts planning how he is going to get it, thereby adding to the word of God.

If, on the other hand, he has no plan or conception as to the fulfillment of his desire, then he compromises his desire by modifying it. He feels that if he will be satisfied with less than his basic desire, then he might have a better chance of realizing it. In doing so he takes from the word of God. Individuals and nations alike are constantly violating this law of their basic desire by plotting and planning the realization of their ambitions; they thereby add to the word of prophecy, or they compromise with their ideals, thus taking from the word of God.

The inevitable result is death and plagues or failure and frustration as promised for such violations.

God speaks to man only through the medium of his basic desires.

Your desires are determined by your conception of yourself. Of themselves they are neither good nor evil. "I know and am persuaded by the Lord Christ Jesus that there is nothing unclean of itself but to him that seeth anything to be unclean to him it is unclean" [Romans 14:14].

Your desires are the natural and automatic result of your present conception of yourself.

God, your unconditioned consciousness, is impersonal and no respecter of persons [Acts 10:34, Romans 2:11].

Your unconditioned consciousness, God, gives to your conditioned consciousness, man, through the medium of your basic desires that which your conditioned state (your present conception of yourself) believes it needs.

As long as you remain in your present conscious state so long will you continue desiring that which you now desire.

Change your conception of yourself and you will automatically change the nature of your desires.

Desires are states of consciousness seeking embodiment. They are formed by man's consciousness and can easily be expressed by the man who has conceived them.

Desires are expressed when the man who has conceived them assumes the attitude of mind that would be his if the states desired were already expressed. Now because desires regardless of their nature can be so easily expressed by fixed attitudes of mind, a word of warning must be given to those who have not yet realized the oneness of life, and who do not know the fundamental truth that consciousness is God, the one and only reality.

This warning was given to man in the famous Golden Rule – "Do unto others that which you would have them do unto you." [Matthew 7:21]

You may desire something for yourself or you may desire for another. If your desire concerns another make sure that the thing desired is acceptable to that other. The reason for this warning is that your consciousness is God, the giver of all gifts.

Therefore, that which you feel and believe to be true of another is a gift you have given him.

The gift that is not accepted returns to the giver.

Be very sure then that you would love to possess the gift yourself for if you fix a belief within yourself as true of another and he does not accept this state as true of himself, this unaccepted gift will embody itself within your world.

Always hear and accept as true of others that which you would desire for yourself. In doing so you are building heaven on earth.

"Do unto others as you would have them do unto you" is based upon this law.

Only accept such states as true of others that you would willingly accept as true of yourself that you may constantly create heaven on earth. Your heaven is defined by the state of consciousness in which you live, which state is made up of all that you accept as true of yourself and true of others.

Your immediate environment is defined by your own conception of yourself plus your convictions regarding others which have not been accepted by them.

Your conception of another which is not his conception of himself is a gift returned to you.

Suggestions, like propaganda, are boomerangs unless they are accepted by those to whom they are sent.

So your world is a gift you have given to yourself.

The nature of the gift is determined by your conception of yourself plus the unaccepted gifts you offered others.

Make no mistake about this; law is no respecter of persons.

Discover the law of self-expression and live by it; then you will be free. With this understanding of the law, define your desire; know exactly what you want; make certain that it is desirable and acceptable.

The wise and disciplined man sees no barrier to the realization of his desire; he sees nothing to destroy. With a fixed attitude of mind he recognizes that the thing desired is already fully expressed, for he knows that a fixed subjective state has ways and means of expressing itself of which no man knows. "Before they ask I have answered" [approx., Isaiah 65:24], "I have ways ye know not of" [approx., Isaia 42:16], "My ways are past finding out" [Romans 11:33].

The undisciplined man, on the other hand, constantly sees opposition to the fulfillment of his desire, and, because of the frustration, he forms desires of destruction which he firmly believes must be expressed before his basic desire can be realized.

When man discovers this law of one consciousness he will understand the great wisdom of the Golden Rule and so he will live by it and prove to himself that the kingdom of heaven is on earth.

You will realize why you should "do unto others that which you would have them do unto you." You will know why you should live by this Golden Rule because you will discover that it is just good common sense to do so since the rule is based upon life's changeless law and is no respecter of persons.

Consciousness is the one and only reality. The world and all within it are states of consciousness objectified.

Your world is defined by your conception of yourself PLUS YOUR CONCEPTIONS OF OTHERS which are not their conceptions of themselves.

The story of the Passover is to help you turn your back on the limitations of the present and pass over into a better and freer state.

The suggestion to "Follow the man with the pitcher of water"

[Mark 14:13; Luke 22:10] was given to the disciples to guide them to the last supper or the feast of the Passover. The man with the pitcher of water is the eleventh disciple, Simon of Canaan, the disciplined quality of mind which hears only dignified, noble and kindly states.

The mind that is disciplined to hear only the good feasts upon good states and so embodies the good on earth.

If you, too, would attend the last supper – the great feast of the Passover – then follow this man. Assume this attitude of mind is symbolized as the "man with the pitcher of water" and you will live in a world that is really heaven on earth.

The feast of the Passover is the secret of changing your consciousness.

You turn your attention from your present conception of yourself and assume the consciousness of being that which you want to be, thereby passing from one state to another.

This feat is accomplished with the help of the twelve disciples, which are the twelve disciplined qualities of mind [see "Your Faith is Your Fortune" by the same author, chapter 18].

Chapter Eight
FAITH

"And Jesus said unto them, Because of your unbelief; for verily I say unto you, if ye have faith as a grain of mustard seed, ye shall say unto this mountain, remove hence to yonder place; and it shall remove; and nothing shall be impossible unto you." [– Matthew 17:20]

This faith of a grain of mustard seed has proved a stumbling block to man [Corinthians 1:23]. He has been taught to believe that a grain of mustard seed signifies a small degree of faith. So he naturally wonders why he, a mature man, should lack this insignificant measure of faith when so small an amount assures success.

"Faith," he is told, "is the substance of things hoped for, the evidence of things not seen" [Hebrews 11:1]. And again, "Through faith… the worlds were framed by the word of God, so that things which are seen were not made of things which do appear" [Hebrews 11:3].

Invisible things were made visible. The grain of mustard seed is not the measure of a small amount of faith. On the contrary, it is the absolute in faith.

A mustard seed is conscious of being a mustard seed and a mustard seed alone. It is not aware of any other seed in the world. It is sealed in the conviction that it is a mustard seed in the same manner that the spermatozoa sealed in the womb is conscious of being man and only man.

A grain of mustard seed is truly the measure of faith necessary to accomplish your every objective; but like the mustard seed you too must lose yourself in the consciousness of being only the thing desired.

You abide within this sealed state until it bursts itself and reveals your conscious claim.

Faith is feeling or living in the consciousness of being the thing desired; faith is the secret of creation, the VAU in the divine name JOD HE VAU HE; faith is the Ham in the family of Noah; faith is the sense of feeling by which Isaac blessed and made real his son Jacob. By faith God (your consciousness) calleth things that are not seen as though they were and makes them seen.

It is faith which enables you to become conscious of being the thing desired; again, it is faith which seals you in this conscious state until your invisible claim ripens to maturity and expresses itself, is made visible.

Faith or feeling is the secret of this appropriation. Through feeling, the consciousness desiring is joined to the thing desired.

How would you feel if you were that which you desire to be?

Wear the mood, this feeling that would be yours if you were already that which you desire to be; and in a little while you will be sealed in the belief that you are. Then without effort this invisible state will objectify itself; the invisible will be made visible.

If you had the faith of a grain of mustard seed you would this day through the magical substance of feeling seal yourself in the consciousness of being that which you desire to be.

In this mental stillness or tomblike state you would remain, confident that you need no one to roll away the stone [Matthew 28:2; Mark 16:3; Luke 24:2;

John 20:1], for all the mountains, stones and inhabitants of earth are nothing in your sight [Isaiah 40:17; Daniel 4:32]. That which you now recognize to be true of yourself (this present conscious state) will do according to its nature among all the inhabitants of earth, and none can stay its hand or say unto it, "What doest Thou?" [Daniel 4:32]. None can stop this conscious state in which you are sealed from embodying itself, nor question its right to be.

This conscious state when properly sealed by faith is a Word of God, I AM, for the man so seated is saying, "I AM so and so," and the Word of God (my fixed conscious state) is spirit and cannot return unto me void but must accomplish whereunto it is sent. God's word (your conscious state) must embody itself that you may know: "I AM the Lord... there is no God beside Me" [Isaiah 45:5]. "The Word was made flesh and dwelt among us" [John 1:14], and "He sent His word and healed him" [Psalm 107:20].

You too can send your word, God's Word, and heal a friend. Is there something that you would like to hear of a friend? Define this something that you know he would love to be or to possess. Now with your desire properly defined you have a Word of God. To send this Word on its way, to speak this Word into being, you simply do this. Sit quietly where you are and assume the mental attitude of listening; recall your friend's voice; with this familiar voice established in your consciousness, imagine that you are actually hearing his voice and that he is telling you that he is or has that which you wanted him to be or to have.

Impress upon your consciousness the fact that you actually heard him and that he told you what you wanted to hear; feel the thrill of having heard. Then drop it completely. This is the mystic's secret of sending words into expression – of making the word flesh. You form within yourself the word, the thing you want to hear; then you listen, and tell it to yourself. "Speak, Lord, for thy servant heareth" [Samuel 3:9,10].

Your consciousness is the Lord speaking through the familiar voice of a friend and impressing on yourself that which you desire to hear. This self-impregnation, the state impressed upon yourself, the Word, has ways and means of expressing itself of which no man knows. As you succeed in making the impression you will be unmoved by appearances for this self-impression is sealed as a grain of mustard seed and will in due season mature to its full expression.

Chapter Nine
THE ANNUNCIATION

The use of a friend's voice to impregnate one's self with a desirable state is beautifully told in the story of the Immaculate Conception.

It is recorded that God sent an angel to Mary to announce the birth of His son. "And the angel said unto her... thou shalt conceive in thy womb, and bring forth a son... Then said Mary unto the angel, How shall this be, seeing I know not a man? And the angel answered and said unto her, The Holy Ghost shall come upon thee, and the power of the highest shall overshadow thee; therefore also that holy thing which shall be born of thee shall be called the son of God. For with God nothing shall be impossible". [Luke 1:30-37]

This is the story that has been told for centuries the world over, but man was not told that it was written about himself so he has failed to receive the benefit it was intended to give him.

The story reveals the method by which the idea or Word was made flesh. God, we are told, germinated or begat an idea, a son, without the aid of another.

Then He placed His germinal idea in the womb of Mary with the help of an angel who made the announcement to her and impregnated her with the idea.

No simpler method was ever recorded of consciousness impregnating itself than is found in the story of the Immaculate Conception.

The four characters in this drama of creation are the Father, the Son, Mary and the Angel.

The Father symbolizes your consciousness; the Son symbolizes your desire; Mary symbolizes your receptive attitude of mind; and the Angel symbolizes the method used to make the impregnation.

The drama unfolds in this manner. The Father begets a Son without the aid of another.

You define your objective – you clarify your desire without the help or suggestion of another.

Then the Father selects that angel who is best qualified to bear this message or germinal possibility to Mary.

You select the person in your world who would be sincerely thrilled in witnessing the fulfillment of your desire.

Then Mary learns through the angel that she has already conceived a Son without the aid of man.

You assume a receptive attitude of mind, a listening attitude, and imagine you are hearing the voice of the one you have chosen to tell you what you desire to know. Imagine that you hear him tell you that you are and have that which you desire to be and to have. You remain in this receptive state until you feel the thrill of having heard the good and wonderful news. Then like Mary of the story, you go about your business in secret telling no one of this wonderful and immaculate self-impregnation, confident that in due season you will express this impression.

The Father generates the seed or germinal possibility of a Son but in a eugenic impregnation; He does not convey the spermatozoa from Himself to the womb. He has it borne through another medium.

Consciousness desiring is the Father generating the seed or idea. A clarified desire is the perfectly formed seed or the only begotten Son. This seed is then carried from the Father (consciousness desiring) to the Mother (consciousness of being and having the state desired).

This change in consciousness is accomplished by the angel or imaginary voice of a friend telling you that you have already achieved your objective.

The use of an angel or friend's voice to make a conscious impression is the shortest, safest and surest way to be self-impregnated.

With your desire properly defined, you assume an attitude of listening. Imagine you are hearing the voice of a friend; then make him tell you (imagine he is telling you) how lucky and fortunate you are to have fully realized your desire.

In this receptive attitude of mind you are receiving the message of an angel; you are receiving the impression that you are and have that which you desire to be and to have. The emotional thrill of having heard that which you desire to hear is the moment of conception. It is the moment you become self-impregnated, the moment you actually feel you are now that or have that which heretofore you but desired to be or to possess.

As you emerge from this subjective experience, you, like Mary of the story, will know by your changed attitude of mind that you have conceived a Son; that you have fixed a definite subjective state and will in a little while express or objectify this state.

This book has been written to show you how to achieve your objectives. Apply the principle expressed herein and all the inhabitants of earth cannot stop you from realizing your desires.

The Law and The Promise

CHAPTER 1
"THE LAW" IMAGINING CREATES REALITY

"Man is all Imagination. God is Man and exists in us and we in Him . . . The Eternal Body of Man is the Imagination, that is, God, Himself"
—Blake

The purpose of the first portion of this book is to show, through actual true stories, how imagining creates reality. Science progresses by way of hypotheses tentatively tested and afterwards accepted or rejected according to the facts of experience. The claim that imagining creates reality needs no more consideration than is allowed by science. It proves itself in performance.

The world in which we live is a world of imagination. In fact, life itself is an activity of imagining, "For Blake," wrote Professor Morrison of the University of St. Andrews, "the world originates in a divine activity identical with what we know ourselves as the activity of imagination;" his task being "to open the immortal eyes of man inward into the worlds of thought, into eternity, ever expanding in the bosom of God, the Human Imagination."

Nothing appears or continues in being by a power of its own. Events happen because comparatively stable imaginal activities created them, and they continue in being only as long as they receive such support. "The secret of imagining," writes Douglas Fawcett, "is the greatest of all problems to the solution of which the mystic aspires. Supreme power, supreme wisdom, supreme delight lie in the far-off solution of this mystery."

When man solves the mystery of imagining, he will have discovered the secret of causation, and that is: Imagining creates reality. Therefore, the man who is aware of what he is imagining knows what he is creating; realizes more and more that the drama of life is imaginal — not physical. All activity is at bottom imaginal. An awakened Imagination works with a purpose. It creates and conserves the desirable, and transforms or destroys the undesirable.

Divine imagining and human imagining are not two powers at all, rather one. The valid distinction which exists between the seeming two lies not in the substance with which they operate but in the degree of intensity of the operant power itself. Acting at high tension, an imaginal act is an immediate objective fact. Keyed low, an imaginal

[106] NEVILLE GODDARD

act is realized in a time process. But whether imagination is keyed high or low, it is the "ultimate, essentially non-objective Reality from which objects are poured forth like sudden fancies." No object is independent of imagining on some level or levels. Everything in the world owes its character to imagination on one of its various levels.

"Objective reality," writes Fichte, "is solely produced through imagination." Objects seem so independent of our perception of them that we incline to forget that they owe their origin to imagination. The world in which we live is a world of imagination, and man—through his imaginal activities—creates the realities and the circumstances of life; this he does either knowingly or unknowingly.

Men pay too little attention to this priceless gift—The Human Imagination—and a gift is practically nonexistent unless there is a conscious possession of it and a readiness to use it. All men possess the power to create reality, but this power sleeps as though dead, when not consciously exercised. Men live in the very heart of creation—The Human Imagination—yet are no wiser for what takes place therein. The future will not be fundamentally different from the imaginal activities of man; therefore, the individual who can summon at will whatever imaginal activity he pleases and to whom the visions of his imagination are as real as the forms of nature, is master of his fate.

The future is the imaginal activity of man in its creative march. Imagining is the creative power not only of the poet, the artist, the actor and orator, but of the scientist, the inventor, the merchant and the artisan. Its abuse in unrestrained unlovely imagemaking is obvious; but its abuse in undue repression breeds a sterility which robs man of actual wealth of experience. Imagining novel solutions to ever more complex problems is far more noble than to run from problems. Life is the continual solution of a continuously synthetic problem. Imagining creates events. The world, created out of men's imagining, comprises un-numbered warring beliefs; therefore, there can never be a perfectly stable or static state. Today's events are bound to disturb yesterday's established order. Imaginative men and women invariably unsettle a preexisting peace of mind.

Do not bow before the dictate of facts and accept life on the basis of the world without. Assert the supremacy of your Imaginal acts over facts and put all things in subjection to them. Hold fast to your ideal in your imagination. Nothing can take it from you but your failure to persist in imagining the ideal realized. Imagine only such states that are of value or promise well.

To attempt to change circumstances before you change your imaginal activity, is to struggle against the very nature of things. There can be no outer change until there is first an imaginal change. Everything you do, unaccompanied by an imaginal change, is but futile readjustment of surfaces. Imagining the wish fulfilled brings about a union with that state, and during that union you behave in keeping with your imaginal change. This shows you that an imaginal change will result in a change of behavior. However, your ordinary imaginal alterations as you pass from one state to another are not transformations because each of them is so rapidly succeeded by another in the reverse direction. But whenever one state grows so stable as to become your constant mood, your habitual attitude, then that habitual state defines your character and is a true transformation.

How do you do it? Self-abandonment! That is the secret. You must abandon yourself mentally to your wish fulfilled in your love for that state, and in so doing, live in the new state and no more in the old state. You can't commit yourself to what you do not love, so the secret of self-commission is faith—plus love. Faith is believing what is unbelievable. Commit yourself to the feeling of the wish fulfilled, in faith that this act of self-commission will become a reality. And it must become a reality because imagining creates reality.

Imagination is both conservative and transformative. It is conservative when it builds its world from images supplied by memory and the evidence of the senses. It is creatively transformative when it imagines things as they ought to be, building its world out of the generous dreams of fancy. In the procession of images, the ones that take precedence—naturally—are those of the senses. Nevertheless, a present sense impression is only an image. It does not differ in nature from a memory image or the image of a wish. What makes a present sense impression so objectively real is the individual's imagination functioning in it and thinking from it; whereas, in a memory image or a wish, the individual's imagination is not functioning in it and thinking from it, but is functioning out of it and thinking of it.

If you would enter into the image in your imagination, then would you know what it is to be creatively transformative: then would you realize your wish; and then you would be happy. Every image can be embodied. But unless you, yourself, enter the image and think from it, it is incapable of birth. Therefore, it is the height of folly to expect the wish to be realized by the mere passage of time. That which requires imaginative occupancy to produce its effect, obviously cannot be effected without such occupancy. You cannot be in one image and not suffer the consequences of not being in another.

Imagination is spiritual sensation. Enter the image of the wish fulfilled, then give it sensory vividness and tones of reality by mentally acting as you would act were it a physical fact. Now, this is what I mean by spiritual sensation. Imagine that you are holding a rose in your hand. Smell it. Do you detect the odor of roses? Well, if the rose is not there, why is its fragrance in the air? Through spiritual sensation—that is—through imaginal sight, sound, scent, taste and touch, you can give to the image sensory vividness. If you do this, all things will conspire to aid your harvesting and upon reflection you will see how subtle were the threads that led to your goal. You could never have devised the means which your imaginal activity employed to fulfill itself.

If you long to escape from your present sense fixation, to transform your present life into a dream of what might well be, you need but imagine that you are already what you want to be and to feel the way you would expect to feel under such circumstances. Like the make-believe of a child who is remaking the world after its own heart, create your world out of pure dreams of fancy. Mentally enter into your dream; mentally do what you would actually do, were it physically true. You will discover that dreams are realized not by the rich, but by the imaginative. Nothing stands between you and the fulfillment of your dreams but facts—and facts are the creations of imagining. If you change your imagining, you will change the facts.

Man and his past are one continuous structure. This structure contains all of the facts which have been conserved and still operate below the threshold of his surface mind. For him it is merely history. For him it seems unalterable—a dead and firmly fixed past. But for itself, it is living—it is part of the living age. He cannot leave behind him the mistakes of the past, for nothing disappears. Everything that has been is still in existence. The past still exists, and it gives—and still gives—its results. Man must go back in memory, seek for and destroy the causes of evil, however far back they lie. This going into the past and replaying a scene of the past in imagination as it ought to have been played the first time, I call revision—and revision results in repeal.

Changing your life means changing the past. The causes of any present evil are the unrevised scenes of the past. The past and the present form the whole structure of man; they are carrying all of its contents with it. Any alteration of content will result in an alteration in the present and future.

Live nobly—so that mind can store a past well worthy of recall. Should you fail to do so, remember, the first act of correction or cure is always—"revise." If the past is recreated into the present, so will the revised past be recreated into the present, or else the claim . . . though your sins are like scarlet, they shall be as white as snow ... is a lie. And it is no lie.

The purpose of the story-to-story Commentary that follows is to link up as briefly as possible the distinct but never disconnected themes of the fourteen chapters into which I have divided the first part of this book. It will serve, I hope, as a thread of coherent thought that binds the whole into proof of its claim! Imagining Creates Reality.

To make such a claim is easily done. To prove it in the experience of others is far sterner. To stir you to use the "Law" constructively in your own life—that is the aim of this book.

CHAPTER 2
"DWELL THEREIN"

"My God, I heard this day, that none doth build a stately habitation, but he that means to dwell therein. What house more stately hath there been, or can be, than is Man? to whose creation all things are in decay." —George Herbert

I wish it were true of man's noble dreams, but unfortunately—perpetual construction, deferred occupancy—is the common fault of man. Why "build a stately habitation," unless you intend to "dwell therein?" Why build a dream house and not "dwell therein?"

This is the secret of those who lie in bed awake while they dream things true. They know how to live in their dream until, in fact, they do just that. Man, through the medium of a controlled, waking dream, can predetermine his future. That imaginal activity, of living in the feeling of the wish fulfilled, leads man across a bridge of incident to the fulfillment of the dream. If we live in the dream—thinking from it, and not of it—then the creative power of imagining will answer our adventurous fancy, and the wish fulfilled will break in upon us and take us unawares.

Man is all imagination; therefore, man must be where he is in imagination, for his imagination is himself. To realize that imagination is not something tied to the senses or enclosed within the spatial boundary of the body is most important. Although man moves about in space by movement of his physical body, he need not be so restricted. He can move by a change in what he is aware of. However real the scene on which sight rests, man can gaze on one never before witnessed. He can always remove the mountain if it upsets his concept of what life ought to be. This ability to mentally move from things as they are to things as they ought to be, is one of the most important discoveries that man can make. It reveals man as a center of imagining with powers of intervention which enable him to alter the course of observed events, moving from success to success through a series of mental transformations of nature, of others, and himself.

For many years a doctor and his wife "dreamed" about their "stately habitation," but not until they imaginatively lived in it, did they manifest it. Here is their story:

"Some fifteen years ago, Mrs. M. and I purchased a lot on which we built a two-story building housing our office and living area. We left ample space on the lot for an apartment building—if and when our finances would permit. All those years we were busy paying off our mortgage, and at the end of that time had no money for the additional building we still desired so much. It was true that we had an ample savings account which meant security for our business, but to use any part of it for a new building would be to jeopardize that security.

"But now your teaching awakened a new concept, boldly telling us we could have what we most desired through the controlled use of our imagination and that realizing a desire was made more convincing 'without money.' We decided to put it to a test to forget about 'money' and concentrate our attention on the thing we desired most in this world—the new apartment building.

"With this principle in mind, we mentally constructed the new building as we wanted it, actually drawing physical plans so we could better formulate our mental picture of the completed structure. Never forgetting to think from the end (in our case, the completed, occupied building,) we took many imaginative trips through our apartment house, renting the units to imaginary tenants, examining in detail every room and enjoying the feeling of pride as friends offered congratulations on the unique planning. We brought into our imaginal scene one friend in particular (I shall call her Mrs. X) a lady we had not seen for some time as she had 'given us up' socially, believing us a bit peculiar in our new way of thinking. In our imaginal scene we took her through the building and asked how she liked it. Hearing her voice distinctly, we had her reply, 'Doctor, I think it is beautiful.'

"One day while talking together of our building, my wife mentioned a contractor who had constructed several apartment houses in our neighborhood. We knew of him only by the name that appeared on signs adjacent to buildings under construction. But realizing that if we were living in the end, we would not be looking for a contractor, we promptly forgot this angle. Continuing these periods of daily imagining for several weeks, we both felt we were now 'fused' with our desire and had successfully been living in the end.

"One day a stranger entered our office and identified himself as the contractor whose name my wife had mentioned weeks before. In an apologetic manner, he said, 'I don't know why I stopped here. I normally don't go to see people, but rather, people come to see me.' He explained that he passed our office often and had wondered why there wasn't an apartment building on the comer lot. We assured him we would like very much to have such a building there but that we had no money to put into the project, not even the few hundred dollars it would take for plans.

"Our negative response did not faze him and seemingly compelled, he began to figure and devise ways and means to carry out the job, unasked and unencouraged by us. Forgetting the incident, we were quite startled when a few days later this man called, informing us that plans were completed and that the proposed building would cost us thirty thousand dollars! We thanked him politely and did absolutely nothing. We knew we had been 'living imaginatively in the end' of a completed building and that Imagination would assemble that building perfectly without any 'outside' assistance from us. So, we were not surprised when the contractor called again the next day to say he had found a set of blueprints in his files that fitted our needs perfectly with few alterations. This, we were informed, would save us the architect's fee for new plans. We thanked him again and still did nothing.

"Logical thinkers would insist that such negative response from prospective customers would completely end the matter. Instead, two days later the contractor again called with the news that he had located a finance company willing to cover the necessary loan with the exception of a few thousand dollars. It sounds incredible, but we still did nothing. For—remember—to us this building was completed and rented, and in our imagination we had not put one penny into its construction.

"The balance of this tale reads like a sequel to 'Alice In Wonderland,' for the contractor came to our office the next day and said, as though presenting us with a gift, 'You people are going to have that new building anyway. I've decided to finance the balance of the loan myself. If this is agreeable, I'll have my lawyer draw up the papers, and you can pay me back out of net profits from rentals.'

"This time we did do something! We signed the papers, and construction began immediately. Most of the apartment units were rented before final completion, and all but one occupied the day of completion. We were so thrilled by the seemingly miraculous events of the past few months that for a while we didn't understand this seeming 'flaw' in our imaginal picture. But knowing what we had already accomplished through the power of imagining, we immediately conceived another imaginal scene and in it, this time, instead of showing the party through the unit and hearing the words 'we'll take it,' we ourselves in imagination visited tenants who had already moved in that apartment. We allowed them to show us through the rooms and heard their pleased and satisfied comments. Three days later that apartment was rented.

"Our original imaginary drama had objectified itself in every detail save one, and that one became a reality when one month later our friend, Mrs. X, surprised us with a long overdue visit, expressing her desire to see our new building. Gladly we took her through, and at the end of the tour heard her speak the line we had heard in our imagination so many weeks before, as with emphasis on each word, she said, 'Doctor, I think it is beautiful.'

"Our dream of fifteen years was realized. And we know, now, that it could have been realized any time within those fifteen years if we had known the secret of imagining and how to 'live in the end' of desire. But now it was realized—our one big desire was objectified. And we did not put one penny of our own money into it." — Dr. M.

Through the medium of a dream—a controlled, waking dream—the Doctor and his wife created reality. They learned how to live in their dream house as, in fact, now they do. Although help seemingly came from without, the course of events was ultimately determined by the imaginal activity of the Doctor and his wife. The participants were drawn into their imaginal drama because it was dramatically necessary that they should be. Their imaginal structure demanded it.

"All things by a law divine In one another's being mingle."

The following story illustrates the way in which a lady prepared her "stately habitation" by imaginatively sleeping in it—or "dwelling therein."

"A few months ago my husband decided to place our home on the market. The main object for the move which we had discussed many times was to find a home large enough for the two of us, my mother and my aunt, in addition to ten cats, three dogs and one parakeet. Believe it or not, the contemplated move was my husband's idea as he loved my mother and aunt and said I was at their house most of the time anyway, so 'why not live together and pay one tax bill?' I liked the idea tremendously, but I knew that this new home would have to be something very special in size, location and arrangement as I insisted on privacy for all concerned.

"So at the moment I was undecided whether to sell our present home or not, but I didn't argue as I knew quite well from past experience with imagining that our house would never sell until I stopped 'sleeping' in it. Two months and four or five real estate brokers later, my husband had 'given up' on the sale of our house and so had the brokers. At this point I had convinced myself I now wanted the change, so for four nights in my imagination I went to sleep in the kind of home I would like to own. On the fifth day, my husband had an appointment at a friend's home and while there, met a stranger who 'just happened' to be looking for a house in the hills. He was, of course, brought swiftly back to see our house which he walked through once and said, 'I'll buy it.' This didn't make us very popular with the brokers, but that was all right with me as I was happy to keep the broker's commission in the family! We moved within ten days and stayed with my mother while looking for our new home.

"We listed our requirements with every agent on the Sunset Strip only (because I wouldn't move out of the area) and each one of them without exception informed us we were both mad. It was entirely impossible, they said, to find an older home of English style with two separate living rooms, separate apartments, a library, and built on a flat knoll with enough ground space to fence for large dogs—and located in one particular area. When we told them the price we would pay for this house they just looked sad.

"I said that wasn't all we wanted. We wanted wood paneling all through the house, a huge fireplace, a magnificent view and seclusion—no close neighbors, please. At this point the lady agent would giggle and remind me that there was no such house, but if there were they would realize five times what we were willing to pay. But I knew there was such a house—because my imagination had been sleeping in it, and if I am my imagination, then I had been sleeping in it.

"By the second week we had exhausted five real estate offices, and the gentleman in the sixth office was looking a little wild when one of his partners who had not spoken until then said, 'Why don't you show them the place up Kings Road?' A third partner in the office laughed sourly and said, 'That property isn't even listed. And besides— the old lady would throw you off the property. She's got two acres up there and you know she wouldn't split.'

"Well, I didn't know what she wouldn't split, but my interest had been aroused by the street name for I liked that particular area best of all. So I asked why not just take a look anyway, for laughs. As we drove up the street and turned off onto a private road, we approached a large two-story house built of redwood and brick, English in appearance, surrounded by tall trees and sitting alone and aloof on its own knoll, viewing the city below from all of its many windows. I felt a peculiar excitement as we walked to the front door and were greeted by a lovely woman who graciously asked us in.

"I do not think I breathed for the next minute or two, for I had walked into the most exquisite room I had ever seen. The solid redwood walls and the brick of a great fireplace rose to a height of twenty-eight feet terminating in an arched ceiling joined together by huge redwood beams. The room was straight out of Dickens, and I could almost hear Christmas carolers singing on the balcony of the upstairs dining room which looked out over the living room. A great cathedral window gave a view of sky, mountains and city far below, and the beautiful old redwood walls glowed in the sunlight. We were shown through a spacious apartment on the lower floor with connecting library, separate entrance and separate patio. Two staircases led upward to a long hall opening into two separated bedrooms and baths, and at the end of the hall was—yes—a second living room, opening out onto a second patio screened by trees and redwood fencing.

"Built on two acres of beautifully landscaped grounds, I began to understand what the agent had meant by saying, 'she wouldn't split' for on one acre stood a large swimming pool and pool house completely separated from the main house but undoubtedly belonging to it. It did, indeed, seem to be an impossible situation as we did not want two acres of highly taxable property plus a swimming pool a block away from the house.

"Before we left, I walked through that magnificent living room, once more going up the stairs to the dining room balcony. I turned, and looking down saw my husband standing by the fireplace, pipe in hand, with an expression of perfect satisfaction on his face. I placed my hands on the balcony railing and watched him for a moment.

"When we were back in the real estate office, the three agents were ready to close for the day, but my husband detained them saying, 'Let's make her an offer anyway. Maybe she will split the property. What can we lose?' One agent left the office without a word. Another said, 'The idea is ridiculous.' The agent we had originally talked to said, 'Forget it. It's a pipe dream.' My husband is not easily annoyed but when he is, there is no more stubborn creature on earth. He was now annoyed. He sat down, slammed his hand on a desk and roared, 'It's your business to submit offers, isn't it?' They agreed that this was so and finally promised to submit our offer on the property.

"We left, and that night—in my imagination—I stood on that dining room balcony and looked down at my husband standing by the fireplace. He looked up at me and said, 'Well, honey, how do you like our new home?' I said, 'I love it.' I continued to see that beautiful room and my husband in it and 'felt' the balcony railing gripped in my hands until I fell asleep.

"The next day as we were having dinner in my mother's house, the telephone rang and the agent, in an unbelieving voice, informed me that we had just purchased a house. The owner had split the property right down the middle, giving us the house and the acre it stood on for the price we offered." . . . J.R.B.

"... dreamers often lie in bed awake, while they do dream things true."

One must adopt either the way of imagination or the way of sense. No compromise or neutrality is possible. "He who is not for me is against me." When man finally identifies himself with his Imagination rather than his senses, he has at long last discovered the core of reality.

I have often been warned by self-styled "realists" that man will never realize his dream by simply imagining that it is already here. Yet, man can realize his dream by simply imagining that it is already here. That is exactly what this collection of stories proves; if only men were prepared to live imaginatively in the feeling of the wish fulfilled, advancing confidently in their controlled waking-dream, then the power of imagining would answer their adventurous fancy and the wish fulfilled would break in upon them and take them unawares.

Nothing is more continuously wonderful than the things that happen every day to the man with imagination sufficiently awake to realize their wonder. Observe your imaginal activities. Imagine better than the best you know, and create a better world for yourself and others. Live as though the wish had come, even though it is yet to come, and you will shorten the period of waiting. The world is imaginal, not mechanistic. Imaginal acts—not blind fate—determine the course of history.

CHAPTER 3
TURN THE WHEEL BACKWARD

"Oh, let your strong imagination turn the great wheel backward, until Troy unburn."

"All life is, throughout the ages nothing but the continuing solution of a continuous synthetic problem." —H. G. Wells

The perfectly stable or static state is always unattainable. The end attained objectively always realizes more than the end the individual originally had in view. This, in turn, creates a new situation of inner conflict, needing novel solutions to force man along the path of creative evolution. "His touch is infinite and lends a yonder to all ends." Today's events are bound to disturb yesterday's established order. The creatively active imagination invariably unsettles a pre-existing peace of mind.

The question may arise as to how, by representing others to ourselves as better than they really were, or mentally rewriting a letter to make it conform to our wish, or by revising the scene of an accident, the interview with the employer, and so on—could change what seems to be the unalterable facts of the past, but remember my claims for imagining: Imagining Creates Reality. What it makes, it can unmake. It is not only conservative, building a life from images supplied by memory—it is also creatively transformative, altering a theme already in being.

The parable of the unjust steward gives the answer to this question. We can alter our world by means of a certain "illegal" imaginal practice, by means of a mental falsification of the facts—that is, by means of a certain intentional imaginal alteration of that which we have experienced. All this is done in one's own imagination. This is a form of falsehood which not only is not condemned, but is actually approved in the gospel teaching. By means of such a falsehood, a man destroys the causes of evil and acquires friends and on the strength of this revision proves, judging by the high praise the unjust steward received from his master, that he is deserving of confidence.

Because imagining creates reality, we can carry revision to the extreme and revise a scene that would be otherwise unforgivable. We learn to distinguish between man— who is all imagination—and those states into which he may enter. An unjust steward, looking at another's distress, will represent the other to himself as he ought to be seen. Were he, himself, in need—he would enter his dream in his

[118] NEVILLE GODDARD

imagination and imagine what he would see and how things would seem and how people would act—'after these things should be.' Then, in this state he would fall asleep, feeling the way he would expect to feel, under such circumstances.

Would that all the Lord's people were unjust stewards—mentally falsifying the facts of life to deliver individuals forevermore. For the imaginal change goes forward, until at length the altered pattern is realized on the heights of attainment. Our future is our imaginal activity in its creative march. Imagine better than the best you know.

To revise the past is to re-construct it with new content. Man should daily relive the day as he wished he had lived it, revising the scenes to make them conform to his ideals. For instance, suppose today's mail brought disappointing news. Revise the letter. Mentally rewrite it and make it conform to the news you wish you had received. Then, in imagination, read the revised letter over and over again and this will arouse the feeling of naturalness; and imaginal acts become facts as soon as we feel natural in the act. This is the essence of revision and revision results in repeal. This is exactly what F.B. did:

"Late in July I wrote to a real estate agent of my desire to sell a piece of land which had been a financial burden to me. His negative reply listed all the reasons why sales were at a standstill in that area, and he forecast a bleak period of waiting until after the first of the year.

"I received his letter on a Tuesday, and—in my imagination—I rewrote it with words indicating that the agent was eager to take my listing. I read this revised letter over and over, and I extended my imaginal drama using your theme of the Four Mighty Ones of our Imagination—from your book 'Seedtime and Harvest.'—the Producer, the Author, the Director, and the Actor.

"In my imaginal scene as Producer, I suggested the theme, 'The lot is sold for a profit. As the Author, I wrote this simple scene which, to me, implied fulfillment: Standing in the real estate office, I extended my hand to the agent and said, 'Thank you, sir,' and he replied, 'It was a pleasure doing business with you.' As Director, I rehearsed myself as Actor until that scene was vividly real and I felt the relief which would be mine if the burden were really lifted.

"Three days later, the agent I had originally written phoned me saying he had a deposit for my lot at the price I had specified. I signed the papers in his office the next day, extended my hand and said, 'Thank you, sir.' The agent replied, 'It was a pleasure doing business with you.'

"Five days after I had constructed and enacted an imaginal scene, it became a physical reality and was played word for word just as I had heard it in my imagination. The feeling of relief and joy came—not so much from selling the property—but from the incontrovertible proof that my imagined drama worked." . . . F.B.

If the thing accomplished were all, how futile! But F.B. discovered a power within himself that can consciously create circumstances.

By mentally falsifying the facts of life, man moves from passive reaction to active creation; this breaks the wheel of recurrence and builds a cumulatively enlarging future. If man does not always create in the full sense of the word, it is because he is not faithful to his vision, or else he thinks of what he wants rather than from his wish fulfilled.

Man is such an extraordinary synthesis, partly tied by his senses, and partly free to dream that his internal conflicts are perennial. The state of conflict in the individual is expressed in society.

Life is a romantic adventure. To live creatively, imagining novel solutions to ever more complex problems is far nobler than to restrain or kill out desire. All that is desired can be imagined into existence.

"Wouldst thou be in a Dream, and yet not sleep?" Try to revise your day every night before falling asleep. Try to visualize clearly and enter into the revised scene which would be the imaginal solution of your problem. The revised imaginal structure may have a great influence on others, but that is not your concern. The "other" influenced in the following story is profoundly grateful for that influence. L. S. E. writes:

"Last August, while on a 'blind date' I met the man I wanted to marry. This happens sometimes, and it happened to me. He was everything I had ever thought of as desirable in a husband. Two days after this enchanted evening, it was necessary for me to change my place of residence because of my work, and that same week the mutual friend who had introduced me to this man, moved away from the city. I realized that the man I had met probably did not know of my new address, and frankly, I was not sure he knew my name.

"After your last lecture, I spoke to you of this situation. Although I had plenty of other 'dates' I could not forget this one man. Your lecture was based on revising outday; and after speaking to you, I determined to revise my day, every day. Before going to sleep that night, I felt I was in a different bed, in my own home, as a married woman — and not as a single working girl, sharing an apartment with three other girls. I twisted an imaginary wedding band on my imaginary left hand, saying over and over to myself, 'This is wonderful! I really am Mrs. J.E.!' and I fell asleep in what was—a moment before—a waking dream.

"I repeated this imaginary scene for one month, night after night. The first week in October he 'found' me. On our second date, I knew my dreams were rightly placed. Your teaching tells us to live in the end of our desire until that desire becomes 'fact' so although I did not know how he felt toward me, I continued, night after night, living in the feeling of my dream realized.

"The results? In November he proposed. In January we announced our engagement; and the following May we were married. The loveliest part of it all, however, is that I am happier than I ever dreamed possible; and I know in my heart, he is too." . . . Mrs. J.E.

By using her imagination radically, instead of conservatively,—by building her world out of pure dreams of fancy—rather than using images supplied by memory, she brought about the fulfillment of her dream. Common sense would have used images supplied by her memory, and thereby perpetuated the fact of lack in her life. Imagination created what she desired out of a dream of fancy. Everyone must live wholly on the level of imagination, and it must be consciously and deliberately undertaken.

". . . Lovers and madmen have such seething brains, Such shaping fantasies, that apprehend more than cool reason over comprehends."

If our time of revision be well spent, we need not worry about results — our fondest hopes will be realized.

"Art thou real, Earth? Am I? In whose dream do we exist? ..."

There is no inevitable permanence in anything. Both past and present continue to exist only because they are sustained by "Imagining" on some level or other; and a radical transformation of life is always possible by man revising the undesirable part of it.

In his letter, Mr. R.S. questions this subject of influence:

"During your current series of lectures, trouble developed with collections on one of my Trust Deeds. The security, a house and lot, was neglected and run down. The owners were apparently spending their money in bars while their two little girls, aged nine and eleven, were noticeably uncared for. However, forgetting appearances, I began to revise the situation. In my imagination I drove my wife past the property and said to her, 'Isn't the yard beautiful? It's so neat and well cared for. Those people really show their love for their home. This is one Trust Deed we will never have to worry about.' I would 'see' the house and lot as I wanted to see it — a place so lovely, it gave me a warm glow of pleasure. Every time the thought of this property came to me, I repeated my imaginal scene.

"After I had been practicing this revision for some time, the woman who lived in the house had an automobile accident; while she was in the hospital her husband disappeared. The children were cared for by neighbors; and I was tempted to visit the mother in the hospital to reassure her of assistance, if necessary. But how could I, when my imaginary scene implied that she and her family were happy, successful and obviously contented? So I did nothing but my daily revision. A short while after leaving the hospital, the woman and her two daughters disappeared also. Payments were sent in on the property and a few months later she reappeared with a wedding certificate and a new husband. At this writing, all payments are right up to date. The two little girls are obviously happy and well cared for, and a room has been added to the property by the owners giving our Trust Deed additional security.

"It was mighty nice to solve my problem without threats, unkind words, eviction, or worry about the little girls; but was there something in my imagining that sent that woman to the hospital?" . . . R.S.

Any imaginal activity acquiring intensity through our concentrated attention to clarity of the end desired tends to overflow into regions beyond where we are; but we must leave it to take care of such imaginal activity itself. It is marvelously resourceful in adapting and adjusting means to realize itself. Once we think in terms of influence rather than of clarity of the end desired, the effort of imagination becomes an effort of will and the great art of imagining is perverted into tyranny.

The buried past usually lies deeper than our surface mind can plumb. But fortunately, for this lady, she remembered and proved that the "made" past can also be "unmade" through revision.

"For thirty-nine years I had suffered from a weak back. The pain would increase and decrease but would never leave completely. The condition had progressed to the point where I used medical treatment almost constantly; the doctor would put the hip right for the moment but the pain simply would not go away. One night I heard you speak of revision and wondered to myself if a condition of almost forty years could be revised. I had remembered that at the age of three or four years I had fallen backward from a very high swing and had been quite ill at that time because of a serious hip injury. From that time on I had never been completely free from pain and had paid many a dollar to alleviate the condition, to no avail.

"This year during the month of August the pain had become more intense and one night I decided to test myself and attempt to revise that 'ancient' accident which had been the cause of so much distress in pain and costly medical fees most of my adult life. Many nights passed before I could 'feel' myself back to the age of childhood play. But I succeeded. One night I actually 'felt' myself on that swing feeling the rush of wind as the swing rose higher and higher. As the swing slowed down, I jumped forward landing solidly and easily on my feet. In the imaginal action I ran to my mother and insisted that she come watch what I could do. I did it again, jumping down from the swing and landing safely on my two feet. I repeated this imaginal act over and over until I fell asleep in the doing of it.

"Within two days the pain in my back and hip began to recede and within two months pain no longer existed for me. A condition that had plagued me for more than thirtynine years, that had cost a small fortune in attempted cure—was no more. . ." L.H.

It is to the pruning shears of revision that we owe our prime fruit. Man and his past are one continuous structure. This structure contains all of the past which has been conserved and still operates below the threshold of his senses to influence the present and the future of his life. The whole is carrying all of its contents with it; any alteration of content will result in an alteration in the present and the future. The first act of correction or cure is always "Revise." If the past can be recreated into the present, so can the revised past. And thus the Revised Past appears within the very heart of her present life; not Fate but a revised past brought her good fortune.

Make results and accomplishment the crucial test of true imagination and your confidence in the power of imagination to create reality will grow gradually from your experiments with revision confronted by experience. Only by this process of experiment can you realize the potential power of your awakened and controlled imagination.

"How much do you owe my master?" He said, "A hundred measures of oil." And he said to him, "Take your bill, and sit down quickly and write fifty!" This parable of the unjust steward urges us to mentally falsify the facts of life, to alter a theme already in being. By means of such imaginative falsehoods a man "acquires friends." As each day falls, mentally revise the facts of life and make them conform to events well worthy of recall; tomorrow will take up the altered pattern and go forward until at length it is realized on the heights of attainment.

The reader will find it worthwhile to follow these clues— imaginal construction of scenes implying the wish fulfilled, and imaginative participation in these scenes until tones of reality are reached. We are dealing with the secret of imagining, in which man is seen awakening into a world completely subject to his imaginative power.

Man can understand recurrence of events well enough (the building of a world from images supplied by memory) — things remaining as they are. This gives him a sense of security in the stability of things. However, the presence within him of a power which awakens and becomes what it wills, radically changing its form, its environment and the circumstances of life, inspires in him a feeling of insecurity, a dreadful fear of the future. Now, "it is high time to awake out of sleep" and put an end to all the unlovely creations of sleeping Man. Revise each day. "Let your strong imagination turn the great wheel backward until Troy unburn."

CHAPTER 4
THERE IS NO FICTION

"The distinction between what is real and what is imaginary is not one that can be finally maintained ... all existing things are, in an intelligible sense, imaginary."

— John S. MacKenzie

There is no fiction. If an imaginal activity can produce a physical effect, our physical world must be essentially imaginal. To prove this would require merely that we observe our imaginal activities and watch to see whether or not they produce corresponding external effects. If they do, then we must conclude that there is no fiction. Today's imaginal drama—fiction—becomes tomorrow's fact.

If we had this wider view of causation—that causation is mental—not physical—that our mental states are causative of physical effects, then we would realize our responsibility as a creator and imagine only the best imaginable.

Fable enacted as a sort of stage-play in the mind is what causes the physical facts of life. Man believes that reality resides in the solid objects he sees around him, that it is in this world that the drama of life originates, that events spring suddenly into existence, created moment by moment out of antecedent physical facts. But causation does not lie in the external world o£ facts. The drama of life originates in the imagination of man. The real act of becoming takes place within man's imagination and not without.

The following stories could define "causation" as the assemblage of mental states, which occurring, creates that which the assemblage implies.

The foreword from Walter Lord's "A Night To Remember" illustrates my claim, "Imagining Creates Reality."

"In 1898 a struggling author, named Morgan Robertson, concocted a novel about a fabulous Atlantic liner, far larger than any that had ever been built. Robertson loaded his ship with rich and complacent people and then wrecked it one cold April night on an iceberg. This somehow showed the futility of everything, and in fact, the book was called 'FUTILITY' when it appeared that year, published by the firm of M. F. Mansfield.

"Fourteen years later a British shipping company, named the White

Star Line, built a steamer remarkably like the one in Robertson's novel. The new liner was 66,000 tons displacement; Robertson's was 70,000 tons.

"The real ship was 882.5 feet long; the fictional one was 800 feet. Both could carry about 3,000 people, and both had enough lifeboats for only a fraction of this number. But, then this didn't seem to matter because both were labelled 'unshakable!'

"On April 19, 1912, the real ship left Southampton on her maiden voyage to New York. Her cargo included a priceless copy of the Rubaiyat of Omar Khayyam and a list of passengers collectively worth $250 million dollars. On her way over she, too, struck an iceberg and went down on a cold April night.

"Robertson called his ship the Titan; the White Star Line called its ship the Titanic."

Had Morgan Robertson known that Imagining Creates Reality, that today's fiction is tomorrow's fact, would he have written the novel Futility? "In the moment of the tragic catastrophe," writes Schopenhauer, "the conviction becomes more distinct to us than ever that life is a bad dream from which we have to awake." And the bad dream is caused by the imaginal activity of sleeping humanity.

Imaginal activities may be remote from their manifestation and unobserved events are only appearance. Causation as seen in this tragedy is elsewhere in space-time. Far off from the scene of action, invisible to all, was Robertson's imaginal activity, like a scientist in a control-room directing his guided missile through Space-Time.

Who paints a picture, writes a play or book

Which others read while he's asleep in bed

O' the other side of the world — when they o'erlook

His page the sleeper might as well be dead;

What knows he of his distant unfelt life?

What knows he of the thoughts his thoughts are raising,

The life his life is giving, or the strife Concerning him — some cavilling, some praising?

Yet which is most alive, he who's asleep Or his quick spirit in some other place,

Or score of other places, that doth keep Attention fixed and sleep from others chase?

Which is the "he"— the "he" that sleeps, or "he"

That his own "he" can neither feel nor see? . . .

— Samuel Butler

Imaginative writers communicate not their vision of the world but their attitudes which result in their vision. Just a short while before Katherine Mansfield died, she said to her friend Orage:

"There are in life as many aspects as attitudes toward it; and aspects change with attitudes. . . Could we change our attitude, we should not only see life differently, but life itself would come to be different. Life would undergo a change of appearance because we ourselves had undergone a change in attitude . . . Perception of a new pattern is what I call a creative attitude towards life."

"Prophets," wrote Blake, "in the modern sense of the word, have never existed. Jonah was no prophet in the modern sense, for his prophesy of Nineveh failed. Every honest man is a prophet; he utters his opinion both of private & public matters. Thus: If you go on So, the result is So. He never says, such a thing shall happen let you do what you will. A Prophet is a Seer, not an Arbitrary Dictator." The function of the Prophet is not to tell us what is inevitable, but to tell us what can be built up out of persistent imaginal activities.

The future is determined by the imaginal activities of humanity, activities in their creative march, activities which can be seen in "Your dreams and the visions of your head as you lay in bed." "Would that all the Lord's people were prophets" in the true sense of the word like this dancer who now, from the summit of his realized ideal, sights yet higher peaks that are to be scaled. After you have read this story you will understand why he is so confident that he can predetermine any materialistic future he desires and why he is equally sure that others give reality to what were otherwise a mere figment of his imagination, that there exists and can exist nothing outside imagining on some level or other. Nothing continues in being save what imagining supports. "... The mind can make Substance, and people planets of its own with beings brighter than have been, and give a breath to forms which can outlive all flesh ..."

"As my story begins at the age of nineteen I was a mildly successful dancing teacher and continued in this static state for almost five years. At the end of this time I met a young lady who talked me into attending your lectures. My thought, upon hearing you say 'Imagining creates reality,' was that the entire idea was ridiculous. However, I decided

[127] THE POWER OF IMAGINATION: THE NEVILLE GODDARD TREASURY

to accept your challenge and disprove your thesis. I bought your book 'Out of This World' and read it many times. Still unconvinced I set myself a rather ambitious goal. My present position was as an instructor with the Arthur Murray Dance Studio and my goal was to own a franchise and be boss of an Arthur Murray studio myself!

"This seemed the most unlikely thing in the world as franchises were extremely difficult to secure, but on top of this fact, I was completely without the necessary funds to begin such an operation. Nevertheless. I assumed the feeling of my wish fulfilled as night after night, in my imagination, I went to sleep managing my own studio. Three weeks later a friend called me from Reno, Nevada. He had the Murray Studio there and said it was too much for him to cope with alone. He offered me a partnership and I was delighted; so delighted, in fact, that I hastened to Reno on borrowed money and promptly forgot all about you and your story of Imagination!

"My partner and I worked hard and were very successful, but after a year I was still not satisfied, I wanted more. I began thinking of ways and means to get another studio. All my efforts failed. One night as I retired, I was restless and decided to read. As I looked through my collection of books I noticed your slender volume, 'Out of This World.' I thought of the 'silly nonsense' I had gone through one year ago before getting my own studio. GETTING MY OWN STUDIO! The words in my mind electrified me! I reread the book that night and later, in my imagination, I heard my superior praise the good job we had done in Reno and suggest we acquire a second studio as he had a second location ready for us if we desired to expand. I re-enacted this imaginal scene nightly without fail. Three weeks from the first night of my imaginal drama, it materialized — almost word for word. My partner accepted the new studio in Bakersfield and I had the Reno Studio alone. Now I was convinced of the truth of your teaching and never again will I forget.

"Now I wanted to share this wonderful knowledge — of imaginal power with my staff. I tried to tell them of the marvels they could accomplish, but I was unable to reach many although one fantastic incident resulted from my efforts to tell this story. A young teacher told me he believed my story but said it would have probably happened anyway in time. He insisted the entire theory was nonsense but stated that if I could tell him something of an incredible nature that would actually happen and which he could witness — then he would believe. I accepted his challenge and conceived a truly fantastic test.

"The Reno Studio is the most insignificant in the entire Murray system because of the small population count in the city itself. There are over three hundred Murray Studios in the country with much larger populations, therefore providing greater possibilities to draw from. So, my test was this. I told the teacher that within the next three months, at the time of a national dance convention, the little Reno Studio would be the foremost topic of conversation at that convention. He calmly stated this was quite impossible.

"That night when I retired, I felt myself standing before a tremendous audience. I was speaking on 'Creative Imagining' and felt the nervousness of being before such a vast audience; but I also felt the wonderful sensation of audience acceptance. I heard the roar of applause and as I left the stage, I saw Mr. Murray, himself come forward and shake my hand. I re-enacted this entire drama night after night. It began to take on the 'tones of reality' and I knew I had done it again!

"My imaginal drama materialized down to the last detail.

"My little Reno Studio was the 'talk' of the convention and I did appear on that stage just as I had done in my imagination. But even after this unbelievable but actual happening, the young teacher who threw me the challenge remained unconvinced. He said it had all happened too naturally! And he was sure it would have happened anyway!

"I did not mind his attitude because his challenge had given me another opportunity to prove, at least to myself, that Imagining does Create Reality. From that time on, I continued with my ambition to own the 'largest Arthur Murray Dance Studio in the world!' Night after night, in my imagination, I heard myself accepting a studio franchise for a great city. Within three weeks Mr. Murray called me and offered a studio in a city of one and a half million people! It is now my goal to make my studio the greatest and biggest in the entire system. And, of course, 'I know it will be done — through my Imagination'!" . . . E.O.L., Jr.

"Imagining," writes Douglas Fawcett, "may be hard to grasp, being 'quicksilver-like' it vanishes into each of its metamorphoses and thereby displays its transformative magic." We must look beyond the physical fact for the imagining which has caused it. For one year E.O.L., Jr. lost himself in his metamorphosis but fortunately he remembered "the silly nonsense" he had gone through before getting his own studio . . . and re-read the book.

Imaginal acts on the human level need a certain interval of time to develop but imaginal acts, whether committed to print or locked in the bosom of a hermit, will realize themselves in time.

Test yourself, if only out of curiosity. You will discover the "Prophet" is your own imagining and you will know "there is no fiction."

"We should never be certain that it was not some woman treading in the wine-press who began that subtle change in men's mind ... or that the passion, because of which so many countries were given to the sword, did not begin in the mind of some shepherd boy, lighting up his eyes for a moment before it ran upon its way." — William Butler Yeats

There is no fiction. Imagining fulfills itself in what our lives become. "And now I have told you before it takes place, so that when it does take place, you may believe." The Greeks were right: "The Gods have come down to us in the likeness of men!" But they have fallen asleep and do not realize the might they wield by their imaginal activities.

"Real are the dreams of Gods, and smoothly pass Their pleasure in a long immortal dream."

E.B., an author, is fully aware that "today's fiction can become tomorrow's fact." In this letter, she writes:

"One Spring, I completed a novelette, sold it and forgot it. Not until many long months later did I sit down and nervously compare some 'facts' in my fiction with some 'facts' in my life! Please read a brief outline of my created story. Then compare it with my personal experience.

"The heroine of my story took a vacation trip to Vermont. To the small city of Stowe, Vermont, to be exact. When she reached her destination she was faced with such unpleasant behavior on the part of her companion that she either had to continue her lifetime pattern of allowing another's selfish demand dominate her or to break that pattern and leave. She broke it and returned to New York. When she returned (and the story continues) events took shape in a proposal of marriage which she happily accepted.

"For my part of this tale ... as small events evolved ... I began to remember the dictates of my own pen and in significant relationship. This is what happened to me! I received an invitation from a friend offering me a vacation at her summer place in Vermont. I accepted and was not startled, at first, when I learned her 'summer place' was in the city of Stowe. When I arrived, I found my hostess in such a highly nervous state I realized I was faced with either a wretched summer or the choice of 'walking out' on her. Never before in my life had I been strong enough to ignore what I thought were the claims of duty and friendship — but this time I did and without ceremony returned to New York. A few days after I returned to my home, I, too, received a proposal of marriage. But at this point fact and fiction

[130] NEVILLE GODDARD

parted. I refused the offer! I know, Neville, there is no such thing as fiction." . . . E.B.

"Forgetful is green earth, the gods alone remember everlastingly ... by their great memories the gods are known."

Ends run true to their imaginal origins — we reap the fruit of forgotten blossom-time. In life the events do not come up always where we have strewn the seed; so that we may not recognize our own harvest. Events are the emergence of a hidden imaginal activity. Man is free to imagine whatever he desires. This is why, despite all fatalists and misguided prophets of doom, all awakened men know that they are free. They know that they are creating reality. Is there a scriptural passage to support this claim? Yes:

"And it came to pass, as he interpreted to us, so it was."

W. B. Yeats must have discovered that "there is no fiction" for after describing some of his experiences in the conscious use of imagination, he writes: "If all who have described events like this have not dreamed, we should rewrite our histories for all men, certainly all imaginative men, must be forever casting forth enchantments, glamours, illusions; and all men, especially tranquil men, who have no powerful egotistic life must be continually passing under their power. Our most elaborate thoughts, elaborate purposes, precise emotions, are often as I think, not really ours, but have on a sudden come up, as it were, out of hell or down out of heaven. . ."

"There is no fiction." Imagine better than the best you know.

CHAPTER 5
SUBTLE THREADS

. . All you behold; tho' it appears Without, it is Within; In your Imagination, of which this World of Mortality is but a Shadow." — Blake

Nothing appears or continues in being by a power of its own. Events happen because comparatively stable imaginal activities created them, and they continue in being by virtue of the support they receive from such imaginal activities. The part which imagining the wish fulfilled plays in consciously creating circumstances is obvious in this series of stories.

You will see how the telling of one story of the successful use of imagination can serve as a spur and a challenge to others to "try" it and "see."

One night a gentleman rose in my audience. He said that he had no question to ask but would like to tell me something. This was his story:

When he came out of the Armed Forces after World War II he got a job that gave him take-home pay of $25.00 a week. After ten years he was making $600.00 a month. At that time he bought my book "Awakened Imagination" and read the chapter "The Pruning Shears of Revision." Through the daily practice of "Revision," as set forth there, he was able to tell my audience two years later that his income was equal to that of the President of the United States.

In my audience sat a man who, by his confession, was broke. He had read the same book, but he suddenly realized he had done nothing with the use of his imagination to solve his financial problem.

He decided he would try to imagine himself as the winner of the 5-10 pool at Caliente Race Track. In his words: "In this pool, one attempts to pick winners in the fifth through the tenth races. So this is what I did: In my imagination I stood, sorting my tickets and feeling as I did so, that I had each of the six winners. I enacted this scene over and over in my imagination, until I actually felt 'goose pimples.' Then I 'saw' the cashier giving me a large sum of money which I placed beneath my imaginary shirt. This was my entire imaginal drama; and for three weeks, night after night, I enacted this scene and fell asleep in the action.

"After three weeks I traveled physically to the Caliente Race Track,

[132] NEVILLE GODDARD

and on that day every detail of my imaginative play was actually realized. The only change in the scene was that the cashier gave me a check for a total of $84,000.00 instead of currency.". . . T.K.

After my lecture the night this story was told, a man in the audience asked me if I thought it possible for him to duplicate T.K.'s experience. I told him he must decide the circumstances of his imaginal scene himself but that whatever scene he chose, he must create a drama he could make natural to himself and imagine the end intently with all the feeling he could muster; he must not labor for the means to the end but live imaginatively in the feeling of the wish fulfilled.

One month later he showed me a check for $16,000.00 which he had won in another 5-10 pool at the same Caliente Race Track the previous day.

This man had a sequel to his most interesting duplication of T.K.'s good fortune. His first win took care of his immediate financial difficulties although he wanted more money for future family security. Also, and more important to him, he wanted to prove that this had not been an "accident." He reasoned that if his good luck could happen a second time in succession, the so-called "law of percentages" would give way to proof for him that his imaginal structures were actually producing this miraculous "reality." And so he dared to put his imagination to a second test. He continues:

"I wanted a sizeable bank account and this, to me, meant 'seeing' a large balance on my bank statements. Therefore, in my imagination I enacted a scene which took me into two banks. In each bank I would 'see' an appreciative smile meant for me from the bank manager as I walked into his establishment and I would 'hear' the teller's cordial greeting. I would ask to see my statement. In one bank I 'saw' a balance of $10,000.00. In the other bank I 'saw' a balance of $15,000.00.

"My imaginal scene did not end there. Immediately after seeing my bank balances I would turn my attention to my horse racing system which, through a progression of ten steps, would bring my winnings to $11,533.00 with a starting capital of $200.00.

"I would divide the winnings into twelve piles on my desk. Counting the money in my imaginary hands I would put $1,000.00 in each of eleven piles and the remaining five-hundred thirty-three dollars in the last pile. My 'imaginative accounting' would amount to $36,533.00 including my bank balances.

"I enacted this entire imaginative scene each morning, afternoon and night for less than one month, and, on March second, I went to the

Caliente track again. I made out my tickets, but strangely enough and not knowing why I did so, I duplicated six more tickets exactly like the six already made out but in the tenth selection I made a 'mistake' and copied two tickets twice. As the winners came in, I held two of them — each paying $16,423.50. I also had six consolation tickets, each paying $656.80. The combined total amounted to $36,788.00. My imaginary accounting one month before had totaled $36,533.00. Two points of interest, most profound to me, were that by seeming accident I had marked two winning tickets identically and also, that at the end of the ninth race (which was one of the major winners) the trainer attempted to 'scratch' the horse, but the Stewards denied the trainer's request." . . . A.J.F.

How subtle were the threads that led to his goal? Results must testify to our imagining or we really are not imagining the end at all. A.J.F. faithfully imagined the end, and all things conspired to aid his harvesting. His "mistake" in copying a winning ticket twice, and the Steward's refusal to allow the trainer's request were events created by the imaginal drama to move the plan of things forward to its goal.

"Chance," wrote Belfort Bax, "may be defined as that element in the reality change — that is, in the flowing synthesis of events — which is irreducible to law or the causal category."

To live wisely we must be aware of our imaginal activities or, at any rate, of the end which they are tending. We must see to it that it is the end we desire. Wise imagining identifies itself only with such activities that are of value or promise well. However much man seems to be dealing with a material world, he is actually living in a world of imagination. When he discovers that it is not the physical world of facts but imaginal activities which shape his life, then the physical world will no longer be the reality, and the world of imagination no longer the dream.

"Does the road wind uphill all the way?

Yes, to the very end.

Will the day's journey take the whole long day?

From morn to night, my friend."

CHAPTER 6
VISIONARY FANCY

"The Nature of Visionary Fancy, or Imagination, is very little known, & the External nature & permanence of its ever Existent Images is consider'd as less permanent than the things of Vegetative & Generative Nature; yet the Oak dies as well as the Lettuce, but Its Eternal image & Individuality never dies, but renews by its seed; just so the Imaginative Image returns by the seed of Contemplative Thought." — Blake

The images of our imagination are the realities of which any physical manifestation is only the shadow. If we are faithful to vision, the image will create for itself the only physical manifestation of itself it has a right to make. We speak of the "reality" of a thing when we mean its material substance. That is exactly what an imaginist means by its "unreality" or shadow.

Imagining is spiritual sensation. Enter into the feeling of your wish fulfilled. Through spiritual sensation—through your use of imaginal sight, sound, scent, taste and touch—you will give to your image the sensory vividness necessary to produce that image in your outer or shadow world.

Here is the story of one who was faithful to his vision. F.B. being a true imaginist, remembered what he had heard in his imagination. Thus he writes:

"A friend who knows my passionate fondness for opera tried to get Kirsten Flagstad's complete recording of Tristan and Isolde for me at Christmas. In over a dozen record stores he was told the same thing: 'RCA Victor is not reissuing this recording and there have been no copies available since June.l On December 27th, I determined to prove your principle again by getting the album I desired so intensely. Eying down in my living room, I mentally walked into a record shop I patronize and asked the one salesman whose face and voice I could recall, 'Do you have Flagstad's complete Isolde?' He replied, 'Yes, I have.' That ended the scene and I repeated it until it was 'real' to me.

"Fate that afternoon I went to that record shop to physically enact the scene. Not one detail supplied by the senses had encouraged me to believe I could walk out o£ that shop with those records. I had been told last September by the same salesman in the same shop the same story my friend had received there before Christmas. Approaching the salesman I had seen in imagination that morning, I said, 'Do you have Flagstad's complete Isolde?' He replied, 'No, we haven't.' Without saying anything audible to him, I said inwardly, 'That's not what I heard you say!'

"As I turned to leave the shop I noticed on a top shelf what I thought to be an advertisement of this set of records and remarked to the salesman, 'If you don't have the merchandise you shouldn't advertise it.' 'That's right,' he replied, and as he reached up to take it down discovered it to be a complete album, with all five records! The scene wasn't played exactly as I had constructed it, but the result confirmed what my imagined scene implied. How can I thank you?" . . . F.B.

After reading F.B.'s letter we must agree with Anthony Eden that "An assumption, though false, if persisted in will harden into fact." F.B.'s fancy, fusing with the sense-field of the record shop, enriched aspects of it and made them 'his' — what he perceived.

Our future is our imagining in its creative march. F.B. used his imagination for a conscious purpose representing life as he desired it to be and thereby affecting life instead of merely reflecting it. So sure, was he that his imaginal drama was the reality — and the physical act but a shadow — that when the salesman said, "No, we haven't" F.B. mentally said, "That's not what I heard you say!" He not only remembered what he had heard, but he was still remembering it. Imagining the wish fulfilled is the seeking that finds, the asking that receives, the knocking to which is opened. He saw and heard what he desired to see and hear; and would not take "No, we haven't" for an answer.

The imagines dream while awake. He is not the servant of his Vision, but the master of the direction of his attention. Imaginative constancy controls perception of events in space-time.

Unfortunately, most men are . . .

"Ever changing, like a joyless eye That finds no object worth its constancy...."

Mrs. G.R., too, had imaginatively heard what she wanted to physically hear and knew the outer world must confirm it. This is her story:

"Some time ago we advertised our home for sale which was necessary for us to buy a larger property on which we had placed a deposit. Several people would have bought our home immediately but we were obliged to explain that we could not close any deal until we learned whether or not our offer for the property we wanted had been accepted. At this time, a broker called and literally begged us to allow him to show our home to a client of his who was eager for this

[136] NEVILLE GODDARD

location and would be glad to pay even more than we were asking. We explained our situation to the broker and to his client; they both stated they did not mind waiting for our deal to be consummated. The broker asked us to sign a paper which he said was not binding in any way but would give him first chance at the sale if our other deal went through. We signed the paper and later learned that in California Real Estate law nothing could have been more binding. A few days later our deal for the new property fell through so we notified this broker and his verbal response was, 'Well, just forget it.' Two weeks later he filed suit against us for fifteen hundred dollars commission. Trial date was set and we asked for a jury trial.

"Our attorney assured us he would do all he could, but that the law on this particular point was so stringent that he could not see any possibility of our winning the case. When time for the trial arrived, my husband was in the hospital and could not appear with me in our defense. I had no witnesses; but the broker brought three attorneys and a number of witnesses into court against us. Our attorney now told me we had not the slightest chance to win.

"I turned to my imagination, and this is what I did. Completely disregarding all that had been said by attorneys, witnesses and the judge who seemed to favor the plaintiff, I thought only of the words I wanted to hear. In my imagination, I listened intently and heard the foreman of the jury say, 'We find the defendant not guilty.' I listened until I knew it was true. I closed my mind's ear to everything said in that courtroom and heard only those words, 'We find the defendant not guilty!' The jury deliberated from noon recess until four-thirty that afternoon, and all during those hours I sat in the courtroom and heard those words over and over in my imagination. When the jurors returned the Judge asked the foreman to stand and give their verdict. The foreman stood up and said, 'We find the defendant NOT guilty'."
. . . Mrs. G.R.

"If there were dreams to sell, what would you buy?"

Would you not buy your wish fulfilled? Your dreams are without price and without money. By locking up the jury in her imagination — hearing only what she wanted to hear, she called the jury to unanimity on her behalf. Imagining being the reality of all that exists, with it the lady achieved her wish fulfilled.

Hebbel's statement that "the poet creates from contemplation" is true of imagines as well. They know how to utilize their video-audio hallucinations to create reality.

Nothing is so fatal as conformity. We must not allow ourselves to be girt about by the ringed fixity of fact. Change the image, and thereby change the fact. R.O. employed the art of seeing and feeling to create her vision in imagination.

"A year ago, I took my children to Europe leaving my furnished apartment in the care of my maid. When we returned a few months later to the United States I found my maid and all my furniture gone. The apartment superintendent stated that the maid had had my furniture moved 'by my request.' There was nothing I could do at the moment, so I took my children and moved into a hotel. I, of course, reported the incident to the police and, also, brought in private detectives on the case. Both organizations investigated every moving company and every storage warehouse in New York City, but to no avail. There seemed to be absolutely no trace of my furniture, nor of my maid.

"Having exhausted all outside sources, I remembered your teaching and decided I would try using my imagination in this matter. So, while seated in my hotel room I closed my eyes and imagined myself in my own apartment sitting in my favorite chair and surrounded by all of my personal furnishings. I looked across the living room at the piano on which I kept pictures of my children. I would continue to stare at my piano until the entire room became vividly real to me. I could see my children's pictures and actually feel the upholstery of the chair in which, in my imagination, I sat.

"The next day, as I came out of my bank, I turned to walk in the direction of my vacant apartment instead of toward my hotel. When I reached the corner, I discovered my 'mistake' and was just about to turn back when my attention was drawn to a very familiar pair of ankles. Yes, the ankles belonged to my maid. I walked up to her and took hold of her arm. She was quite frightened, but I assured her all I wanted from her was my furniture. I called a taxi and she took me to the place in which her friends had stored my furnishings. In one day, my imagination had found what an entire big city police force and private investigators could not find in weeks." . . . R.O.

This lady knew of the secret of imagining before she called in the police, but imagining—in spite of its importance—was forgotten owing to attention being fixed on facts. However, what reason failed to find by force, imagining found without effort. Nothing merely goes on—including the sense of loss—without its imaginal support. By imagining that she was seated in her own chair, in her own living room, surrounded by all of her own furnishings, she withdrew the imaginal support she had given to her sense of loss; and by this imaginal change she recovered her lost furniture and re-established her home.

Your imagination is most creative when you imagine things as you desire them to be, building a new experience out of a dream of fancy. To build such a dream of fancy in her imagination, F.G. brought to play all of her senses—sight, sound, touch, smell— even taste. This is her story:

"Since childhood I have dreamed of visiting far-away places. The West Indies, particularly, fired my fancy, and I would revel in the feeling of actually being there. Dreams are wonderfully inexpensive and as an adult I continued to dream my dreams, for I had no money or time to make them 'come true.' Last year I was taken to the hospital in need of surgery. I had heard your teaching and, while recuperating, had decided to intensify my favorite daydream while I had time on my hands. I actually wrote to the Alcoa Steamship Line asking for free travel folders and pored over them, hour after hour, choosing the ship and the stateroom and the seven ports I desired most to see. I would close my eyes and, in my imagination, would walk up the gangplank of that ship and feel the movement of water as the great liner pushed its way into free ocean. I heard the thud of waves breaking against the sides of the ship, felt the steaming warmth of a tropical sun on my face and smelled and tasted salt in the air as we all sailed through blue waters.

"For one solid week, confined to a hospital bed, I lived the free and happy experience of actually being on that ship. Then, the day before my release from the hospital, I tucked the colored folders away and forgot them. Two months later I received a telegram from an advertising agency telling me I had won a contest. I remembered having deposited a contest coupon some months before in a neighborhood supermarket but had completely forgotten the act. I had won first prize and—wonder of wonders—it entitled me to a Caribbean cruise sponsored by the Alcoa Steamship Line. But the wonder didn't stop there. The very stateroom I had imaginatively lived in and moved about in while confined to a hospital bed had been assigned to me. And to make an unbelievable story even more unbelievable, I sailed on the one ship I had chosen — which stopped in not one, but all of the seven ports I had desired to visit!" . . . F.G.

"To travel is the privilege, not of the rich but of the imaginative."

CHAPTER 7
MOODS

"This is an age in which the mood decides the fortunes of people rather than the fortunes decide the mood." —Sir Winston Churchill

Men regard their moods far too much as effects and not sufficiently as causes. Moods are imaginal activities without which no creation is possible. We say that we are happy because we have achieved our goal; we do not realize that the process works equally well in the reverse direction—that we shall achieve our goal because we have assumed the happy feeling of the wish fulfilled.

Moods are not only the result of the conditions of our life; they are also the causes of those conditions. In "The Psychology of Emotions," Professor Ribot writes, "An idea which is only an idea produces nothing and does nothing; it only acts if it is felt, if it is accompanied by an effective state, if it awakens tendencies, that is to say, motor elements."

The lady in the following story so successfully felt the feeling of her wish fulfilled, she made her mood the character of the night—frozen in a delightful dream.

"Most of us read and love fairy stories, but we all know that stories of improbable riches and good fortune are for the delight of the very young. But are they? I want to tell you of something unbelievably wonderful that happened to me through the power of my imagination — and I am not 'young' in years. We live in an age which believes in neither fable nor magic, and yet everything I could possibly want in my wildest day-dreams was given to me by the simple use of what you teach — that 'imagining creates reality' and that 'feeling' is the secret of imagining.

"At the time this wonderful thing happened to me I was out of a job and had no family to fall back upon for support. I needed just about everything. To find a decent job I needed a car to look for it, and though I had a car it was so worn out it was ready to fall apart. I was behind in my rent; I had no proper clothes to seek a job; and today it's no fun for a woman of fifty-five to apply for a job of any kind. My bank account was almost depleted and there was no friend to whom I could turn.

"But I had been attending your lectures for almost a year and my desperation forced me to put my imagination to the test. Indeed, I

[140] NEVILLE GODDARD

had nothing to lose. It was natural for me, I suppose, to begin by imagining myself having everything I needed. But I needed so many things and in such short order that I found myself exhausted when I finally got through the list, and by that time I was so nervous I could not sleep. One lecture night I heard you tell of an artist who captured the 'feeling,' or 'word,' as you called it, of 'isn't it wonderful!' in his personal experience. I began to apply this idea to my case. Instead of thinking of and imagining every article I needed, I tried to capture the 'feeling' that something wonderful was happening to me—not tomorrow, not next week—but right now. I would say over and over to myself as I fell asleep, 'Isn't it wonderful! Something marvelous is happening to me now!' And as I fell asleep I would feel the way I would expect to feel under such circumstances.

"I repeated that imaginary action and feeling for two months, night after night, and one day in early October I met a casual friend I hadn't seen for months who informed me he was about to leave on a trip to New York. I had lived in New York many years ago and we talked of the city a few moments and then parted. I completely forgot the incident. One month later, to the day, this man called at my apartment and simply handed me a Certified Check in my name for twenty-five hundred dollars. After I got over the initial shock of seeing my name on a check for so much money, the story that unfolded seemed to me like a dream. It concerned a friend I had not seen nor heard from in more than twenty-five years. This friend of my past, I now learned, had become extremely wealthy in those twenty-five years. Our mutual acquaintance who had brought the check to me had met him quite by accident during the trip to New York last month. During their conversation they spoke of me, and for reasons I was not to know (for to this day I have not heard from him personally and have never attempted to contact him) this old friend decided to share a portion of his great wealth with me.

"For the next two years, from the office of his attorney, I received monthly checks so generous in amount they not only covered every necessary requirement of daily living, but left much over for all the lovely things of life: a car, clothes, a spacious apartment — and best of all, no need to earn my daily bread.

"This past month I received a letter and some legal papers to be signed which provide the continuation of this monthly income for the rest of my natural life!" . . . T.K.

"If the fool would persist in his folly He would become wise."

Sir Winston calls on us to act on the assumption that we already possess that which we sought, to "assume a virtue," if we have it not.

Is this not the secret of "miracles"? Thus the man with palsy was told to rise, to take up his bed and walk — to mentally act as if he were healed; and when the actions of his imagination corresponded with the actions which he would physically perform were he healed — he was healed.

"This is a story about which some may say, 'it would have happened anyway,' but those who read it carefully will find room to wonder. It begins one year ago as I left Los Angeles to visit my daughter in San Francisco. Instead of the happy-natured individual she had always been, I found her in deep distress. Not knowing the cause of her anguish and not wishing to ask, I waited until she told me that she was in great financial trouble and must have three thousand dollars immediately. I am not a poor woman but I didn't have much cash I could put my hands on that quickly. Knowing my daughter, I knew she would not have accepted it anyway. I offered to borrow the money for her, but she refused and instead asked me to help her in 'my way' . . . she meant using my imagination, for I had often told her of your teaching and some of my words must have struck home.

"I immediately agreed on this plan with the provision that she would help me help her. We decided on an imaginal scene we could both practice that involved 'seeing' money coming to her from everywhere. We felt money was flooding toward her from every corner, until she was in the middle of a 'sea' of money, but we did this always with the feeling of 'Joy' for anyone concerned and we had no thought of means, only happiness for all.

"The idea seemed to catch fire with her, and I know she was responsible for what happened a few days later. She was certainly transformed back to the happy, confident mood that was natural to her, though there was no evidence of any real money coming in at the time. I left to return home in the East.

"When I arrived home I called my mother (a lovely young lady of ninety-one) who immediately asked me to come and see her. I wanted a day's rest but she couldn't wait; it had to be now. Of course I went, and after greeting me, she handed me a check for three thousand dollars made out to my daughter! Before I could speak, she handed be three additional checks totaling fifteen hundred dollars made in favor of my daughter's children. Her reason? She explained that she had suddenly decided the day before to give what she had in cash to those she loved while she was still 'here' to know of their happiness in receiving it!

"It would have happened anyway? No—not like this. Not within days of my daughter's frantic need, and then her sudden transformation

[142] NEVILLE GODDARD

to a mood of joy. I know that her imaginal act caused this wonderful change—bringing not only great joy to the receiver but to the giver as well."

"P.S. ... I almost forgot to add that among the checks so lavishly given, was one for me too, for three thousand dollars!" ... M.B.

The boundless opportunities opened by recognizing the shift of the focus of imagining is beyond measure. There are no boundaries. The drama of life is an imaginal activity in which we bring to pass by our moods rather than by our physical acts. Moods so ably guide all towards that which they affirm, they may be said to create the circumstances of life and dictate the events. The mood of the wish fulfilled is the high tide which lifts us easily off the bar of the senses where we usually lie stranded. If we are aware of the mood and know this secret of imagining, we may announce that all that our mood affirms will come to pass.

The following story is by a mother who succeeded in sustaining a seemingly "playful" mood with startling results.

"Surely you've heard the 'old wives' tale about warts: That, if a wart is bought, it will disappear? I've known this story from childhood but not until I heard your lectures did I realize the truth hidden in the old tale. My boy, a lad of ten, had many large ugly warts on his legs causing an irritation which had plagued him for years. I decided that my sudden 'insight' could be used to his advantage. A boy has a lot of faith in his mother as a rule so I asked him if he would like to be rid of his warts. He quickly said, 'Yes,' but he did not want to go to a doctor. I asked him to play a little game with me, that I would pay him a sum of money for each wart. This suited him fine; he said—'he didn't see how he could lose!' We arrived at a fair price, he thought, and then I said, 'Now, I'm paying you good money for those warts; they no longer belong to you. You never keep property belonging to someone else so you can no longer keep those warts. They will disappear. It may take a day, two days or a month; but remember, that I've bought them and they belong to me.'

"My son was delighted with our game and the results sound like something read in old musty books on magic. But, believe me, within ten days the warts began to fade, and, at the end of one month every wart on his body had completely disappeared!

"There is a sequel to this story for I've bought warts from many people. They, too, thought it great fun and accepted my five, seven or ten cents a wart. In each case the wart disappeared—but really—only one person believes me when I tell him his Imagination, alone, took away the warts. That one person is my young son. . . . J.R.

Man imagining himself into a mood takes on himself the results of the mood. If he does not imagine himself into the mood, he is ever free of the result. The great Irish mystic, A.E., wrote in "The Candle of Vision": "I became aware of a swift echo or response to my own moods in circumstance which had seemed hitherto immutable in its indifference ... I could prophesy from the uprising of new moods in myself that I, without search, would soon meet people of a certain character, and so I met them. Even inanimate things were under the sway of these affinities." But man need not wait for the uprising of new moods in himself; he can create happy moods at will.

CHAPTER 8
THROUGH THE LOOKING GLASS

"A man that looks on glasse,

On it may stay his eye;

Or if he pleaseth, through it passe,

And then the heav'n espie."

—George Herbert

Objects, to be perceived, must first penetrate in some manner our brain; but we are not—because of this—interlocked with our environment. Although normal consciousness is focused on the senses and is usually restricted to them, it is possible for man to pass through his sense fixation into any imaginal structure which he conceives and so fully occupy it that it is more alive and more responsive than that on which his senses "stay his eye." If this were not true, man would be an automaton reflecting life, never affecting it. Man, who is all Imagination, is not tenant to the brain but landlord; he need not rest content with the appearance of things; he can go beyond perceptual to conceptual awareness.

This ability, to pass through the mechanical reflective structure of the senses, is the most important discovery man can make. It reveals man as a center of imagining with powers of intervention which enable him to alter the course of observed events moving from success to success through a series of mental transformations in himself. Attention, the spearhead of imagining, may be either attracted from without as his senses "stay his eye" or directed from within "if he pleases" and through the senses pass into the wish fulfilled.

To move from perceptual awareness, or things as they seem, to conceptual awareness, or things as they ought to be, we imagine as vivid and as life-like a representation as possible of what we would see, hear, and do, were we physically present, and physically experiencing things as they ought to be and imaginatively participate in that scene.

The following story tells of one who went "through the glass" and broke the chains that bound her.

"Two years ago I was taken to the hospital with a serious blood clot condition which apparently had affected the entire vascular system causing hardening of arteries and arthritis. A nerve in my head was damaged and my thyroid enlarged. Doctors could not agree on the cause of this condition, and all their treatments were completely ineffective. I was forced to give up my every enjoyable activity and remain in bed most of the time. My body, from hips to toes, felt as though it was encased and bound

by tight wires, and I couldn't put my feet on the floor without wearing heavy hiplength elastic stockings.

"I knew something of your teaching and tried very hard to apply what I had heard, but as my condition grew worse and I could no longer attend any of your lectures, my despondency grew deeper. One day a friend sent me a postcard picturing the scene of a lovely beach by the ocean. The picture was so beautiful I looked and looked at it and began to remember past summer days at the seashore with my parents. For a moment, the postcard picture seemed to become animated and flooding memories of myself running free on the beach filled my mind. I felt the impact of my bare feet against the hard wet sand; I felt the icy water running over my toes and heard the crash of waves breaking on shore. This imaginal activity was so satisfying to me as I lay in bed that I continued to imagine this wonderful scene, day after day, for about one week.

"One morning I moved from my bed to a couch and had started to sit up when I was seized with such an excruciating pain my entire body became paralyzed. I could neither sit up nor lie down. This terrible pain lasted for more than a full minute, but when it stopped — I was free! It seemed as if all the wires binding my legs had been cut. One moment I was bound; the next moment I was free. Not by degrees, but instantly." . . . V.H.

"We walk by faith, not by sight." —2 Cor. 5:7

When we walk by sight, we know our way by objects which our eyes see. When we walk by faith we order our life by scenes and actions which only imagination sees.

Man perceives by the Eye of Imagination or by Sense. But two mental attitudes to perception are possible, the creative imaginative effort which meets with an imaginative response, or the unimaginative "staying of the eye" which merely reflects.

Man has within him the principle of life and the principle of death. One is the imagination building its imaginal structures out of the generous dreams of fancy. The other is the imagination building its imaginal structures from images reflected by the chill wind of fact. One creates. The other perpetuates. Man must adopt either the way of faith or the way of sight. To the extent that man builds from dreams of fancy, he is alive; and, therefore, the development of the faculty to pass through the reflective glass of the senses is an increase of life. It follows that restricting the imagination by "staying the eye" on the reflective glass of the senses is a reduction of life.

The specious surface of fact reflects rather than discloses, deflecting the "Eye of Imagination" from the truth that sets man free. "The Eye of Imagination," if not deflected, looks on what ought to be there, not what is. However familiar the scene on which sight rests, the "Eye of Imagination" could gaze on one never before witnessed. It is this "Eye of Imagination" and only this that can free us from the sense fixation of outer things which completely dominates our ordinary existence and keeps us looking on the reflective glass of facts.

It is possible to pass from thinking of to thinking from; but the crucial matter is thinking from, i.e., experiencing the state, for that experience means unification; whereas in thinking of there is always subject and object — the thinking individual and the thing thought of.

Self-abandonment. That is the secret. We have to abandon ourselves to the state, in our love for the state, and in so doing live the life of the state and no more our present state. Imagination seizes upon the life of the state and gives itself to the expression of the life of that state.

Faith plus Love is self-commission. We can't commit ourselves to what we do not love. "Never would you have made anything if you had not loved it." And to make the state alive, one must become it. "I live, yet not I, God lives in me: and the life I now live in the flesh, I live by the faith of God, who loved me and gave Himself for me." God loved man, His created, and became man in faith that this act of self-commission would transform the created into the creative.

We must be "imitators of God as dear children" and commit ourselves to what we love, as God who loved us committed Himself to us. We must BE the state to experience the state.

The center of conscious imagining can be shifted and what are now mere wishes — imaginal activities keyed low — brought into penetrative focus and entered. Entrance commits us to the state. The possibilities of such shifting of the center of imagining are startling. The activities concerned are psychical throughout. The shifting of the center of imagining is not brought about by spatial travel but by a change in what we are aware of. The boundary of the world of sense is a subjective barrier. So long as the senses take notice, the Eye of Imagination is deflected from the truth. We do not get far unless we let go. This lady "let go" with immediate and miraculous results.

"Thank you for the 'golden key.' It has released my brother from the hospital, from pain and probable death, for he was facing a fourth major operation with little hope of recovery, I was very concerned and attempting to use what I had learned about my Imagination, I first asked myself what my brother truly desired: 'Does he want to continue in this body or does he desire to be free of it?' The question revolved itself over and over in my mind and suddenly I felt that he would like to continue remodeling his kitchen which he had been contemplating before his confinement in the hospital. I knew my question had been answered, so I began to imagine from that point.

"Attempting to 'see' my brother in the busy activity of remodeling, I suddenly found myself gripping the back of a kitchen chair I had used many times when 'something' happened, then suddenly I found myself standing beside my brother's bed in the hospital. This was the last place I would have wanted to be, physically or mentally, but there I was and my brother's hand reached up and clasped my hand tightly as I heard him say, 'I knew you would come, Jo.' It was a well hand I clasped, strong and sure, and the joy that filled and spilled over in my voice as I heard myself say, 'It's all better now. You know it.' My brother didn't answer, but I distinctly heard a voice say to me, 'Remember this moment.' I seemed to awake then, back in my own home.

"This took place the night after he had entered the hospital. The following day his wife telephoned me saying, 'It is unbelievable! The doctor can't account for it, Jo, but no operation is necessary. He's so improved that they have agreed to release him tomorrow.' The following Monday my brother went back to his work and has been perfectly well since that day." . . . J.S.

Not facts — but dreams of fancy shape our lives. She needed no compass to find her brother, nor tools to operate, only the "Eye of Imagination." In the world of sense we see what we have to see; in the world of Imagination we see what we want to see; And seeing it, we create it for the world of sense to see. We see the outer world automatically. Seeing what we want to see demands voluntary and conscious imaginative effort. Our future is our own imaginal activity in its creative march. Common sense assures us that we are living in a solid and sensible world but this so seemingly solid world is — in reality — imaginal through and through.

The following story proves that it is possible for an individual to transfer the center of imagining to some greater or lesser degree to a distant area, and not only do so without moving physically, but to be visible to others who are present at that point in space-time. And, if this be a dream, then,

"Is all that we see or seem But a dream within a dream?"

"Seated in my living room in San Francisco, I imagined I was in my daughter's living room in London, England. I surrounded myself so completely with that room which I knew intimately, that I suddenly found myself actually standing in it. My daughter was standing by her fireplace, her face turned away from me. A moment later she turned and our eyes met. I saw such a startled, frightened expression on her face that I, too, became emotionally upset and immediately found myself back in my own living room in San Francisco.

"Five days later I received an airmail letter from my daughter which had been written on the day of my experiment with imaginal travel. In her letter she told me she had 'seen' me in her living room that day just as real as though I were actually standing there in the flesh. She confessed she had been very frightened and that before she could speak, I had vanished. The time of this 'visitation,' as she gave it in her letter, was exactly the time I had begun the imaginative action allowing, of course, for the difference in time between the two points. She explained that she told her husband of this amazing experience and he insisted that she write to me immediately as he stated, 'Your mother must have died or is dying.' But I wasn't 'dead' or 'dying,' but very much alive and very excited by this marvelous experience." . . .M.L.J.

"Nothing can act but where it is: with all my heart; only where is it?"

—Thomas Carlyle

Man is All Imagination. Therefore, a man must be where he is in imagination, for his Imagination is himself. Imagination is active at and through any state that it is aware of. If we take shifting of awareness seriously, there are possibilities beyond belief. The senses join man in forced and unholy wedlock to what, were he imaginatively awake, he would put asunder. We need not feed on sense-data. Shift the focus of awareness and see what happens. However little we move mentally we should perceive the world under a slightly changed aspect. Awareness is usually moved about in space by movement of the physical organism but it need not be so restricted. It can be moved by a change in what we are aware of.

Man is manifesting the power of Imagination whose limits he cannot define. To realize that the Real Self—Imagination—is not something enclosed within the spatial boundary of the body is most important. The foregoing; story proves, that when we meet a person in the flesh, that his Real Self need not be present in space where his body is. It also shows that sense-perception can be thrown into operation outside of the normal physical means, and that the sense-data produced is of the same kind as those which occur in normal perception. The idea in the mother's mind which started the whole process going was the very definite idea of being in the place where her daughter lived. And if the mother really were in that place, and if the daughter were present, then she would have to be perceptible to her daughter.

We can only hope to understand this experience in imaginal, and not in mechanical or materialistic terms. The mother imagined 'elsewhere' as being 'here.' London was just as 'here' to her daughter living 'there' as San Francisco was 'here' to the mother living 'there.'

It hardly ever crosses our minds that this world might be different in essence from what common sense tells us it so obviously is. Blake writes: "I question not my Corporeal or Vegatative Eye any more than I would Question a Window concerning a Sight. I look thro' it and not with it." This looking through the eye not only shifts consciousness to other parts of "this world" but to "other worlds" as well. Astronomers must wish they knew more of this "looking through the eye"; this mental traveling that mystics practice so easily.

"I travel'd thro' a land of men, A land of men and women too, And heard and saw such dreadful things As cold earth wanderers never knew."

Mental traveling has been practiced by awakened men and women since the earliest days. Paul states: "I know a man in Christ who fourteen years ago was caught up to the third heaven — whether in the body or out of the body I do not know, God knows." 2.Cor. 12: Paul is telling us that he is that man and that he traveled by the power of imagination or Christ. In his next letter to the Corinthians he writes: "Test yourselves. Do you not realize that Jesus Christ is in you?" We need not be 'dead' in order to enjoy spiritual privileges. "Man is All Imagination and God is Man." Test yourselves as this mother did.

Sir Arthur Eddington said that all we have a right to say of the external world is that it is a "shared experience." Things are more or less 'real' according to the extent to which they are capable of being shared with others or with ourselves at another time. But there is no hard and fast line.

Accepting Eddington's definition of reality as "shared experience," the above story is as 'real' as the earth or a color for it was shared by both mother and daughter. The range of imagining is such that I must confess that I do not know what limits, if any, there are to its ability to create reality.

All these stories show us one thing — that an imaginal activity implying the wish fulfilled must start in the imagination apart from the evidence of the senses in that Journey that leads to the realization of desire.

CHAPTER 9
ENTER INTO

"If the Spectator would Enter into these Images in his Imagination, approaching them on the Fiery Chariot of his Contemplative Thought, if he could . . . make a Friend & Companion of one of these Images of wonder, which always entreats him to leave mortal things (as he must know) then would he arise from his Grave, then would he meet the Ford in the Air & then he would be happy." —BLAKE

Imagination it seems will do nothing that we wish until we enter into the image of the wish fulfilled. Does not this entering into the image of the wish fulfilled resemble Blake's "Void outside of Existence which if enter'd into Englobes itself & becomes a Womb?" Is this not the true interpretation of the mythical story of Adam and Eve? Man and his emanation? Are not man's dreams of fancy his Emanation, his Eve in whom "He plants himself in all her Nerves, just as a Husbandman his mould; And she becomes his dwelling place and garden fruitful seventy fold?"

The secret of creation is the secret of imagining — first, desiring and then assuming the feeling of the wish fulfilled until the dream of fancy, 'the Void outside existence,' is enter'd and 'englobes itself and becomes a womb, a dwelling place and garden fruitful seventy fold.' Note well that Blake urges us to enter info these images. This entering into the image makes it 'englobe itself and become a womb.' Man, by entering a state impregnates it and causes it to create what the union implies. Blake tells us that these images are 'Shadowy to those who dwell not in them, mere possibilities; but to those who enter into them they seem the only substances. . . .'

On my way to the West Coast I stopped in Chicago to spend the day with friends. My host was recovering from a severe illness and his doctor advised him to move to a one-story house. Acting upon the doctor's advice, he had purchased a one-story house suited to his needs; but he now was confronted with the fact that there seemed to be no buyer for his large three-story home. When I arrived he was very discouraged. In trying to explain the law of constructive imagining to my host and his wife, I told them the story of a very prominent New York woman who had come to see me concerning the rental of her apartment. She maintained a lovely city apartment and a country home, but it was absolutely essential that she rent her apartment if she and her family were to spend the summer at their country home.

In previous years the apartment had been rented without any difficulty early in the Spring, but at the time she came to see me the season for summer sublets was seemingly over. Although the apartment had been in the hands of good real estate agents, no one had seemed interested in renting it. I told her what to do in her imagination. She did it and in less than twenty-four hours her apartment was rented.

I explained how she, by the constructive use of her imagination, had rented her apartment. At my suggestion, before she went to sleep that night in her apartment in the city, she imagined she was lying in her bed in her country home. In her imagination she viewed the world from the country house rather than from the city apartment. She smelled the fresh country air. She made this so real that she actually drifted off to sleep feeling that she was in the country. That was on a Thursday night. At nine o'clock the following Saturday morning, she phoned me from her country home and told me that on Friday a highly desirable tenant, who met all of her requirements, not only rented her apartment but rented it on the one condition that he could move in that very day.

I suggested to my friends that they build an imaginal structure as this woman had done, and that was to sleep, imagining they were physically present in their new home, feeling they had sold their old home. I explained to them the wide difference between thinking of the image of their new house, and thinking from the image of their new house. Thinking of it is a confession they are not in it; thinking from it is proof that they are in it. Entering into the image would give substance to the image. Their physical occupancy of the new house would follow automatically.

I explained that what the world looks like depends entirely on where man is when he makes his observation. And man, being "All Imagination," must be where he is in imagination. This concept of causation disturbed them, for it smacked of magic or superstition, but they promised they would try it. I left that night for California and the following evening the conductor on the train in which I was traveling handed me a telegram. It read: "House sold midnight last." One week later they wrote and told me that the very night I left Chicago they fell asleep physically in the old house but mentally in the new, viewing the world from the new home, imagining how things would "sound" if this were true. They were awakened that very night from their sleep to be told the house was sold.

Not until the image is entered, until Eve is known, does the event burst upon the world. The wish fulfilled must be conceived in the imagination of man before the event can evolve out of what Blake calls 'the Void.'

This next story proves that by shifting the focus of her imagining, Mrs. A. F. entered physically into where she had persisted in being imaginatively.

"Soon after our marriage, my husband and I decided that our greatest joint desire was a year in Europe. This objective may seem reasonable to a lot of people, but to us— tied to a narrow sphere of limited finances—it seemed not only unreasonable but completely ridiculous. Europe might as well have been another planet. But I had heard your teaching, so I persisted in falling asleep in England! Why England necessarily, I cannot tell, except that I had seen a current motion picture featuring the area around Buckingham Palace and had promptly fallen in love with the scene. All I did in my imagination was to stand quietly outside the great iron gates and feel the cold metal bars gripped tightly in my hands as I viewed the Palace.

"For many, many nights I felt an intense joy at 'being' there and fell asleep in this happy state. Soon after, my husband met a stranger at a party who, within one month, was instrumental in securing a teaching fellowship for him at a great university. Imagine my excitement when I heard the university was in England! Tied to a narrow sphere? Within another month we were crossing the Atlantic and our supposedly insurmountable difficulties melted as though they never existed. We had our year in Europe, one of the happiest years of my life." . . . M.F.

What the world looks like depends entirely on where man is when he makes his observations. And man, being 'All Imagination,' must be where he is in imagination.

"The stone which the builders rejected has become the chief corner-stone." That stone is Imagining. I acquaint you with this secret and leave you to Act or Re-act.

"This is the famous stone That turneth all to gold; For that which God doth touch and own Cannot for lesse be told."

—George Herbert

"My home is old but it is mine. I wanted the exterior painted and the interior redecorated, yet I had no money to accomplish either objective. You told us to 'live' as though our desire is already a reality, and this I began to do — imagining my old house with a brand-new coat of paint, new furnishings, new decoration and all the trimmings. I walked, in my imagination, through the newly decorated rooms. I walked around the outside admiring the fresh paint; and, at the end of my imaginal act, I handed the contractor a check for payment in full. I entered this imaginal scene faithfully as often as I could during the day and each night before I fell asleep.

"Within two weeks I received a registered letter from Lloyd's of London, telling me I had inherited seven thousand dollars from a woman I had never met! I had known her brother slightly almost forty years before and had performed a small service fifteen years ago for the lady when this brother had died in our country, and she had written to me asking for particulars regarding his death which I was able to provide. I had not heard from her since that time.

"Now, here was the check for seven thousand dollars — more than enough to cover the cost of my house restoration, plus many, many other things I desired." . . . E.C.A.

"He who does not imagine in stronger and better lineaments, and in stronger and better light than his perishing and mortal eye can see, does not imagine at all."

—Blake

Unless the individual imagines himself someone else, or somewhere else, the present conditions and circumstances of his life will continue in being and his problems recur, for all events renew themselves from his constant images. By him they were made; by him they continue in being; and by him they can cease to be.

The secret of causation is in the assembled imagery—but a word of warning—the assemblage must have meaning; it must imply something or it will not form the creative activity — The Word.

CHAPTER 10
THINGS WHICH DO NOT APPEAR

. . what is seen was made out of things which do not appear." —Heb. 11:3

"Human history, with its forms of governments, its revolutions, its wars, and in fact the rise and fall of nations, could be written in terms of the rise and fall of ideas implanted in the minds of men." —Herbert Hoover

"The secret of imagining is the greatest of all problems to the solution of which the mystic aspires. Supreme power, supreme wisdom, supreme delight He in the far-off solution of this mystery." —Douglas Fawcett

To refuse to recognize the creative power of man's invisible, imaginal activity, is too great to be argued with. Man, through his imaginal activity, literally "calls into existence the things that do not exist." By man's imaginal activity, all things are made, and without such activity, "was not anything made that was made."

Such causal activity could be defined as, an imaginal assemblage of images, which occurring, some physical event invariably takes place. It is for us to assemble the images of happy outcome and then keep from interfering. The event must not be forced but allowed to happen.

If imagination is the only thing that acts, or is, in existing beings or men (as Blake believed) then we should never be certain that it was not some woman treading in the wine press who began that subtle change in men's minds.

This grandmother is daily treading the wine press for her little grand-daughter. She writes:

"This is one of those things that make my family and friends say, 'we just don't understand it.' Kim is two-and-a-half years old now. I took care of her for a month after she was born and did not see her again until a year ago, and then, only for two weeks. However, during this past year every day I have taken her on my lap—in my imagination—and cuddled her and talked to her.

"In these imaginal acts I go over all the wonderful things about Kim: 'God is growing through me; God is loving through me,' etc. At first, I would get the response of a very young child. When I started 'God is growing through me'—she would reply, 'Me.' Now—as I start she

[156] NEVILLE GODDARD

completes the whole sentence. Another thing that has happened is, as the months have passed, as I take her—in my imagination—on my lap she has grown constantly larger and heavier.

"Kim hasn't even seen a picture of me in this past year. At the most, I could only be a name to her. Now, some time each day, her family tells me, she starts talking about me—to no one in particular—just talking. Sometimes it goes on for an hour; or she goes to the phone and pretends to call. In her monologue are such bits as: 'My Dee Dee loves me. My Dee Dee always comes to see me every day.'

"Even though I know what I have been doing in my imagination, it has caused me, too, 'to wonder much.' "... U.K.

All imaginative men and women are forever casting forth enchantments, and all passive men and women, who have no powerful imaginative lives, are continually passing under the spell of their power.

There is no form in nature, which is not produced by, and sustained by some imaginal activity. Therefore, any change in the imaginal activity must result in a corresponding change in form. To imagine a substitute-image for unwanted or defective content is to create it. If only we persist in our ideal imaginal activity and do not let lesser satisfactions suffice, ours shall be the victory.

"When I read in 'Seedtime and Harvest' the story of the school teacher who, through her imagination, in daily revision, transformed a delinquent pupil into a lovely girl, I decided to 'do' something about a young boy in my husband's school.

"To tell all the problems involved would take pages, for my husband has never had such a difficult child nor such a trying parent situation. The lad was too young to be expelled, yet the teachers refused to have him in their classes. To make matters worse, the mother and grandmother literally 'camped' on the school grounds making trouble for everyone.

"I wanted to help the boy, but, I also, wanted to help my husband. So, nightly, I constructed two scenes in my imagination: one, I 'saw' a perfectly normal, happy child; two, I 'heard' my husband say, 'I can't believe it, dear, but do you know "R" is acting like a normal boy, now, and it is heaven not having those two women around.'

"After two months of persisting in my imaginal play, night after night, my husband came home and said, 'It's like heaven around school' — not exactly the same words but close enough for me. The grandmother had become involved in something that took her out of town and the mother had to accompany her.

"At the same time a new teacher had welcomed the challenge of 'R' and he was progressing wonderfully well into all I imagined for him." . . . G.B.

It is useless to hold standards that we do not apply. Unlike Portia, who said: "I can easier teach twenty what were good to be done, than be one of the twenty to follow mine own teaching."

G. B. followed her own teaching. It is fatally easy to make the acceptance of the imaginal faith a substitute for living by it.

". . . he has sent me to bind up the brokenhearted, to proclaim liberty to the captives, and the opening of the prison to those who are bound. . . ." —Isaiah 61:1

CHAPTER 11
THE POTTER

"Arise, and go down to the potter's house, and there I will let you hear my words. So, / went down to the potter's house, and there he was working at his wheel. And the vessel he was making of clay was spoiled in the potter's hand, and he reworked it into another vessel, as it seemed good to the potter to do." —Jeremiah 18:2-4

The word translated Potter means imagination. Out of material others would have thrown away as useless, an awakened imagination refashions it as it ought to be. "O Lord, thou art our father, we are the clay, and thou art our potter; we are all the work of thy hand." Isaiah 64:8

This conception of creation as a work of imagination, and the Lord our Father as our imagination, will take us further into the mystery of creation than any other guide.

The only reason people do not believe in this identity of God and human imagination is that they are unwilling to assume the responsibility for their frightful misuse of imagination. Divine Imagination has descended to the level of human imagination, that human imagination may ascend to Divine Imagination.

The 8th Psalm says that man was made a little lower than God—not a little lower than the angels—as the King James Version mistakenly translates it. Angels are the emotional dispositions of man and are therefore his servant—and not his superior—as the author of Hebrews tells us. (Heb. 1:14.)

Imagination is the Real Man and is one with God.

Imagination creates, conserves and transforms. Imagination is radically creative when all imaginative activity based on memory disappears.

Imagination is conservative when its imaginal activity is fed with images supplied mainly by memory. Imagination is transformative when it varies a theme already in being; when it mentally alters a fact of life; when it leaves the fact out of the remembered experience or puts something in its place if it upsets the harmony it desires.

Through the use of her imagination this talented young artist has made her dream a reality.

"Ever since I entered into the art field I have enjoyed doing sketches and paintings for children's rooms. However, I have been discouraged by advisers and friends who were far more experienced in the 'field' than I. They liked my work, admired my talent, but said I would not get recognition nor pay for this type of work.

"Somehow, I always felt I would — but how? Then last fall I heard your lectures and read your books and I decided to let my imagination create the reality I desired. This is what I did daily: I imagined I was in a gallery — there was a great deal of excitement about me — on the walls hung my 'art' — only mine (a one-woman show) — and I saw red stars on many of the pictures. This would indicate that they had been sold.

"This is what happened: Just before Christmas I did a mobile for a friend who showed it in turn to a friend of hers who owns an art-import shop in Pasadena. He expressed a desire to meet me — so I took a few samples of my work along. When he looked at the very first painting he said he would like to give me 'a one-woman show' in the spring.

"The night of the opening, April 17, an interior decorator came and liked and commissioned me to do a collage for a little boy's room, which will appear in the September issue of Good Housekeeping for the 1961 House of the Year.

"Later, during the showing another decorator came and admired my work so much, he asked if he might arrange for me to meet the 'right' interior decorators and the 'right' owners of galleries who would buy and display my work properly. Incidentally, the show was a financial success for the owner of the gallery, as well as for me.

"The interesting thing about this is that seemingly these three men came to me 'out of the blue.' Certainly, I made no effort during the time of my 'imagining' to contact anyone; but, now, I am getting recognition and have a market for my work. And, now, I know without a shadow of doubt that there is no 'no' when you seriously apply this principle that 'imagining creates reality.' "... G.L.

She tested the Potter and proved His creativity in performance. Only the indolent mind would fail to rise to this challenge. Paul states, "the spirit of God dwells in you," now, "Examine yourselves to see whether you are holding to your faith. Test yourselves. Do you not realize that Jesus Christ is in you? Unless indeed you fail to meet the test! I hope you will find out that we have not failed." 2.Cor: 13.5-6

If "all things were made through him, and without him was not anything made that was made," it should not be difficult for man to test himself to find out who this creator in himself is. The test will prove to man that his imagination is the One, "who gives life to the dead and calls into existence the things that do not exist." Rom:4.17

The Potter's presence in us is inferred from what He does there. We cannot see Him there as One not ourselves. The nature of the Potter— Jesus Christ—is to create and there is no creation without Him.

Every recorded story in this book is just such a test as Paul asked the Corinthians to make. God really and truly exists in man — in every human being. God wholly becomes us. He is not our virtue but our Real Selves — Our Imagination.

The following illustrations from the mineral world may help us to see how Supreme Imagining and Human Imagining could be one and the same power and yet be vastly different in their creativity. Diamond is the world's hardest mineral. Graphite, used in 'lead' pencils, is one of the softest. Yet both minerals are pure carbon. The vast difference in the properties of the two forms of carbon is believed to be caused by a different arrangement of the carbon atoms. But whether the difference is produced by a different arrangement of the carbon atoms or not — all agree that Diamond and Graphite are one substance, pure carbon.

The purpose of life is the creative realization of desire. Man, lacking desire, could not exist efficiently in a world of continuous problems requiring continuing solutions. A desire is an awareness of something we lack or need to make life more enjoyable. Desires always have some personal gain in view. The greater the anticipated gain, the more intense the desire. There is no really unselfish desire. Even when our desire is for another, we are still seeking to gratify desire. To attain our desire we should imagine scenes implying their fulfillment, and enact the scene in our imagination, if only momentarily, with a joy sufficiently felt within its limits to make it natural. It is like a child dressing up and playing "Queen." We must imagine we are what we would like to be. We must play it in imagination first—not as a spectator—as an actor.

This lady imaginatively played "Queen" by being where she wanted to be in her imagination. She was the true actor in this theatre.

"My desire was to attend a matinee performance of a famous pantomimist currently playing in one of the largest theatres of our city. Because of the intimate nature of this art, I wanted to sit in the orchestra; but I didn't have even the price of a balcony ticket. The night I determined to have this pleasure for myself, in my imagination, I fell asleep watching the wondrous performer. In my imaginal act I sat in an orchestracenter seat, heard the applause as the curtain rose and the artist came on stage, and I actually felt the intense excitement of this experience.

"The next day—the day of the matinee performance—my financial condition had not changed. I had exactly one dollar and thirty-seven cents in my purse. I knew I must use the dollar to buy gas for my car which would leave me with thirty-seven cents, but I also knew I had faithfully slept in the feeling of being at that performance, so I dressed myself for the theatre. While changing articles from one purse to another, I found a dollar bill and forty-five cents in change hidden in the pocket of my seldomused opera purse. I grinned to myself, realizing that gasoline money had been given to me; so would the balance of my theatre ticket be given to me. Gaily I finished dressing and left for the theatre.

"Standing before the ticket window, my confidence dwindled as I gazed at the prices and saw three-seventy-five for orchestra seats. With a feeling of dismay I turned away quickly and walked across the street to a cafe for a cup of tea. I had spent sixteen cents on my tea before I remembered seeing the price of balcony seats on the ticket window list. Hurriedly, I counted my change and found I had one dollar and sixty-six cents left. Running back to the theatre, I bought the cheapest seat available which cost a dollar and fifty-five cents. With one dime left in my purse, I went through the entrance and the usher tore my ticket in half saying, "Upstairs, left, please." The performance was about to begin, but ignoring the usher's instructions, I walked into the main floor lady's restroom.

Still determined to sit in the orchestra section, I sat down, closed my eyes and kept my inward 'sight' riveted on the stage from the direction of the orchestra. At that moment, a group of women walked into the restroom, all talking at once, but I heard only one conversation as a woman speaking to her companion, said, 'But I waited and waited until the last moment. Then she called and said she couldn't make it. I would have given her ticket away but it's too late now. Not realizing it, I handed the usher both tickets and he tore them in half before I could stop him.' I almost laughed aloud. Getting up, I walked over to this lady and asked if I might use the extra ticket she had, instead of the balcony seat I had bought. She was charming and kindly invited me to join her party. The ticket she handed me was for the orchestra section, center seat, six rows from the stage. I sat in that seat only moments before the curtain rose on a performance I had witnessed the night before from that seat — in my Imagination.". . . J.R.

We must actually BE, in Imagination. It is one thing to think of the end, and another thing to think from the end. To think from the end; to enact the end, is to create reality. The inner actions must correspond to the actions we would physically perform "after these things should be."

To live wisely we must be aware of our imaginal activity, and see to it that it is faithfully shaping the end we desire. The world is clay; our Imagination is the Potter. We should always imagine ends that are of value or promise well.

"He who desires but acts not breeds pestilence."

What's done flows from what's imagined. Outward forms reveal the imaginings of Man.

"Man is the shuttle, to whose winding quest and passage through these looms God ordered motion, but ordained no rest."

"I run a small business, solely owned, and a few years ago it seemed that my venture would end in failure. For some months, sales had fallen steadily and I found myself in a financial 'jam'—along with thousands of other small businessmen, as this period spanned one of our country's minor recessions. I was badly in debt and needed at least three thousand dollars almost immediately. My auditors advised me to close my doors and try to salvage what I could. Instead, I turned to my Imagination. I knew your teaching but had never actually attempted to solve any problem in this manner. I was frankly skeptical of the entire idea that imagination can create reality but I was also desperate; and desperation forced me to test your teaching.

"I imagined my office receiving four thousand dollars unexpectedly in remittances due. This money would have to come from new orders as my accounts receivable were practically nonexistent, but this seemed far-fetched as I hadn't received this much in sales during the last four months or more. Nevertheless, I kept my imaginal picture of receiving this amount of money steadily before me for three days. Early the fourth morning a customer I had not heard from in months called me on the telephone asking me to come and see him personally. I was to bring a quotation previously given him for machinery needed by his factory. The quotation was months old, but I dug it out of my files and lost no time in arriving at his office that day. I wrote out the order which he signed, but I saw no immediate help for me in the transaction as the equipment he wanted would take from four to six months for factory delivery, and of course, my customer did not have to pay for it until delivered.

"I thanked him for the order and rose to leave. He stopped me at the door and handed me a check for a little over four thousand dollars, saying, 'I want to pay for the merchandise now, in advance — for tax puiposes, you know. You don't mind?' No, I didn't mind. I realized what had happened the moment I took that check into my hands.

Within three days my imaginal act had done for me what I hadn't been able to do in months of desperate financial shuffling. I know, now, that imagination could have brought forty thousand dollars into my business just as easily as four thousands." . . . L.N.C.

"O Lord, thou art our Father; we are the clay, and thou art our potter; we are all the work of thy hand."

CHAPTER 12
ATTITUDES

"Mental Things are alone Real; what is call'd Corporeal, Nobody Knows of its Dwelling Place: it is in Fallacy, and its Existence an Imposture. Where is the Existence Out of Mind or Thought? Where is it but in the Mind of a Fool?" — Blake

Memory, though faulty, is adequate to the call for sameness. If we remember another as we have known him, we recreate him in that image, and the past will be recognized in the present. Imagining creates reality. If there is room for improvement, we should reconstruct him with new content; visualize him as we would like him to be, rather than have him bear the burden of our memory of him. "Everything possible to be believed is an image of truth."

The following story is by one who believes that imagining creates reality and acting on this belief changed his attitude toward a stranger and bore witness to this change in reality.

"More than twenty years ago, when I was a 'green' farm boy newly arrived in Boston to attend school, a 'panhandler' asked me for money for a meal. Although the money I had was pitifully insufficient for my own needs, I gave him what was in my pocket. A few hours later the same man, by this time staggering drunk, stopped me again and asked for money. I was so outraged to think the money I could so ill afford had been put to such use, I made myself a solemn pledge that I would never again listen to the plea of a street beggar. Through the years I kept my pledge, but every time I refused anyone, my conscience needled me. I felt guilty even to the point of developing a sharp pain in my stomach, but I couldn't bring myself to unbend.

"The early part of this year, a man stopped me as I was walking my dog and asked for money so he could eat. True to the old pledge, I refused him. His manner was gracious as he accepted my refusal. He even admired my dog and spoke of a family in New York state he knew that raised cocker spaniels. This time my conscience was really pricking me! As he went on his way, I determined to remake that scene as I wished it had been, so I stopped right there on the street, closed my eyes for only a few moments and enacted the scene differently. In my imagination I had the same man approach me, only this time he opened the conversation by admiring my dog. After we had talked a moment, I had him say, 'I don't like to ask you this, but I really need something to eat. I have a job that begins tomorrow morning, but I've been out of work and tonight I'm hungry.' I then reached into my imaginary pocket, pulled out an imaginary five-dollar bill and gladly gave it to him. This imaginal act immediately dissolved the guilty feeling and the pain.

"I know from your teaching that an imaginal act is fact, so I knew I could grant anyone what he asked and by faith in the imaginal act, consent to the reality of his having it.

"Four months later as I was again walking my dog, the same man approached me and opened the conversation by admiring my dog. 'Here's a beautiful dog,' he said. 'Young man, I don't suppose you remember me, but awhile back I asked you for some money and you very kindly said "no." I say "kindly," because if you had given it to me I would still be asking for money. Instead, I got a job that very next morning, and now I'm on my feet and have some self-respect again.'

"I knew his job was a fact when I imagined it that night some four months before, but I won't deny there was immense satisfaction in having him appear in the flesh to confirm it!" . . . F.B.

"I have no silver and gold, but I give you what I have." . . . Acts 3:6

None is to be discarded, all must be saved, and our Imagination reshaping memory is the process whereby this salvation is brought to pass. To condemn the man for having lost his way is to punish the already punished. "O whom should I pity if I pity not the sinner who is gone astray?" Not what the man was but what he may become should be our imaginal activity.

"Don't you remember sweet Alice, Ben Bolt—

Sweet Alice whose hair was so brown,

Who wept with delight when you gave her a smile,

And trembled with fear at your frown?"

If we imagine no worse of him than he of himself, he would pass as excellent. It's not the man at his best, but the imaginist exercising the spirit of forgiveness that performs the miracle. Imagining with new content transformed both the man who asked and the man who gave. Imagining has not yet had its due in the systems either of moralists or educators. When it does, there will be "the opening of the prison to those who are bound."

Nothing has existence for us save through the memory we have of it, therefore we should remember it not as it was—unless of course, it was altogether desirable—but as we desire it to be. Inasmuch

[166] NEVILLE GODDARD

as imagining is creative, our memory of another either furthers or hinders him, and makes his upward or downward way easier and swifter.

"There is no coal of character so dead that it will not glow and flame if but slightly turned."

The following story shows that imagining can make rings, and husbands, and move people "to China!

"My husband, child of a broken home and raised by beloved grandparents, was never 'close' to his mother — nor she to him. A woman of sixty-three and a divorcee for thirty-two of those years, she was lonely and embittered; and my relationship with her was strained as I attempted to 'stay in the middle.' By her own admission her great desire was to remarry for companionship, but she believed this to be impossible at her age. My husband would often state to me that he hoped she would remarry and, as he fervently put it, 'perhaps live way out of town!'

"I had the same wish and, as I put it, 'perhaps move to China?' Being wary of my personal motive for this wish, I knew I must change my feeling toward her in my imaginal drama and at the same time 'give' her what she wanted. I began by seeing her in my imagination as a completely changed personality — a happy, joyous woman, secure and contented in a new relationship. Every time I thought of her, I would see her mentally as a 'new' woman.

"About three weeks later, she came to our house for a visit bringing a friend she had met many months previously. The man had recently become a widower; he was her age, secure financially and had grown children and grandchildren. We liked him and I was excited because it was obvious they liked each other. But my husband still thought 'it' was impossible. I didn't.

"From that day on, every time her image rose in my mind, I 'saw' her extending her left hand toward me; and I admired the 'ring' on her finger. One month later, she and her friend came to visit us and as I walked forward to greet them, she proudly extended her left hand. The ring was on her finger.

"Two weeks later she was married — and we haven't seen her since. She lives in a brand-new home . . . 'way out of town' and as her new husband dislikes the long drive to our house, she might as well have 'moved to China'!" . . . J.B.

There is a wide difference between the will to resist an activity and the decision to change it. He who changes an activity acts; whereas he who resists an activity, reacts. One creates; the other perpetuates.

Nothing is real beyond the imaginative patterns we make of it. Memory, no less than desire, resembles a day-dream. Why make it a day-mare? Man can forgive only if he treats memory as a day-dream, and shapes it to his heart's desire.

R.K. learned that we may rob others of their abilities by our attitudes toward them. He changed his attitude and thereby changed a fact.

"I am not a money lender nor am I in the investment business as such, but a friend and business acquaintance came to me for a substantial loan in order to expand his plant. Because of personal friendship, I granted the loan with reasonable interest rates and gave my friend the right of renewal at the end of one year. When the first year term expired, he was behind in his interest payments and requested a thirty-day extension on the note. I granted this request, but at the end of thirty days he was still unable to meet the note and asked for an additional extension.

"As I previously stated, I am not in the business of lending money. Within twenty days I needed full payment of the loan to meet debts of my own. But I consented again to extend the note although my own credit was now in serious jeopardy. The natural thing to do was to apply legal pressure to collect and a few years ago I would have done just that. Instead, I remembered your warning 'not to rob others of their ability,' and I realized that I had been robbing my friend of his ability to pay what he owed.

"For three nights I constructed a scene in my imagination in which I heard my friend tell me that unexpected orders had flooded his desk so rapidly, he was now able to pay the loan in full. The fourth day I received a telephone call from him. He told me that by what he called 'a miracle' he had received so many orders, and big ones, too, he was now able to pay back my loan including all interest due and, in fact, had just mailed a check to me for the entire amount." . . . R.K.

There is nothing more fundamental to the secret of imagining than the distinction between imagining and the state imagined.

"Mental Things are alone Real..." "Every thing possible to be believ'd is an image of truth."

CHAPTER 13
ALL TRIVIA

"General knowledge is remote knowledge; It is in particulars that wisdom consists And happiness too." — Blake

We must use our imagination to achieve particular ends, even if the ends are all trivia. Because men do not clearly define and imagine particular ends the results are uncertain, while they might be perfectly certain. To imagine particular ends is to discriminate clearly. "How do we distinguish the oak from the beech, the horse from the ox, but by the bounding outline?" Definition asserts the reality of the particular thing against the formless generalizations which flood the mind.

Life on earth is a kindergarten for image making. The bigness or littleness of the object to be created is not in itself important. "The great and golden rule of art, as well as of life," said Blake, "is this: That the more distinct, sharp and wirey the bounding line, the more perfect the work of art, and the less keen and sharp, the greater is the evidence of weak imitation. What is it that builds a house and plants a garden but the definite and determinate? . . . leave out this line, and you leave out life itself."

The following stories are concerned with the acquiring of seemingly little things, or 'toys' as I call them, but they are important because of the clear imaginal images that created the toys. The author of the first story is one of whom it is said, 'she has everything.' This is true. She has financial, social and intellectual security.

She writes:

"As you know, through your teaching and through my practice of that teaching, I have completely changed myself and my life. Two weeks ago when you spoke of 'toys' I realized I had never used my imagination for the getting of 'things' and I decided it would be fun to try it. You told of a young woman who was given a hat by merely wearing that hat in her imagination. The last thing on earth I needed was a hat, but I wanted to test my imagination for this 'getting of things,' so I selected a hat pictured in a fashion magazine. I cut the picture out and stuck it on the mirror of my dressing table. I studied the picture carefully. Then, I shut my eyes, and in my imagination, I put that hat on my head and 'wore' it as I walked out of the house. I did this just once.

[169] THE POWER OF IMAGINATION: THE NEVILLE GODDARD TREASURY

"The following week I met some friends for luncheon and one of them was wearing 'the' hat. We all admired it. The very next day, I received a parcel by special delivery messenger. 'The' hat was in the parcel. The friend who had worn it the day before had sent the hat to me with a note saying she did not particularly care for the hat and didn't know why she had bought it in the first place, but for some reason she thought it would look well on me — and would I please accept it!" . . . G.L.

Movement from 'dreams to things' is the power driving humanity.

"We must live wholly on the level of Imagination. And it must be consciously and deliberately undertaken."

"All my life I have loved birds. I enjoy watching them—hearing their chatter— feeding them; and I am particularly fond of the small sparrow. For many months I have fed them crumbs of morning bread, wild bird seed and anything I believed they would eat.

"And for all those months I have been frustrated as I watched the larger birds— particularly the pigeons—command the area, gobbling up most of the good seed and leaving the husks for my sparrows.

"To use my imagination on this problem seemed facetious to me at first, but the more I thought of it, the more interesting the idea became. So, one night I set about 'seeing' the little birds come in for their full share of daily offerings, and I would 'tell' my wife that the pigeons no longer interfered with my sparrows but took their share like gentlemen and then left the area. I continued this imaginary action for almost one month. Then one morning I noticed that the pigeons had disappeared. The sparrows had breakfast all to themselves for a few days; for those few days no larger bird entered the area. They did return eventually, but to this day they have never again infringed on the area occupied by my sparrows. They stay together, eating what I put out for them, leaving a full share of the area to my tiny friends. And do you know . . . I actually believe the sparrows understand; they no longer seem to be afraid when I walk among them." . . . R.K.

This lady proves that unless our heart is in the task, unless we imagine ourselves right into the feeling of our wish fulfilled, we are not there — for we are all imagination, and must be where, and what we are in imagination.

"In early February my husband and I had been in our new house one month — a home lovely beyond telling, perched on a rugged cliff with the ocean for our front yard, wind and sky for neighbors and seagulls for guests — we were ecstatic. If you have experienced the joy and woe of building your own home, you know how completely filled with happiness you are and how completely empty your purse is: A hundred lovely things clamored to be bought for that house, but the one thing we wanted most of all was the most useless — a picture. Not just any picture but a wild wonderful scene of the sea dominated by a great white clipper ship. This picture had been in our thoughts all the months of building and we left one living room wall free of paneling to hold it. My husband mounted decorative red and green ship lanterns on the wall to frame our picture, but the picture— itself —would have to wait. Draperies, carpeting — all the practical items must come first. Perhaps so, but that didn't stop either one of us from 'seeing' that picture, in our imagination, on that wall.

"One day while shopping, I strolled into a small art gallery and as I walked through the door I stopped so suddenly a gentleman walking behind me crashed into an easel. I apologized and pointed to a painting hanging at head-height across the room.

"'That's what did it! I've never seen anything so wonderful!' He introduced himself as the owner of the gallery and said, 'Yes, an original by the greatest English painter of clipper ships the world has known.' He went on to tell me about the artist, but I wasn't listening. I could not take my eyes from that wonderful ship; and suddenly I experienced a very strange thing. It was only a moment in time, but the art gallery faded and I 'saw' that picture on my wall. I'm afraid the owner thought me a little giddy, and I was, but I finally managed to return my attention to his voice when he mentioned an astronomical price. I smiled and said, 'Perhaps some day. . .' He continued to tell me about the painter and also about an American artist who was the only living lithographer capable of copying the great English master. He said, 'If you're very lucky, you may pick up one of his prints. I've seen his work. It's perfect down to the last detail. Many people prefer prints to paintings.'

" 'Prints' or 'paintings,' I knew nothing about the values of either, and anyway, all I wanted was that scene. When my husband returned home that evening, I talked of nothing but that painting and pleaded with him to visit the gallery and see it. 'Maybe we could find a print of it somewhere. The man said . . .' 'Yes,' he interrupted, 'but you know we can't afford any picture now . . .' Our conversation ended there, but that night after dinner, I stood in our living room and 'saw' that picture on our wall.

"The next day my husband had an appointment with a client which he did not want to keep. But the appointment was kept, and my husband did not return home until after dark, When he walked through the front door, I was busy in another part of the house and called a greeting to him. A few minutes later I heard hammering and walked into the living room to see what he was doing. On our wall hung my picture. In my first moment of intense joy I remembered the man in the art gallery, saying ... 'If you're very lucky, you may pick up one of his prints. . .' Lucky? Well, here is my husband's part of this story:

"Making the call already mentioned, he entered one of the poorest, meanest little houses he had ever been in. The client introduced himself and led my husband into a tiny dark dining area where the two of them sat down at a bare table. As my husband put his brief case on the table top, he looked up and saw the picture on a wall. He confessed to me he had conducted a very sloppy interview because he couldn't take his eyes from that picture. The client signed the contract and gave a check as down payment which, as my husband believed at the time, was ten dollars short. Mentioning this fact to the client, he said the check given was every cent he could afford but added . . . "I've noticed your interest in that picture. It was here when I took this place. I don't know to whom it belonged, but I don't want it. If you'll put the ten dollars in for me, I'll give you the picture.'

"When my husband returned to his company's main office, he learned he had been in error about the amount. He was not charged ten dollars. Our picture is on our wall. And it costs us nothing." . . . A.A.

Of R. L. who writes the following letter it must be said:

"In faith. Lady, you have a merry heart."

"One day, during a bus strike, I needed to go into the downtown area and had to walk ten blocks from my home to the nearest bus in operation. Before starting home I recalled there was no food market on this new route and I wouldn't be able to shop for dinner. I had enough to manage a 'pot luck' meal but I would need bread. After shopping all day, the ten blocks back from the bus line was all I could manage and to go still farther to shop for bread was out of the question.

"I stood very still for a moment and allowed a vision of bread to 'dance in my head.' Then I started for home. When I boarded the bus I was so tired I grabbed the first available seat and almost sat on a paper bag. Now, on a crowded bus tired passengers rarely look directly at one another, so being naturally curious, I peeked into the bag. Of course it was a loaf of bread — not just any bread but the very same brand of bread I always buy!" . . . R.L.

Trifles: all trifles — but they produced their trivia without price. Imagining accomplished these things without the means generally reputed necessary to do so. Man rates wealth in a way that bears no relation to real values.

[172] NEVILLE GODDARD

"Come, buy wine and milk without money and without price." — Isaiah. 55:1

CHAPTER 14
THE CREATIVE MOMENT

"The natural man does not receive the gifts of the Spirit of God, for they are folly to him, and he is not able to understand them because they are spiritually discerned." . . . I Cor. 2:14.

"There is a Moment in each Day that Satan cannot find, Nor can his Watch Fiends find it; but the Industrious find This Moment & it multiply, & when it once is found It renovates every Moment of the Day if rightly placed." — Blake

Whenever we imagine things as they ought to be, rather than as they seem to be, is "The Moment." For in that moment the spiritual man's work is done and all the great events of time start forth to mould a world in harmony with that moment's altered pattern.

Satan, Blake writes, is a "Reactor." He never acts; he only reacts. And if our attitude to the happenings of the day is "reactionary" are we not playing Satan's part? Man is only reacting in his natural or Satan state; he never acts or creates, he only re-acts or re-creates. One real creative moment, one real feeling of the wish fulfilled, is worth more than the whole natural life of re-action. In such a moment God's work is done. Once more we may say with Blake,

"God only Acts and Is, in existing beings or Men."

There is an imaginal past and an imaginal future. If, by reacting, the past is re-created into the present—so—by acting out our dreams of fancy can the future be brought into the present.

"I feel now the future in the instant."

The spiritual man Acts: for him, anything that he wants to do, he can do and do at once — in his imagination — and his motto is always, "The Moment is Now."

"Behold, now is the acceptable time; behold, now is the day of salvation." —2 Cor. 6:2

Nothing stands between man and the fulfillment of his dream but facts: And facts are the creations of imagining. If man changes his imagining, he will change the facts.

This story tells of a young woman who found the Moment and, by acting out her dream of fancy, brought the future into the instant, not realizing what she had done until the final scene.

"The incident related below must appear to be coincidence to those never exposed to your teaching — but I know I observed an imaginative act take solid form in, perhaps, four minutes. I believe you will be interested in reading this account, written down, exactly as it happened, a few minutes after the actual occurrence, yesterday morning.

"I was driving my car east on Sunset Boulevard, in the center lane of traffic, braking slowly to stop for a red signal at a three-way intersection, when my attention was caught by the sight of an elderly lady, dressed all in grey, running across the street in front of my car. Her arm was raised, signaling to the driver of a bus which was beginning to pull away from the curb. She was obviously attempting to cross in front of the bus to delay it. The driver slowed his vehicle and I thought would allow her to enter. Instead, as she jumped on to the curb, the bus pulled away leaving her standing just in the act of lowering her arm. She turned and walked swiftly toward a nearby phone booth.

"As my signal changed to green and I put my car in motion, I wished I had been behind the bus and had been able to offer her a ride. Her extreme agitation was obvious even from the distance I was away from her. My wish instantly fulfilled itself in a mental drama, and as I drove away, the fancy played itself out in the following scene . . .

". . . I opened the car door and a lady dressed in grey stepped in, smilingly relieved and thanking me profusely. She was out of breath from running and said, 'I only have a few blocks to go. I'm meeting friends and I was so afraid they would leave without me when I missed my bus.' I left my imaginary lady out a few blocks farther on and she was delighted to observe her friends still waiting for her. She thanked me again and walked away ...'"

"The entire mental scene was spanned in the time it takes to drive one block at a normal rate of speed. The fancy satisfied my feelings regarding the 'real' incident, and I immediately forgot it. Four blocks farther, I was still in the center lane and again had to stop for a red signal. My attention at this time was turned inward on something I have now forgotten, when suddenly someone tapped on the closed window of my car and I looked up to see a lovely-appearing elderly lady with grey hair, dressed all in grey. Smiling, she asked if she might ride a few blocks with me as she had missed her bus. She was out of breath, as though from running, and I was so stunned by her sudden appearance in the middle of a busy street at my window that for a moment I could only react physically, and without answering, leaned over and opened my car door. She got in and said, 'It's so annoying to rush so and then miss a bus. I wouldn't have imposed on you like this, but I'm supposed to meet some friends a few blocks down the street and if I had to walk now, I would miss them.' Six blocks farther on, she exclaimed, 'Oh, good! They're still waiting for me.' I let her out and she thanked me again and walked away.

"I'm afraid I drove to my own destination by automatic reflex, for I had fully recognized that I had just observed a waking dream take form in physical action. I recognized what was happening while it was happening. As soon as I could, I wrote down each part of the incident and found a startling consistency between the 'waking dream' and the subsequent 'reality.' Both women were elderly, gracious in manner, dressed all in grey, and out of breath from hurrying to catch a bus and missing it. Both wished to meet friends (who for some reason could not wait for them much longer) and both left my car within the space of a few blocks after successfully completing their contact with their friends.

"I am amazed, confounded and elated! If there is no such thing as coincidence or accident — then I witnessed imagination become 'reality' almost instantaneously." . . . J.R.B.

"There is a Moment in each Day that Satan cannot find. Nor can his Watch Fiends find it; but the Industrious find This Moment & it multiply, & when it once is found It renovates every Moment of the Day if rightly placed."

"From the first time I read your 'Search' I have longed to experience a vision. Since you have told us of the 'Promise' this desire has been intensified. I want to tell you of my vision which was a glorious answer to my prayer; but I am sure I would not have had this experience were it not for something that occurred two weeks ago.

"It was necessary for me to park my car some distance from the University Building where I was scheduled to conduct my class. As I left my car I was conscious of the stillness about me. The street was completely deserted; no one was in sight.

"Suddenly I heard a most frightful cursing voice. I looked toward the sound and saw a man brandishing a cane, yelling, between vile words, 'I'll kill you. I'll kill you.' I continued on as he approached me, for at that moment I thought 'Now I can test what I have professed to believe; if I do believe we are one, The Father, this derelict and I, no harm can come to me. At that moment I had no fear. Instead of seeing a man coming toward me, I felt a light. He stopped yelling, dropped his cane and walked quietly as we passed with less than a foot between us.

"Having tested my faith at that moment, everything about me had seemed more alive than before — flowers brighter and trees greener. I have had a sense of peace and the 'oneness' of life I had not known before.

"Last Friday I drove to our country home — nothing was unusual about the day or evening. I worked on a manuscript and not being tired did not try to fall off to sleep until around two the following morning. Then I turned off the light and drifted into that floating sensation, not asleep but drowsy, as I call it, half awake and half asleep.

Often, while in this state — lovely, unknown faces float before me — but this morning the experience was different. A perfect face of a child came before me in profile — then it turned and smiled at me. It was glowing with light and seemed to fill my own head with light.

"I was aglow and excited and thought 'this must be the Christos'; but something within me, without sound, said, 'No, this is you.' I feel I will never be the same again and some day I may experience the 'Promise.' "... G.B.

Our dreams will all be realized from the time that we know that Imagining Creates Reality — and Act. But Imagination seeks from us something much deeper and more fundamental than creating things: nothing less indeed than the recognition of its own oneness, with God; that what it does is, in reality, God Himself doing it in and through Man who is All Imagination.

CHAPTER 15
"THE PROMISE"

Four Mystical Experiences

In all I have related thus far — with the exception of G.B.'s Vision of the child — imagination was consciously exercised. Men and women created stage plays in their imagination, plays implying the fulfillment of their desires. Then, by imagining themselves participating in these dramas they created that which their imaginal acts implied. This is the wise use of God's law. But "No man is justified before God by the law." Gal. 3.11.

Many people are interested in Imaginism as a way of life, but are not at all interested in its framework of faith, a faith leading to the fulfillment of God's promise. "I will raise up your son after you, who shall come forth from your body ... I will be his father, and he shall be my son." 2 Sam. 7:12-14.

The promise that God will bring forth from our body a son who will be "born, not of blood nor of the will of the flesh nor of the will of man, but of God" does not concern them. They want to know God's law, not His promise. However, this miraculous birth has been stated clearly as a must for all mankind from the earliest days of the Christian fellowship. "You must be bom from above," John. 3.7. My purpose here is to state it again and to state it in such language and with such reference to my own personal mystical experiences that the reader will see that this birth "from above" is far more than a part of a dispensable superstructure, that it is the sole puipose for God's creation.

Specifically, my purpose in recording these four mystical experiences is to show what "Jesus Christ the faithful witness, the firstborn from the dead" (Rev. 1.5) was trying to say about this birth from above. "How can men preach unless they are sent?" Rom. 10.15.

Many years ago, I was taken in spirit into a Divine Society, a Society of men in whom God is awake. Though it may seem strange, the gods do truly meet. As I entered this society, the first to greet me was the embodiment of infinite Might. His was a power unknown to mortals. I was then taken to meet infinite Love. He asked me, "What is the greatest thing in the world?" I answered him in the words of Paul, "faith, hope, and love, these three; but the greatest of these is love." At that moment, he embraced me and our bodies fused and became one body. I was knit to him and loved him as my own soul.

[178] NEVILLE GODDARD

The words, "love of God" so often a mere phrase, were now a reality with a tremendous meaning. Nothing ever imagined by man could be compared with this love which man feels through his union with Love. The most intimate relationship on earth is like living in separate cells compared with this union.

While I was in this state of supreme delight, a voice from outer space shouted, "Down with the blue bloods!" At this blast, I found myself standing before the one who had first greeted me, he who embodied infinite Might. He looked into my eyes and without the use of words or mouth, I heard what he told me: "Time to act." I was suddenly whisked out of that Divine Society and returned to earth. I was tormented by my limitations of understanding but I knew that on that day the Divine Society had chosen me as a companion and sent me to preach Christ — God's promise to man.

My mystical experiences have brought me to accept literally, the saying that all the world's a stage. And to believe that God plays all the parts. The puipose of the play? To transform man, the created, into God, the creator. God loved man, his created, and became man in faith that this act of self-commission would transform man — the created, into God — the creator.

The play begins with the crucifixion of God on man — as man — and ends with the resurrection of man — as God. God becomes as we are, that we may be as He is. God becomes man that man may become, first — a living being, and secondly — a lifegiving spirit.

"I have been crucified with Christ; it is no longer I who live, but Christ who lives in me; and the life I now live in the flesh I live by faith in the Son of God, who loved me and gave himself for me." — Gal.2:20

God took upon Himself the form of man and became obedient unto death — even death on the cross of man — and is crucified on Golgotha, the skull of man. God himself enters death's door — the human skull — and lies down in the grave of man to make man a living being. God's mercy turned death into sleep. Then began the prodigious and unthinkable metamoiphosis of man, the transformation of man into God.

No man, unaided by the crucifixion of God, could cross the threshold that admits to conscious life, but now we have union with God in His crucified self. He lives in us as our wonderful human imagination. "Man is all imagination, and God is man, and exists in us and we in him. The eternal body of man is the imagination — that is, God, himself." When He rises in us we will be like Him and He will be like us. Then all impossibilities will dissolve in us at that touch of exaltation which His rising in us will impart to our nature.

Here is the secret of the world: God died to give man life and to set man free, for however clearly God is aware of His creation, it does not follow that man, imaginatively created, is aware of God. To work this miracle God had to die, then rise again as man, and none has ever expressed it so clearly as William Blake. Blake says — or rather has Jesus say — "Unless I die, thou canst not live; but if I die I shall arise again and thou with me. Wouldest thou love one who never died for thee, or ever die for one who had not died for thee? And if God dieth not for man and giveth not himself eternally for man, man could not exist."

So God dies — that is to say — God has freely given himself for man. Deliberately, He has become man and has forgotten that He is God, in the hope that man, thus created, will eventually rise as God. God has so completely offered His own self for man, that He cries out on the cross of man, "My God, my God; why hast thou forsaken me?" He has completely forgotten that He is God. But after God rises in one man, that man will say to his brothers, "Why stand we here, trembling around, calling on God for help, and not ourselves, in whom God dwells?"

This first man that has been raised from the dead is known as Jesus Christ — the first fruits of those who have fallen asleep, the first-born of the dead. For man God died; now, by a man, has come also the resurrection of the dead. Jesus Christ resurrects his dead Father by becoming his father. In Adam — the universal man — God sleeps. In Jesus Christ—the individualized God —God wakes. In waking, man the created, has become God, the creator, and can truly say, "Before the world was, I am." Just as God in His love for man so completely identified Himself with man that He forgot that He was God, so man in his love for God must so completely identify himself with God that he lives the life of God, that is, Imaginatively.

God's play which transforms man into God is revealed to us in the Bible. It is completely consistent in imagery and symbolism. The New Testament is hid in the Old Testament, and the old is manifested in the new. The Bible is a vision of God's Law and His Promise. It was never intended to teach history but rather to lead man in faith through the furnaces of affliction to the fulfillment of God's promise, to rouse man from this profound sleep and awaken him as God. Its characters live not in the past but in an imaginative eternity. They are personifications of the eternal spiritual states of the soul. They mark man's journey through eternal death and his awakening to eternal life.

The Old Testament tells us of God's promise. The New Testament tells us not how this promise was fulfilled but how it is fulfilled. The central theme of the Bible is the direct, individual, mystical experience of the birth of the child, that child of whom the prophet spoke "... to us a child is born, to us a son is given; and the government will be upon his shoulder; and his name will be called, Wonderful Counselor, Mighty God, Everlasting Father, Prince of Peace. Of the increase of his government and of peace, there will be no end ..." Isaiah 9:6-7

When the child is revealed to us we see it, we experience it, and the response to this revelation can be stated in the words of Job, "I have heard of thee by the hearing of the ear, but now my eye sees thee." The story of the incarnation is not fable, allegory or some carefully contrived fiction to enslave the minds of men, but mystical fact. It is a personal mystical experience of the birth of oneself out of one's own skull, symbolized in the birth of a child, wrapped in swaddling clothes and lying on the floor.

There is a distinction between hearing of this birth of a child from one's own skull — a birth which no scientist or historian could ever possibly explain — and actually experiencing the birth — holding in your own hands and seeing with your own eyes this miraculous child — a child born from above out of your own skull, a birth contrary to all the laws of nature. The question as it is posed in the Old Testament, "Ask now, and see, can a male bear a child? Why then do I see every man with his hands delivering himself like a woman in labor? Why has every face turned pale?" Jer: 30.6. The Hebrew word "chalats" mistranslated "loins" means: to draw out, to deliver, to withdraw self. The drawing of oneself out of one's own skull was exactly what the prophet foresaw as the necessary birth from above, a birth giving man entrance into the kingdom of God and reflective perception on the highest levels of Being. Throughout the ages "Deep calls to deep . . . Rouse thyself! Why sleepest thou, O Lord? Awake!"

The event, as it is recorded in the Gospels, actually takes place in man. But of that day or that hour when the time will come for the individual to be delivered, no one knows but the Father. "Do not marvel that I said to you, You must be born from above. The wind blows where it wills, and you hear the sound of it, but you do not know whence it comes or whither it goes; so it is with every one who is born of the Spirit." John: 3:7-8

This revelation in the Gospel of John is true. Here is my experience of this birth from above. Like Paul, I did not receive it from man — nor was I taught it. It came through the actual mystical experience of being born from above. None can speak truly of this mystical birth from above but one who has experienced it. I had no idea that this birth from above was literally true. Who, before the experience, could believe that the child, the Wonderful Counselor, the Mighty God, the Everlasting Father, the Prince of Peace was inwoven in his own skull? Who, before the experience, would understand that his Maker is his Husband and the Lord of Hosts is His Name? Who would believe that the creator went in unto His own creation, man, and knew it to be Himself and that this entrance into the skull of man — this union of God and man — resulted in the birth of a Son out of the skull of man; which birth gave to that man eternal life and union with his creator forever?

If I now tell what I experienced that night I do so not to impose my ideas on others but that I may give hope to those who, like Nicodemus, wonder how can a man be born when he is old? How can he enter a second time into his mother's womb and be born? How can this be? This is how it happened to me. Therefore, I will now "write the vision"; and "make it plain upon tablets, so he may run who reads it. For still the vision awaits its time; it hastens to the end — it will not lie. If it seem slow, wait for it; it will surely come, it will not delay. Behold, he whose soul is not upright in him shall fail, but the righteous shall live by his faith." Hab. 2:2-4.

In the early hours of the morning on July 20, 1959, in the city of San Francisco, a heavenly dream in which the arts flourished was suddenly interrupted by the most intense vibration centered at the base of my skull. Then a drama, as real as those I experience when I am fully awake, began to unfold. I awoke from a dream to find myself completely entombed within my skull. I tried to force my way out through its base. Something gave way and I felt myself move head downward, through the base of my skull. I squeezed myself out, inch by inch. When I was almost out, I held what I took to be the foot of the bed and pulled the remaining portion of me out of my skull. There, on the floor, I lay for a few seconds.

Then I rose and looked at my body on the bed. It was pale of face lying on its back and tossing from side to side like one in recovery from a great ordeal. As I contemplated it, hoping that it would not fall off the bed, I became aware that the vibration which started the whole drama was not only in my head but now was also coming from the corner of the room. As I looked over to that corner I wondered if that vibration could be caused by a very high wind, a wind strong enough to vibrate the window. I did not realize that the vibration which I still felt within my head was related to that which seemed to be coming from the corner of the room.

Looking back to the bed, I discovered that my body was gone but in its place sat my three older brothers. My oldest brother sat where the head was. My second and third brothers sat where the feet were. None seemed to be aware of me, although I was aware of them and could discern their thoughts. I suddenly became aware of the reality of my own invisibility. I noticed that they, too, were disturbed by the vibration coming from the corner of the room. My third brother was the most disturbed and went over to investigate the cause of the disturbance. His attention was attracted by something on the floor and looking down he announced, "It's Neville's baby." My other two brothers, in most incredulous voices, asked "How can Neville have a baby?"

My brother lifted the infant wrapped in swaddling clothes and laid him on the bed. I, then, with my invisible hands lifted the babe and asked him "How is my sweetheart?" He looked into my eyes and smiled and I awoke in this world — to ponder this greatest of my many mystical experiences.

Tennyson has a description of Death as a warrior — a skeleton "high on a night-black horse," issuing forth at midnight. But when Gareth's sword cut through the skull, there was in it. . .

". . . the bright face of a blooming boy Fresh as a flower new-born." (Idylls of the King)

Two other visions I will tell because they bear out the truth of my assertion that the Bible is mystical fact, that everything written about the promised child in the law of Moses and the Prophets and the Psalms must be mystically experienced in the imagination of the individual. The child's birth is a sign and a portent, signalling the resurrection of David, the Lord's anointed, of whom He said, "You are my son, today I have begotten you." —Psalms 2:7

Five months after the birth of the child, on the morning of December 6, 1959, in the city of Los Angeles, a vibration similar to the one which preceded his birth started in my head. This time its intensity was centered at the top of my head. Then came a sudden explosion and I found myself in a modestly furnished room. There, leaning against the side of an open door was my son David of Biblical fame. He was a lad in his early teens. What struck me forcibly about him was the unusual beauty of his face and figure. He was — as he is described in the first book of Samuel — ruddy, with beautiful eyes and very handsome.

Not for one moment did I feel myself to be anyone other than who I am now. Yet, I knew that this lad, David, was my son, and he knew that I was his father; for "the wisdom from above is without uncertainty." As I sat there contemplating the beauty of my son, the vision faded and I awoke.

" 'I and the children whom the Lord has given me are signs and portents in Israel from the Lord of hosts, who dwells on Mount Zion.' Is. 8.18. God gave me David as my very own son. 'I will raise up your son after you, who shall come forth from your body ... I will be his father, and he shall be my son.' 2 Sam. 7.12-14. God is known in no other way than through the Son.

" 'No one knows who the Son is except the Father, or who the Father is except the Son and any one to whom the Son chooses to reveal Him.' Luke. 10.22. The experience of being David's Father is the end of man's pilgrimage on earth. The purpose of life is to find the Father of David, the Lord's anointed, the Christ. 'Abner, whose son is this youth?' And Abner said, 'As your soul lives, O king, I cannot tell.' And the king said, 'Inquire whose son the stripling is.' And as David returned from the slaughter of the Philistine, Abner took him and brought him before Saul with the head of the Philistine in his hand. And Saul said to him, 'Whose son are you, young man?' And David answered, 'I am the son of your servant Jesse the Bethlehemite.' 1 Sam: 17:55-58. Jesse is any form of the verb 'to be.' In other words, I Am the Son of who I Am, I am self begotten, I Am the Son of God, the Father. I And my Father are one. I am the image of the invisible God. He who has seen me has seen the Father.

" 'Whose son . . . ?' is not about David but about David's Father, whom the king had promised (1 Sam: 17:25) to make free in Israel. Note: in all these passages (1 Sam: 17:55,56,58) the king's inquiry is not about David but about David's Father. 'I have found David, my servant; ... He shall cry to me, "Thou art my Father, my God, and the Rock of my salvation. And I will make him the first-born, the highest of the kings of the earth.' " —Psalms. 89.

The individual who is born from above will find David and know him to be his very own son. Then he will ask the Pharisees — who are always with us — "What do you think of the Christ? Whose son is he?" And when they say to him, "The son of David." He will say to them, "How is it then that David, in the Spirit, calls him Lord . . . If David thus calls him Lord, how is he his son?" Matt: 22.41-45. Man's misconception of the role of the Son — which is only a sign and a portent — has made the Son an idol. "Little children, keep yourselves from idols." 1 John. 5.21.

God awakes; and that man in whom he awakes becomes his own father's father. He who was David's son, "Jesus Christ, the son of David" Matt: 1.1. has become David's Father.

No longer will I cry to "our father David, thy child." Acts. 4.25. "I have found David." He has cried to me, "Thou art my Father." Ps. 89.

Now I know myself to be one of the Elohim, the God who became man, that man may become God. "Great indeed, we confess, is the mystery of our religion." 1 Tim. 3.16. If the Bible were history it would not be a mystery. "Wait for the promise of the Father." Acts. 1.4. that is, for David—God's Son—who will reveal you as the Father. This promise, says Jesus, you heard from me (Luke 24:49) and to its fulfillment at that moment in time when it pleases God to give you his Son — as "your offspring, which is Christ." Gal. 3.16.

A figure of speech is used for the purpose of calling attention to, emphasizing and intensifying the reality of the literal sense. The truth is literal; the words used are figurative. "The curtain of the temple was torn in two, from top to bottom, and the earth shook and the rocks were split." Matt: 27.51.

On the morning of April 8, 1960—four months after it was revealed to me that I am David's father—a bolt of lightning out of my skull split me in two from the top of my skull to the base of my spine. I was cleft as though I were a tree that had been struck by lightning. Then I felt and saw myself as a golden liquid light moving up my spine in a serpentine motion; as I entered my skull it vibrated like an earthquake. "Every word of God proves true; he is a shield to those who take refuge in him. Do not add to his words, lest he rebuke you, and you be found a liar." "And as Moses lifted up the serpent in the wilderness, so must the Son of man be lifted up." John. 3.14.

These mystical experiences will help to rescue the Bible from the externals of history, persons and events, and to restore it to its real significance in the life of man. Scripture must be fulfilled "in" us. God's promise will be fulfilled. You will have these experiences: "And you shall be my witnesses in Jerusalem and in all Judea and Sa-ma-ri-a and to the end of the earth." Acts. 1:8.

The widening circle — Jerusalem . . . Judea . . . Samaria the end of the earth — is God's plan.

The Promise is still maturing to its time, its appointed time, but how long, vast and severe the trials e're you find David, your son, who will reveal you as God, The Father, were long to tell; but it hastens to the end; it will not fail. So wait, for there will be no postponement.

"Is anything too wonderful for the Lord? At the appointed time I will return to you, in the spring, and Sarah shall have a son." Gen. 18:14.

Out Of This World

CHAPTER ONE
THINKING FOURTH-DIMENSIONALLY

And now I have told you before it come to pass, that, when it is come to pass, ye might believe.

[John 14:29]

MANY persons, myself included, have observed events before they occurred; that is, before they occurred in this world of three dimensions. Since man can observe an event before it occurs in the three dimensions of space, life on earth must proceed according to plan, and this plan must exist elsewhere in another dimension and be slowly moving through our space.

If the occurring events were not in this world when they were observed, then, to be perfectly logical, they must have been out of this world.

And whatever is there to be seen before it occurs here must be "Predetermined" from the point of view of man awake in a three-dimensional world.

Thus the question arises: —Are we able to alter our future?

My object in writing these pages is to indicate possibilities inherent in man, to show that man can alter his future; but, thus altered, it forms again a deterministic sequence starting from the point of interference

– a future that will be consistent with the alteration.

The most remarkable feature of man's future is its flexibility.

It is determined by his attitudes rather than by his acts.

The cornerstone on which all things are based is man's concept of himself. He acts as he does and has the experiences that he does, because his concept of himself is what it is, and for no other reason. Had he a different concept of self, he would act differently. A change of concept of self automatically alters his future: and a change in any term of his future series of experiences reciprocally alters his concept of self.

Man's assumptions which he regards as insignificant produce effects that are considerable; therefore man should revise his estimate of an assumption, and recognize its creative power.

All changes take place in consciousness. The future, although prepared in every detail in advance, has several outcomes.

At every moment of our lives we have before us the choice of which of several futures we will choose.

There are two actual outlooks on the world possessed by every-one

– a natural focus and a spiritual focus. The ancient teachers called the one "the carnal mind," the other "the mind of Christ."

We may differentiate them as ordinary waking consciousness – governed by our senses, and a controlled imagination – governed by desire.

We recognize these two distinct centers of thought in the statement:

"The natural man receiveth not the things of the spirit of God for they are foolishness unto him; neither can he know them for they are spiritually discerned" [Corinthians 2:14].

The natural view confines reality to the moment called now. To the natural view, the past and future are purely imaginary.

The spiritual view, on the other hand, sees the contents of time. It sees events as distinct and separated as objects in space. The past and future are a present whole to the spiritual view. What is mental and subjective to the natural man is concrete and objective to the spiritual man.

The habit of seeing only that which our senses permit, renders us totally blind to what we otherwise could see.

To cultivate the faculty of seeing the invisible, we should often deliberately disentangle our minds from the evidence of the senses and focus our attention on an invisible state, mentally feeling it and sensing it until it has all the distinctness of reality.

Earnest, concentrated thought focused in a particular direction shuts out other sensations and causes them to disappear.

We have but to concentrate on the state desired in order to see it.

The habit of withdrawing attention from the region of sensation and concentrating it on the invisible develops our spiritual outlook and enables us to penetrate beyond the world of sense and to see that which is invisible.

"For the invisible things of him from the creation of the world are clearly seen" – Romans 1:20.

This vision is completely independent of the natural faculties. Open it and quicken it! Without it, these instructions are useless, for "the things of the spirit are spiritually discerned."

A little practice will convince us that we can, by controlling our imagination, reshape our future in harmony with our desire. Desire is the mainspring of action. We could not move a single finger unless we had a desire to move it. No matter what we do, we follow the desire which at the moment dominates our minds. When we break a habit, our desire to break it is greater than our desire to continue in the habit.

The desires which impel us to action are those that hold our attention. A desire is but an awareness of something we lack or need to make our life more enjoyable.

Desires always have some personal gain in view, the greater the anticipated gain, the more intense is the desire. There is no absolutely unselfish desire. Where there is nothing to gain there is no desire, and consequently no action.

The spiritual man speaks to the natural man through the language of desire.

The key to progress in life and to the fulfillment of dreams lies in

ready obedience to its voice.

Unhesitating obedience to its voice is an immediate assumption of

the wish was fulfilled. To desire a state is to have it.

As Pascal has said, —You would not have sought me had you not already found me. Man, by assuming the feeling of his wish being fulfilled, and then living and acting on this conviction, alters the future in harmony with his assumption.

Assumptions awaken what they affirm.

As soon as man assumes the feeling of his wish being fulfilled, his four- dimensional self finds ways for the attainment of this end, discovers methods for its realization.

I know of no clearer definition of the means by which we realize our desires than to experience in imagination what we would experience

in the flesh were we to achieve our goal.

This experience of the end wills the means.

With its larger outlook the four-dimensional self then constructs the means necessary to realize the accepted end.

The undisciplined mind finds it difficult to assume a state which is denied by the senses.

Here is a technique that makes it easy to encounter events before they occur, to "call things which are not seen as though they were" [Romans 4:17].

People have a habit of slighting the importance of simple things; but this simple formula for changing the future was discovered after years of searching and experimenting.

The first step in changing the future is desire – that is: define your objective – know definitely what you want.

Secondly: construct an event which you believe you would encounter following the fulfillment of your desire – an event which implies fulfillment of your desire – something that will have the action of self predominant.

Thirdly: immobilize the physical body and induce a condition akin to sleep – lie on a bed or relax in a chair and imagine that you are sleepy; then, with eyelids closed and your attention focused on the action you intend to experience – in imagination – mentally feel yourself right into the proposed action – imagining all the while that you are actually performing the action here and now. You must always participate in the imaginary action, not merely stand back and look on, but you must feel that you are actually performing the action so that the imaginary sensation is real to you.

It is important always to remember that the proposed action must be one which follows the fulfillment of your desire; and, also, you must feel yourself into the action until it has all the vividness and distinctness of reality.

For example: suppose you desired promotion in office. Being congratulated would be an event you would encounter following the fulfillment of your desire. Having selected this action as the one you will experience in imagination, immobilize the physical body, and induce a state akin to sleep – a drowsy state – but one in which you are still able to control the direction of your thoughts – a state in which you are attentive without effort. Now, imagine that a friend is standing before you. Put your imaginary hand into his. First feel it to be solid and real, then carry on an imaginary conversation with him in harmony with the action. Do not visualize yourself at a distance in point of space and at a distance in point of time being congratulated on your good fortune. Instead, make elsewhere here, and the future now. The future event is a reality now in a dimensionally larger world; and, oddly enough, now in a dimensionally larger world, is equivalent to here in the ordinary three-dimensional space of everyday life.

The difference between feeling yourself in action, here and now, and visualizing yourself in action, as though you were on a motion-picture screen, is the difference between success and failure.

The difference will be appreciated if you will now visualize yourself climbing a ladder. Then with eyelids closed imagine that a ladder is right in front of you and feel you are actually climbing it.

Desire, physical immobility bordering on sleep, and imaginary action in which self feelingly predominates, here and now, are not only important factors in altering the future, but they are essential conditions in consciously projecting the spiritual self. If, when the physical body is immobilized we become possessed of the idea to do something – and imagine that we are doing it here and now and keep the imaginary action feelingly going right up until sleep ensues – we are likely to awaken out of the physical body to find ourselves in a dimensionally larger world with a dimensionally larger focus and actually doing what we desired and imagined we were doing in the flesh.

But whether we awaken there or not, we are actually performing the action in the fourth-dimensional world, and we will re-enact it in the future, here in the third-dimensional world.

Experience has taught me to restrict the imaginary action, to condense the idea which is to be the object of our meditation into a single act, and to re-enact it over and over again until it has the feeling of reality. Otherwise, the attention will wander off along an associational track, and hosts of associated images will be presented to our attention. In a few seconds they will lead us hundreds of miles away from our objective in point of space, and years away in point of time.

If we decide to climb a particular flight of stairs, because that is the likely event to follow the realization of our desire, then we must restrict the action to climbing that particular flight of stairs. Should our attention wander off, we must bring it back to its task of climbing that flight of stairs and keep on doing so until the imaginary action has all the solidity and distinctness of reality. The idea must be maintained in the field of presentation without any sensible effort on our part. We must, with the minimum of effort, permeate the mind with the feeling of the wish fulfilled.

Drowsiness facilitates change because it favors attention without effort, but it must not be pushed to the stage of sleep, in which we shall no longer be able to control the movements of our attention, but rather a moderate degree of drowsiness in which we are still able to direct our thoughts.

A most effective way to embody a desire is to assume the feeling of the wish fulfilled and then, in a relaxed and sleepy state, repeat over and over again, like a lullaby, any short phrase which implies fulfillment of our desire, such as "Thank you" as though we addressed a higher power for having done it for us.

If, however, we seek a conscious projection into a dimensionally larger world, then we must keep the action going right up until sleep ensues.

Experience in imagination, with all the distinctness of reality, what would be experienced in the flesh were you to achieve your goal; and you shall, in time, meet it in the flesh as you met it in your imagination.

Feed the mind with premises – that is, assertions presumed to be true, because assumptions, though unreal to the senses, if persisted in, until they have the feeling of reality, will harden into facts. To an assumption all means which promote its realization are good. It influences the behavior of all by inspiring in all the movements, the actions, and the words which tend towards its fulfillment.

To understand how man molds his future in harmony with his assumption we must know what we mean by a dimensionally larger world, for it is to a dimensionally larger world that we go to alter our future. The observation of an event before it occurs implies that the event is predetermined from the point of view of man in the three-dimensional world. Therefore, to change the conditions here in the three dimensions of space we must first change them in the four dimensions of space.

Man does not know exactly what is meant by a dimensionally larger world, and would no doubt deny the existence of a dimensionally larger self.

He is quite familiar with the three dimensions of length, width and height, and he feels that if there were a fourth dimension, it should be just as obvious to him as the dimensions of length, width and height.

A dimension is not a line; it is any way in which a thing can be measured that is entirely different from all other ways.

That is, to measure a solid fourth-dimensionally, we simply measure it in any direction except that of its length, width and height.

Is there another way of measuring an object other than those of its length, width and height?

Time measures my life without employing the three dimensions of length, width and height.

There is no such thing as an instantaneous object. Its appearance and disappearance are measurable.

It endures for a definite length of time. We can measure its life span

without using the dimensions of length, width and height.

Time is definitely a fourth way of measuring an object.

The more dimensions an object has, the more substantial and real it becomes. A straight line, which lies entirely in one dimension, acquires shape, mass and substance by the addition of dimensions. What new quality would time, the fourth dimension, give which would make it just as vastly superior to solids as solids are to surfaces and surfaces are to lines?

Time is a medium for changes in experience because all changes take time. The new quality is changeability.

Observe that if we bisect a solid, its cross section will be a surface; by bisecting a surface, we obtain a line; and by bisecting a line, we get a point. This means that a point is but a cross section of a line, which is, in turn, but a cross section of a surface, which is, in turn, but a cross section of a solid, which is, in turn, if carried to its logical conclusion, but a cross section of a four-dimensional object.

We cannot avoid the inference that all three-dimensional objects are but cross sections of four-dimensional bodies. Which means: when I meet you, I meet a cross section of the four-dimensional you

– the four-dimension self that is not seen.

To see the four-dimensional self I must see every cross section or moment of your life from birth to death and see them all as coexisting.

My focus should take in the entire array of sensory impressions which you have experienced on earth plus those you might encounter.

I should see them, not in the order in which they were experienced by you, but as a present whole. Because change is the characteristic of the fourth dimension, I should see them in a state of flux as a living, animated whole.

If we have all this clearly fixed in our minds, what does it mean to us in this three-dimensional world?

It means that, if we can move along time's length, we can see the future and alter it as we so desire.

This world, which we think so solidly real, is a shadow out of which and beyond which we may at any time pass.

It is an abstraction from a more fundamental and dimensionally larger world – a more fundamental world abstracted from a still more fundamental and dimensionally larger world and so on to infinity.

The absolute is unattainable by any means or analysis, no matter how many dimensions we add to the world.

Man can prove the existence of a dimensionally larger world simply by focusing his attention on an invisible state and imagining that he sees and feels it. If he remains concentrated in this state, his present environment will pass away, and he will awaken in a dimensionally larger world where the object of his contemplation will be seen as a concrete objective reality.

Intuitively I feel that, were he to abstract his thoughts from this dimensionally larger world and retreat still further within his mind, he would again bring about an externalization of time. He would discover that every time he retreats into his inner mind and brings about an externalization of time, space becomes dimensionally larger.

And he would, therefore, conclude that both time and space are serial, and that the drama of life is but the climbing of a multitudinous dimensional time block.

Scientists will one day explain why there is a Serial Universe.

But in practice how we use this Serial Universe to change the future is more important.

To change the future, we need only concern ourselves with two worlds in the infinite series, the world we know by reason of our bodily organs, and the world we perceive independently of our bodily organs.

CHAPTER TWO
ASSUMPTIONS BECOME FACTS

Men believe in the reality of the external world because they do not know how to focus and condense their powers to penetrate its thin crust.

This book has only one purpose – the removing of the veil of the senses – the traveling into another world.

To remove the veil of the senses we do not employ great effort; the objective world vanishes by turning our attention away from it.

We have only to concentrate on the state desired in order to mentally see it, but to give it reality so that it will become an objective fact, we must focus attention upon the invisible state until it has the feeling of reality.

When, through concentrated attention, our desire appears to possess the distinctness and feeling of reality, we have given it the right to become a visible concrete fact.

If it is difficult to control the direction of your attention while in a state akin to sleep, you may find gazing fixedly into an object very helpful. Do not look at its surface but into and beyond any plain object such as a wall, a carpet, or any other object which possesses depth.

Arrange it to return as little reflection as possible. Imagine then that in this depth you are seeing and hearing what you want to see and hear until your attention is exclusively occupied by the imagined state.

At the end of your meditation, when you awake from your — controlled waking dream, you feel as though you had returned from a great distance.

The visible world which you had shut out returns to consciousness and by its very presence informs you that you have been self-deceived into believing that the object of your contemplation was real.

But, if you know that consciousness is the one and only reality,

you will remain faithful to your vision, and by this sustained mental attitude confirm your gift of reality, and prove that you have the power to give reality to your desires that they may become visible concrete facts.

Define your ideal and concentrate your attention upon the idea of identifying yourself with your ideal. Assume the feeling of being it, the feeling that would be yours were you already the embodiment of your ideal. Then live and act upon this conviction. This assumption, though denied by the senses, if persisted in, will become fact. You will know when you have succeeded in fixing the desired state in consciousness by simply looking mentally at the people you know.

In dialogues with yourself you are less inhibited and more sincere than in actual conversations with others, therefore the opportunity for self-analysis arises when you are surprised by your mental conversations with others.

If you see them as you formerly saw them, you have not changed your concept of self, for all changes of concepts of self result in a changed relationship to your world.

In your meditation allow others to see you as they would see you were this new concept of self a concrete fact. You always seem to others an embodiment of the ideal you inspire. Therefore, in meditation, when you contemplate others, you must be seen by them mentally as you would be seen by them physically were your concept of self an objective fact; that is, in meditation you imagine that they see you expressing that which you desire to be.

If you assume that you are what you want to be your desire is fulfilled, and, in fulfillment, all longing is neutralized. You cannot continue desiring what you have already realized. Your desire is not something you labor to fulfill, it is recognizing something you already possess. It is assuming the feeling of being that which you desire to be. Believing and being are one.

The conceiver and his conception are one, therefore that which you conceive yourself to be can never be so far off as even to be near, for nearness implies separation. "If thou canst believe, all things are possible to him that believeth‖ [Mark 9:23].

Being is the substance of things hoped, the evidence of things not yet seen [cf. Hebrews 11:1].

If you assume that you are what you want to be, then you will see others as they are related to your assumption If, however, it is the good of others that you desire, then, in meditation, you must represent them to yourself as already being that which you desire them to be.

It is through desire that you rise above your present sphere and the road from longing to fulfillment is shortened as you experience in imagination what you would experience in the flesh were you already the embodiment of the ideal you desire to be.

I have stated that man has at every moment of time the choice before him which of several futures he will encounter; but the question arises; —How is that possible when the experiences of man, awake in the three-dimensional world, are predetermined?" as his observation of an event before it occurs implies. This ability to change the future will be seen if we liken the experiences of life on earth to this printed page.

Man experiences events on earth singly and successively in the same way that you are now experiencing the words of this page.

Imagine that every word on this page represents a single sensory impression. To get the context, to understand my meaning, you focus your vision of the first word in the upper left-hand corner and then move your focus across the page from left to right, letting it fall on the words singly and successively. By the time your eyes reach the last word on this page you have extracted my meaning. Suppose, however, on looking at the page, with all the printed words thereon equally present, you decided to rearrange them. You could, by rearranging them, tell an entirely different story; in fact; you could tell many different stories.

A dream is nothing more than uncontrolled four-dimensional thinking, or the rearrangement of both past and future sensory impressions. Man seldom dreams of events in the order in which he experiences them when awake.

He usually dreams of two or more events which are separated in time, fused into a single sensory impression; or, in his dream, he so completely rearranges his single waking sensory impressions that he does not recognize them when he encounters them in his waking state.

For example; I dreamed that I delivered a package to the restaurant in my apartment building. The hostess said to me, —You can't leave that there‖; whereupon, the elevator operator gave me a few letters and as I thanked him for them, he, in turn, thanked me. At this point, the night elevator operator appeared and waved a greeting to me.

The following day, as I left my apartment, I picked up a few letters which had been placed at my door. On my way down I gave the day elevator operator a tip and thanked hem for taking care of my mail; whereupon, he thanked me for the tip. On my return home that day I overheard a doorman say to a delivery man, —You can't leave that there.‖ As I was about to take the elevator up to my apartment, I was attracted by a familiar face in the restaurant, and, as I looked in, the hostess greeted me with a smile. Late that night I escorted my dinner guests to the elevator and as I said good-bye to them, the night operator waved good-night to me.

By simply rearranging a few of the single sensory impressions I was destined to encounter, and by fusing two or more of them into single sensory impressions, I constructed a dream which differed quite a bit from my waking experience.

When we have learned to control the movements of our attention in the four-dimensional world, we shall be able to consciously create circumstances in the three-dimensional world.

We learn this control through the waking dream, where our attention can be maintained without effort, for attention minus effort is indispensable to changing the future. We can, in a controlled waking dream, consciously construct an event which we desire to experience in the three-dimensional world.

The sensory impressions we use to construct our waking dream are present realities displaced in time or the four-dimensional world. All that we do in constructing the waking dream is to select from the vast array of sensory impressions those, which, when they are properly arranged, imply that we have realized our desire. With the dream clearly defined we relax in a chair and induce a state of consciousness akin to sleep – a state, which, although bordering on sleep, leaves us in conscious control of the movements of our attention. When we have achieved that state, we experience in imagination what we would experience in reality were this waking dream an objective fact. In applying this technique to change the future it is important always to remember that the only thing which occupies the mind during the waking dream is the waking dream, the predetermined action which implies the fulfillment of our desire.

How the waking dream becomes physical fact is not our concern.

Our acceptance of the waking dream as physical reality wills the means for its fulfillment.

Let me again lay the foundation of changing the future, which is nothing more than a controlled waking dream.

Define your objective–know definitely what you want.

Construct an event which you believe you will encounter following the fulfillment of your desire – something which will have the action of self predominant – an event which implies the fulfillment of your desire.

Immobilize the physical body and induce a state of consciousness akin to sleep; then, mentally feel yourself right into the proposed action – imagining all the while that you are actually performing the action here and now so that you experience in imagination what you would experience in the flesh were you now to realize your goal.

Experience has convinced me that this is the perfect way to achieve my goal.

However, my own many failures would convict me were I to imply that I have completely mastered the movements of my attention.

I can, however, with the ancient teacher say: "This one thing I do, forgetting those things which are behind, and reaching forth unto those things which are before, I press toward the mark for the prize." [Philippians 3:13,14.]

CHAPTER THREE
POWER OF IMAGINATION

"Ye shall know the truth and the truth shall make you free" – [John 8:32]

Men claim that a true judgment must conform to the external reality to which it relates. This means that if I, while imprisoned, suggest to myself that I am free and succeed in believing that I am free, it is true that I believe in my freedom; but it does not follow that I am free for I may be the victim of illusion.

But, because of my own experiences, I have come to believe in so many strange things that I see little reason to doubt the truth of things that are beyond my experience.

The ancient teachers warned us not to judge from appearances because, said they, the truth need not conform to the external reality to which it relates.

They claimed that we bore false witness if we imagined evil against another – that no matter how real our belief appears to be – how truly it conforms to the external reality to which it relates – if it does not make free the one of whom we hold the belief, it is untrue and therefore a false judgment.

We are called upon to deny the evidence of our senses and to imagine as true of our neighbor that which makes him free. —Ye shall know the truth, and the truth shall make you free.

To know the truth of our neighbor we must assume that he is already that which he desires to be. Any concept we hold of another that is short of his fulfilled desire will not make him free and therefore cannot be the truth.

Instead of learning my craft in schools where attending courses and seminars is considered a substitute for self-acquired knowledge, my schooling was devoted almost exclusively to the power of imagination.

I stayed for hours imagining myself to be other than that which my

reason and my senses dictated until the imagined states were vivid as reality – so vivid that passer-by became but a part of my imagination and acted as I would have them. By the power of imagination my fantasy led theirs and dictated to them their behavior and the discourse they held together while I was identified with my imagined state.

[200] NEVILLE GODDARD

Man's imagination is the man himself, and the world as imagination sees it is the real world, but it is our duty to imagine all that is lovely and of good report [Philippians 4:8].

"For the Lord seeth not as man seeth; for man looketh on the outward appearance, but the Lord looketh on the heart" [1 Samuel 16:7].

"As a man thinketh in his heart so is he" [Proverbs 23:7].

In meditation, when the brain grows luminous, I find my imagination endowed with the magnetic power to attract to me whatsoever I desire. Desire is the power imagination uses to fashion life about me as I fashion it within myself.

I first desire to see a certain person or scene, and then I look at though I were seeing that which I want to see, and the imagined state becomes

objectively real. I desire to hear, and then I listen as though I were hearing, and the imagined voice speaks that which I dictate as though it had initiated the message.

I could give you many examples to prove my arguments, to prove that these imagined states do become physical realities; but I know that my examples will awaken in all who have not met the like or who are not inclined towards my arguments, a most natural incredulity.

Nevertheless, experience has convinced me of the truth of the statement, "He calleth those things which be not as though they were." [Romans 4:17]

For I have, in intense meditation, called things that were not seen as though they were, and the unseen not only became seen, but eventually became physical realities.

By this method – first desiring and then imagining that we are experiencing that which we desire to experience – we can mold the future in harmony with our desire. But let us follow the advice of the prophet and think only the lovely and the good, for the imagination waits on us as indifferently and as swiftly when our nature is evil as when it is good. From us spring forth good and evil. —I have set before thee this day life and good, and death and evil. [Deuteronomy 30:15]

Desire and imagination are the enchanter's wand of fable and they draw to themselves their own affinities. They break forth best when the mind is in a state akin to sleep.

I have written with some care and detail the method I use to enter the dimensionally larger world, but I shall give one more formula for opening the door of the larger world.

"In a dream, in a vision of the night, when deep sleep falleth upon men, in slumberings upon the bed; Then he openeth the ears of men, and sealeth their instruction." [Job 33:15,16]

In dream we are usually the servant of our vision rather than its master, but the internal fantasy of dream can be turned into an external reality. In dream, as in mediation, we slip from this world into a dimensionally larger world, and I know that the forms in dream are not flat two-dimensional images which modern psychologists believe them to be. They are substantial realities of the dimensionally larger world, and I can lay hold of them. I have discovered that, if I surprise myself dreaming, I can lay hold of any inanimate or stationary form of the dream – a chair – a table – a stairway – a tree – and command to awake, while firmly holding on the object of the dream, I am pulled through myself with the distinct feeling of awakening from dream. I awaken in another sphere holding the object of my dream, to find that I am no longer the servant of my vision but its master, for I am fully conscious and in control of the movements of my attention. It is in this fully conscious state, when we are in control of the direction of thought, that we call things that are not seen as though they were. In this state we call things by wishing and assuming the feeling of our wish fulfilled.

Unlike the world of three dimensions where there is an interval between our assumption and its fulfillment, in the dimensionally larger world there is an immediate realization of our assumption. The external reality instantly mirrors our assumption. Here there is no need to wait four months till harvest [see John 4:35]. We look again as though we saw, and lo and behold, the fields are already white to harvest.

In this dimensionally larger world —Ye shall not need to fight, set yourselves, stand ye still and see the salvation of the Lord with you, [Chronicles 20:17].

And because that greater world is slowly passing through our three-dimensional world, we can by the power of imagination mold our world in harmony with our desire.

Look as though you saw; listen as though you heard; stretch forth your imaginary hand as though you touched…. And your assumptions will harden into facts.

To those who believe that a true judgment must conform to the external reality to which it relates, this will be foolishness and a stumbling block [1Corinthians 1:23].

But I preach and practice the fixing in consciousness of that which man desires to realize. Experience convinces me that fixed attitudes of mind which do not conform to the external reality to which they relate and are therefore called imaginary – "things which are not"

– will, nevertheless, "bring to nought things that are" [1Corinthians 1:28].

I do not wish to write a book of wonders, but rather to turn man's mind back to the one and only reality that the ancient teachers worshipped as God.

All that was said of God was in reality said of man's consciousness so we may say, "that, according as it is written, He that glorieth, let him glory in his own consciousness" [1Corinthians 1:31; 2Corinthians 10:17,18; "But let him that glorieth glory in this, that he understandeth and knoweth Me, that I am the LORD which exercise lovingkindness, judgment, and righteousness, in the earth", Jeremiah 9:24].

No man needs help to direct him in the application of this law of consciousness. "I am" is the self-definition of the absolute. The root out of which everything grows. "I am the vine"

[John 15:1; 15:5].

What is your answer to the eternal question, "who am I?"

Your answer determines the part you play in the world's drama. Your answer – that is, your concept of self – need not conform to the external reality to which it relates. This great truth is revealed in the statements, "Let the weak say, I am strong." [Joel 3:10]

Look back over the good resolutions with which many past new years are encumbered. They lived a little while and then they died. Why? Because they were severed from their root. Assume that you are that which you want to be.

Experience in imagination what you would experience in the flesh were you already that which you want to be. Remain faithful to your assumption, so that you define yourself as that which you have assumed.

Things have no life if they are severed from their roots, and our consciousness, our "I AM-ness" is the root of all that springs in our world.

"If we believe not that I am he, ye shall die in your sins" – John 8:24 –, that is, if I do not believe that I am already that which I desire to be, then I remain as I am and die in my present concept of self.

[203] THE POWER OF IMAGINATION: THE NEVILLE GODDARD TREASURY

There is no power, outside of the consciousness of man, to resurrect and make alive that which man desires to experience.

That man who is accustomed to call up at will whatever images he pleases, will be, by virtue of the power of his imagination, master of his fate.

—I am the resurrection, and the life; he that believeth in Me, though he were dead, yet shall he live. [John 11:25]

"Ye shall know the truth, and the truth shall make you free."

CHAPTER FOUR
NO ONE TO CHANGE BUT SELF

—And for their sake I sanctify myself, that they also might be sanctified through the truth. [John 17:19]

The ideal we serve and strive to attain could never be evolved from us were it not potentially involved in our nature.

It is now my purpose to retell and to emphasize an experience of mine printed by me two years ago. I believe these quotations from "THE SEARCH" will help us to understand the operation of the law of consciousness, and show us that we have no one to change but ourselves.

—Once in an idle interval at sea I meditated on, —the perfect state,‖ and wondered what I would be, were I of too pure eyes to behold iniquity, if to me all things were pure and were I without condemnation. As I became lost in this fiery brooding, I found myself lifted above the dark environment of the senses. So intense was the feeling I felt myself being a fire dwelling in a body of air. Voices from a heavenly chorus, with the exaltation of those who had been conquerors in a conflict with death were singing, —He is risen – He is risen, and intuitively I knew they meant me. Then I seemed to be walking in the night. I soon came upon a scene that might have been the ancient Pool of Bethesda for in this place lay a great multitude of impotent folk –blind, halt, withered – waiting not for the moving of the water as of tradition, but waiting for me. As I came near, without thought or effort on my part they were, one after the other, molded as by the Magician of the Beautiful. Eyes, hands, feet – all missing members – were drawn from some invisible reservoir and molded in harmony with that perfection which I felt springing within me. When all were made perfect, the chorus exulted, "It is finished. Then the scene dissolved and I awoke.

I know the vision was the result of my intense meditation upon the idea of perfection, for my meditations invariably bring about union with the state contemplated. I had been so completely absorbed within the idea that for a while I had become what I contemplated, and the high purpose with which I had for that moment identified myself drew the companionship of high things and fashioned the vision in harmony with my inner nature. The ideal with which we are united works by association of ideals to awaken a thousand moods to create a drama in keeping with the central idea.

My mystical experiences have convinced me that there is no way to bring about the outer perfection we seek other than by the transformation of ourselves.

In the divine economy nothing is lost. We cannot lose anything save by descent from the sphere where the thing has its natural life. There is no transforming power in death and, whether we are here or there, we fashion the world that surrounds us by the intensity of our imagination and feeling, and we illuminate or darken our lives by the concepts we hold of ourselves. Nothing is more important to us than our conception of ourselves, and especially is this true of our concept of the dimensionally great One within us.

Those who help or hinder us, whether they know it or not, are the servants of that law which shapes outward circumstances in harmony with our inner nature.

It is our conception of ourselves which frees or constrains us, though it may use material agencies to achieve its purpose.

Because life molds the outer world to reflect the inner arrangement of our minds, there is no way of bringing about the outer perfection we seek other than by the transformation of ourselves. No help cometh from without; the hills to which we lift our eyes are those of an inner range. It is thus to our own consciousness that we must turn to the only reality, the only foundation on which all phenomena can be explained. We can rely absolutely on the justice of this law to give us only that which is of the nature of ourselves.

To attempt to change the world before we change our concept of ourselves is to struggle against the nature of things.

There can be no outer change until there is first an inner change. As within, so without. I am not advocating philosophical indifference when I suggest that we should imagine ourselves as already that which we want to be, living in a mental atmosphere of greatness, rather than using physical means and arguments to bring about the desired change.

Everything we do, unaccompanied by a change of consciousness, is but futile readjustment of surfaces.

However we toil or struggle, we can receive no more than our assumptions affirm. To protest against anything which happens to us is to protest against the law of our being and our rulership over our own destiny.

The circumstances of my life are too closely related to my conception of myself not to have been formed by my own spirit from some dimensionally larger storehouse of my being. If there is pain to me in these happenings, I should look within myself for the cause, for I am moved here and there and made to live in a world in harmony with my concept of myself.

Intense meditation brings about a union with the state contemplated, and during this union we see visions, have experiences and behave in keeping with our change of consciousness. This shows us that a transformation of consciousness will result in a change of environment and behavior. All wars prove that violent emotions are extremely potent in precipitating mental rearrangements. Every great conflict has been followed by an era of materialism and greed in which the ideals for which the conflict ostensibly were waged are submerged. This is inevitable because war evokes hate which impels a descent in consciousness from the plane of the ideal to the level where the conflict is waged. If we could become as emotionally aroused over our ideals as we become over our dislikes, we would ascend to the plane of our ideal as easily as we now descend to the level or our hates. Love and hate have a magical transforming power, and we grow through their exercise into the likeness of what we contemplate. By intensity of hatred we create in ourselves the character we imagine in our enemies. Qualities die for want of attention, so the unlovely states might best be rubbed out by imaging —beauty for ashes and joy for mourning [Isaiah 61:3] rather than by direct attacks on the state from which we would be free. —Whatsoever things are lovely and of good report, think on these things [Philippians 4:8], for we become that with which we are in rapport.

There is nothing to change but our concept of self. As soon as we succeed in transforming ourselves, our world will dissolve and reshape itself in harmony with that which our change affirms.

Prayer: The Art Of Believing

Chapter 1
LAW OF REVERSIBILITY

"Pray for my soul, more things are wrought by prayer than this world dreams of" (Tennyson).

PRAYER is an art and requires practice. The first requirement is a controlled imagination. Parade and vain repetitions are foreign to prayer. Its exercise requires tranquillity and peace of mind, "Use not vain repetitions," for prayer is done in secret and "thy Father which seeth in secret shall reward thee openly." The ceremonies that are customarily used in prayer are mere superstitions and have been invented to give prayer an air of solemnity. Those who do practice the art of prayer are often ignorant of the laws that control it. They attribute the results obtained to the ceremonies and mistake the letter for the spirit. The essence of prayer is faith; but faith must be permeated with understanding to be given that active quality which it does not possess when standing alone. "Therefore, get wisdom; and with all thy getting get understanding."

This book is an attempt to reduce the unknown to the known, by pointing out the conditions on which prayers are answered, and without which they cannot be answered. It defines the conditions governing prayer in laws that are simply a generalization of our observations.

The universal law of reversibility is the foundation on which its claims are based.

Mechanical motion caused by speech was known for a long time before anyone dreamed of the possibility of an inverse transformation, that is, the reproduction of speech by mechanical motion (the phonograph). For a long time electricity was produced by friction without ever a thought that friction, in turn, could be produced by electricity. Whether or not man succeeds in reversing the transformation of a force, he knows, nevertheless, that all transformations of force are reversible. If heat can produce mechanical motion, so mechanical motion can produce heat. If electricity produces magnetism, magnetism too can develop electric currents. If the voice can cause undulatory currents, so can such currents reproduce the voice, and so on. Cause and effect, energy and matter, action and reaction are the same and interconvertible.

This law is of the highest importance, because it enables you to foresee the inverse transformation once the direct transformation is verified.

If you knew how you would feel were you to realize your objective, then, inversely, you would know what state you could realize were you to awaken in yourself such feeling. The injunction, to pray believing that you already possess what you pray for, is based upon a knowledge of the law of inverse transformation. If your realized prayer produces in you a definite feeling or state of consciousness, then, inversely, that particular feeling or state of consciousness must produce your realized prayer. Because all transformations of force are reversible, you should always assume the feeling of your fulfilled wish. You should awaken within you the feeling that you are and have that which heretofore you desired to be and possess. This is easily done by contemplating the joy that would be yours were your objective an accomplished fact, so that you live and move and have your being in the feeling that your wish is realized.

The feeling of the wish fulfilled, if assumed and sustained, must objectify the state that would have created it. This law explains why "Faith is the substance of things hoped for, the evidence of things not seen" and why "He calleth things that are not seen as though they were and things that were not seen become seen." Assume the feeling of your wish fulfilled and continue feeling that it is fulfilled until that which you feel objectifies itself.

If a physical fact can produce a psychological state, a psychological state can produce a physical fact. If the effect (a) can be produced by the cause (b), then inversely, the effect (b) can be produced by the cause (a).

Therefore I say unto you, "What things soever ye desire, when ye pray, believe that ye have received them, and ye shall have them" (Mark 11:24).

Chapter 2
DUAL NATURE OF CONSCIOUSNESS

A clear concept of the dual nature of man's consciousness must be the basis of all true prayer. Consciousness includes a subconscious as well as a conscious part. The infinitely greater part of consciousness lies below the sphere of objective consciousness. The subconscious is the most important part of consciousness. It is the cause of voluntary action. The subconscious is what a man is. The conscious is what a man knows. "I and my Father are one but my Father is greater than I." The conscious and subconscious are one, but the subconscious is greater than the conscious.

"I of myself can do nothing, the Father within me He doeth the work." I, objective consciousness, of myself can do nothing; the Father, the subconscious, He doeth the work. The subconscious is that in which everything is known, in which everything is possible, to which everything goes, from which everything comes, which belongs to all, to which all have access.

What we are conscious of is constructed out of what we are not conscious of. Not only do our subconscious assumptions influence our behavior but they also fashion the pattern of our objective existence. They alone have the power to say, "Let us make man—objective manifestations—in our image, after our likeness." The whole of creation is asleep within the deep of man and is awakened to objective existence by his subconscious assumptions. Within that blankness we call sleep there is a consciousness in unsleeping vigilance, and while the body sleeps this unsleeping being releases from the treasure house of eternity the subconscious assumptions of man.

Prayer is the key which unlocks the infinite storehouse. "Prove me now herewith, saith the Lord of hosts, if I will not open you the windows of heaven, and pour you out a blessing, that there shall not be room enough to receive it." Prayer modifies or completely changes our subconscious assumptions, and a change of assumption is a change of expression.

The conscious mind reasons inductively from observation, experience and education. It therefore finds it difficult to believe what the five senses and inductive reason deny. The subconscious reasons deductively and is never concerned with the truth or falsity of the premise, but proceeds on the assumption of the correctness of the premise and objectifies results which are consistent with the premise.

This distinction must be clearly seen by all who would master the art of praying. No true grasp of the science of prayer can be really obtained until the laws governing the dual nature of consciousness are understood and the importance of the subconscious realized.

Prayer—the art of believing what is denied by the senses—deals almost entirely with the subconscious. Through prayer, the subconscious is suggested into acceptance of the wish fulfilled, and, reasoning deductively, logically unfolds it to its legitimate end. "Far greater is He that is in you than he that is in the world."

The subjective mind is the diffused consciousness that animates the world; it is the spirit that giveth life. In all substance is a single soul—subjective mind. Through all creation runs this one unbroken subjective mind. Thought and feeling fused into beliefs impress modifications upon it, charge it with a mission, which mission it faithfully executes.

The conscious mind originates premises. The subjective mind unfolds them to their logical ends. Were the subjective mind not so limited in its initiative power of reasoning, objective man could not be held responsible for his actions in the world. Man transmits ideas to the subconscious through his feelings. The subconscious transmits ideas from mind to mind through telepathy. Your unexpressed convictions of others are transmitted to them without their conscious knowledge or consent, and if subconsciously accepted by them will influence their behavior.

The only ideas they subconsciously reject are your ideas of them which they could not wish to be true of anyone. Whatever they could wish for others can be believed of them, and by the law of belief which governs subjective reasoning they are compelled to subjectively accept, and therefore objectively express, accordingly.

The subjective mind is completely controlled by suggestion. Ideas are best suggested when the objective mind is partly subjective, that is, when the objective senses are diminished or held in abeyance. This partly subjective state can best be described as controlled reverie, wherein the mind is passive but capable of functioning with absorption. It is a concentration of attention. There must be no conflict in your mind when you are praying. Turn from what is to what ought to be. Assume the mood of fulfilled desire, and by the universal law of reversibility you will realize your desire.

Chapter 3
IMAGINATION AND FAITH

PRAYERS are not successfully made unless there is rapport between the conscious and subconscious mind of the operator. This is done through imagination and faith.

By the power of imagination all men, certainly imaginative men, are forever casting forth enchantments, and all men, especially unimaginative men, are continually passing under their power. Can we ever be certain that it was not our mother while darning our socks who began that subtle change in our minds? If I can unintentionally cast an enchantment over persons, there is no reason to doubt that I am able to cast intentionally a far stronger enchantment.

Everything, that can be seen, touched, explained, argued over, is to the imaginative man nothing more than a means, for he functions, by reason of his controlled imagination, in the deep of himself where every idea exists in itself and not in relation to something else. In him there is no need for the restraints of reason, for the only restraint he can obey is the mysterious instinct that teaches him to eliminate all moods other than the mood of fulfilled desire.

Imagination and faith are the only faculties of mind needed to create objective conditions. The faith required for the successful operation of the law of consciousness is a purely subjective faith and is attainable upon the cessation of active opposition on the part of the objective mind of the operator. It depends upon your ability to feel and accept as true what your objective senses deny. Neither the passivity of the subject nor his conscious agreement with your suggestion is necessary, for without his consent or knowledge he can be given a subjective order which he must objectively express. It is a fundamental law of consciousness that by telepathy we can have immediate communion with another.

To establish rapport you call the subject mentally. Focus your attention on him and mentally shout his name just as you would to attract the attention of anyone. Imagine that he has answered, and mentally hear his voice. Represent him to yourself inwardly in the state you want him to obtain. Then imagine that he is telling you in the tones of ordinary conversation what you want to hear. Mentally answer him. Tell him of your joy in witnessing his good fortune. Having mentally heard with all the distinctness of reality that which you wanted to hear, and having thrilled to the news heard, return to objective consciousness. Your subjective conversation must awaken what it affirmed.

"Thou shalt decree a thing and it shall be established unto thee." It is not a strong will that sends the subjective word on its mission so much as it is clear thinking and feeling the truth of the state affirmed. When belief and will are in conflict, belief invariably wins. "Not by might, nor by power, but by my spirit, saith the Lord of hosts." It is not what you want that you attract; you attract what you believe to be true. Therefore, get into the spirit of these mental conversations and give them the same degree of reality that you would a telephone conversation. "If thou canst believe, all things are possible to him that believeth. Therefore, I say unto you, what things soever ye desire, when ye pray, believe that ye have received them, and ye shall have them." The acceptance of the end wills the means. And the wisest reflection could not devise more effective means than those which are willed by the acceptance of the end. Mentally talk to your friends as though your desires for them were already realized.

Imagination is the beginning of the growth of all forms, and faith is the substance out of which they are formed. By imagination, that which exists in latency or is asleep within the deep of consciousness is awakened and is given a form. The cures attributed to the influence of certain medicines, relics and places are the effects of imagination and faith. The curative power is not in the spirit that is in them, it is in the spirit in which they are accepted. "The letter killeth, but the spirit giveth life."

The subjective mind is completely controlled by suggestion, so, whether the object of your faith be true or false, you will get the same results. There is nothing unsound in the theory of medicine or in the claims of the priesthood for their relics and holy places. The subjective mind of the patient accepts the suggestion of health conditioned on such states, and as soon as these conditions are met proceeds to realize health. "According to your faith be it done unto you for all things are possible to him that believeth." Confident expectation of a state is the most potent means of bringing it about. The confident expectation of a cure does that which no medical treatment can accomplish.

Failure is always due to an antagonistic auto-suggestion by the patient, arising from objective doubt of the power of the medicine or relic, or from doubt of the truth of the theory. Many of us, either from too little emotion or too much intellect, both of which are stumbling blocks in the way of prayer, cannot believe that which our senses deny. To force ourselves to believe will end in greater doubt. To avoid such counter-suggestions the patient should be unaware, objectively, of the suggestions which are made to him. The most effective method of healing or influencing the behavior of others consists in what is known as "the silent or absent treatment." When the subject is unaware, objectively, of the suggestion given him there is no possibility of him setting up an antagonistic belief. It is not necessary that the patient know, objectively, that anything is being done for him. From what is known of the subjective and objective processes of reasoning, it is better that he should not know objectively of that which is being done for him. The more completely the objective mind is kept in ignorance of the suggestion, the better will the subjective mind perform its functions. The subject subconsciously accepts the suggestion and thinks he originates it, proving the truth of Spinoza's dictum that we know not the causes that determine our actions.

The subconscious mind is the universal conductor which the operator modifies with his thoughts and feelings. Visible states are either the vibratory effects of subconscious vibrations within you or they are the vibratory causes of corresponding vibrations within you. A disciplined man never permits them to be causes unless they awaken in him desirable states of consciousness. With a knowledge of the law of reversibility, the disciplined man transforms his world by imagining and feeling only what is lovely and of good report. The beautiful idea he awakens within himself shall not fail to arouse its affinity in others. He knows the savior of the world is not a man but the manifestation that would save. The sick man's savior is health, the hungry man's savior is food, the thirsty man's savior is water. He walks in the company of the savior by assuming the feeling of his wish fulfilled. By the laws of reversibility, that all transformations of force are reversible, the energy or feeling awakened transforms itself into the state imagined. He never waits four months for the harvest. If in four months the harvest will awaken in him a state of joy, then, inversely, the joy of harvest now will awaken the harvest now. "Now is the acceptable time to give beauty for ashes, joy for mourning, praise for the spirit of heaviness; that they might be called trees of righteousness, the planting of the Lord that he might be glorified."

Chapter 4
CONTROLLED REVERIE

EVERYONE is amenable to the same psychological laws which govern the ordinary hypnotic subject. He is amenable to control by suggestion. In hypnosis, the objective senses are partly or totally suspended. However, no matter how profoundly the objective senses are locked in hypnosis, the subjective faculties are alert, and the subject recognizes everything that goes on around him. The activity and power of the subjective mind are proportionate to the sleep of the objective mind. Suggestions which appear powerless when presented directly to objective consciousness are highly efficacious when the subject is in the hypnotic state. The hypnotic state is simply being unaware, objectively. In hypnotism, the conscious mind is put to sleep and the subconscious powers are exposed so as to be directly reached by suggestion. It is easy to see from this, providing you accept the truth of mental suggestions, that anyone not objectively aware of you is in a profound hypnotic state relative to you. Therefore, "Curse not the king, no not in thy thought; and curse not the rich in thy bedchamber; for a bird of the air shall carry the voice, and that which hath wings shall tell the matter" (Ecc. 10:20). What you sincerely believe as true of another you awaken within him.

No one need be entranced, in the ordinary manner, to be helped. If the subject is consciously unaware ot the suggestion, and if the suggestion is given with conviction and confidently accepted by the operator as true, then you have the ideal setting for a successful prayer. Represent the subject to yourself mentally as though he had already done that which you desire him to do. Mentally speak to him and congratulate him on having done what you want him to do. Mentally see him in the state you want him to obtain. Within the circle of its action, every word subjectively spoken awakens, objectively, what it affirms. Incredulity on the part of the subject is no hindrance when you are in control of your reverie.

Bold assertion by you, while you are in a partly subjective state, awakens what you affirm. Self-confidence on your part and the thorough belief in the truth of your mental assertion are all that is needed to produce results. Visualize the subject and imagine that you hear his voice. This establishes contact with his subjective mind. Then imagine that he is telling you what you want to hear. If you want to send him words of health and wealth, then imagine that he is telling you, "I have never felt better and I have never had more," and mentally tell him of your joy in witnessing his good fortune. Imagine that you see and hear his joy.

A mental conversation with the subjective image of another must be in a manner which does not express the slightest doubt as to the truth of what you hear and say. If you have the least idea that you do not believe what you have imagined you have heard and seen, the subject will not comply, for your subjective mind will transmit only your fixed ideas. Only fixed ideas can awaken their vibratory correlates in those toward whom they are directed. In the controlled reverie, ideas must be suggested with the utmost care. If you do not control your imagination in the reverie, your imagination will control you. Whatever you suggest with confidence is law to the subjective mind; it is under obligation to objectify that which you mentally affirm. Not only does the subject execute the state affirmed but he does it as though the decision had come of itself, or the idea had been originated by him.

Control of the subconscious is dominion over all. Each state obeys one mind's control. Control of the subconscious is accomplished through control of your beliefs, which in turn is the all-potent factor in the production of visible states. Imagination and faith are the secrets of creation.

Chapter 5
LAW OF THOUGHT TRANSMISSION

"HE sent his word and healed them, and delivered them from their destructions." He transmitted the consciousness of health and it awoke its vibratory correlate in the one toward whom it was directed. He mentally represented the subject to himself in a state of health and imagined he heard the subject confirm it. "For no word of God shall be void of power; therefore hold fast the pattern of healthful words which thou hast heard."

To pray successfully you must have clearly defined objectives. You must know what you want before you can ask for it. You must know what you want before you can feel that you have it, and prayer is the feeling of fulfilled desire. It does not matter what it is you seek in prayer, or where it is, or whom it concerns. You have nothing to do but convince yourself of the truth of that which you desire to see manifested. When you emerge from prayer you no longer seek, for you have—if you have prayed correctly—subconsciously assumed the reality of the state sought, and by the law of reversibility your subconscious assumption must objectify that which it affirms.

You must have a conductor to transmit a force. You may employ a wire, a jet of water, a current of air, a ray of light or any intermediary whatsoever. The principle of the photophone or the transmission of voice by light will help you to understand thought transmission, or the sending of a word to heal another. There is a strong analogy between a spoken voice and a mental voice. To think is to speak low, to speak is to think aloud. The principle of the photophone is this: A ray of light is reflected by a mirror and projected to a receiver at a distant point. Back of the mirror is a mouthpiece. By speaking into the mouthpiece you cause the mirror to vibrate. A vibrating mirror modifies the light reflected on it. The modified light has your speech to carry, not as speech, but as represented in its mechanical correlate. It reaches the distant station and impinges on a disk within the receiver; it causes the disk to vibrate according to the modification it undergoes—and it reproduces your voice.

"I am the light of the world." I am, the knowledge that I exist, is a light by means of which what passes in my mind is rendered visible. Memory, or my ability to mentally see what is not objectively present, proves that my mind is a mirror, and so sensitive a mirror that it can reflect a thought. The reperception of an image in memory in no way differs as a visual act from the perception of my image in a mirror.

[218] NEVILLE GODDARD

The same principle of seeing is involved in both.

Your consciousness is the light reflected on the mirror of your mind and projected in space to the one of whom you think. By mentally speaking to the subjective image in your mind you cause the mirror of your mind to vibrate. Your vibrating mind modifies the light of consciousness reflected on it. The modified light of consciousness reaches the one toward whom it is directed and impinges on the mirror of his mind; it causes his mind to vibrate according to the modifications it undergoes. Thus, it reproduces in him what was mentally affirmed by you.

Your beliefs, your fixed attitudes of mind, constantly modify your consciousness as it is reflected on the mirror of your mind. Your consciousness, modified by your beliefs, objectifies itself in the conditions of your world. To change the world, you must first change your conception of it. To change a man, you must change your conception of him. You must believe him to be the man you want him to be and mentally talk to him as though he were. All men are sufficiently sensitive to reproduce your beliefs of them. Therefore, if your word is not reproduced visibly in him toward whom it is sent, the cause is to be found in you, not in the subject. As soon as you believe in the truth of the state affirmed, results follow. Everyone can be transformed; every thought can be transmitted; every thought can be visibly embodied.

Subjective words—subconscious assumptions—awaken what they affirm. "They are living and active and shall not return unto me void, but shall accomplish that which I please, and shall prosper in the thing whereto I sent them." They are endowed with the intelligence pertaining to their mission and will persist until the object of their existence is realized; they persist until they awaken the vibratory correlates of themselves within the one toward whom they are directed, but the moment the object of their creation is accomplished they cease to be. The word spoken subjectively in quiet confidence will always awaken a corresponding state in the one for whom it was spoken; but the moment its task is accomplished it ceases to be, permitting the one in whom the state is realized to remain in the consciousness of the state affirmed or to return to his former state.

Whatever state has your attention holds your life. Therefore, to become attentive to a former state is to return to that condition. "Remember not the former things, neither consider the things of old."

Nothing can be added to man, for the whole of creation is already perfected within him. "The kingdom of heaven is within you." "Man can receive nothing, except it be given him from heaven." Heaven is your subconsciousness. Not even a sunburn is given from without. The rays without only awaken corresponding rays within. Were the burning rays not contained within man, all the concentrated rays in the universe could not burn him. Were the tones of health not contained within the consciousness of the one of whom they are affirmed, they could not be vibrated by the word which is sent. You do not really give to another—you resurrect that which is asleep within him. "The damsel is not dead, but sleepeth." Death is merely a sleeping and a forgetting. Age and decay are the sleep—not death—of youth and health. Recognition of a state vibrates or awakens it.

Distance, as it is cognized by your objective senses, does not exist for the subjective mind. "If I take the wings of the morning, and dwell in the uttermost parts of the sea; even there shall thy hand lead me." Time and space are conditions of thought; the imagination can transcend them and move in a psychological time and space. Although physically separated from a place by thousands of miles, you can mentally live in the distant place as though it were here. Your imagination can easily transform winter into summer, New York into Florida, and so on. Whether the object of your desire be near or far, results will be the same. Subjectively, the object of your desire is never far off; its intense nearness makes it remote from observation of the senses. It dwells in consciousness, and consciousness is closer than breathing and nearer than hands and feet.

Consciousness is the one and only reality. All phenomena are formed of the same substance vibrating at different rates. All is consciousness modified by belief. Out of consciousness I as man came, and to consciousness I as man return. In consciousness all states exist subjectively, and are awakened to their objective existence by belief. The only thing that prevents us from making a successful subjective impression on one at a great distance, or transforming there into here, is our habit of regarding space as an obstacle.

A friend a thousand miles away is rooted in your consciousness through your fixed ideas of him. To think of him and represent him to yourself inwardly in the state you desire him to be, confident that this subjective image is as true as though it were already objectified, awakens in him a corresponding state which he must objectify. The results will be as obvious as the cause was hidden. The subject will express the awakened state within him and remain unaware of the true cause of his action. Your illusion of free will is but ignorance of the causes which make you act. Prayers depend upon your attitude of mind for their success and not upon the attitude of the subject. The subject has no power to resist your controlled subjective ideas of him unless the state affirmed by you to be true of him is a state he is incapable of wishing as true of another. In that case, it returns to you, the sender, and will realize itself in you. Provided the idea is acceptable, success depends entirely on the operator not upon the subjects who, like compass needles on their pivots, are quite indifferent as to what direction you choose to give them. If your fixed idea is not subjectively accepted by the one toward whom it is directed, it rebounds to you from whom it came. "Who is he that will harm you, if ye be followers of that which is good? I have been young, and now am old; yet have I not seen the righteous forsaken, nor his seed begging bread." "There shall no evil happen to the just." Nothing befalls us that is not of the nature of ourselves.

A person who directs a malicious thought to another will be injured by its rebound if he fails to get subconscious acceptance of the other. "As ye sow, so shall ye reap." Furthermore, what you can wish and believe of another can be wished and believed of you, and you have no power to reject it if the one who desires it for you accepts it as true of you. The only power to reject a subjective word is to be incapable of wishing a similar state of another—to give presupposes the ability to receive. The possibility to impress an idea upon another mind presupposes the ability of that mind to receive that impression. Fools exploit the world; the wise transfigure it. It is the highest wisdom to know that in the living universe there is no destiny other than that created out of the imagination of man. There is no influence outside of the mind of man.

"Whatsoever things are lovely, whatsoever things are of good report; if there be any virtue, and if there be any praise, think on these things." Never accept as true of others what you would not want to be true of you. To awaken a state within another it first must be awake within you. The state you would transmit to another can be transmitted only if it is believed by you. Therefore, to give is to receive. You cannot give what you do not have and you have only what you believe. So to believe a state as true of another not only awakens that state within the other but it makes it alive within you. You are what you believe.

"Give and ye shall receive, full measure, pressed down and running over." Giving is simply believing, for what you truly believe of others you awaken within them. The vibratory state transmitted by your belief persists until it awakens its corresponding vibration in him of whom it is believed. But before it can be transmitted it must first be awake within the consciousness of the transmitter. Whatever is awake within your consciousness, you are. Whether the belief pertains to self or another does not matter, for the believer is defined by the sum total of his beliefs or subconscious assumptions.

"As a man thinketh in his heart"—in the deep subconscious of himself—"so is he." Disregard appearances and subjectively affirm as true that which you wish to be true. This awakens in you the tone of the state affirmed which in turn realizes itself in you and in the one of whom it is affirmed. Give and ye shall receive. Beliefs invariably awaken what they affirm. The world is a mirror wherein everyone sees himself reflected. The objective world reflects the beliefs of the subjective mind.

Some people are self-impressed best by visual images, others by mental sounds, and still others by mental actions. The form of mental activity which allows the whole power of your attention to be focused in one chosen direction is the one to cultivate, until you can bring all to play on your objective at the same time.

Should you have some difficulty in understanding the terms, "visual images," "mental sounds" and "mental actions," here is an illustration that should make their meanings clear: A imagines he sees a piece of music, knowing nothing at all about musical notations. The impression in his mind is a purely visual image. B imagines he sees the same piece, but he can read music and can imagine how it would sound when played on the piano; that imagination is mental sound. C also reads music and is a pianist; as he reads, he imagines himself playing the piece. The imaginary action is mental action.

The visual images, mental sounds and mental actions are creations of your imagination, and though they appear to come from without, they actually come from within yourself. They move as if moved by another but are really launched by your own spirit from the magical storehouse of imagination. They are projected into space by the same vibratory law that governs the sending of a voice or picture. Speech and images are projected not as speech or images but as vibratory correlates. Subjective mind vibrates according to the modifications it undergoes by the thought and feelings of the operator. The visible state created is the effect of the subjective vibrations. A feeling is always accompanied by a corresponding vibration, that is, a change in expression or sensation in the operator.

There is no thought or feeling without expression. No matter how motionless you appear to be if you reflect with any degree of intensity, there is always an execution of slight muscular movements. The eye, though shut, follows the movements of the imaginary objects and the pupil is dilated or contracted according to the brightness or the remoteness of those objects; respiration is accelerated or slowed, according to the course of your thoughts; the muscles contract correspondingly to your mental movements.

This change of vibration persists until it awakens a corresponding vibration in the subject, which vibration then expresses itself in a physical fact. "And the word was made flesh." Energy, as you see in the case of radio, is transmitted and received in a "field," a place where changes in space occur. The field and energy are one and inseparable. The field or subject becomes the embodiment of the word or energy received. The thinker and the thought, the operator and the subject, the energy and the field are one. Were you still enough to hear the sound of your beliefs you would know what is meant by "the music of the spheres." The mental sounds you hear in prayer as coming from without are really produced by yourself. Self-observation will reveal this fact. As the music of the spheres is defined as the harmony heard by the gods alone, and is supposed to be produced by the movements of the celestial spheres, so, too, is the harmony you subjectively hear for others heard by you alone and is produced by the movements of your thoughts and feelings in the true kingdom or "heaven within you."

Chapter 6
GOOD TIDINGS

"How beautiful upon the mountains are the feet of him that bringeth good tidings, that publisheth peace, that bringeth good tidings of good, that publisheth salvation."

A very effective way to bring good tidings to another is to call before your mind's eye the subjective image of the person you wish to help and have him affirm that he has done that which you desired him to do. Mentally hear him tell you that he has done it. This awakens within him the vibratory correlate of the state affirmed, which vibration persists until its mission is accomplished. It does not matter what it is you desire to have done, or whom you select to do it. As soon as you subjectively affirm that it is done, results follow. Failure can result only if you fail to accept the truth of your assertion or if the state affirmed would not be desired by the subject for himself or another. In the latter event, the state would realize itself in you, the operator.

The seemingly harmless habit of "talking to yourself" is the most fruitful form of prayer. A mental argument with the subjective image of another is the surest way to pray for an argument. You are asking to be offended by the other when you objectively meet. He is compelled to act in a manner displeasing to you, unless before the meeting you countermand or modify your order by subjectively affirming a change.

Unfortunately, man forgets his subjective arguments, his daily mental conversations with others, and so is at a loss for an explanation of the conflicts and misfortunes of his life. As mental arguments produce conflicts, so happy mental conversation produce corresponding visible states of good tidings. Man creates himself out of his own imagination.

If the state desired is for yourself, and you find it difficult to accept as true what your senses deny, call before your mind's eye the subjective image of a friend and have him mentally affirm that you are already that which you desire to be. This establishes in him, without his conscious consent or knowledge, the subconscious assumption that you are that which he mentally affirmed, which assumption, because it is unconsciously assumed, will persist until it fulfills its mission. Its mission is to awaken in you its vibratory correlate, which vibration when awakened in you realizes itself as an objective fact.

Another very effective way to pray for oneself is to use the formula of Job who found that his own captivity was removed as he prayed for his friends. Fix your attention on a friend and have the imaginary voice of your friend tell you that he is, or has that which is comparable to that which you desire to be or have. As you mentally hear and see him, feel the thrill of his good fortune and sincerely wish him well. This awakens in him the corresponding vibration of the state affirmed, which vibration must then objectify itself as a physical fact. You will discover the truth of the statement, "Blessed are the merciful for they shall receive mercy." "The quality of mercy is twice blessed—it blesses him who taketh and him who giveth." The good you subjectively accept as true of others will not only be expressed by them, but a full share will be realized by you.

Transformations are never total. Force A is always transformed into more than a force B. A blow with a hammer produces not only a mechanical concussion, but also heat, electricity, a sound, a magnetic change and so on. The vibratory correlate in the subject is not the entire transformation of the sentiment communicated. The gift transmitted to another is like the divine measure, pressed down, shaken together and running over, so that after the five thousand are fed from the five loaves and two fish, twelve baskets full are left over.

Chapter 7

THE GREATEST PRAYER

IMAGINATION is the beginning of creation. You imagine what you desire, and then you believe it to be true. Every dream could be realized by those self-disciplined enough to believe it. People are what you choose to make them; a man is according to the manner in which you look at him. You must look at him with different eyes before he will objectively change. "Two men looked from the prison bars, one saw the mud and the other saw the stars." Centuries ago, Isaiah asked the question: "Who is blind, but my servant, or deaf, as my messenger that I sent?" "Who is blind as he that is perfect, and blind as the Lord's servant?" The perfect man judges not after appearances, but judges righteously. He sees others as he desires them to be; he hears only what he wants to hear. He sees only the good in others. In him is no condemnation for he transforms the world with his seeing and hearing.

"The king that sitteth on the throne scattereth the evil with his eye." Sympathy for living things—agreement with human limitations—is not in the consciousness of the king because he has learned to separate their false concepts from their true being. To him poverty is but the sleep of wealth. He does not see caterpillars, but painted butterflies to be; not winter, but summer sleeping; not man in want, but Jesus sleeping. Jesus of Nazareth, who scattereth the evil with his eye, is asleep in the imagination of every man, and out of his own imagination must man awaken him by subjectively affirming "I AM Jesus." Then and only then will he see Jesus, for man can only see what is awake within himself. The holy womb is man's imagination. The holy child is that conception of himself which fits Isaiah's definition of perfection. Heed the words of St. Augustine, "Too late have I loved thee, for behold thou wert within and it was without that I did seek thee." It is to your own consciousness that you must turn as to the only reality. There, and there alone, you awaken that which is asleep. "Though Christ a thousand times in Bethlehem be bom, if He is not born in thee thy soul is still forlorn."

Creation is finished. You call your creation into being by feeling the reality of the state you would call. A mood attracts its affinities but it does not create what it attracts. As sleep is called by feeling "I am sleepy," so, too, is Jesus Christ called by the feeling, "I am Jesus Christ." Man sees only himself. Nothing befalls man that is not of the nature of himself. People emerge out of the mass betraying their close affinity to your moods as they are engendered. You meet them

[226] NEVILLE GODDARD

seemingly by accident but find they are intimates of your moods. Because your moods continually externalize themselves you could prophesy from your moods, that you, without search, would soon meet certain characters and encounter certain conditions. Therefore call the perfect one into being by living in the feeling, "I am Christ," for Christ is the one concept of self through which can be seen the unveiled realities of eternity.

Our behavior is influenced by our subconscious assumption respecting our own social and intellectual rank and that of the one we are addressing. Let us seek for and evoke the greatest rank, and the noblest of all is that which disrobes man of his mortality and clothes him with uncurbed immortal glory. Let us assume the feeling, "I am Christ," and our whole behavior will subtly and unconsciously change in accordance with that assumption.

Our subconscious assumptions continually externalize themselves that others may consciously see us as we subconsciously see ourselves, and tell us by their actions what we have subconsciously assumed ourselves to be. Therefore let us assume the feeling, "I AM Christ," until our conscious claim becomes our subconscious assumption that "We all with open face beholding as in a glass the glory of the Lord are changed into the same image from glory to glory." Let God awake and His enemies be destroyed. There is no greater prayer for man.

Seedtime And Harvest

THE FOUR MIGHTY ONES

"And a river went out of Eden to water the garden; and from thence it was parted, and became into four heads.". . . Genesis 2:10

"And every one had four faces: Ezekiel 10:14

"I see four men loose, walking in the midst of the fire, and they have no hurt; and the form of the fourth is like the Son of God." . . . Daniel 3:25

"Four Mighty Ones are in every man." . . . Blake

The "Four Mighty Ones" constitute the selfhood of man, or God in man. There are "Four Mighty Ones" in every man, but these "Four Mighty Ones" are not four separate beings, separated one from the other as are the fingers of his hand. The "Four Mighty Ones" are four different aspects of his mind, and differ from one another in function and character without being four separate selves inhabiting one man's body.

The "Four Mighty Ones" may be equated with the four Hebrew characters: (characters here) which form the four-lettered mystery-name of the Creative Power from and combining within itself the past, present and future forms of the verb "to be." The Tetragrammaton is revered as the symbol of the Creative Power in man -1 AM - the creative four functions in man reaching forth to realize in actual material phenomena qualities latent in Itself.

We can best understand the "Four Mighty Ones" by comparing them to the four most important characters in the production of a play.

"All the world's a stage, And all the men and women merely players; They have their exits and their entrances; And one man in his time plays many parts . . ."

- As You Like It Act II, Scene VII

The producer, the author, the director and the actor are the four most important characters in the production of a play. In the drama of life, the producer's function is to suggest the theme of a play. This he does in the form of a wish, such as, "I wish I were successful"; "I wish I could take a trip"; "I wish I were married:, and so on. But to appear on the world's stage, these general themes must somehow be specified and worked out in detail. It is not enough to say, "I wish I were successful"

- that is too vague. Successful at what? However, the first "Mighty

One" only suggests a theme.

The dramatization of the theme is left to the originality of the second "Might One", the author. In dramatizing the theme, the author writes only the last scene of the play - but this scene he writes in detail. The scene must dramatize the wish fulfilled. He mentally constructs as life-like a scene as possible of what he would experience had he realized his wish. When the scene is clearly visualized, the author's work is done.

The third "Mighty One" in the production of life's play is the director. The director's tasks are to see that the actor remains faithful to the script and to rehearse him over and over again until he is natural in the part. This function may be likened to a controlled and consciously directed attention - an attention focused exclusively on the action which implies that the wish is already realized.

"The form of the Fourth is like the Son of God" - human imagination, the actor. This fourth "Mighty One" performs within himself, in imagination, the pre-determined action which implies the fulfillment of the wish. This function does not visualize or observe the action. This function actually enacts the drama, and does it over and over again until it takes on the tones of reality. Without the dramatized vision of fulfilled desire, the theme remains a mere theme and sleeps forever in the vast chambers of unborn themes. Nor without the co-operant attention, obedient to the dramatized vision of fulfilled desire, will the vision perceived attain objective reality.

The "Four Mighty Ones" are the four quarters of the human soul. The first is Jehovah's King, who suggests the theme; the second is Jehovah's servant, who faithfully works out the theme in a dramatic vision; the third is Jehovah's man, who was attentive and obedient to the vision of fulfilled desire, who brings the wandering imagination back to the script "seventy times seven". The "Form of the Fourth" is Jehovah himself, who enacts the dramatized theme on the stage of the mind.

"Let this mind be in you, which was also in Christ Jesus: Who, being in the form of God, thought it not robbery to be equal with God: ..." - Philippians 2:5,6

The drama of life is a joint effort of the four quarters of the human soul.

"All that you behold, tho' it appears without, it is within, in your imagination, of which this world of mortality is but a shadow." - Blake

All that we behold is a visual construction contrived to express a theme - a theme which has been dramatized, rehearsed and performed elsewhere. What we are witnessing on the stage of the world is an optical construction devised to express the themes which have been dramatized, rehearsed and performed in the imagination of men.

The "Four Mighty Ones" constitute the Selfhood of man, or God in man: and all that man beholds, tho' it appears without, are but shadows cast upon the screen of space - optical constructions contrived by Selfhood to inform him in regard to the themes which he has conceived, dramatized, rehearsed and performed within himself.

"The creature was made subject unto vanity" that he may become conscious of Selfhood and its functions, for with consciousness of Selfhood and its functions, he can act to a purpose; he can have a consciously self-determined history. Without consciousness, he acts unconsciously, and cries to an objective God to save him from his own creation.

"O Lord, how long shall I cry, and Thou wilt not hear! Even cry out unto Thee of violence, and Thou wilt not save!" - Habakkuk 1:2

When man discovers that life is a play which he, himself, is consciously or unconsciously writing, he will cease from the blind, self-torture of executing judgment upon others. Instead, he will rewrite the play to conform to his ideal, for he will realize that all changes in the play must come from the cooperation of the "Four Mighty Ones" within himself. They alone can alter the script and produce the change.

All the men and women in his world are merely players and are as helpless to change his play as are the players on the screen of the theatre to change the picture. The desired change must be conceived, dramatized, rehearsed and performed in the theatre of his mind. When the fourth function, the imagination, has completed its task of rehearsing the revised version of the play until it is natural, then the curtain will rise upon this so seemingly solid world and the "Mighty Four" will cast a shadow of the real play upon the screen of space. Men and women will automatically play their parts to bring about the fulfillment of the dramatized theme. The players, by reason of their various parts in the world's drama, become relevant to the individual's dramatized theme and, because relevant, are drawn into his drama. They will play their parts, faithfully believing all the while that it was they themselves who initiated the parts they play. This they do because:

"Thou, Father, art in me, and I in thee, ... I in them, and thou in me." - John 17:21,23

I am involved in mankind. We are one. We are all playing the four parts of producer, author, director and actor in the drama of life. Some of us are doing it consciously, others unconsciously. It is necessary that we do it consciously. Only in this way can we be certain of a perfect ending to our play. Then we shall understand why we must become conscious of the four functions of the one God within ourselves that w may have the companionship of God as His Sons.

"Man should not stay a man:

Hs aim should higher be.

For God will only gods Accept as company."

- Angelus Silesius

In January of 1946, I took my wife and little daughter to Barbados in the British West Indies for a holiday. Not knowing there were any difficulties in getting a return passage, I had not booked ours before leaving New York. Upon our arrival in Barbados I discovered that there were only two ships serving the islands, one from Boston and one from New York. I was told there was no available space on either ship before September. As I had commitments in New York for the first week in May, I put my name on the long waiting list for the April sailing.

A few days later, the ship from New York was anchored in the harbor. I observed it very carefully, and decided that this was the ship we should take. I returned to my hotel and determined on an inner action that would be mine were we actually sailing on that ship. I settled down in an easy chair in my bedroom, to lose myself in this imaginative action.

I Barbados, we take a motor launch or rowboat out into the deep harbor when we embark on a large steamer. I knew I must catch the feeling that we were sailing on that ship. I chose the inner action of stepping from the tender and climbing up the gangplank of the steamer. The first time I tried, my attention wandered after I had reached the top of the gangplank. I brought myself back down, and tried again and again. I do not recall how many times I carried out this action in my imagination until I reached the deck and looked back at the port with the feeling of sweet sadness at departing. I was happy to be returning to my home in New York, but nostalgic in saying goodby to the lovely island and our family and friends. I do recall that in one of my many attempts at walking up the gangplank in the feeling that I was sailing, I fell asleep. After I awoke, I went about the usual social activities of the day and evening.

The following morning, I received a call from the steamship company requesting me to come down to their office and pick up our tickets for the April sailing. I was curious to know why Barbados had been chosen to receive the cancellation and why I, at the end of the long waiting list, was to have the reservation, but all that the agent could tell me was that a cable had been received that morning from New York, offering passage for three. I was not the first the agent had called, but for reasons she could not explain, those she had called said that now they found it inconvenient to sail in April. We sailed on April 20th and arrived in New York on the morning of May the first.

In the production of my play - the sailing on a boat that would bring me to New York by the first of May -1 played the four most important characters in my drama. As the producer, I decided to sail on a specific ship at a certain time. Playing the part of the author, I wrote the script -1 visualized the inner action which conformed to the outer action I would take if my desire were realized. As the director, I rehearsed myself, the actor, in that imagined action of climbing the gangplank until that action felt completely natural.

This being done, events and people moved swiftly to conform, in the outer world, to the play I had constructed and enacted in my imagination.

"I saw the mystic vision flow

And live in men and woods and streams.

Until I could no longer know

The stream of life from my own dreams."

- George William Russell (AE)

I told this story to an audience of mine in San Francisco, and a lady in the audience told me how she had unconsciously used the same technique, when she was a young girl.

The incident occurred on Christmas Eve. She was feeling very sad and tired and sorry for herself. Her father, whom she adored, had died suddenly. Not only did she feel this loss at the Christmas season, but necessity had forced her to give up her planned college years and go to work. This rainy Christmas Eve she was riding home on a San Diego street car. The car was filled with gay chatter of happy young people home for the holidays. To hide her tears from those round about her, she stood on the open part at the front of the car and turned her face into the skies to mingle her tears with the rain. With her eyes closed, and holding the rail of the car firmly, this is what she said to herself: "This is not the salt of the tears that I taste, but the salt of the sea in the wind. This is not San Diego, this is the South Pacific and I am sailing into the Bay of Samoa". And looking up, in her imagination, she constructed what she imagined to be the Southern Cross. She lost herself in this contemplation so that all faded round about her. Suddenly she was at the end of the line, and home.

Two weeks later, she received word from a lawyer in Chicago that he was holding three thousand dollars in American bonds for her. Several years before, an aunt of hers had gone to Europe, with instructions that these bonds be turned over to her niece if she did not return to the United States. The lawyer had just received word of the aunt's death, and was now carrying out her instructions.

A month later, this girl sailed for the islands in the South Pacific. It was night when she entered the Bay of Samoa. Looking down, she could see the white foam like a "bone in the lady's mouth" as the ship ploughed through the waves, and brought the salt of the sea in the wind. An officer on duty said to her: "There is the Southern Cross", and looking up, she saw the Southern Cross as she had imagined it.

In the intervening years, she had many opportunities to use her imagination constructively, but as she had done this unconsciously, she did not realize there was a Law behind it all. Now that she understands, she, too, is consciously playing her four major roles in the daily drama of her life, producing plays for the good of others as well as herself.

"Then the soldiers, when they had crucified Jesus, took his garments, and made four parts, to every soldier a part; and also his coat; now the coat was without seam, woven from the top throughout." - John 19:23

THE GIFT OF FAITH

"And the Lord had respect unto Abel and in his offerings; But unto Cain and to his offering he had no respect." - Genesis 4:4, 5

If we search the Scriptures, we will become aware of a far deeper meaning in the above quotation than that which a literal reading would give us. The Lord is non other than your own consciousness ". . . say unto the children of Israel, I AM hath sent me unto you . . .Exodus 3:14." "I AM" is the self-definition of the Lord.

Cain and Abel, as the grandchildren of the Lord, can be only personifications of two distinct functions of your own consciousness. The author is really concerned to show the "Two Contrary States of the Human Soul," and he has used two brothers to show these states. The two brothers represent two distinct outlooks on the world possessed by everyone. One is the limited perception of the senses, and the other is an imaginative view of the world. Cain - the first view - is a passive surrender to appearances and an acceptance of life on the basis of the world without: a view which inevitably leads to unsatisfied longing or a contentment with disillusion. Abel - the second view - is a vision of fulfilled desire, lifting man above the evidence of the senses to that state of relief where he no longer pines with desire. Ignorance of the second view is a soul on fire. Knowledge of the second view is the wing whereby it flies to the Heaven of fulfilled desire.

"Come, eat my bread and drink of the wind that I have mingled, forsake the foolish and live." Proverbs 9:56

In the epistle to the Hebrews, the writer tells us that Abel's offering was faith and, states the author, "Without faith it is impossible to please Him . . .Hebrews 11:6."

"Now faith is the substance of things hoped for, the evidence of things not seen. . . Through faith we understand that the worlds were framed by the word of God, so that things which are seen were not made of things which do appear." - Hebrews 11:1,3

Cain offers the evidence of the senses which consciousness, the Lord, rejects, because acceptance of this gift as a mold of the future would mean the fixation and perpetuation of the present state forever. The sick would be sick, the poor would be poor, the thief would be a thief, the murderer a murderer, and so on, without hope of redemption.

The Lord, or consciousness, has no respect for such passive use of imagination - which is the gift of Cain. He delights in the gift of Abel, the active, voluntary, loving exercise of the imagination on behalf of man for himself and others.

"Let the weak man say, I am strong.: - Joel 3:10

Let man disregard appearances and declare himself to be the man he wants to be. Let him imagine beauty where his senses reveal ashes, joy where they testify to mourning, riches where they bear witness to poverty. Only by such active, voluntary use of imagination can man be lifted up and Eden restored.

The ideal is always waiting to be incarnated, but unless we ourselves offer the ideal to the Lord, our consciousness, by assuming that we are already that which we seek to embody, it is incapable of birth. The Lord needs his daily lamb of faith to mold the world in harmony with our dreams.

"By faith Abel offered unto God a more excellent sacrifice than Cain." - Hebrews 11:4

Faith sacrifices the apparent fact for the unapparent truth. Faith holds fast to the fundamental truth that through the medium of an assumption, invisible states become visible facts.

For what is faith unless it is to believe what you do not see?" - St. Augustine

Just recently, I had the opportunity to observe the wonderful results of one who had the faith to believe what she did not see.

A young woman asked me to meet her sister and her three-year-old nephew. He was a fine, healthy lad with clear blue eyes and an exceptionally fine unblemished skin. Then, she told me her story.

At birth, the boy was perfect in every way save for a large, ugly birthmark covering one side of his face. Their doctor advised them that nothing could be done for this type of scar. Visits to many specialists only confirmed his statement. Hearing the verdict, the aunt set herself the task of proving he faith - that an assumption, though denied by the evidence of the senses, if persisted in, will harden into fact.

Every time she thought of the baby, which was often, she saw, in her imagination, an eightmonth-old baby with a perfect face - without any trace of a scar. This was not easy, but she knew that in this case, that was the gift of Abel which pleased God. She persisted in her faith - she believed what was not there to be seen. The result was that she visited her sister on the child's eight-month birthday and found him to have a perfect, unblemished skin with no trace of a birthmark ever having been present. "Luck! Coincidence! Shouts Cain. No. Abel knows that these are names given by those who have no faith, to the works of faith.

"We walk by faith, not by sight." - II Corinthians 5:7

When reason and the facts of life oppose the idea you desire to realize and you accept the evidence of your senses and the dictates of reason as the truth, you have brought the Lord - your consciousness - the gift of Cain. It is obvious that such offerings do not please Him.

Life on earth is a training ground for image making. If you use only the molds which your senses dictate, there will be no change in your life. You are here to live the more abundant life, so you must use the invisible molds of imagination and make results and accomplishments the crucial test of your power to create. Only as you assume the feeling of the wish fulfilled and continue therein are you offering the gift that pleases.

"When Abel's gift is my attire Then I'll realize my desire."

The Prophet Malachi complains that man has robbed God:

"But ye say, Wherein have we robbed thee? In tithes and offerings." - Malachi 3:8

Facts based upon reason and the evidence of the senses which oppose the idea seeking expression, rob you of the belief in the reality of the invisible state. But "faith is the evidence of things not seen", and through it "Good calleth those things which be not as though they were . . . Romans 4:17." Call the thing not seen; assume the feeling of your wish fulfilled.

". . .that there may be meat in mine house, and prove me now herewith, sayeth the Lord of hosts, if I will not open you the windows of heaven, and pour you out a blessing, that there shall not be room enough to receive it." - Malachi 3:10

This is the story of a couple living in Sacramento, California, who refused to accept the evidence of their senses, who refused to be robbed, in spite of a seeming loss. The wife had given her husband a very valuable wristwatch. The gift doubled its value because of the sentiment he attached to it. They had a little ritual with the watch. Every night as he removed the watch he gave it to her and she put it away in a special box in the bureau. Every morning she took the watch and gave it to him to put on.

One morning the watch was missing. They both remembered playing their usual parts the night before, therefore the watch was not lost or misplaced, but stolen. Then and there, they determined not to accept the fact that it was really gone. They said to each other, "This is an opportunity to practice what we believe." They decided that, in their imagination, they would enact their customary ritual as though the watch were actually there. In his imagination, every night the husband took off the watch and gave it to his wife, while in her imagination she accepted the watch and carefully put it away. Every morning she removed the watch from its box and gave it to her husband and he, in turn, put it on. This they did faithfully for two weeks.

After their fourteen-day vigil, a man went into the one and only jewelry store in Sacramento where the watch would be recognized. As he offered a gem for appraisal, the owner of the store noticed the wristwatch he was wearing. Under the pretext of needing a closer examination of the stone, he went into an inner office and called the police. After the police arrested the man, they found in his apartment over ten thousand dollars worth of stolen jewelry. In walking "by faith, not by sight", this couple attained their desire - the watch - and also aided many others in regaining what had seemed to be lost forever.

"If one advances confidently in the direction of his dream, and endeavors to live the life which he has imagined, he will meet with a success unexpected in common hours." - Thoreau

THE SCALE OF BEING

"And he dreamed, and behold a ladder set up on the earth, and the top of it reached to heaven: and behold the angels of God ascending and descending on it. And, behold, the Lord stood above it. . ." - Genesis 28:12, 13

In a dream, in a vision of the night, when deep sleep fell upon Jacob, his inner eye was opened and he beheld the world as a series of ascending and descending levels of awareness. It was a revelation of the deepest insight into the mysteries of the world. Jacob saw a vertical scale of ascending and descending values, or states of consciousness. This gave meaning to everything in the outer world, for without such a scale of values there would be no meaning to life.

At every moment of time, man stands upon the eternal scale of meaning. There is no object or event that has ever taken place or is taking place now that is without significance. The significance of an object or event for the individual is a direct index to the level of his consciousness.

You are holding this book, for example. On one level of consciousness, it is an object in space.

On a higher level, it is a series of letters on paper, arranged according to certain rules. On a still higher level, it is an expression of meaning.

Looking outwardly, you see the book first, but actually, the meaning comes first. It occupies a higher grade of significance than the letter arrangement on paper or the book as an object in space. Meaning determined the arrangement of letters; the arrangement of letters only expresses the meaning. The meaning is invisible and above the level of the visible arrangement of letters. If there had been on meaning to be expressed, no book would have been written and published.

"And, behold, the Lord stood above it."

The Lord and meaning are one - the Creator, the cause of the phenomena of life.

"In the beginning was the Word, and the Word was with God, and the Word was God." - John 1:1

In the beginning was the intention - the meaning - and the intention was with the intender, and the intention was the intender. The objects and events in time and space occupy a lower level of significance than the level of meaning which produced them. All things were made by meaning, and without meaning was not anything made that was made. The fact that everything seen can be regarded as the effect, on a lower level of significance, of an unseen higher order of significance is a very important one to grasp.

Our usual mode of procedure is to attempt to explain the higher levels of significance - why things happen - in terms of the lower - what and how things happen. For example, let us take an actual accident and try to explain it.

Most of us live on the level of what happened - the accident was an event in space - one automobile struck another and practically demolished it. Some of us live on the higher level of "how" the accident happened - it was a rainy night, the roads were slippery and the second car skidded into the first. On rare occasions, a few of us reach the highest or causal level of "why" such an accident occurs. Then we become aware of the invisible, the state of consciousness which produced the visible event.

In this case, the ruined car was driven by a widow, who, though she felt she could not afford to, greatly desired to change her environment. Having heard that, by the proper use of her imagination, she could do and be all she wished to be, this widow had been imagining herself actually living in the city of her desire. At the same time, she was living in a consciousness of loss, both personal and financial. Therefore, she brought upon herself an event which was seemingly another loss, but the sum of money the insurance company paid her allowed her to make the desired change in her life.

When we see the "why" behind the seeming accident, the state of consciousness that produced the accident, we are led to the conclusion that there is no accident. Everything in life has its invisible meaning.

The man who learns of an accident, the man who knows "how" it happened, and the man who knows "why" it happened are on three different levels of awareness in regard to that accident. On the ascending scale, each higher level carries us a step in advance towards the truth of the accident.

We should strive constantly to lift ourselves to the higher level of meaning, the meaning that is always invisible and above the physical event. But, remember, the meaning or cause of the phenomena of life can be found only within the consciousness of man.

Man is so engrossed in the visible side of the drama of life - the side of "what" has happened, and "how" it happened - that he rarely rises to the invisible side of "why" it happened. He refuses to accept the Prophet's warning that:

"Things which are seen were not made of things that do appear." - Hebrews 11:3

His descriptions of "what" has happened and "how" it happened are true in terms of his corresponding level of thought, but when he asks "why" it happened, all physical explanations break down and he is forced to seek the "why", or meaning of it, on the invisible and higher level. The mechanical analysis of events deals only with external relationships of things. Such a course will never reach the level which holds the secret of why the events happen. Man must recognize that the lower and visible sides flow from the invisible and higher level of meaning.

Intuition is needed to lift us up to the level of meaning - to the level of why things happen. Let us follow the advice of the Hebrew prophet of old and "lift up our eyes unto the hills" within ourselves, and observe what is taking place there. See what ideas we have accepted as true, what states we have consented to, what dreams, what desires - and, above all, what intentions. It is from these hills that all things come to reveal our stature - our height - on the vertical scale of meaning. If we lift our eyes to "the Thee in Me who works behind the Veil", we will see the meaning of the phenomena of life.

Events appear on the screen of space to express the different levels of consciousness of man. A change in the level of his consciousness automatically results in a change of the phenomena of his life. To attempt to change conditions before he changes the level of consciousness from whence they came, is to struggle in vain. Man redeems the world as he ascends the vertical scale of meaning.

We saw, in the analogy of the book, that as consciousness was lifted up to the level where man could see meaning expressed in the arrangement of its letters, it also included the knowledge that the letters were arranged according to certain rules, and that such arrangements, when printed on paper and bound together, formed a book. What is true of the book is true of every event in the world.

"They shall not hurt or destroy in all my holy mountain: for the earth shall be full of the knowledge of the Lord, as the waters cover the sea." - Isaiah 11:9

Nothing is to be discarded; all is to be redeemed. Our lives, ascending the vertical scale of meaning towards an ever increasing awareness - an awareness of things of higher significance - are the process whereby this redemption is brought to pass. As man arranges letters into words, and words into sentences to express meaning, in like manner, life arranges circumstances, conditions and events to express the unseen meanings or attitudes of men. Nothing is without significance. But man, not knowing the higher level of inner meaning, looks out upon a moving panorama of events and sees no meaning to life. There is always a level of meaning determining events and their essential relationship to our lives.

Here is a story that will enable us to seize the good in things seeming evil; to withhold judgment, and to act aright amid unsolved problems.

Just a few years ago, our country was shocked by a seeming injustice in our midst. The story was told on radio and television, as well as in the newspapers. You may recall the incident. The body of a young American soldier killed in Korea was returned to his home for burial. Just before the service, his wife was asked a routine question: Was her husband a Caucasian? When she replied that he was an Indian, burial was refused. This refusal was in accordance with the laws of that community, but it aroused the entire nation. We felt incensed that anyone who had been killed in the service of his country should be denied burial anywhere in his country. The story reached the attention of the President of the United States, and he offered burial with full military honors in Arlington National Cemetery. After the service, the wife told reporters that her husband had always dreamed of dying a hero, and having a hero's burial service with full military honors.

When, we in America, had to explain why progressive, intelligent people like ourselves, not only enacted but supported such laws in our great land of the free and the brave, we were hard put for an explanation. We, as observers, had seen only "what" happened, and "how" it happened. We failed to see "why" it happened.

That burial had to be refused if that lad was to realize his dream. We tried to explain the drama in terms of the lower level of "how" it happened, which explanation could not satisfy the one who had asked "why" it happened.

The true answer, viewed from the level of higher meaning, would be such a reversal of our common habits of thinking that it would be instantly rejected. The truth is that future states are causative of present facts - the Indian boy dreaming of a hero's death, with full military honors, was like Lady Macbeth transported "beyond this ignorant present", and could "feel now the future in the instant."

". . . and by it he being dead yet speaketh." - Hebrews 11:4

THE GAME OF LIFE

"I can easier teach twenty what were good to be done, than be one of the twenty to follow mine own teaching." - Shakespeare

With this confession off my mind, I will now teach you how to play the game of life. Life is a game and, like all games, it has its aims and its rules.

In the little games that men concoct, such as cricket, tennis, baseball, football, and so on, the rules may be changed from time to time. After the changes are agreed upon, man must learn the new rules and play the game within the framework of the accepted rules.

However, in the game of life, the rules cannot be changed or broken. Only within the framework of its universal and everlastingly fixed rules can the game of life be played.

The game of life is played on the playing field of the mind. In playing a game, the first thing we ask is: "What is its aim and purpose?" and the second, "What are the rules governing the game?" In the game of life, our chief aim is towards increasing awareness - an awareness of things of greater significance; and our second aim is towards achieving our goals, realizing our desires.

As to our desires, the rules reach only so far as to indicate the way in which we should go to realize them, but the desires themselves must be the individual's own concern. The rules governing the game of life are simple, but it takes a lifetime of practice to use them wisely. Here is one of the rules:

"As he thinketh in his heart, so is he." - Proverbs 23:7

Thinking is usually believed to be a function entirely untrammeled and free, without any rules to constrain it. But that is not true. Thinking moves by its own processes in a bounded territory, with definite paths and patterns.

"Thinking follows the tracks laid down in one's own inner conversations."

All of us can realize our objectives by the wise use of mind and speech. Most of us are totally unaware of the mental activity which goes on within us. But to play the game of life successfully, we must become aware of our every mental activity, for this activity, in the form of inner conversations, is the cause of the outer phenomena of our life.

". . . every idle word that man shall speak, they shall give account thereof in the day of judgment. For by thy words thou shall be justified, and by thy words thou shalt be condemned." - Matthew 12:36,37

The law of the Word cannot be broken.

". . .A bone of him shall not be broken." - John 19:36

The law of the Word never overlooks an inner word nor makes the smallest allowance for our ignorance of its power. It fashions life about us as we, by our inner conversations, fashion life within ourselves. This is done to reveal to us our position on the playing field of life. There is no opponent in the game of life; there is only the goal.

Not long ago, I was discussing this with a successful and philanthropic business man. He told me a though-provoking story about himself.

He said, "You know, Neville, I first learned about goals in life when I was fourteen, and it was on the playing field at school. I was good at track and had a fine day, but there was one more race to run and I had stiff competition in one other boy. I was determined to beat him. I beat him, it is true, but, while I was keeping my eye on him, a third boy, who was considered no competition at all, won the race."

"That experience taught me a lesson I have used throughout my life. When people ask me about my success, I must say, that I believe it is because I have never made 'making money' my goal: 'My goal is the wise, productive use of money'."

This man's inner conversations are based on the premise that he already has money, his constant inner question: the proper use of it. The inner conversations of the man struggling to 'get' money only prove his lack of money. In his ignorance of the power of the word, he is building barriers in the way of the attainment of his goal; he has his eye on the competition rather than on the goal itself.

"The fault, dear Brutus, is not in our stars, But in ourselves, that we are underlings."

- Julius Caesar: Act I, Scene II

As "the worlds were framed by the Word of God", so we as "imitators of God as dear children" create the conditions and circumstances of our lives by our all-powerful human inner words. Without practice, the most profound knowledge of the game would produce no desired results.

"To him that knoweth to do good" - that is, knoweth the rules - and doeth it not, to him it is sin". In other words, he will miss his mark and fail to realize his goal.

In the parable of the Talents, the Master's condemnation of the servant who neglected to use his gift is clear and unmistakable, and having discovered one of the rules of the game of life, we risk failure by ignoring it. The talent not used, like the limb not exercised, slumbers and finally atrophies. We must be "doers of the Word, and not hearers only". Since thinking follows the tracks laid down in one's own inner conversations, not only can we see where we are going on the playing field of life by observing our inner conversations, but also, we can determine where we will go by controlling and directing our inner talking.

What would you think and say and do were you already the one you want to be? Begin to think and say and do this inwardly. You are told that "there is a rod in heaven that revealeth secrets," and, you must always remember that heaven is within you; and to make it crystal clear who God is, where He is, and what His secrets are, Daniel continues, "Thy dream, and the visions of thy head are these". They reveal the tracks to which you are tied, and point the direction in which you are going.

This is what one woman did to turn the tracks to which she had been unhappily tied in the direction in which she wanted to go. For two years, she had kept herself estranged from the three people she loved most. She had had a quarrel with her daughter-in-law, who ordered her from her home. For those two years, she had not seen or heard from her son, her daughter-in-law or her grandson, though she had sent her grandson numerous gifts in the meantime. Every time she thought of her family, which was daily, she carried on a mental conversation with her daughter-inlaw, blaming her for the quarrel and accusing her of being selfish.

Upon hearing a lecture of mine one night - it was this very lecture on the game of life and how to play it - she suddenly realized she was the cause of the prolonged silence and that she, and she alone, must do something about it. Recognizing that her goal was to have the former loving relationship, she set herself the task of completely changing her inner talking.

That very night, in her imagination, she constructed two loving, tender letters written to her, one from her daughter-in-law and the other from her grandson. In her imagination, she read them over and over again until she fell asleep in the joyful mood of having received the letters. She repeated this imaginary act each night for eight nights. On the morning of the ninth day, she received one envelope containing two letters, one from her daughter-in-law, one from her grandson. They were loving, tender letters inviting her to visit them, almost replicas of those she had constructed mentally. By using her imagination consciously and lovingly, she had turned the tracks to which she was tied, in the direction she wanted to go, towards a happy family reunion.

A change of attitude is a change of position on the playing field of life. The game of life is not being played out there in what is called space and time; the real moves in the game of life take place within, on the playing field of the mind.

"Losing thy soul, thy soul Again to find;

Rendering toward that goal Thy separate mind."

- Laurence Housman

"TIME, TIMES, AND AN HALF"

"And one said to the man clothed in linen, which was upon the waters of the river, How long shall it be to the end of these wonders?

And I heard the man clothed in linen, which was upon the waters of the river, when he held up his right hand and his left hand unto heaven, and swear by him that liveth forever that it shall be for a time, times, and an half." - Daniel 12:6, 7

At one of my lectures given in Los Angeles on the subject of the hidden meaning behind the stories of the Bible, someone asked me to interpret the above quotation from the Book of Daniel. After I confessed I did not know the meaning of that particular passage, a lady in the audience said to herself, "If the mind behaves according to the assumption with which it starts, then I will find the true answer to that question and tell it to Neville." And this is what she told me.

"Last night the question was asked: 'What is the meaning of "time, times, and an half" as recorded in Daniel 12:7?' Before going to sleep last night I said to myself, 'Now there is a simple answer to this question, so I will assume that I know it and while I am sleeping my greater self will find the answer and reveal it to my lesser self in dream or vision.'"

"Around five A.M. I awakened. It was too early to rise, so remaining in bed I quickly fell into that half dreamy state between waking and sleeping, and while in that state a picture came into my mind of an old lady. She was sitting in a rocking chair and rocking back and forth, back and forth. Then a voice which sounded like your voice said to me: 'Do it over and over and over again until it takes on the tones of reality.'"

"I jumped out of bed and re-read the Twelfth Chapter of Daniel, and this is the intuitive answer I received. Taking the sixth and seventh verses, for they constituted last night's question, I felt that if the garments with which Biblical characters are clothed correspond to their level of consciousness, as you teach, then linen must represent a very high level of consciousness indeed, for the 'man clothed in linen' was standing 'upon the waters of the river' and if, as you teach, water symbolizes a high level of psychological truth, then the individual who could walk upon it must truly represent an exalted state of consciousness. I therefore felt that what he had to say must indeed be very significant. Now the question asked of him was 'How long shall it be to the end of these wonders?' And his answer was, 'A time, times, and an half.' Remembering my vision of the old lady rocking

[247] THE POWER OF IMAGINATION: THE NEVILLE GODDARD TREASURY

back and forth, and your voice telling me to 'do it over and over and over again until it takes on the tones of reality', and remembering that this vision and your instruction came to me in response to my assumption that I knew the answer, I intuitively felt that the question asked the 'man clothed in linen' meant how long shall it be until the wonderful dreams that I am dreaming become a reality. And his answer is, 'Do it over and over and over again until it takes on the tones of reality'. 'A time' means to perform the imaginary action which implies the fulfillment of the wish;

'Times' mean to repeat the imaginary action over and over again, and 'an half means the moment of falling asleep while performing the imaginary action, for such a moment usually arrives before the pre-determined action is completed and, therefore, can be said to be a half, or part, of a time."

To get such inner understanding of the Scriptures by the simple assumption that she did know the answer, was a wonderful experience for this woman. However, to know the true meaning of "time, times, and an half" she must apply her understanding in her daily life. We are never at a loss in an opportunity to test this understanding, either for ourselves or for another.

A number of years ago, a widow living in the same apartment house as we, came to see me about her cat. The cat was her constant companion and dear to her heart. He was, however, eight years old, very ill and in great pain. He had not eaten for days and would not move from under her bed. Two veterinarians had seen the cat and advised the woman that the cat could not be cured, and that he should be put to sleep immediately. I suggested that that night, before retiring, she create in her imagination some action that would indicate the cat was its former healthy self. I advised her to do it over and over again until it took on the tones of reality.

This, she promised to do. However, either from lack of faith in my advice or from lack of faith in her own ability to carry out the imaginary action, she asked her niece to spend the night with her. This request was made so that if the cat were not well by morning, the niece could take it to the veterinarian's and she, the owner, would not have to face such a dreaded task herself. That night, she settled herself in an easy chair and began to imagine the cat was romping beside her, scratching at the furniture and doing many things she would not normally have allowed. Each time she found that her mind had wandered from its pre-determined task to see a normal, healthy, frisky cat, she brought her attention back to the room and started her imaginary action over again. This she did over and over again until, finally, in a feeling of relief, she dropped off to sleep, still seated in her chair.

At about four o'clock in the morning, she was awakened by the cry of her cat. He was standing by her chair. After attracting her attention, he led her to the kitchen where he begged for food. She fixed him a little warm milk which he quickly drank, and cried for more.

That cat lived comfortably for five more years, when, without pain or illness, he died naturally in his sleep.

"How long shall it be to the end of these wonders?. . .

A time, times, and an half.

In a dream in a vision of the night, when deep sleep falleth upon men, in slumberings upon the bed;

Then he openeth the ears of men, and sealeth their instructions."

-Job 33:15, 16

BE YE WISE AS SERPENTS

". . .be ye therefore wise as serpents, and harmless as doves." - Matthew 10:16

The serpent's ability to form its skin by ossifying a portion of itself, and its skill in shedding each skin as it outgrew it, caused man to regard this reptile as a symbol of the power of endless growth and self-reproduction. Man is told, therefore, to be "wise as the serpent" and learn how to shed his skin - his environment - which is his solidified self; man must learn how to "loose him, and let him go". . . how to "put off the old man". . .how to die to the old and yet know, like the serpent, that he "shall not surely die".

Man has not learned as yet that all that is outside his physical body is also a part of himself, that his world and all the conditions of his life are but the outpicturing of his state of consciousness. When he knows this truth, he will stop the futile struggle of self-contention and, like the serpent, let the old go and grow a new environment.

"Man is immortal; therefore he must die endlessly. For life is a creative idea; it can only find itself in changing forms." - Tagore

In ancient times, serpents were also associated with the guardianship of treasure or wealth. The injunction to be "wise as serpents" is the advice to man to awaken the power of his subtilized body - his imagination - that he, like the serpent, may grow and outgrow, die and yet not die, for from such deaths and resurrections alone, shedding the old and putting on the new, shall come fulfillment of his dreams and the finding of his treasures. As "the serpent was more subtil than any beast of the field which the Lord God had made" - Genesis 3:1 - even so, imagination is more subtile than any creature of the heavens which the Lord God had created. Imagination is the creature that:

". . .was made subject to vanity, not willingly, but by reason of him who hath subjected the same in hope. . .For we are saved by hope: but hope that is seen is not hope: for what a man seeth, why doth he yet hope for it? But if we hope for that we see not, then do we have patience wait for it." - Romans 8:20, 24, 25

Although the outer, or "natural", man of the senses is interlocked with his environment, the inner, or spiritual, man of imagination is not thus interlocked. If the interlocking were complete, the charge to be "wise as serpents" would be in vain. Were we completely interlocked with our environment, we could not withdraw our attention from the evidence of the senses and feel ourselves into the situation of our fulfilled desire, in hope that that unseen state would solidify as our new environment. But:

"There is a natural body, and there is a spiritual body." -1 Corinthians 15:44

The spiritual body of imagination is not interlocked with man's environment. The spiritual body can withdraw from the outer man of sense and environment and imagine itself to be what it wants to be. And if it remains faithful to the vision, imagination will build for man a new environment in which to live. This is what is meant by the statement:

. .1 go to prepare a place for you. And if I go and prepare a place for you, I will come again, and receive you unto myself; that where I am, there ye may be also."

-John 14:2, 3

The place that is prepared for you need not be a place in space. It can be health, wealth, companionship, anything that you desire in this world. Now, how is the place prepared?

You must first construct as life-like a representation as possible of what you would see and hear and do if you were physically present and physically moving about in that "place." Then, with your physical body immobilized, you must imagine that you are actually in that "place" and are seeing and hearing and doing all that you would see and hear and do if you were there physically. This you must do over and over again until it takes on the tones of reality. When it feels natural, the "place" has been prepared as the new environment for your outer or physical self. Now you may open your physical eyes and return to your former state. The "place" is prepared, and where you have been in imagination, there you shall be in the body also.

How this imagined state is realized physically is not the concern of you, the natural or outer man. The spiritual body, on its return from the imagined state to its former physical state, created an invisible bridge of incident to link the two states. Although the curious feeling that you were actually there and that the state was real is gone, as soon as you open your eyes upon the old familiar environment, nevertheless, you are haunted with the sense of a double identity - with the knowledge that "there is a natural body, and there is a spiritual body." When you, the natural man, have had this experience you will go automatically across the bridge of events which leads to the physical realization of your invisibly prepared place.

This concept - that man is dual and that the inner man of imagination can dwell in future states and return to the present moment with a bridge of events to link the two - clashes violently with the widely accepted view about the human personality and the cause and nature of phenomena. Such a concept demands a revolution in current ideas about the human personality, and about space, time and matter. The concept that man, consciously or unconsciously, determines the conditions of life by imagining himself into these mental states, leads to the conclusion that this supposedly solid world is a construction of Mind - a concept which, at first, common sense rejects. However, we should remember that most of the concepts which common sense at first rejected, man was afterward forced to accept. These never-ending reversals of judgment which experience has forced upon man led Professor Whitehead to write: "Heaven knows what seeming nonsense may not tomorrow be demonstrated truth."

The creative power in man sleeps and needs to be awakened.

"Awake thou that sleepest, and arise from the dead." - Ephesians 5:14

Wake from the sleep that tells you the outer world is the cause of the conditions of your life. Rise from the dead past and create a new environment.

"Know ye not that ye are the temple of God, and that the Spirit of God dwelleth in you?"

-1 Corinthians 3:16

The Spirit of God in you is your imagination, but it sleeps and needs to be awakened, in order to lift you off the bar of the senses where you have so long lain stranded.

The boundless possibilities open to you as you become "wise as serpents" is beyond measure. You will select the ideal conditions you want to experience and the ideal environment you want to live in. Experiencing these states in imagination until they have sensory vividness, you will externalize them as surely as the serpent now externalizes its skin.

After you have outgrown them, then, you will cast them off as easily as "the snake throws her enamell'd skin". The more abundant life - the whole purpose of Creation - cannot be saved through death and resurrection.

God desired form, so He became man: and it is not enough for us to recognize His spirit at work in creation, we must see His work in form and say that it is good, even though we outgrow the form, forever and ever.

"He leads

Through widening chambers of delight to where Throbs rapture near an end that aye recedes,

Because His touch is Infinite and lends A yonder to all ends."

"And, I, if I be lifted up from the earth, will draw all men unto me."
- John 12:32

If I be lifted up from the evidence of the senses to the state of consciousness I desire to realize and remain in that state until it feels natural. I will form that state around me and all men will see it. But how to persuade man this is true - that imaginative life is the only living; that assuming the feeling of the wish fulfilled is the way to the more abundant life and not the compensation of the escapist - that is the problem. To see as "though widening chambers of delight" what living in the realms of imagination means, to appreciate and enjoy the world, one must live imaginatively; one must dream and occupy his dream, then grow and outgrow the dream, forever and ever. The unimaginative man, who will not lose his life on one level that he may find it on a higher level, is nothing but a Lot's wife - a pillar of self-satisfied salt. On the other hand, those who refuse form as being unspiritual and who reject incarnation as separate from God are ignorant of the great mystery: "Great is the mystery, God was manifest in the flesh."

Your life expresses one thing, and one thing only, your state of consciousness. Everything is dependent upon that. As you, through the medium of imagination, assume a state of consciousness, that state begins to clothe itself in form, It solidifies around you as the serpent's skin ossifies around it. But you must be faithful to the state. You must not go from state to state, but, rather, wait patiently in the one invisible state until it takes on form and becomes an objective fact. Patience is necessary, but patience will be easy after your first success in shedding the old and growing the new, for we are able to wait according as we have been rewarded by understanding in the past. Understanding is the secret of patience. What natural joy and spontaneous delight lie in seeing the world - not with, but as Blake says - through the eye! Imagine that you are seeing what you want to see, and remain faithful to your vision. Your imagination will make for itself a corresponding form in which to live.

All things are made by imagination's power. Nothing begins except in the imagination of man. "From within out" is the law of the universe. "As within, so without." Man turns outward in his search for truth, but the essential thing is to look within.

"Truth is within ourselves; it takes no rise From outward things, what e'er you may believe.

There is an inmost center in us all,

Where truth abides in fullness .. . and to know,

Rather consist in opening out a way Whence the imprisoned splendor may escape,

Than in effecting entry for a light Supposed to be without."

- Browning: "Paracelsus"

I think you will be interested in an instance of how a young woman shed the skin of resentment and put on a far different kind of skin. The parents of this woman had separated when she was six years old and she had lived with her mother. She rarely saw her father. But once a year he sent her a five dollar check for Christmas. Following her marriage, he did increase the Christmas gift to ten dollars.

After one of my lectures, she was dwelling on my statement that man's suspicion of another is only a measure of his own deceitfulness, and she recognized that she had been harboring a resentment towards her father for years. That night she resolved to let go her resentment and put a fond reaction in its place. In her imagination, she felt she was embracing her father in the warmest way. She did it over and over again until she caught the spirit of her imaginary act, and then she fell asleep in a very contented mood.

The following day she happened to pass through the fur department of one of our large stores in California. For some time she had been toying with the idea of having a new fur scarf, but felt she could not afford it. This time her eye was caught by a stone marten scarf, and she picked it up and tired it on. After feeling it and seeing herself in it, reluctantly she took off the scarf and returned it to the salesman, telling herself she really could not afford it. As she was leaving the department, she stopped and thought, "Neville tells we can have whatever we desire if we will only capture the feeling of already having it." In her imagination, she put the scarf back on, felt the reality of it, and went about her shopping, all the while enjoying the imagined wearing of it.

This young woman never associated these two imaginary acts. In fact, she had almost forgotten what she had done until, a few weeks later, on Mother's Day, the doorbell rang unexpectedly.

There was her father. As she embraced him, she remembered her first imaginary action. As she opened the package he had brought her - the first gift in these many years - she remembered her second imaginary action, for the box contained a beautiful stone marten scarf.

"Ye are gods; and all of you are children of the most High." - Psalms 82:6

". . .be ye therefore wise as serpents, and harmless as doves." - Matthew 10:16

Power Of Awareness

I AM

Leave the mirror and change your face. Leave the world alone and change your conceptions of yourself.

I AM

All things, when they are admitted, are made manifest by the light: for everything that is made manifest is light. Ephesians 5:13

THE "LIGHT" is consciousness. Consciousness is one, manifesting in legions of forms or levels of consciousness.

There is no one that is not all that is, for consciousness, though expressed in an infinite series of levels, is not divisional. There is no real separation or gap in consciousness. I AM cannot be divided. I may conceive myself to be a rich man, a poor man, a beggar man or a thief, but the center of my being remains the same, regardless of the concept I hold of myself. At the center of manifestation, there is only one I AM manifesting in legions of forms or concepts of itself and "I am that I am".

I AM is the self-definition of the absolute, the foundation on which everything rests. I AM is the first cause-substance. I AM is the self-definition of God.

I AM hath sent me unto you. [Exodus 3:14] I AM THAT I AM. [Exodus 3:14]

Be still and know that I AM God. [Psalm 46:10]

I AM is a feeling of permanent awareness. The very center of consciousness is the feeling of I AM. I may forget who I am, where I am, what I am, but I cannot forget that I AM. The awareness of being remains, regardless of the degree of forgetfulness of who, where and what I am.

I AM is that which, amid unnumbered forms, is ever the same.

This great discovery of cause reveals that, good or bad, man is actually the arbiter of his own fate, and that it is his concept of himself that determines the world in which he lives [and his concept of himself is his reactions to life]. In other words, if you are experiencing ill health, knowing the truth about cause, you cannot attribute the illness to anything other than to the particular arrangement of the basic cause-substance, an arrangement which [was produced by your reactions to life, and] is defined by your concept "I am unwell". This is why you are told "Let the weak man say, 'I am strong'" (Joel 3:10), for by his assumption, the cause-substance – I AM – is rearranged and must, therefore, manifest that which its rearrangement affirms. This principle governs every aspect of your life, be it social, financial, intellectual, or spiritual.

I AM is that reality to which, whatever happens, we must turn for an explanation of the phenomena of life. It is I AM's concept of itself that determines the form and scenery of its existence.

Everything depends upon its attitude towards itself; that which it will not affirm as true of itself cannot awaken in its world.

That is, your concept of yourself, such as "I am strong", "I am secure", "I am loved", determines the world in which you live. In other words, when you say, "I am a man, I am a father, I am an American", you are not defining different I AM's; you are defining different concepts or arrangements of the one causc-substance – the one I AM.

Even in the phenomena of nature, if the tree were articulate, it would say, "I am a tree, an apple tree, a fruitful tree".

When you know that consciousness is the one and only reality – conceiving itself to be something good, bad or indifferent, and becoming that which it conceived itself to be – you are free from the tyranny of second causes, free from the belief that there are causes outside of your own mind that can affect your life.

In the state of consciousness of the individual is found the explanation of the phenomena of life.

If man's concept of himself were different, everything in his world would be different.

His concept of himself being what it is, everything in his world must be as it is.

Thus it is abundantly clear that there is only one I AM and you are that I AM.

And while I AM is infinite, you, by your concept of yourself, are displaying only a limited aspect of the infinite I AM.

Build thee more stately mansions, O, my soul,

As the swift seasons roll! Leave thy low-vaulted past!

Let each new temple, nobler than the last,

Shut thee from heaven with a dome more vast

Till thou at length art free, Leaving thine outgrown shell by life's unresting sea!

[Oliver Wendell Holmes, Sr., "The Chambered Nautilus"]

1.CONSCIOUSNESS

IT IS only by a change of consciousness, by actually changing your concept of yourself, that you can "build more stately mansions" – the manifestations of higher and higher concepts.

(By manifesting is meant experiencing the results of these concepts in your world.)

It is of vital importance to understand clearly just what consciousness is.

The reason lies in the fact that consciousness is the one and only reality, it is the first and only cause-substance of the phenomena of life.

Nothing has existence for man save through the consciousness he has of it.

Therefore, it is to consciousness you must turn, for it is the only foundation on which the phenomena of life can be explained.

If we accept the idea of a first cause, it would follow that the evolution of that cause could never result in anything foreign to itself. That is, if the first cause-substance is light, all its evolutions, fruits and manifestations would remain light.

The first cause-substance being consciousness, all its evolutions, fruits and phenomena must remain consciousness.

All that could be observed would be a higher or lower form or variation of the same thing. In other words, if your consciousness is the only reality, it must also be the only substance.

Consequently, what appears to you as circumstances, conditions and even material objects is really only the product of your own consciousness.

Nature, then, as a thing or a complex of things external to your mind, must be rejected.

You and your environment cannot be regarded as existing separately. You and your world are one.

Therefore, you must turn from the objective appearance of things to the subjective center of things, your consciousness, if you truly desire to know the cause of the phenomena of life, and how to use this knowledge to realize your fondest dreams.

In the midst of the apparent contradictions, antagonisms and contrasts of your life, there is only one principle at work, only your consciousness operating.

Difference does not consist in variety of substance, but in variety of arrangement of the same cause-substance, your consciousness.

The world moves with motiveless necessity. By this is meant that it has no motive of its own, but is under the necessity of manifesting your concept, the arrangement of your mind, and your mind is always arranged in the image of all you believe and consent to as true.

The rich man, poor man, beggar man or thief are not different minds, but different arrangements of the same mind, in the same sense that a piece of steel, when magnetized, differs not in substance from its demagnetized state, but in the arrangement and order of its molecules. A single electron revolving in a specified orbit constitutes the unit of magnetism. When a piece of steel or anything else is demagnetized, the revolving electrons have not stopped. Therefore, the magnetism has not gone out of existence.

There is only a rearrangement of the particles, so that they produce no outside or perceptible effect. When particles are arranged at random, mixed up in all directions, the substance is said to be demagnetized; but when particles are marshaled in ranks so that a number of them face in one direction, the substance is a magnet. Magnetism is not generated; it is displayed.

Health, wealth, beauty and genius are not created; they are only manifested by the arrangement of your mind – that is, by your concept of yourself [and your concept of yourself is all that you accept and consent to as true. What you consent to can only be discovered by an uncritical observation of your reactions to life. Your reactions reveal where you live psychologically; and where you live psychologically determines how you live here in the outer visible world].

The importance of this in your daily life should be immediately apparent. The basic nature of the primal cause is consciousness.

Therefore, the ultimate substance of all things is consciousness.

2.POWER OF ASSUMPTION

MAN'S CHIEF delusion is his conviction that there are causes other than his own state of consciousness.

All that befalls a man – all that is done by him, all that comes from him – happens as a result of his state of consciousness.

A man's consciousness is all that he thinks and desires and loves, all that he believes is true and consents to. That is why a change of consciousness is necessary before you can change your outer world.

Rain falls as a result of a change in the temperature in the higher regions of the atmosphere, so, in like manner, a change of circumstance happens as a result of a change in your state of consciousness.

Be ye transformed by the renewing of your mind. [Romans 12:2]

To be transformed, the whole basis of your thoughts must change. But your thoughts cannot change unless you have new ideas, for you think from your ideas.

All transformation begins with an intense, burning desire to be transformed. The first step in the "renewing of the mind" is desire.

You must want to be different [and intend to be] before you can begin to change yourself.

Then you must make your future dream a present fact. You do this by assuming the feeling of your wish fulfilled. By desiring to be other than what you are, you can create an ideal of the person you want to be and assume that you are already that person. If this assumption is persisted in until it becomes your dominant feeling, the attainment of your ideal is inevitable.

The ideal you hope to achieve is always ready for an incarnation, but unless you yourself offer it human parentage, it is incapable of birth.

Therefore, your attitude should be one in which having desired to express a higher state – you alone accept the task of incarnating this new and greater value of yourself.

In giving birth to your ideal, you must bear in mind that the methods of mental and spiritual knowledge are entirely different.

This is a point that is truly understood by probably not more than one person in a million.

You know a thing mentally by looking at it from the outside, by comparing it with other things, by analyzing it and defining it [by thinking of it]; whereas you can know a thing spiritually only by becoming it [only by thinking from it].

You must be the thing itself and not merely talk about it or look at it.

You must be like the moth in search of his idol, the flame, who spurred with true desire, plunging at once into the sacred fire, folded his wings within, till he became one color and one substance with the flame.

He only knew the flame who in it burned,

and only he could tell who ne'er to tell returned.

["Bird Parliament", by Farid ud-Din Attar, tr. by Edward FitzGerald (1889), apud William Ralph Inge, "Faith: Personal Religion and the Life of Devotion"]

Just as the moth in his desire to know the flame was willing to destroy himself, so must you in becoming a new person be willing to die to your present self.

You must be conscious of being healthy if you are to know what health is. You must be conscious of being secure if you are to know what security is.

Therefore, to incarnate a new and greater value of yourself, you must assume that you already are what you want to be and then live by faith in this assumption – which is not yet incarnate in the body of your life – in confidence that this new value or state of consciousness will become incarnated through your absolute fidelity to the assumption that you are that which you desire to be.

This is what wholeness means, what integrity means. They mean submission of the whole self to the feeling of the wish fulfilled in certainty that that new state of consciousness is the renewing of mind which transforms.

There is no order in Nature corresponding to this willing submission of the self to the ideal beyond the self.

Therefore, it is the height of folly to expect the incarnation of a new and greater concept of self to come about by natural evolutionary process.

That which requires a state of consciousness to produce its effect obviously cannot be effected without such a state of consciousness, and in your ability to assume the feeling of a greater life, to assume a new concept of yourself, you possess what the rest of Nature does not possess – imagination – the instrument by which you create your world.

Your imagination is the instrument, the means, whereby your redemption from slavery, sickness, and poverty is effected.

If you refuse to assume the responsibility of the incarnation of a new and higher concept of yourself, then you reject the means, the only means, whereby your redemption – that is, the attainment of your ideal – can be effected.

Imagination is the only redemptive power in the universe.

However, your nature is such that it is optional to you whether you remain in your present concept of yourself (a hungry being longing for freedom, health, and security) or choose to become the instrument of your own redemption, imagining yourself as that which you want to be, and thereby satisfying your hunger and redeeming yourself.

O, be strong then, and brave, pure, patient and true;

The work that is yours let no other hand do.

For the strength for all need is faithfully given

From the fountain within you – The Kingdom of Heaven.

DESIRE

THE CHANGES which take place in your life as a result of your changed concept of yourself always appear to the unenlightened to be the result, not of a change of your consciousness, but of chance, outer cause, or coincidence.

However, the only fate governing your life is the fate determined by your own concepts, your own assumptions; for an assumption, though false, if persisted in, will harden into fact.

The ideal you seek and hope to attain will not manifest itself, will not be realized by you until you have imagined that you are already that ideal.

There is no escape for you except by a radical psychological transformation of yourself, except by your assumption of the feeling of your wish fulfilled.

Therefore, make results or accomplishments the crucial test of your ability to use your imagination.

Everything depends on your attitude towards yourself.

That which you will not affirm as true of yourself can never be realized by you, for that attitude alone is the necessary condition by which you realize your goal.

All transformation is based upon suggestion, and this can work only where you lay yourself completely open to an influence. You must abandon yourself to your ideal as a woman abandons herself to love, for complete abandonment of self to it is the way to union with your ideal.

You must assume the feeling of the wish fulfilled until your assumption has all the sensory vividness of reality.

You must imagine that you are already experiencing what you desire. That is, you must assume the feeling of the fulfillment of your desire until you are possessed by it and this feeling crowds all other ideas out of your consciousness.

The man who is not prepared for the conscious plunge into the assumption of the wish fulfilled in the faith that it is the only way to the realization of his dream is not yet ready to live consciously by the law of assumption, although there is no doubt that he does live by the law of assumption unconsciously.

But for you, who accept this principle and are ready to live by consciously assuming that your wish is already fulfilled, the adventure of life begins.

To reach a higher level of being, you must assume a higher concept of yourself.

If you will not imagine yourself as other than what you are, then you remain as you are, for if ye believe not that I am He, ye shall die in your sins. [John 8:24]

If you do not believe that you are He (the person you want to be), then you remain as you are.

Through the faithful systematic cultivation of the feeling of the wish fulfilled, desire becomes the promise of its own fulfillment.

The assumption of the feeling of the wish fulfilled makes the future dream a present fact.

3.THE TRUTH THAT SETS YOU FREE

THE DRAMA of life is a psychological one, in which all the conditions, circumstances and events of your life are brought to pass by your assumptions.

Since your life is determined by your assumptions, you are forced to recognize the fact that you are either a slave to your assumptions or their master.

To become the master of your assumptions is the key to undreamed-of freedom and happiness.

You can attain this mastery by deliberate conscious control of your imagination. You determine your assumptions in this way:

Form a mental image, a picture of the state desired, of the person you want to be. Concentrate your attention upon the feeling that you are already that person. First, visualize the picture in your consciousness. Then feel yourself to be in that state as though it actually formed your surrounding world. By your imagination that which was a mere mental image is changed into a seemingly solid reality.

The great secret is a controlled imagination and a well-sustained attention firmly and repeatedly focused on the object to be accomplished. It cannot be emphasized too much that, by creating an ideal within your mental sphere, by assuming that you are already that ideal, you identify yourself with it and thereby transform yourself into its image [thinking FROM the ideal instead OF thinking of the ideal. Every state is already there as "mere possibilities" as long as we think OF them, but as overpoweringly real when we think FROM them].

This was called by the ancient teachers "Subjection to the will of God" or "Resting in the Lord", and the only true test of "Resting in the Lord" is that all who do rest are inevitably transformed into the image of that in which they rest [thinking FROM the wish fulfilled].

You become according to your resigned will, and your resigned will is your concept of yourself and all that you consent to and accept as true.

You, assuming the feeling of your wish fulfilled and continuing therein, take upon yourself the results of that state; not assuming the feeling of your wish fulfilled, you are ever free of the results.

When you understand the redemptive function of imagination, you hold in your hands the key to the solution of all your problems.

Every phase of your life is made by the exercise of your imagination. Determined imagination alone is the means of your progress, of the fulfilling of your dreams. It is the beginning and end of all creating.

The great secret is a controlled imagination and a well-sustained attention firmly and repeatedly focused on the feeling of the wish fulfilled until it fills the mind and crowds all other ideas out of consciousness.

What greater gifts could be given you than to be told the Truth that will set you free John 8:32]?

The Truth that sets you free is that you can experience in imagination what you desire to experience in reality, and by maintaining this experience in imagination, your desire will become an actuality.

You are limited only by your uncontrolled imagination and lack of attention to the feeling of your wish fulfilled.

When the imagination is not controlled and the attention not steadied on the feeling of the wish fulfilled, then no amount of prayer or piety or invocation will produce the desired effect.

When you can call up at will whatsoever image you please, when the forms of your imagination are as vivid to you as the forms of nature, you are master of your fate. [You must stop spending your thoughts, your time and your money. Everything in life must be an investment.*]

Visions of beauty and splendor, Forms of a long-lost race, Sounds and faces and voices,

From the fourth dimension of space – And on through the universe boundless, Our thoughts go lightning shod –

Some call it imagination, And others call it God.

[Dr. George W. Carey, "The New Name"]

* Neville follows this with the date April 12, [19]53. In Awakened Imagination (1954), he would write, "On the morning of April 12, 1953, my wife was awakened by the sound of a great voice of authority speaking within her and saying, 'You must stop spending your thoughts, time, and money.

Everything in life must be an investment'. To spend is to waste, to squander, to layout without return. To invest is to lay out for a purpose from which a profit is expected. This revelation of my wife is about the importance of the moment. It is about the transformation of the moment… It is only what is done now that counts… Whenever we assume the feeling of being what we want to be, we are investing". (Ch. 5) – Ed.

4.ATTENTION

A double-minded man is unstable in all his ways. James 1:8

ATTENTION IS forceful in proportion to the narrowness of its focus, that is, when it is obsessed with a single idea or sensation. It is steadied and powerfully focused only by such an adjustment of the mind as permits you to see one thing only, for you steady the attention and increase its power by confining it. The desire which realizes itself is always a desire upon which attention is exclusively concentrated, for an idea is endowed with power only in proportion to the degree of attention fixed on it. Concentrated observation is the attentive attitude directed from1 some specific end. The attentive attitude involves selection, for when you pay attention, it signifies that you have decided to focus your attention on one object or state rather than on another.

Therefore, when you know what you want, you must deliberately focus your attention on the feeling of your wish fulfilled until that feeling fills the mind and crowds all other ideas out of consciousness.

The power of attention is the measure of your inner force.

Concentrated observation of one thing shuts out other things and causes them to disappear.

The great secret of success is to focus the attention on the feeling of the wish fulfilled without permitting any distraction. All progress depends upon an increase of attention. The ideas which impel you to action are those which dominate the consciousness, those which possess the attention. [The idea which excludes all others from the field of attention discharges in action.]

This one thing I do, forgetting those things that are behind, I press toward the mark. [Approx., Philippians 3:13,14]

This means you, this one thing you can do, "forgetting those things that are behind". You can press toward the mark of filling your mind with the feeling of the wish fulfilled.

To the unenlightened man, this will seem to be all fantasy, yet all progress comes from those who do not take the accepted view, nor accept the world as it is. As was stated heretofore, if you can imagine what you please, and if the forms of your thought are as vivid as the forms of nature, you are, by virtue of the power of your imagination, master of your fate.

Your imagination is you yourself, and the world as your imagination sees it is the real world.

When you set out to master the movements of attention, which must be done if you would successfully alter the course of observed events, it is then you realize how little control you exercise over your imagination and how much it is dominated by sensory impressions and by a drifting on the tides of idle moods.

To aid in mastering the control of your attention, practice this exercise:

Night after night, just before you drift off to sleep, strive to hold your attention on the activities of the day in reverse order. Focus your attention on the last thing you did, that is, getting in to bed, and then move it backward in time over the events until you reach the first event of the day, getting out of bed. This is no easy exercise, but just as specific exercises greatly help in developing specific muscles, this will greatly help in developing the "muscle" of your attention.

Your attention must be developed, controlled, and concentrated in order to change your concept of yourself successfully and thereby change your future.

Imagination is able to do anything, but only according to the internal direction of your attention.

If you persist night after night, sooner or later you will awaken in yourself a centre of power and become conscious of your greater self, the real you.

Attention is developed by repeated exercise or habit.

Through habit, an action becomes easier, and so, in course of time, gives rise to a facility or faculty, which can then be put to higher uses.

When you attain control of the internal direction of your attention, you will no longer stand in shallow water, but will launch out into the deep of life.

You will walk in the assumption of the wish fulfilled as on a foundation more solid even than earth.

5.ATTITUDE

EXPERIMENTS RECENTLY conducted by Merle Lawrence (Princeton) and Adelbert Ames (Dartmouth) in the latter's psychology laboratory at Hanover, N.H., prove that what you see when you look at something depends not so much on what is there as on the assumption you make when you look.

Since what we believe to be the "real" physical world is actually only an "assumptive" world, it is not surprising that these experiments prove that what appears to be solid reality is actually the result of "expectations" or "assumptions".

Your assumptions determine not only what you see, but also what you do, for they govern all your conscious and subconscious movements towards the fulfillment of themselves.

Over a century ago, this truth was stated by Emerson as follows:

As the world was plastic and fluid in the hands of God, so it is ever to so much of his attributes as we bring to it. To ignorance and sin, it is flint. They adapt themselves to it as they may, but in proportion as a man has anything in him divine, the firmament flows before him and takes his signet and form.

Your assumption is the hand of God moulding the firmament into the image of that which you assume.

The assumption of the wish fulfilled is the high tide which lifts you easily off the bar of the senses where you have so long lain stranded.

It lifts the mind into prophecy in the full right sense of the word; and if you have that controlled imagination and absorbed attention which it is possible to attain, you may be sure that all your assumption implies will come to pass.

When William Blake wrote,

What seems to be, is, to those to whom it seems to be, he was only repeating the eternal truth, there is nothing unclean of itself; but to him that esteemeth anything to be unclean, to him it is unclean.

Romans 14:14

Because there is nothing unclean of itself (or clean of itself), you should assume the best and think only of that which is lovely and of good report [Philippians 4:8].

It is not superior insight, but ignorance of this law of assumption, if you read into the greatness of men some littleness with which you may be familiar – or into some situation or circumstance an unfavorable conviction. Your particular relationship to another influences your assumption with respect to that other and makes you see in him that which you do see. If you can change your opinion of another, then what you now believe of him cannot be absolutely true but is only relatively true. The following is an actual case history illustrating how the law of assumption works:

One day, a costume designer described to me her difficulties in working with a prominent theatrical producer. She was convinced that he unjustly criticized and rejected her best work and that often he was deliberately rude and unfair to her.

Upon hearing her story, I explained that if she found the other rude and unfair, it was a sure sign that she, herself, was wanting and that it was not the producer, but herself that was in need of a new attitude.

I told her that the power of this law of assumption and its practical application could be discovered only through experience, and that only by assuming that the situation was already what she wanted it to be could she prove that she could bring about the change desired.

Her employer was merely bearing witness, telling her by his behavior what her concept of him was.

I suggested that it was quite probable that she was carrying on conversations with him in her mind which were filled with criticism and recriminations.

There was no doubt but that she was mentally arguing with the producer, for others only echo that which we whisper to them in secret.

I asked her if it was not true that she talked to him mentally, and, if so, what those conversations were like.

She confessed that every morning on her way to the theatre she told him just what she thought of him in a way she would never have dared address him in person. The intensity and force of her mental arguments with him automatically established his behavior towards her.

She began to realize that all of us carry on mental conversations, but, unfortunately, on most occasions, these conversations are argumentative... that we have only to observe the passerby on the street to prove this assertion... that so many people are mentally engrossed in conversation and few appear to be happy about it, but the very intensity of their feeling must lead them quickly to the unpleasant incident they themselves have mentally created and therefore must now encounter.

When she realized what she had been doing, she agreed to change her attitude and to live this law faithfully by assuming that her job was highly satisfactory and her relationship with the producer was a very happy one. To do this, she agreed that, before going to sleep at night, on her way to work, and at other intervals during the day, she would imagine that he had congratulated her on her fine designs and that she, in turn, had thanked him for his praise and kindness.

To her great delight, she soon discovered for herself that her own attitude was the cause of all that befell her.

The behavior of her employer miraculously reversed itself. His attitude, echoing as it had always done, that which she had assumed, now reflected her changed concept of him.

What she did was by the power of her imagination.

Her persistent assumption influenced his behavior and determined his attitude toward her.

With the passport of desire on the wings of a controlled imagination, she traveled into the future of her own predetermined experience.

Thus we see it is not facts, but that which we create in our imagination, which shapes our lives, for most of the conflicts of the day are due to the want of a little imagination to cast the beam out of our own eye.

It is the exact and literal-minded who live in a fictitious world.

As this designer, by her controlled imagination, started the subtle change in her employer's mind, so can we, by the control of our own imagination and wisely directed feeling, solve our problems.

By the intensity of her imagination and feeling, the designer cast a kind of enchantment on her producer's mind and caused him to think that his generous praise originated with him.

Often our most elaborate and original thoughts are determined by another.

We should never be certain that it was not some woman treading in the winepress who began that subtle change in men's mind, or that the passion did not begin in the mind of some shepherd boy, lighting up his eyes for a moment before it ran upon its way.

William Butler Yeats

6.RENUNCIATION

There is no coal of character so dead that it will not glow and flame if but slightly turned.

Resist not evil.

Whosoever shall smite thee on thy right cheek, turn to him the other also. [Matthew 5:39]

THERE IS a great difference between resisting evil and renouncing it. When you resist evil, you give it your attention; you continue to make it real. When you renounce evil, you take your attention from it and give your attention to what you want. Now is the time to control your imagination and

Give beauty for ashes, joy for mourning, praise for the spirit of heaviness, that they might be called trees of righteousness, the planting of the Lord that He might be glorified. [Approx., Isaiah 61:3]

You give beauty for ashes when you concentrate your attention on things as you would like them to be rather than on things as they are.

You give joy for mourning when you maintain a joyous attitude regardless of unfavorable circumstances. You give praise for the spirit of heaviness when you maintain a confident attitude instead of succumbing to despondency.

In this quotation, the Bible uses the word tree as a synonym for man. You become a tree of righteousness when the above mental states are a permanent part of your consciousness. You are a planting of the Lord when all your thoughts are true thoughts.

He is "I AM" as described in Chapter One. "I AM" is glorified when your highest concept of yourself is manifested.

When you have discovered your own controlled imagination to be your saviour, your attitude will be completely altered without any diminution of religious feeling, and you will say of your controlled imagination,

Behold this vine. I found it a wild tree, whose wanton strength had swollen into irregular twigs. But I pruned the plant and it grew temperate in its vain expense of useless leaves, and knotted as you see into these clean full clusters to repay the hand that wisely wounded it. [Robert Southey, "Thalaba the Destroyer"]

By vine is meant your imagination, which, in its uncontrolled state, expends its energy in useless or destructive thoughts and feelings. But you, just as the vine is pruned by cutting away its useless branches and roots, prune your imagination by withdrawing your attention from all unlovely and destructive ideas and concentrating on the ideal you wish to attain.

The happier, more noble life you will experience will be the result of wisely pruning your own imagination.

Yes, be pruned of all unlovely thoughts and feelings, that you may Think truly, and thy thoughts shall the world's famine feed; Speak truly, and each word of thine shall be a fruitful seed; Live truly, and thy life shall be a great and noble creed. [Horatio Bonar, "Hymns of Faith and Hope"]

7.PREPARING YOUR PLACE

And all mine are thine, and thine are mine. John 17:10

Thrust in thy sickle, and reap; for the time is come for thee to reap; for the harvest of the earth is ripe. Revelation 14:15

ALL IS yours. Do not go seeking for that which you are. Appropriate it, claim it, assume it.

Everything depends upon your concept of yourself. That which you do not claim as true of yourself cannot be realized by you.

The promise is, Whosoever hath, to him it shall be given, and he shall have more abundance; but whosoever hath not, from him shall be taken away even that which he seemeth to have. [Approx., Matthew 25:29; Luke 8:18]

Hold fast, in your imagination, to all that is lovely and of good report, for the lovely and the good are essential in your life if it is to be worthwhile.

Assume it. You do this by imagining that you already are what you want to be – and already have what you want to have.

As a man thinketh in his heart, so is he. [Proverbs 23:7]

Be still and know that you are that which you desire to be, and you will never have to search for it.

In spite of your appearance of freedom of action, you obey, as everything else does, the law of assumption.

Whatever you may think of the question of free will, the truth is your experiences throughout your life are determined by your assumptions – whether conscious or unconscious.

An assumption builds a bridge of incidents that lead inevitably to the fulfillment of itself.

Man believes the future to be the natural development of the past. But the law of assumption clearly shows that this is not the case.

Your assumption places you psychologically where you are not physically; then your senses pull you back from where you were psychologically to where you are physically.

It is these psychological forward motions that produce your physical forward motions in time.

Precognition permeates all the scriptures of the world.

In my Father's house are many mansions; If it were not so, I would have told you. I go to prepare a place for you. And if I go and prepare a place for you, I will come again and receive you unto myself: that where I am, there ye may be also… And now I have told you before it came to pass, that, when it is come to pass, ye might believe. John 14:2,3; 29

The "I" in this quotation is your imagination, which goes into the future, into one of the many mansions.

Mansion is the state desired… telling of an event before it occurs physically is simply feeling yourself into the state desired until it has the tone of reality.

You go and prepare a place for yourself by imagining yourself into the feeling of your wish fulfilled.

Then, you speed from this state of the wish fulfilled – where you have not been physically – back to where you were physically a moment ago. Then, with an irresistible forward movement, you move forward across a series of events to the physical realization of your wish, that where you have been in imagination, there you will be in the flesh also.

Unto the place from whence the rivers come, thither they return again. Ecclesiastes 1:7

8.CREATION

I am God, declaring the end from the beginning, and from ancient times, things that are not yet done.

Isaiah 46:9, 10

CREATION IS finished. Creativeness is only a deeper receptiveness, for the entire contents of all time and all space, while experienced in a time sequence, actually coexist in an infinite and eternal now.

In other words, all that you ever have been or ever will be – in fact, all that mankind ever was or ever will be – exists now.

This is what is meant by creation, and the statement that creation is finished means nothing is ever to be created, it is only to be manifested.

What is called creativeness is only becoming aware of what already is.

You simply become aware of increasing portions of that which already exists.

The fact that you can never be anything that you are not already or experience anything not already existing explains the experience of having an acute feeling of having heard before what is being said, or having met before the person being met for the first time, or having seen before a place or thing being seen for the first time.

The whole of creation exists in you, and it is your destiny to become increasingly aware of its infinite wonders and to experience ever greater and grander portions of it.

If creation is finished, and all events are taking place now, the question that springs naturally to the mind is "what determines your time track?"

That is, what determines the events which you encounter? And the answer is your concept of yourself.

Concepts determine the route that attention follows. Here is a good test to prove this fact. Assume the feeling of your wish fulfilled and observe the route that your attention follows. You will observe that as long as you remain faithful to your assumption, so long will your attention be confronted with images clearly related to that assumption.

For example; if you assume that you have a wonderful business, you will notice how in your imagination, your attention is focused on incident after incident relating to that assumption.

Friends congratulate you, tell you how lucky you are. Others are envious and critical. From there, your attention goes to larger offices, bigger bank balances, and many other similarly related events.

Persistence in this assumption will result in actually experiencing in fact that which you assumed.

The same is true regarding any concept.

If your concept of yourself is that you are a failure, you would encounter in your imagination a whole series of incidents in conformance to that concept. Thus it is clearly seen how you, by your concept of yourself, determine your present, that is, the particular portion of creation which you now experience, and your future, that is, the particular portion of creation which you will experience.

9.INTERFERENCE

YOU ARE free to choose the concept you will accept of yourself.

Therefore, you possess the power of intervention, the power which enables you to alter the course of your future. The process of rising from your present concept to a higher concept of yourself is the means of all true progress. The higher concept is waiting for you to incarnate it in the world of experience.

Now unto Him that is able to do exceeding abundantly above all that we ask or think, according to the power that worketh in us, unto Him be glory.

Ephesians 3:20

Him, that is able to do more than you can ask or think, is your imagination, and the power that worketh in us is your attention. Understanding imagination to be HIM that is able to do all that you ask, and attention to be the power by which you create your world, you can now build your ideal world.

Imagine yourself to be the ideal you dream of and desire. Remain attentive to this imagined state, and as fast as you completely feel that you are already this ideal it will manifest itself as reality in your world.

He was in the world, and the world was made by Him and the world knew Him not. [John 1:10]

The mystery hid from the ages; Christ in you, the hope of glory. [Approx., Colossians 1:26,27]

The "He" in the first of these quotations is your imagination. As previously explained, there is only one substance. This substance is consciousness. It is your imagination which forms this substance into concepts, which concepts are then manifested as conditions, circumstances, and physical objects. Thus imagination made your world.

This supreme truth, with but few exceptions, man is not conscious of.

The mystery, Christ in you, referred to in the second quotation, is your imagination, by which your world is molded. The hope of glory is your awareness of the ability to rise perpetually to higher levels.

Christ is not to be found in history, nor in external forms. You find Christ only when you become aware of the fact that your imagination is the only redemptive power. When this is discovered, the "towers of dogma will have heard the trumpets of Truth, and, like the walls of Jericho, crumble to dust".

10.SUBJECTIVE CONTROL

YOUR IMAGINATION is able to do all that you ask in proportion to the degree of your attention. All progress, all fulfillment of desire depend upon the control and concentration of your attention.

Attention may be either attracted from without or directed from within.

Attention is attracted from without when you are consciously occupied with the external impressions of the immediate present. The very lines of this page are attracting your attention from without.

Your attention is directed from within when you deliberately choose what you will be preoccupied with mentally.

It is obvious that, in the objective world, your attention is not only attracted by, but is constantly directed to external impressions.

But, your control in the subjective state is almost nonexistent, for in this state, attention is usually the servant and not the master – the passenger and not the navigator – of your world.

There is an enormous difference between attention directed objectively and attention directed subjectively, and the capacity to change your future depends on the latter.

When you are able to control the movements of your attention in the subjective world, you can modify or alter your life as you please. But this control cannot be achieved if you allow your attention to be attracted constantly from without.

Each day, set yourself the task of deliberately withdrawing your attention from the objective world and of focusing it subjectively.

In other words, concentrate on those thoughts or moods which you deliberately determine. Then those things that now restrict you will fade and drop away.

The day you achieve control of the movements of your attention in the subjective world, you are master of your fate.

You will no longer accept the dominance of outside conditions or circumstances.

You will not accept life on the basis of the world without.

Having achieved control of the movements of your attention, and having discovered the mystery hid from the ages, that Christ in you is your imagination, you will assert the supremacy of imagination and put all things in subjection to it.

11.ACCEPTANCE

Man's Perceptions are not bounded by organs of Perception: he perceives more than sense (though ever so acute) can discover. [William Blake]

HOWEVER MUCH you seem to be living in a material world, you are actually living in a world of imagination.

The outer, physical events of life are the fruit of forgotten blossom-times – results of previous and usually forgotten states of consciousness.

They are the ends running true to oft-times forgotten imaginative origins.

Whenever you become completely absorbed in an emotional state, you are at that moment assuming the feeling of the state fulfilled. If persisted in, whatsoever you are intensely emotional about, you will experience in your world.

These periods of absorption, of concentrated attention, are the beginnings of the things you harvest.

It is in such moments that you are exercising your creative power – the only creative power there is. At the end of these periods, or moments of absorption, you speed from these imaginative states (where you have not been physically) to where you were physically an instant ago. In these periods, the imagined state is so real that, when you return to the objective world and find that it is not the same as the imagined state, it is an actual shock. You have seen something in imagination with such vividness that you now wonder whether the evidence of your senses can now be believed, and, like Keats, you ask, was it a vision or a waking dream?

Fled is that music… Do I wake or sleep?

This shock reverses your time sense. By this is meant that instead of your experience resulting from your past, it now becomes the result of being in imagination where you have not yet been physically.

In effect, this moves you across a bridge of incident to the physical realization of your imagined state.

The man who at will can assume whatever state he pleases has found the keys to the Kingdom of Heaven.

The keys are desire, imagination, and a steadily focused attention on the feeling of the wish fulfilled. To such a man, any undesirable objective fact is no longer a reality and the ardent wish no longer a dream.

Prove Me now herewith, saith the Lord of hosts, if I will not open you the windows of heaven, and pour you out a blessing, that there shall not be room enough to receive it. Malachi 3:10

The windows of heaven may not be opened and the treasures seized by a strong will, but they open of themselves and present their treasures as a free gift – a gift that comes when absorption reaches such a degree that it results in a feeling of complete acceptance.

The passage from your present state to the feeling of your wish fulfilled is not across a gap.

There is continuity between the so-called real and unreal.

To cross from one state to the other, you simply extend your feelers, trust your touch and enter fully into the spirit of what you are doing.

Not by might nor by power, but by My Spirit, saith the Lord of hosts. [Zecharian 4:6]

Assume the spirit, the feeling of the wish fulfilled, and you will have opened the windows to receive the blessing. To assume a state is to get into the spirit of it.

Your triumphs will be a surprise only to those who did not know your hidden passage from the state of longing to the assumption of the wish fulfilled.

The Lord of hosts will not respond to your wish until you have assumed the feeling of already being what you want to be, for acceptance is the channel of His action.

Acceptance is the Lord of hosts in action.

12.THE EFFORTLESS WAY

THE PRINCIPLE of "Least Action" governs everything in physics, from the path of a planet to the path of a pulse of light. Least Action is the minimum of energy, multiplied by the minimum of time. Therefore, in moving from your present state to the state desired, you must use the minimum of energy and take the shortest possible time.

Your journey from one state of consciousness to another is a psychological one, so, to make the journey, you must employ the psychological equivalent of "Least Action" and the psychological equivalent is mere assumption.

The day you fully realize the power of assumption, you discover that it works in complete conformity with this principle. It works by means of attention, minus effort.

Thus, with least action, through an assumption, you hurry without haste and reach your goal without effort.

Because creation is finished, what you desire already exists. It is excluded from view because you can see only the contents of your own consciousness.

It is the function of an assumption to call back the excluded view and restore full vision. It is not the world, but your assumptions that change.

An assumption brings the invisible into sight. It is nothing more nor less than seeing with the eye of God, i.e., imagination.

For the Lord seeth not as a man seeth, for man looketh on the outward appearance, but the Lord looketh on the heart. [1Samuel 16:7]

The heart is the primary organ of sense, hence the first cause of experience. When you look "on the heart", you are looking at your assumptions: assumptions determine your experience.

Watch your assumption with all diligence, for out of it are the issues of life. Assumptions have the power of objective realization. Every event in the visible world is the result of an assumption or idea in the unseen world.

The present moment is all-important, for it is only in the present moment that our assumptions can be controlled.

The future must become the present in your mind if you would wisely operate the law of assumption.

The future becomes the present when you imagine that you already are what you will be when your assumption is fulfilled.

Be still (least action) and know that you are that which you desire to be. The end of longing should be Being.

Translate your dream into Being. Perpetual construction of future states without the consciousness of already being them, that is, picturing your desire without actually assuming the feeling of the wish fulfilled, is the fallacy and mirage of mankind.

It is simply futile day-dreaming.

13. THE CROWN OF THE MYSTERIES

THE ASSUMPTION of the wish fulfilled is the ship that carries you over the unknown seas to the fulfillment of your dream.

The assumption is everything; realization is subconscious and effortless. Assume a virtue if you have it not. [William Shakespeare, "Hamlet"]

Act on the assumption that you already possess that which you sought.

Blessed is she that believed; for there shall be a performance of those things which were told her from the Lord. [Luke 1:45]

As the Immaculate Conception is the foundation of the Christian mysteries, so the Assumption is their crown. Psychologically, the Immaculate Conception means the birth of an idea in your own consciousness, unaided by another.

For instance, when you have a specific wish or hunger or longing, it is an immaculate conception in the sense that no physical person or thing plants it in your mind. It is self-conceived. Every man is the Mary of the Immaculate Conception and birth to his idea must give.

The Assumption is the crown of the mysteries because it is the highest use of consciousness.

When in imagination you assume the feeling of the wish fulfilled, you are mentally lifted up to a higher level.

When, through your persistence, this assumption becomes actual fact, you automatically find yourself on a higher level (that is, you have achieved your desire) in your objective world.

Your assumption guides all your conscious and subconscious movements towards its suggested end so inevitably that it actually dictates the events.

The drama of life is a psychological one and the whole of it is written and produced by your assumptions.

Learn the art of assumption, for only in this way can you create your own happiness.

14.PERSONAL IMPOTENCE

SELF-SURRENDER IS essential, and by that is meant the confession of personal impotence.

I can of mine own self do nothing. [John 5:30]

Since creation is finished, it is impossible to force anything into being.

The example of magnetism previously given is a good illustration. You cannot make magnetism; it can only be displayed. You cannot make the law of magnetism. If you want to build a magnet, you can do so only by conforming to the law of magnetism. In other words, you surrender yourself, or yield to the law.

In like manner, when you use the faculty of assumption, you are conforming to a law just as real as the law governing magnetism.

You can neither create nor change the law of assumption.

It is in this respect that you are impotent. You can only yield or conform, and since all of your experiences are the result of your assumptions (consciously or unconsciously), the value of consciously using the power of assumption surely must be obvious.

Willingly identify yourself with that which you most desire, knowing that it will find expression through you.

Yield to the feeling of the wish fulfilled and be consumed as its victim, then rise as the prophet of the law of assumption.

15.ALL THINGS ARE POSSIBLE

IT IS of great significance that the truth of the principles outlined in this book have been proven time and again by the personal experiences of the Author.

Throughout the past twenty-five years, he has applied these principles and proved them successful in innumerable instances. He attributes to an unwavering assumption of his wish already being fulfilled every success that he has achieved.

He was confident that, by these fixed assumptions, his desires were predestined to be fulfilled. Time and again, he assumed the feeling of his wish fulfilled and continued in his assumption until that which he desired was completely realized.

Live your life in a sublime spirit of confidence and determination; disregard appearances, conditions, in fact all evidence of your senses that deny the fulfillment of your desire. Rest in the assumption that you are already what you want to be, for, in that determined assumption, you and your Infinite Being are merged in creative unity, and with your Infinite Being (God) all things are possible.

God never fails.

For who can stay His hand or say unto Him, What doest thou? [Daniel 4:35]

Through the mastery of your assumptions, you are in very truth enabled to master life.

It is thus that the ladder of life is ascended: thus the ideal is realized.

The clue to the real purpose of life is to surrender yourself to your ideal with such awareness of its reality that you begin to live the life of the ideal and no longer your own life as it was prior to this surrender.

He calleth things that are not seen as though they were, and the unseen becomes seen. [Approx., Romans 4:17]

Each assumption has its corresponding world. If you are truly observant, you will notice the power of your assumptions to change circumstances which appear wholly immutable.

You, by your conscious assumptions, determine the nature of the world in which you live.

Ignore the present state and assume the wish fulfilled. Claim it; it will respond.

The law of assumption is the means by which the fulfillment of your desires may be realized.

Every moment of your life, consciously or unconsciously, you are assuming a feeling.

You can no more avoid assuming a feeling than you can avoid eating and drinking.

All you can do is control the nature of your assumptions.

Thus it is clearly seen that the control of your assumption is the key you now hold to an ever expanding, happier, more noble life.

16.BE YE DOERS

Be ye doers of the word and not hearers only, deceiving your own selves. For if any be a hearer of the word, and not a doer, he is like unto a man beholding his natural face in a glass and goeth his way, and straightway forgetteth what manner of man he was. But whoso looketh into the perfect law of liberty, and continue therein, he being not a forgetful hearer but a doer of the work, this man shall be blessed in his deed. James 1:22-25

THE WORD in this quotation means idea, concept, or desire. You deceive yourself by "hearing only" when you expect your desire to be fulfilled through mere wishful thinking. Your desire is what you want to be, and looking at yourself "in a glass" is seeing yourself in imagination as that person.

Forgetting "what manner of man" you are is failing to persist in your assumption. The "perfect law of liberty" is the law which makes possible liberation from limitation, that is, the law of assumption.

To continue in the perfect law of liberty is to persist in the assumption that your desire is already fulfilled.

You are not a "forgetful hearer" when you keep the feeling of your wish fulfilled constantly alive in your consciousness.

This makes you a "doer of the work", and you are blessed in your deed by the inevitable realization of your desire.

You must be doers of the law of assumption, for without application, the most profound understanding will not produce any desired result.

Frequent reiteration and repetition of important basic truths runs through these pages.

Where the law of assumption is concerned – the law that sets man free – this is a good thing. It should be made clear again and again even at the risk of repetition.

The real truth-seeker will welcome this aid in concentrating his attention upon the law which sets him free.

The parable of the Master's condemnation of the servant who neglected to use the talent given him [Matthew 25:14-30] is clear and unmistakable.

Having discovered within yourself the key to the Treasure House, you should be like the good servant who, by wise use, multiplied by many times the talents entrusted to him. The talent entrusted to you is the power to consciously determine your assumption.

The talent not used, like the limb not exercised, withers and finally atrophies.

What you must strive after is being.

In order to do, it is necessary to be. The end of yearning is to be.

Your concept of yourself can only be driven out of consciousness by another concept of yourself.

By creating an ideal in your mind, you can identify yourself with it until you become one and the same with the ideal, thereby transforming yourself into it.

The dynamic prevails over the static; the active over the passive.

One who is a doer is magnetic and therefore infinitely more creative than any who merely hear. Be among the doers.

17.ESSENTIALS

THE ESSENTIAL points in the successful use of the law of assumption are these:

First, and above all, yearning; longing; intense, burning desire.

With all your heart you must want to be different from what you are. Intense, burning desire [combined with intention to make good] is the mainspring of action, the beginning of all successful ventures. In every great passion [which achieves its objective], desire is concentrated [and intentioned. You must first desire and then intend to succeed].

As the hart panteth after the water brooks, so panteth my soul after Thee, O God. [Psalm 42:1]

Blessed are they that hunger and thirst after righteousness for they shall be filled. [Matthew 5:6]

Here, the soul is interpreted as the sum total of all you believe, think, feel, and accept as true; in other words, your present level of awareness, God[,]5 I AM [the power of awareness], the source and fulfillment of all desires [understood psychologically, I am an infinite series of levels of awareness and I am what I am according to where I am in the series]. This quotation describes how your present level of awareness longs to transcend itself.

Righteousness is the consciousness of already being what you want to be.

Second, cultivate physical immobility, a physical incapacity not unlike the state described by Keats in his "Ode to a Nightingale":

A drowsy numbness pains my senses, as though of hemlock I had drunk.

It is a state akin to sleep, but one in which you are still in control of the direction of attention. You must learn to induce this state at will, but experience has taught that it is more easily induced after a substantial meal, or when you wake in the morning feeling very loath to arise.

Then you are naturally disposed to enter this state. The value of physical immobility shows itself in the accumulation of mental force which absolute stillness brings with it. It increases your power of concentration.

Be still and know that I am God. [Psalm 46:10]

In fact, the greater energies of the mind seldom break forth save when the body is stilled and the door of the senses closed to the objective world.

The third and last thing to do is to experience in your imagination what you would experience in reality had you achieved your goal. [You must gain it in imagination first, for imagination is the very door to the reality of that which you seek. But use imagination masterfully and not as an onlooker thinking of the end, but as a partaker thinking from the end.]

Imagine that you possess a quality or something you desire which hitherto has not been yours.

Surrender yourself completely to this feeling until your whole being is possessed by it. This state differs from reverie in this respect: it is the result of a controlled imagination and a steadied, concentrated attention, whereas reverie is the result of an uncontrolled imagination – usually just a daydream.

In the controlled state, a minimum of effort suffices to keep your consciousness filled with the feeling of the wish fulfilled. The physical and mental immobility of this state is a powerful aid to voluntary attention and a major factor of minimum effort.

The application of these three points:

Desire

Physical immobility

The assumption of the wish already fulfilled is the way to at-one-ment or union with your objective. [The first point is thinking of the end, with intention to realize it. The third point is thinking from the end with the feeling of accomplishment. The secret of thinking from the end is to enjoy being it. The minute you make it pleasurable and imagine that you are it, you start thinking from the end.]

One of the most prevalent misunderstandings is that this law works only for those having a devout or a religious objective. This is a fallacy.

It works just as impersonally as the law of electricity works.

It can be used for greedy, selfish purposes as well as noble ones. But it should always be borne in mind that ignoble thoughts and actions inevitably result in unhappy consequences.

18.RIGHTEOUSNESS

IN THE preceding chapter, righteousness was defined as the consciousness of already being what you want to be. This is the true psychological meaning and obviously does not refer to adherence to moral codes, civil law or religious precepts. You cannot attach too much importance to being righteous.

In fact, the entire Bible is permeated with admonition and exhortations on this subject.

Break off thy sins by righteousness. Daniel 4:27

My righteousness I hold fast, and will not let it go: my heart shall not reproach me so long as I live. Job 27:6

My righteousness shall answer for me in time to come. Genesis 30:33

Very often the words sin and righteousness are used in the same quotation. This is a logical contrast of opposites and becomes enormously significant in the light of the psychological meaning of righteousness and the psychological meaning of sin.

Sin means to miss the mark. Not to attain your desire, not to be the person you want to be is sinning. Righteousness is the consciousness of already being what you want to be.

It is a changeless educative law that effects must follow causes. Only by righteousness can you be saved from sinning.

There is a widespread misunderstanding as to what it means to be "saved from sin".

The following example will suffice to demonstrate this misunderstanding and to establish the truth.

A person living in abject poverty may believe that by means of some religious or philosophical activity he can be "saved from sin" and his life improved as a result.

If, however, he continues to live in the same state of poverty, it is obvious that what he believed was not the truth, and, in fact, he was not "saved".

On the other hand, he can be saved by righteousness.

The successful use of the law of assumption would have the inevitable result of an actual change in his life. He would no longer live in poverty. He would no longer miss the mark. He would be saved from sin.

Except your righteousness shall exceed the righteousness of the scribes and Pharisees, ye shall in no wise enter into the Kingdom of Heaven.

Matthew 5:20

Scribes and Pharisees means those who are influenced and governed by the outer appearances the rules and customs of the society in which they live, the vain desire to be thought well of by other men. Unless this state of mind is exceeded, your life will be one of limitation – of failure to attain your desires – of missing the mark – of sin. This righteousness is exceeded by true righteousness, which is always the consciousness of already being that which you want to be.

One of the greatest pitfalls in attempting to use the law of assumption is focusing your attention on things, on a new home, a better job, a bigger bank balance.

This is not the righteousness without which you "die in your sins" [John 8:24].

Righteousness is not the thing itself; it is the consciousness, the feeling of already being the person you want to be, of already having the thing you desire.

Seek ye first the Kingdom of God and His righteousness; and all these things shall be added unto you. Matthew 6:33

The kingdom (entire creation) of God (your I AM) is within you.

Righteousness is the awareness that you already possess it all.

19.FREE WILL

THE QUESTION is often asked, "What should be done between the assumption of the wish fulfilled and its realization?"

Nothing. It is a delusion that, other than assuming the feeling of the wish fulfilled, you can do anything to aid the realization of your desire.

You think that you can do something, you want to do something; but actually you can do nothing. The illusion of the free will to do is but ignorance of the law of assumption upon which all action is based.

Everything happens automatically.

All that befalls you, all that is done by you – happens.

Your assumptions, conscious or unconscious, direct all thought and action to their fulfillment.

To understand the law of assumption, to be convinced of its truth, means getting rid of all the illusions about free will to act. Free will actually means freedom to select any idea you desire.

By assuming the idea already to be a fact, it is converted into reality. Beyond that, free will ends, and everything happens in harmony with the concept assumed.

I can of Mine Own Self do nothing… because I seek not Mine Own Will,

but the Will of the Father which hath sent Me. [John 5:30]

In this quotation, the Father obviously refers to God. In an earlier chapter, God is defined as I AM.

Since creation is finished, the Father is never in a position of saying "I will be". In other words, everything exists, and the infinite I AM consciousness can speak only in the present tense.

Not My Will, but Thine be done. [Luke 22:42]

"I will be" is a confession that "I am not". The Father's Will is always "I AM".

Until you realize that YOU are the Father (there is only one I AM, and your infinite self is that I AM), your will is always "I will be".

In the law of assumption, your consciousness of being is the Father's will. The mere wish without this consciousness is the "my will". This

[299] THE POWER OF IMAGINATION: THE NEVILLE GODDARD TREASURY

great quotation, so little understood, is a perfect statement of the law of assumption.

It is impossible to do anything. You must be in order to do.

If you had a different concept of yourself, everything would be different. You are what you are, so everything is as it is.

The events which you observe are determined by the concept you have of yourself.

If you change your concept of yourself, the events ahead of you in time are altered, but, thus altered, they form again a deterministic sequence starting from the moment of this changed concept. You are a being with powers of intervention, which enable you, by a change of consciousness, to alter the course of observed events – in fact, to change your future.

Deny the evidence of the senses, and assume the feeling of the wish fulfilled.

Inasmuch as your assumption is creative and forms an atmosphere, your assumption, if it be a noble one, increases your assurance and helps you to reach a higher level of being.

If, on the other hand, your assumption be an unlovely one, it hinders you and makes your downward way swifter. Just as the lovely assumptions create a harmonious atmosphere, so the hard and bitter feelings create a hard and bitter atmosphere.

Whatsoever things are pure, just, lovely, of good report, think on these things. [Approx., Philippians 4:8]

This means to make your assumptions the highest, noblest, happiest concepts. There is no better time to start than now. The present moment is always the most opportune in which to eliminate all unlovely assumptions and to concentrate only on the good.

As well as yourself, claim for others their Divine inheritance.

See only their good and the good in them. Stir the highest in others to confidence and self-assertion by your sincere assumption of their good, and you will be their prophet and their healer, for an inevitable fulfillment awaits all sustained assumptions.

You win by assumption what you can never win by force.

An assumption is a certain motion of consciousness. This motion, like all motion, exercises an influence on the surrounding substance causing it to take the shape of, echo, and reflect the assumption. A change of fortune is a new direction and outlook, merely a change in arrangement of the same mind substance – consciousness.

If you would change your life, you must begin at the very source with your own basic concept of self.

Outer change, becoming part of organizations, political bodies, religious bodies, is not enough. The cause goes deeper. The essential change must take place in yourself, in your own concept of self.

You must assume that you are what you want to be and continue therein, for the reality of your assumption has its being in complete independence of objective fact and will clothe itself in flesh if you persist in the feeling of the wish fulfilled.

When you know that assumptions, if persisted in, harden into facts, then events which seem to the uninitiated mere accidents will be understood by you to be the logical and inevitable effects of your assumption.

The important thing to bear in mind is that you have infinite free will in choosing your assumptions, but no power to determine conditions and events.

You can create nothing, but your assumption determines what portion of creation you will experience.

20. PERSISTENCE

And He said unto them, Which of you shall have a friend, and shall go unto him at midnight, and say unto him, Friend, lend me three loaves; for a friend of mine in his journey is come to me, and I have nothing to set before him? And he from within shall answer and say, Trouble me not; the door is now shut, and my children are with me in bed; I cannot rise and give thee. I say unto you, Though he will not rise and give him, because he is his friend, yet because of his importunity he will rise and give him as many as he needeth. And I say unto you, Ask, and it shall be given you; seek, and ye shall find; knock, and it shall be opened unto you.

Luke 11:5-9

THERE ARE three principal characters in this quotation, you and the two friends mentioned.

The first friend is a desired state of consciousness. The second friend is a desire seeking fulfillment.

Three is the symbol of wholeness, completion. Loaves symbolize substance.

The shut door symbolizes the senses which separate the seen from the unseen.

Children in bed means ideas that are dormant.

Inability to rise means a desired state of consciousness cannot rise to you, you must rise to it.

Importunity means demanding persistency, a kind of brazen impudence.

Ask, seek, and knock mean assuming the consciousness of already having what you desire.

Thus the scriptures tell you that you must persist in rising to (assuming) the consciousness of your wish already being fulfilled. The promise is definite that if you are shameless in your impudence in assuming that you already have that which your senses deny, it shall be given unto you – your desire shall be attained.

The Bible teaches the necessity of persistence by the use of many stories. When Jacob sought a blessing from the Angel with whom he wrestled, he said,

I will not let thee go, except thou bless me. [Genesis 32:26]

When the Shunammite sought the help of Elisha, she said,

As the Lord liveth, and as thy soul liveth, I will not leave thee, and he arose and followed her. [2Kings 4:30]

The same idea is expressed in another passage:

And he spake a parable unto them that men ought always to pray, and not to faint; saying, There was in a city a Judge, which feared not God, neither regarded man and there was a widow in that city; and she came unto him, saying, Avenge me of mine adversary. And he would not for a while; but afterward he said within himself, Though I fear not God, nor regard man; yet because this widow troubleth me, I will avenge her, lest she weary me by her continual coming.

Luke 18:1-5

The basic truth underlying each of these stories is that desire springs from the awareness of ultimate attainment and that persistence in maintaining the consciousness of the desire already being fulfilled results in its fulfillment.

It is not enough to feel yourself into the state of the answered prayer; you must persist in that state.

That is the reason for the injunction Man ought always to pray and not to faint. [Luke 18:1]

Here, to pray means to give thanks for already having what you desire. Only persistency in the assumption of the wish fulfilled can cause those subtle changes in your mind which result in the desired change in your life. It matters not whether they be "Angels", "Elisha", or "reluctant judges"; all must respond in harmony with your persistent assumption.

When it appears that people other than yourself in your world do not act toward you as you would like, it is not due to reluctance on their part, but a lack of persistence in your assumption of your life already being as you want it to be.

Your assumption, to be effective, cannot be a single isolated act; it must be a maintained attitude of the wish fulfilled. [And that maintained attitude that gets you there, so that you think from your wish fulfilled instead of thinking about your wish, is aided by assuming the feeling of the wish fulfilled frequently. It is the frequency, not the length of time, that makes it natural. That to which you constantly return constitutes your truest self. Frequent occupancy of the feeling of the wish fulfilled is the secret of success.]

21.CASE HISTORIES

IT WILL be extremely helpful at this point to cite a number of specific examples of the successful application of this law. Actual case histories are given. In each of these, the problem is clearly defined and the way imagination was used to attain the required state of consciousness is fully described. In each of these instances, the author of this book was either personally concerned or was told the facts by the person involved.

1

This is a story with every detail of which I am personally familiar.

In the spring of 1943, a recently drafted soldier was stationed in a large army camp in Louisiana. He was intensely eager to get out of the army, but only in an entirely honorable way.

The only way he could do this was to apply for a discharge. The application then required the approval of his commanding officer to become effective. Based on army regulations, the decision of the commanding officer was final and could not be appealed. The soldier, following all the necessary procedure, applied for a discharge.

Within four hours, this application was returned – marked "disapproved". Convinced he could not appeal the decision to any higher authority, military or civilian, he turned within to his own consciousness, determined to rely on the law of assumption.

The soldier realized that his consciousness was the only reality, that his particular state of consciousness determined the events he would encounter.

That night, in the interval between getting into bed and falling asleep, he concentrated on consciously using the law of assumption. In imagination, he felt himself to be in his own apartment in New York City. He visualized his apartment, that is, in his mind's eye he actually saw his own apartment, mentally picturing each one of the familiar rooms with all the furnishings vividly real.

With this picture clearly visualized, and lying flat on his back, he completely relaxed physically. In this way, he induced a state bordering on sleep, at the same time retaining control of the direction of his attention. When his body was completely immobilized, he assumed that he was in his own room and felt himself to be lying in his own bed – a very different feeling from that of lying on an army cot.

In imagination, he rose from the bed, walked from room to room, touching various pieces of furniture. He then went to the window and, with his hands resting on the sill, looked out on the street on which his apartment faced. So vivid was all this in his imagination that he saw in detail the pavement, the railings, the trees and the familiar red brick of the building on the opposite side of the street. He then returned to his bed and felt himself drifting off to sleep.

He knew that it was most important in the successful use of this law that at the actual point of falling asleep, his consciousness be filled with the assumption that he was already what he wanted to be. All that he did in imagination was based on the assumption that he was no longer in the army. Night after night, the soldier enacted this drama. Night after night, in imagination, he felt himself, honorably discharged, back in his home, seeing all the familiar surroundings and falling asleep in his own bed. This continued for eight nights.

For eight days, his objective experience continued to be directly opposite to his subjective experience in consciousness each night, before going to sleep. On the ninth day, orders came through from Battalion headquarters for the soldier to fill out a new application for his discharge.

Shortly after this was done, he was ordered to report to the Colonel's office. During the discussion, the Colonel asked him if he was still desirous of getting out of the army.

Upon receiving an affirmative reply, the Colonel said that he personally disagreed, and while he had strong objections to approving of the discharge, he had decided to overlook these objections and to approve it. Within a few hours, the application was approved and the soldier, now a civilian, was on a train bound for home.

2

This is a striking story of an extremely successful businessman demonstrating the power of imagination and the law of assumption. I know this family intimately, and all the details were told to me by the son described herein.

The story begins when he was twenty years old.

He was next to the oldest in a large family of nine brothers and one sister. The father was one of the partners in a small merchandising business. In his eighteenth year, the brother referred to in this story left the country in which they lived and traveled two thousand miles to enter college and complete his education. Shortly after his first year in college, he was called home because of a tragic event in connection with his father's business.

Through the machinations of his associates, the father was not only forced out of his business, but was the object of false accusations impugning his character and integrity.

At the same time, he was deprived of his rightful share in the equity of the business.

The result was he found himself largely discredited and almost penniless. It was under these circumstances that the son was called home from college.

He returned, his heart filled with one great resolution.

He was determined that he would become outstandingly successful in business. The first thing he and his father did was to use the little money they had to start their own business. They rented a small store on a side street not far from the large business of which the father had been one of the principal owners. There they started a business bent upon real service to the community. It was shortly thereafter that the son, with instinctive awareness that it was bound to work, deliberately used imagination to attain an almost fantastic objective.

Every day, on the way to and from work, he passed the building of his father's former business – the biggest business of its kind in the country. It was one of the largest buildings, with the most prominent location in the heart of the city. On the outside of the building was a huge sign on which the name of the firm was painted in large bold letters.

Day after day, as he passed by, a great dream took shape in the son's mind. He thought of how wonderful it would be if it was his family that had this great building – his family that owned and operated this great business.

One day, as he stood gazing at the building, in his imagination, he saw a completely different name on the huge sign across the entrance. Now the large letters spelled out his family name (in these case histories actual names are not used; for the sake of clarity, in this story we will use hypothetical names and assume that the son's family name was Lordard).

Where the sign read F. N. Moth & Co., in imagination, he actually saw the name, letter by letter, N. Lordard & Sons. He remained looking at the sign with his eyes wide open, imagining that it read N. Lordard & Sons. Twice a day, week after week, month after month, for two years, he saw his family name over the front of that building. He was convinced that if he felt strongly enough that a thing was true,

[306] NEVILLE GODDARD

it was bound to be the case, and by seeing in imagination his family name on the sign – which implied that they owned the business – he became convinced that one day they would own it.

During this period, he told only one person what he was doing. He confided in his mother, who with loving concern tried to discourage him in order to protect him from what might be a great disappointment.

Despite this, he persisted day after day.

Two years later, the large company failed and the coveted building was up for sale.

On the day of the sale, he seemed no nearer ownership than he had been two years before when he began to apply the law of assumption. During this period, they had worked hard, and their customers had implicit confidence in them. However, they had not earned anything like the amount of money required for the purchase of the property. Nor did they have any source from which they could borrow the necessary capital. Making even more remote their chance of getting it was the fact that this was regarded as the most desirable property in the city and a number of wealthy business people were prepared to buy it. On the actual day of the sale, to their complete surprise, a man, almost a total stranger, came into their shop and offered to buy the property for them. (Due to some unusual conditions involved in this transaction, the son's family could not even make a bid for the property.)

They thought the man was joking. However, this was not the case. The man explained that he had watched them for some time, admired their ability, believed in their integrity, and that supplying the capital for them to go into business on a large scale was an extremely sound investment for him. That very day the property was theirs. What the son had persisted in seeing in his imagination was now a reality. The hunch of the stranger was more than justified.

Today, this family owns not only the particular business referred to, but owns many of the largest industries in the country in which they live.

The son, seeing his family name over the entrance of this great building, long before it was actually there, was using exactly the technique that produces results. By assuming the feeling that he already had what he desired – by making this a vivid reality in his imagination, by determined persistence, regardless of appearance or circumstance –, he inevitably caused his dream to become a reality.

3

This is the story of a very unexpected result of an interview with a lady who came to consult me.

One afternoon, a young grandmother, a businesswoman in New York, came to see me. She brought along her nine-year-old grandson, who was visiting her from his home in Pennsylvania. In response to her questions, I explained the law of assumption, describing in detail the procedure to be followed in attaining an objective. The boy sat quietly, apparently absorbed in a small toy truck, while I explained to the grandmother the method of assuming the state of consciousness that would be hers were her desire already fulfilled.

I told her the story of the soldier in camp, who, each night, fell asleep, imagining himself to be in his own bed in his own home.

When the boy and his grandmother were leaving, he looked up at me with great excitement and said, "I know what I want and, now, I know how to get it". Surprised, I asked him what it was he wanted; he told me he had his heart set on a puppy.

To this, the grandmother vigorously protested, telling the boy that it had been made clear repeatedly that he could not have a dog under any circumstances… that his father and mother would not allow it, that the boy was too young to care for it properly, and furthermore, the father had a deep dislike for dogs – he actually hated to have one around.

All these were arguments the boy, passionately desirous of having a dog, refused to understand. "Now I know what to do", he said. "Every night, just as I am going off to sleep, I am going to pretend that I have a dog and we are going for a walk". "No", said the grandmother, "that is not what Mr.

Neville means. This was not meant for you. You cannot have a dog".

Approximately six weeks later, the grandmother told me what was to her an astonishing story. The boy's desire to own a dog was so intense that he had absorbed all that I had told his grandmother of how to attain one's desire – and he believed implicitly that at last he knew how to get a dog.

Putting this belief into practice, for many nights, the boy imagined a dog was lying in his bed beside him. In imagination, he petted the dog, actually feeling its fur. Things like playing with the dog and taking it for a walk filled his mind.

Within a few weeks, it happened. A newspaper in the city in which the boy lived organized a special program in connection with Kindness to Animals Week. All schoolchildren were requested to write an essay on "Why I Would Like to Own a Dog".

After entries from all the schools were submitted and judged, the winner of the contest was announced. The very same boy who weeks before in my apartment in New York had told me "Now I know how to get a dog" was the winner. In an elaborate ceremony, which was publicized with stories and pictures in the newspaper, the boy was awarded a beautiful collie puppy.

In relating this story, the grandmother told me that if the boy had been given the money with which to buy a dog, the parents would have refused to do so and would have used it to buy a bond for the boy or put it in the savings bank for him. Furthermore, if someone had made the boy a gift of a dog, they would have refused it or given it away.

But the dramatic manner in which they boy got the dog, the way he won the city-wide contest, the stories and pictures in the newspaper, the pride of achievement and joy of the boy himself all combined to bring about a change of heart in the parents, and they found themselves doing that which they never conceived possible – they allowed him to keep the dog.

All this the grandmother explained to me, and she concluded by saying that there was one particular kind of dog on which the boy had set his heart. It was a collie.

4

This was told by the aunt in the story to the entire audience at the conclusion of one of my lectures.

During the question period following my lecture on the law of assumption, a lady who had attended many lectures and had had personal consultation with me on a number of occasions, rose and asked permission to tell a story illustrating how she had successfully used the law.

She said that upon returning home from the lecture the week before, she had found her niece distressed and terribly upset. The husband of the niece, who was an officer in the Army Air Force stationed in Atlantic City, had just been ordered, along with the rest of his unit, to active duty in Europe. She tearfully told her aunt that the reason she was upset was that she had been hoping her husband would be assigned to Florida as an Instructor.

They both loved Florida and were anxious to be stationed there and not to be separated. Upon hearing this story, the aunt stated that there was only one thing to do and that was to apply immediately the law of assumption.

"Let's actualize it", she said. "If you were actually in Florida, what would you do? You would feel the warm breeze. You would smell the salt air. You would feel your toes sinking down into the sand. Well, let's do all that right now".

They took off their shoes and, turning out the lights, in imagination, they felt themselves actually in Florida, feeling the warm breeze, smelling the sea air, pushing their toes into the sand.

Forty-eight hours later, the husband received a change of orders. His new instructions were to report immediately to Florida as an Air Force Instructor. Five days later, his wife was on a train to join him. While the aunt, in order to help her niece to attain her desire, joined in with the niece in assuming the state of consciousness required, she did not go to Florida. That was not her desire. On the other hand, that was the intense longing of the niece.

5

This case is especially interesting because of the short interval of time between the application of this law of assumption and its visible manifestation.

A very prominent woman came to me in deep concern. She maintained a lovely city apartment and a large country home; but because the many demands made upon her were greater than her modest income, it was absolutely essential that she rent her apartment if she and her family were to spend the summer at their country home.

In previous years, the apartment had been rented without difficulty early in the spring, but the day she came to me, the rental season for summer sublets was over. The apartment had been in the hands of the best real estate agents for months, but no one had been interested even in coming to see it.

When she had described her predicament, I explained how the law of assumption could be brought to bear on solving her problem. I suggested that, by imagining the apartment had been rented by a person desiring immediate occupancy and by assuming that this was the case, her apartment actually would be rented. In order to create the necessary feeling of naturalness – the feeling that it was already a fact that her apartment was rented – I suggested that she drift off into sleep that very night, imagining herself, not in her apartment, but in whatever place she would sleep were the apartment suddenly rented. She quickly grasped the idea and said that in such a situation she would sleep in her country home, even though it was not yet opened for the summer.

This interview took place on Thursday. At nine o'clock the following Saturday morning, she phoned me from her home in the country – excited and happy.

She told me that on Thursday night she had fallen asleep actually imagining and feeling that she was sleeping in her other bed in her country home many miles away from the city apartment she was occupying. On Friday, the very next day, a highly desirable tenant, one who met all her requirements as a responsible person, not only rented the apartment, but rented it on the condition that he could move in that very day.

6

Only the most complete and intense use of the law of assumption could have produced such results in this extreme situation.

Four years ago, a friend of our family asked that I talk with his twenty-eight- year-old son, who was not expected to live.

He was suffering from a rare heart disease. This disease resulted in a disintegration of the organ.

Long and costly medical care had been of no avail.

Doctors held out no hope for recovery. For a long time, the son had been confined to his bed. His body had shrunk to almost a skeleton, and he could talk and breathe only with great difficulty. His wife and two small children were home when I called, and his wife was present throughout our discussion.

I started by telling him that there was only one solution to any problem, and that solution was a change of attitude. Since talking exhausted him, I asked him to nod in agreement if he understood clearly what I said. This he agreed to do.

I described the facts underlying the law of consciousness – in fact that consciousness was the only reality. I told him that the way to change any condition was to change his state of consciousness concerning it. As a specific aid in helping him to assume the feeling of already being well, I suggested that in imagination, he see the doctor's face expressing incredulous amazement in finding him recovered, contrary

[311] THE POWER OF IMAGINATION: THE NEVILLE GODDARD TREASURY

to all reason, from the last stages of an incurable disease, that he see him double checking in his examination and hear him saying over and over, "It's a miracle – it's a miracle".

He not only understood all this clearly, but he believed it implicitly. He promised that he would faithfully follow this procedure. His wife, who had been listening intently, assured me that she, too, would diligently use the law of assumption and her imagination in the same way as her husband. The following day I sailed for New York – all this taking place during a winter vacation in the tropics.

Several months later, I received a letter saying the son had made a miraculous recovery. On my next visit, I met him in person. He was in perfect health, actively engaged in business and thoroughly enjoying the many social activities of his friends and family.

He told me that from the day I left, he never had any doubt that "it" would work. He described how he had faithfully followed the suggestion I had made to him and day after day had lived completely in the assumption of already being well and strong.

Now, four years after his recovery, he is convinced that the only reason he is here today is due to his successful use of the law of assumption.

7

This story illustrates the successful use of the law by a New York business executive.

In the fall of 1950, an executive of one of New York's prominent banks discussed with me a serious problem with which he was confronted.

He told me that the outlook for his personal progress and advancement was very dim. Having reached middle age and feeling that a marked improvement in position and income was justified, he had "talked it out" with his superiors. They frankly told him that any major improvement was impossible and intimated that if he was dissatisfied, he could seek another job. This, of course, only increased his uneasiness.

In our talk, he explained that he had no great desire for really big money, but that he had to have a substantial income in order to maintain his home comfortably and to provide for the education of his children in good preparatory schools and colleges. This he found impossible on his present income. The refusal of the bank to assure him of any advancement in the near future resulted in a feeling of discontent and an intense desire to secure a better position with considerably more money.

He confided in me that the kind of job he would like better than anything in the world was one in which he managed the investment funds of a large institution such as a foundation or great university.

In explaining the law of assumption, I stated that his present situation was only a manifestation of his concept of himself and declared that if he wanted to change the circumstances in which he found himself, he could do so by changing his concept of himself. In order to bring about this change of consciousness, and thereby a change in his situation, I asked him to follow this procedure every night just before he fell asleep:

In imagination, he was to feel he was retiring at the end of one of the most important and successful days of his life. He was to imagine that he had actually closed a deal that very day to join the kind of organization he yearned to be with and in exactly the capacity he wanted.

I suggested to him that if he succeeded in completely filling his mind with this feeling, he would experience a definite sense of relief. In this mood, his uneasiness and discontent would be a thing of the past. He would feel the contentment that comes with the fulfillment of desire. I wound up by assuring him that if he did this faithfully, he would inevitably get the kind of position he wanted.

This was the first week of December. Night after night, without exception, he followed this procedure.

Early in February, a director of one of the wealthiest foundations in the world asked this executive if he would be interested in joining the foundation in an executive capacity handling investments. After some brief discussion, he accepted.

Today, at a substantially higher income and with the assurance of steady progress, this man is in a position far exceeding all that he had hoped for.

8

The man and wife in this story have attended my lectures for a number of years. It is an interesting illustration of the conscious use of this law by two people concentrating on the same objective at one time.

This man and wife were an exceptionally devoted couple. Their life was completely happy and entirely free from any problems or frustrations.

For some time, they had planned to move into a larger apartment. The more they thought about it, the more they realized that what they had their hearts set on was a beautiful penthouse. In discussing it together, the husband explained that he wanted one with a huge window looking out on a magnificent view. The wife said she would like to have one side of the walls mirrored from top to bottom. They both wanted to have a wood- burning fireplace. It was a "must" that the apartment be in New York City.

For months, they had searched for just such an apartment in vain. In fact, the situation in the city was such that the securing of any kind of apartment was almost an impossibility. They were so scarce that not only were there waiting lists for them, but all sorts of special deals including premiums, the buying of furniture etc. were involved.

New apartments were being leased long before they were completed, many being rented from the blueprints of the building.

Early in the spring, after months of fruitless seeking, they finally located one which they seriously considered. It was a penthouse apartment in a building just being completed on upper Fifth Avenue facing Central Park. It had one serious drawback.

Being a new building, it was not subject to rent control, and the couple felt the yearly rental was exorbitant. In fact, it was several thousand dollars a year more than they had considered paying.

During the spring months of March and April, they continued looking at various penthouses throughout the city, but they always came back to this one.

Finally, they decided to increase the amount they would pay substantially and made a proposition which the agent for the building agreed to forward to the owners for consideration.

It was at this point, without discussing it with each other, each determined to apply the law of assumption. It was not until later that each learned what the other had done.

Night after night, they both fell asleep in imagination in the apartment they were considering. The husband, lying with his eyes closed, would imagine that his bedroom windows were overlooking the park. He would imagine going to the window the first thing in the morning and enjoying the view. He felt himself sitting on the terrace overlooking the park, having cocktails with his wife and friends, all thoroughly enjoying it. He filled his mind with actually feeling himself in the penthouse and on the terrace. During all this time, unknown to him, his wife was doing the same thing.

Several weeks went by without any decision on the part of the owners, but they continued to imagine as they fell asleep each night that they were actually sleeping in the penthouse.

One day, to their complete surprise, one of the employees in the apartment building in which they lived told them that the penthouse there was vacant. They were astonished, because theirs was one of the most desirable buildings in the city with a perfect location right on Central Park. They knew there was a long waiting list of people trying to get an apartment in their building. The fact that a penthouse had unexpectedly become available was kept quiet by the management because they were not in a position to consider any applicants for it. Upon learning that it was vacant, this couple immediately made a request that it be rented to them, only to be told that this was impossible. The fact was that not only were there several people on a waiting list for a penthouse in the building, but it was actually promised to one family. Despite this, the couple had a series of meetings with the management, at the conclusion of which the apartment was theirs.

The building being subject to rent control, their rental was just about what they had planned to pay when they first started looking for a penthouse.

The location, the apartment itself, and the large terrace surrounding it on the South, West, and North was beyond all their expectations – and in the living room, on one side, is a giant window 15 feet by 8 feet with a magnificent view of Central Park; one wall is mirrored from floor to ceiling, and there is a wood-burning fireplace.

22.FAILURE

THIS BOOK would not be complete without some discussion of failure in the attempted use of the law of assumption.

It is entirely possible that you either have had or will have a number of failures in this respect – many of them in really important matters.

If, having read this book, having a thorough knowledge of the application and working of the law of assumption, you faithfully apply it in an effort to attain some intense desire and fail, what is the reason? If, to the question "Did you persist enough?", you can answer "Yes" – and still the attainment of your desire was not realized, what is the reason for failure?

The answer to this is the most important factor in the successful use of the law of assumption.

The time it takes your assumption to become fact, your desire to be fulfilled, is directly proportionate to the naturalness of your feeling of already being what you want to be – of already having what you desire.

The fact that it does not feel natural to you to be what you imagine yourself to be is the secret of your failure.

Regardless of your desire, regardless of how faithfully and intelligently you follow the law, if you do not feel natural about what you want to be, you will not be it. If it does not feel natural to you to get a better job, you will not get a better job. The whole principle is vividly expressed by the Bible phrase "you die in your sins" [John 8:24] – you do not transcend from your present level to the state desired.

How can this feeling of naturalness be achieved?

The secret lies in one word – imagination. For example, this is a very simple illustration: assume that you are securely chained to a large heavy iron bench. You could not possibly run, in fact you could not even walk. In these circumstances, it would not be natural for you to run. You could not even feel that it was natural for you to run. But you could easily imagine yourself running. In that instant, while your consciousness is filled with your imagined running, you have forgotten that you are bound. In imagination, your running was completely natural.

The essential feeling of naturalness can be achieved by persistently filling your consciousness with imagination – imagining yourself

[316] NEVILLE GODDARD

being what you want to be or having what you desire.

Progress can spring only from your imagination, from your desire to transcend your present level.

What you truly and literally must feel is that with your imagination, all things are possible.

You must realize that changes are not caused by caprice, but by a change of consciousness. You may fail to achieve or sustain the particular state of consciousness necessary to produce the effect you desire.

But, once you know that consciousness is the only reality and is the sole creator of your particular world and have burnt this truth into your whole being, then you know that success or failure is entirely in your own hands.

Whether or not you are disciplined enough to sustain the required state of consciousness in specific instances has no bearing on the truth of the law itself – that an assumption, if persisted in, will harden into fact.

The certainty of the truth of this law must remain despite great disappointment and tragedy – even when you "see the light of life go out and all the world go on as though it were still day". You must not believe that because your assumption failed to materialize, the truth that assumptions do materialize is a lie. If your assumptions are not fulfilled, it is because of some error or weakness in your consciousness.

However, these errors and weaknesses can be overcome.

Therefore, press on to the attainment of ever higher levels by feeling that you already are the person you want to be. And remember that the time it takes your assumption to become reality is proportionate to the naturalness of being it.

Man surrounds himself with the true image of himself. Every spirit builds itself a house and beyond its house a world, and beyond its world a heaven. Know then that the world exists for you. For you the phenomenon is perfect. What we are, that only can we see. All that Adam had, all that Caesar could, you have and can do. Adam called his house, heaven and earth. Caesar called his house, Rome; you perhaps call yours a cobbler's trade; a hundred acres of land, or a scholar's garret. Yet line for line and point for point, your dominion is as great as theirs, though without fine name. Build therefore your own world. As fast as you conform your life to the pure idea in your mind, that will unfold its great proportion.

23.FAITH

A miracle is the name given, by those who have no faith, to the works of faith.

Faith is the substance of things hoped for, the evidence of things not seen.

Hebrews 11:1

THE VERY reason for the law of assumption is contained in this quotation.

If there were not a deep-seated awareness that that which you hope for had substance and was possible of attainment, it would be impossible to assume the consciousness of being or having it. It is the fact that creation is finished and everything exists that stirs you to hope –and hope, in turn, implies expectation, and without expectation of success it would be impossible to use consciously the law of assumption. "Evidence" is a sign of actuality.

Thus, this quotation means that faith is the awareness of the reality of that which you assume, [a conviction of the reality of things which you do not see, the mental perception of the reality of the invisible].

Consequently, it is obvious that a lack of faith means disbelief in the existence of that which you desire.

Inasmuch as that which you experience is the faithful reproduction of your state of consciousness, lack of faith will mean perpetual failure in any conscious use of the law of assumption.

In all the ages of history, faith has played a major role. It permeates all the great religions of the world, it is woven all through mythology, and yet today it is almost universally misunderstood.

Contrary to popular opinion, the efficacy of faith is not due to the work of any outside agency.

It is from first to last an activity of your own consciousness.

The Bible is full of many statements about faith, of the true meaning of which few are aware. Here are some typical examples:

Unto us was the gospel preached, as well as unto them: but the word preached did not profit them, not being mixed with faith in them that heard it. Hebrews 4:2

In this quotation, the "us" and "them" make clear that all of us hear

[318] NEVILLE GODDARD

the gospel.

"Gospel" means "good news". Very obviously, good news for you would be that you had attained your desire. This is always being "preached" to you by your infinite self. To hear that which you desire does exist and you need only to accept it in consciousness is good news. Not "mixing with faith" means to deny the reality of that which you desire. Hence there is no "profit" (attainment) possible.

O, faithless and perverse generation, how long shall I be with you? Matthew 17:17

The meaning of "faithless" has been made clear.

"Perverse" means turned the wrong way, in other words, the consciousness of not being what you want to be. To be faithless, that is, to disbelieve in the reality of that which you assume, is to be perverse.

"How long shall I be with you" means that the fulfillment of your desire is predicated upon your change to the right state of consciousness.

It is just as though that which you desire is telling you that it will not be yours until you turn from being faithless and perverse to righteousness. As already stated, righteousness is the consciousness of already being what you want to be.

By faith he forsook Egypt, not fearing the wrath of the king: for he endured, as seeing Him Who is invisible.

Hebrews 11:27

"Egypt" means darkness, belief in many gods (causes). The "king" symbolizes the power of outside conditions or circumstances. "He" is your concept of yourself as already being what you want to be. "Enduring as seeing Him Who is invisible" means persisting in the assumption that your desire is already fulfilled. Thus, this quotation means that, by persisting in the assumption that you already are the person you want to be, you rise above all doubt, fear, and belief in the power of outside conditions or circumstances; and your world inevitably conforms to your assumption.

The dictionary definitions of faith, "the ascent of the mind or understanding to the truth" – "unwavering adherence to principle", are so pertinent that they might well have been written with the law of assumption in mind.

Faith does not question – Faith knows.

24.DESTINY

YOUR DESTINY is that which you must inevitably experience. Really it is an infinite number of individual destinies, each of which when attained is the starting place for a new destiny.

Since life is infinite, the concept of an ultimate destiny is inconceivable. When we understand that consciousness is the only reality, we know that it is the only creator. This means that your consciousness is the creator of your destiny. The fact is, you are creating your destiny every moment, whether you know it or not.

Much that is good and even wonderful has come into your life without your having any inkling that you were the creator of it.

However, the understanding of the causes of your experience, and the knowledge that you are the sole creator of the contents of your life, both good and bad, not only make you a much keener observer of all phenomena, but through the awareness of the power of your own consciousness, intensify your appreciation of the richness and grandeur of life.

Regardless of occasional experiences to the contrary, it is your destiny to rise to higher and higher states of consciousness, and to bring into manifestation more and more of creation's infinite wonders.

Actually, you are destined to reach the point where you realize that, through your own desire, you can consciously create your successive destinies.

The study of this book, with its detailed exposition of consciousness and the operation of the law of assumption, is the master key to the conscious attainment of your highest destiny.

This very day start your new life. Approach every experience in a new frame of mind – with a new state of consciousness.

Assume the noblest and the best for yourself in every respect and continue therein.

Make believe – great wonders are possible.

Your Faith Is Your Fortune

CHAPTER ONE - BEFORE ABRAHAM WAS

Verily, verily, I say unto you, before Abraham was, I AM. – John 8:58

"In the beginning was the Word, and the Word was with God, and the Word was God" [John 1:1].

In the beginning was the unconditioned awareness of being, and the unconditioned awareness of being became conditioned by imagining itself to be something, and the unconditioned awareness of being became that which it had imagined itself to be; so did creation begin.

By this law – first conceiving, then becoming that conceived – all things evolve out of No-thing; and without this sequence there is not anything made that is made.

Before Abraham or the world was – I AM. When all of time shall cease to be – I AM. I AM the formless awareness of being conceiving myself to be man. By my everlasting law of being I am compelled to be and to express all that I believe myself to be.

I AM the eternal No-thingness containing within my formless self the capacity to be all things.

I AM that in which all my conceptions of myself live and move and have their being, and apart from which they are not.

I dwell within every conception of myself; from this withinness, I ever seek to transcend all conceptions of myself. By the very law of my being, I transcend my conceptions of myself, only as I believe myself to be that which does transcend.

I AM the law of being and beside ME there is no law. I AM that I AM.

CHAPTER TWO - YOU SHALL DECREE

[Thou shalt also decree a thing and it shall be established unto thee and the light shall shine upon thy ways.

You will also decree a thing, and it will be established for you; And light will shine on your ways. Thou shalt decree a thing, and it I shall come to thee, and light shall shine in thy ways. – Job 22:28]

So shall My word be that goeth forth out of My mouth; it shall not return unto Me void, but it shall accomplish that which I please, and it shall prosper in the thing whereto I sent it. – Isaiah 55:11

Man can decree a thing and it will come to pass.

Man has always decreed that which has appeared in his world. He is today decreeing that which is appearing in his world and he shall continue to do so as long as man is conscious of being man.

Nothing has ever appeared in man's world, but what man decreed that it should. This you may deny; but try as you will, you cannot disprove it for this decreeing is based upon a changeless principle.

Man does not command things to appear by his words, which are, more often than not, a confession of his doubts and fears.

Decreeing is ever done in consciousness.

Every man automatically expresses that which he is conscious of being. Without effort or the use of words, at every moment of time, man is commanding himself to be and to possess that which he is conscious of being and possessing.

This changeless principle of expression is dramatized in all the Bibles of the world. The writers of our sacred books were illumined mystics, past masters in the art of psychology. In telling the story of the soul, they personified this impersonal principle in the form of a historical document both to preserve it and to hide it from the eyes of the uninitiated.

Today, those to whom this great treasure has been entrusted, namely, the priesthoods of the world, have forgotten that the Bibles are psychological dramas representing the consciousness of man; in their blind forgetfulness, they now teach their followers to worship its characters as men and women who actually lived in time and space.

When man sees the Bible as a great psychological drama, with all of its characters and actors as the personified qualities and attributes of his own consciousness, then – and then only – will the Bible reveal to

[323] THE POWER OF IMAGINATION: THE NEVILLE GODDARD TREASURY

him the light of its symbology.

This Impersonal principle of life which made all things is personified as God.

This Lord God, creator of heaven and earth, is discovered to be man's awareness of being.

If man were less bound by orthodoxy and more intuitively observant, he could not fail to notice in the reading of the Bibles that the awareness of being is revealed hundreds of times throughout this literature.

To name a few: "I AM hath sent me unto you" [Exodus 3:14]. "Be still and know that I AM God" [Psalm 46:10]. "I AM the Lord and there is no other God" ["I am the LORD, and there is none else, there is no God beside Me", Isaiah 45:5; "I am the LORD your God, And there is no other", Joel 2:27]. "I AM the shepherd" ["I am the good shepherd: the good shepherd giveth His life for the sheep", John 10:11; "I am the good shepherd, and know My sheep, and am known of Mine", John 10:14;]. "I AM the door" ["I am the door: by Me if any man enter in, he shall be saved, and shall go in and out, and find pasture", John 10:9; "Verily, verily, I say unto you, I am the door of the sheep", John 10:7]. "I AM the resurrection and the life" [John 11:25]. "I AM the way" ["I am the way, and the truth, and the life; no one cometh to the Father but through Me", John 14:6]. "I AM the beginning and the end" ["I am Alpha and Omega, the beginning and the end, the first and the last", Revelation 22:13; "I am Alpha and Omega, the beginning and the ending, saith the Lord, Which is, and Which was, and Which is to come, the Almighty", Revelation 1:8].

I AM; man's unconditioned awareness of being is revealed as Lord and Creator of every conditioned state of being.

If man would give up his belief in a God apart from himself, recognize his awareness of being to be God (this awareness fashions itself in the likeness and image of its conception of itself), he would transform his world from a barren waste to a fertile field of his own liking.

The day man does this he will know that he and his Father are one, but his Father is greater than he. He will know that his consciousness of being is one with that which he is conscious of being, but that his unconditioned consciousness of being is greater than his conditioned state or his conception of himself.

When man discovers his consciousness to be the impersonal power of expression, which power eternally personifies itself in his conceptions of himself, he will assume and appropriate that state of consciousness which he desires to express; in so doing he will become that state in expression.

"Ye shall decree a thing and it shall come to pass" can now be told in this manner: You shall become conscious of being or possessing a thing and you shall express or possess that which you are conscious of being.

The law of consciousness is the only law of expression. "I AM the way". "I AM the resurrection".

Consciousness is the way as well as the power which resurrects and expresses all that man will ever be conscious of being.

Turn from the blindness of the uninitiated man who attempts to express and possess those qualities and things which he is not conscious of being and possessing; and be as the illumined mystic who decrees on the basis of this changeless law. Consciously claim yourself to be that which you seek; appropriate the consciousness of that which you see; and you too will know the status of the true mystic, as follows:

I became conscious of being it. I am still conscious of being it. And I shall continue to be conscious of being it until that which I am conscious of being is perfectly expressed.

Yes, I shall decree a thing and it shall come to pass.

CHAPTER THREE - THE PRINCIPLE OF TRUTH

"Ye shall know the truth and the truth shall set you free". – John 8:32

The truth that sets man free is the knowledge that his consciousness is the resurrection and the life, that his consciousness both resurrects and makes alive all that he is conscious of being.

Apart from consciousness, there is neither resurrection nor life.

When man gives up his belief in a God apart from himself and begins to recognize his awareness of being to be God, as did Jesus and the prophets, he will transform his world with the realization, "I and My Father are one" [John 10:30], but "My Father is greater than I" [John 14:28].

He will know that his consciousness is God and that which he is conscious of being is the Son bearing witness of God, the Father.

The conceiver and the conception are one, but the conceiver is greater than his conception. Before Abraham was, I AM. Yes, I was aware of being before I became aware of being man, and in that day when I shall cease to be conscious of being man I shall still be conscious of being.

The consciousness of being is not dependent upon being anything.

It preceded all conceptions of itself and shall be when all conceptions of itself shall cease to be. "I AM the beginning and the end". That is, all things or conceptions of myself begin and end in me, but I, the formless awareness, remain forever.

Jesus discovered this glorious truth and declared Himself to be one with God, not the God that man had fashioned, for He never recognized such a God.

Jesus found God to be His awareness of being and so told man that the Kingdom of God and Heaven were within [Luke 17:21,23].

When it is recorded that Jesus left the world and went to His Father ["He was received up into heaven", Mark 16:19, Luke 24:51], it is simply stating that He turned His attention from the world of the senses and rose in consciousness to that level which He desired to express.

There He remained until He became one with the consciousness to which He ascended. When He returned to the world of man, He could act with the positive assurance of that which He was conscious of being, a state of consciousness no one but Himself felt or knew that He possessed.

Man who is ignorant of this everlasting law of expression looks upon such happenings as miracles.

To rise in consciousness to the level of the thing desired and to remain there until such level becomes your nature is the way of all seeming miracles. "And I, if I be lifted up, I shall draw all men unto Me" ["And I, if I be lifted up from the earth, will draw all men unto Me", John 12:32]. If I be lifted up in consciousness to the naturalness of the thing desired, I shall draw the manifestation of that desire to me.

"No man comes unto Me save the Father within Me draws him" [John 6:44], and "I and My Father are one" [John 10:30].

My consciousness is the Father who draws the manifestation of life to me. The nature of the manifestation is determined by the state of consciousness in which I dwell. I am always drawing into my world that which I am conscious of being.

If you are dissatisfied with your present expression of life, then you must be born again [John 3:7]. Rebirth is the dropping of that level with which you are dissatisfied and rising to that level of consciousness which you desire to express and possess.

You cannot serve two masters [Matthew 6:24, Luke 16:13] or opposing states of consciousness at the same time.

Taking your attention from one state and placing it upon the other, you die to the one from which you have taken it and you live and express the one with which you are united.

Man cannot see how it would be possible to express that which he desires to be by so simple a law as acquiring the consciousness of the thing desired.

The reason for this lack of faith on the part of man is that he looks at the desired state through the consciousness of his present limitations. Therefore, he naturally sees it as impossible of accomplishment.

One of the first things man must realize is that it is impossible, in dealing with this spiritual law of consciousness, to put new wine into old bottles or new patches on old garments [Matthew 9:16,17; Mark 2:21,22; Luke 5:36-39].

That is, you cannot take any part of the present consciousness into the new state. For the state sought is complete in itself and needs no patching. Every level of consciousness automatically expresses itself.

To rise to the level of any state is to automatically become that state in expression. But, in order to rise to the level that you are not now expressing, you must completely drop the consciousness with which you are now identified.

Until your present consciousness is dropped, you will not be able to rise to another level.

Do not be dismayed. This letting go of your present identity is not as difficult as it might appear to be.

The invitation of the scriptures, "To be absent from the body and be present with the Lord" [Corinthians 5:8, Corinthians 5:3, Colossians 2:5], is not given to a select few; it is a sweeping call to all mankind. The body from which you are invited to escape is your present conception of yourself with all of its limitations, while the Lord with whom you are to be present is your awareness of being.

To accomplish this seemingly impossible feat, you take your attention away from your problem and place it upon just being. You say silently but feelingly, "I AM". Do not condition this awareness but continue declaring quietly, "I AM – I AM". Simply feel that you are faceless and formless and continue doing so until you feel yourself floating.

"Floating" is a psychological state which completely denies the physical. Through practice in relaxation and willfully refusing to react to sensory impressions, it is possible to develop a state of consciousness of pure receptivity. It is a surprisingly easy accomplishment. In this state of complete detachment, a definite singleness of purposeful thought can be indelibly engraved upon your unmodified consciousness. This state of consciousness is necessary for true meditation.

This wonderful experience of rising and floating is the signal that you are absent from the body or problem and are now present with the Lord; in this expanded state you are not conscious of being anything but I AM – I AM; you are only conscious of being.

When this expansion of consciousness is attained, within this formless deep of yourself, give form to the new conception by claiming and feeling yourself to be that which you, before you entered into this state, desired to be. You will find that within this formless deep of yourself all things appear to be divinely possible. Anything that you sincerely feel yourself to be while in this expanded state becomes, in time, your natural expression.

And God said, "Let there be a firmament in the midst of the waters"

[Genesis 1:6]. Yes, let there be a firmness or conviction in the midst of this expanded consciousness by knowing and feeling I AM that, the thing desired.

As you claim and feel yourself to be the thing desired, you are crystallizing this formless liquid light that you are into the image and likeness [Genesis 1:26] of that which you are conscious of being.

Now that the law of your being has been revealed to you, begin this day to change your world by revaluing yourself. Too long has man held to the belief that he is born of sorrow and must work out his salvation by the sweat of his brow. God is impersonal and no respecter of persons [Acts 10:34; Romans 2:11]. So long as man continues to walk in this belief of sorrow, so long will he walk. In a world of sorrow and confusion, for the world in its every detail is man's consciousness crystallized.

In the Book of Numbers it is recorded, "There were giants in the land and we were in our own sight as grasshoppers, and we were in their sight as grasshoppers" [13:33].

Today is the day, the eternal now, when conditions in the world have attained the appearance of giants. The unemployed, the armies of the enemy, business competition etc. are the giants which make you feel yourself to be a helpless grasshopper.

We are told we were first in our own sight helpless grasshoppers and because of this conception of ourselves were to the enemy helpless grasshoppers.

We can be to others only that which we are to ourselves.

Therefore, as we revalue ourselves and begin to feel ourselves to be the giant, a center of power, we automatically change our relationship to the giants, reducing these former monsters to their true place, making them appear to be the helpless grasshoppers.

Paul said of this principle, "It is to the Greeks (or the so-called wise men of the world) foolishness; and to the Jews (or those who look for signs) a stumbling block" ["For the Jews require a sign, and the Greeks seek after wisdom: But we preach Christ crucified, unto the Jews a stumbling block, and unto the Greeks foolishness; But unto them which are called, both Jews and Greeks, Christ the power of God, and the wisdom of God. Because the foolishness of God is wiser than men; and the weakness of God is stronger than men", 1Corinthians 1:22-25]; with the result that man continues to walk in darkness rather than awake to the realization, "I AM the light of the world" [Matthew 5:14; John 8:12].

Man has so long worshipped the images of his own making that at first he finds this revelation blasphemous, but the day man discovers and accepts this principle as the basis of his life, that day man slays his belief in a God apart from himself.

The story of Jesus' betrayal in the Garden of Gethsemane is the perfect illustration of man's discovery of this principle. We are told, the crowds armed with staves and lanterns sought Jesus in the dark of night.

As they inquired after the whereabouts of Jesus (salvation), the voice answered, "I AM"; whereupon the entire crowd fell to the ground. On regaining their composure, they again asked to be shown the hiding place of the savior and again the savior said, "I have told you that I AM, therefore if ye seek Me, let all else go" [John 18:8].

Man in the darkness of human ignorance sets out on his search for God, aided by the flickering light of human wisdom.

As it is revealed to man that his I AM or awareness of being is his savior, the shock is so great, he mentally falls to the ground, for every belief that he has ever entertained tumbles as he realizes that his consciousness is the one and only savior.

The knowledge that his I AM is God compels man to let all others go for he finds it impossible to serve two Gods. Man cannot accept his awareness of being as God and at the same time believe in another deity.

With this discovery, man's human ear or hearing (understanding) is cut off by the sword of faith (Peter) as his perfect disciplined hearing (understanding) is restored by (Jesus) the knowledge that I AM is Lord and Savior.

Before man can transform his world, he must first lay this foundation or understanding. "I AM the Lord [and there is none else", Isaiah 45:5].

Man must know that his awareness of being is God.

Until this is firmly established so that no suggestion or argument of others can shake him, he will find himself returning to the slavery of his former belief.

"If ye believe not that I AM He, ye shall die in your sins" [John 8:24].

Unless man discovers that his consciousness is the cause of every expression of his life, he will continue seeking the cause of his confusion in the world of effects, and so shall die in his fruitless search.

"I AM the vine and ye are the branches" [John 15:5].

Consciousness is the vine and that which you are conscious of being is as branches that you feed and keep alive. Just as a branch has no life except it be rooted in the vine, likewise things have no life except you be conscious of them.

Just as a branch withers and dies if the sap of the vine ceases to flow towards it, so do things and qualities pass away if you take your attention from them; because your attention is the sap of life which sustains the expression of your life.

CHAPTER FOUR - WHOM SEEK YE?

"I have told you that I AM; if therefore ye seek Me, let these go their way." – John 18:8

"As soon then as He had said unto them, I AM, they went backward and fell to the ground." – John 18:6

Today there is so much said about Masters, Elder Brothers, Adepts and initiates that numberless truth seekers are being constantly misled by seeking these false lights.

For a price, most of these pseudo-teachers offer their students initiation into the mysteries, promising them guidance and direction. Man's weakness for leaders, as well as his worship of idols, makes him an easy prey of these schools and teachers.

Good will come to most of these enrolled students; they will discover after years of awaiting and sacrificing that they were following a mirage.

They will then become disillusioned in their schools and teachers, and this disappointment will be worth the effort and price they have paid for their fruitless search.

They will then turn from their worship of man and in so doing discover that which they are seeking is not to be found in another, for the Kingdom of Heaven is within [Luke 17:21].

This realization will be their first real initiation.

The lesson learned will be this: There is only one Master and this Master is God, the I AM within themselves.

"I AM the Lord thy God who led thee out of the land of darkness; out of the house of bondage" [Exodus 20:2, Deuteronomy 5:6].

I AM, your awareness, is Lord and Master and besides your awareness there is neither Lord nor Master.

You are Master of all that you will ever be aware of being.

You know that you are, do you not? Knowing that you are is the Lord and Master of that which you know that you are.

You could be completely isolated by man from that which you are conscious of being; yet you would, in spite of all human barriers, effortlessly draw to yourself all that you were conscious of being.

The man who is conscious of being poor does not need the assistance of anyone to express his poverty. The man who is conscious of being sick, though isolated in the most hermetically sealed germ-proof area in the world, would express sickness.

There is no barrier to God, for God is your awareness of being.

Regardless of what you are aware of being, you can and do express it without effort.

Stop looking for the Master to come; he is with you always. "I AM with you always, even unto the end of the world" [Matthew 28:20].

You will from time to time know yourself to be many things, but you need not be anything to know that you are.

You can, if you so desire, disentangle yourself from the body you wear; in so doing, you realize that you are a faceless, formless awareness and not dependent on the form you are in your expression.

You will know that you are; you will also discover that this knowing that you are is God, the Father, which preceded all that you ever knew yourself to be.

Before the world was, you were aware of being and so you were saying "I AM", and I AM will be, after all that you know yourself to be shall cease to be.

There are no Ascended Masters. Banish this superstition.

You will forever rise from one level of consciousness (master) to another; in so doing, you manifest the ascended level, expressing this newly acquired consciousness.

Consciousness being Lord and Master, you are the Master Magician conjuring that which you are now conscious of being.

"For God (consciousness) calleth those things which be not as though they were" [Romans 4:17]: things that are not now seen will be seen the moment you become conscious of being that which is not now seen.

This rising from one level of consciousness to another is the only ascension that you will ever experience.

No man can lift you to the level you desire. The power to ascend is within yourself; it is your consciousness.

You appropriate the consciousness of the level you desire to express by claiming that you are now expressing such a level.

This is the ascension. It is limitless, for you will never exhaust your capacity to ascend.

Turn from the human superstition of ascension with its belief in masters, and find the only and everlasting master within yourself.

"Far greater is he that is in you than he that is in the world" [1John 4:4]. Believe this.

Do not continue in blindness, following after the mirage of masters. I assure you your search can end only in disappointment.

"If you deny Me (your awareness of being), I shall deny you also" [Matthew 10:33]. "Thou shalt have no other God beside ME" [Isaiah 45:5; Joel 2:27]. "Be still and know that I AM God"

[Psalm 46:10]. "Come prove me and see if I will not open you the windows of Heaven and pour you out a blessing, that there shall not be room enough to receive it" [Malachi 3:10].

Do you believe that the I AM is able to do this?

Then claim ME to be that which you want to see poured out.

Claim yourself to be that which you want to be and that you shall be.

Not because of masters will I give it unto you, but, because you have recognized ME (yourself) to be that, I will give it unto you for I AM all things to all.

Jesus would not permit Himself to be called Good Master. He knew that there is but one good and one master. He knew this one to be His Father in Heaven, the awareness of being. "The Kingdom of God" (Good) and the Kingdom of Heaven are within you [Luke 17:21].

Your belief in masters is a confession of your slavery. Only slaves have masters.

Change your conception of yourself and you will, without the aid of masters or anyone else, automatically transform your world to conform to your changed conception of yourself.

You are told in the Book of Numbers that there was a time when men were in their own eyes as grasshoppers and because of this conception of themselves, they saw giants in the land. This is as true of man today as it was the day it was recorded. Man's conception of himself is so grasshopper-like, that he automatically makes the conditions round about him appear gigantic; in his blindness he cries out for masters to help him fight his giant problems.

Jesus tried to show man that salvation was within himself and warned him not to look for his savior in places or people.

If anyone should come saying look here or look there, believe him not, for the Kingdom of Heaven is within you [Luke 17:21].

Jesus not only refused to permit Himself to be called Good Master, He warned his followers, "Salute no man along the highway" ["and greet no man along the way", Luke 10:4; 2Kings 4:29]. He made it clear that they should not recognize any authority or superior other than God, the Father.

Jesus established the identity of the Father as man's awareness of being. "I and My Father are one, but My Father is greater than I" [John 10:30 & John 14:28]. I AM one with all that I am conscious of being. I AM greater than that which I am aware of being. The creator is ever greater than his creation.

"As Moses lifted up the serpent in the wilderness even so must the Son of Man be lifted up" [John 3:14]. The serpent symbolizes man's present conception of himself as a worm of the dust, living in the wilderness of human confusion. Just as Moses lifted himself from his worm-of-the-dust conception of himself to discover God to be his awareness of being, "I AM hath sent me" [Exodus 3:14], so must you be lifted up. The day you claim, as did Moses, "I AM that I AM" [Exodus 3:14], that day your claim will blossom in the wilderness.

Your awareness is the master magician who conjures all things by being that which he would conjure. This Lord and Master that you are can and does make all that you are conscious of being appear in your world.

"No man (manifestation) cometh unto Me save My Father draw him and I and My Father are one" ["No man can come to Me, except the Father which hath sent Me draw him: and I will raise him up at the last day", John 6:44; "My Father, which gave them Me, is greater than all; and no man is able to pluck them out of My Father''s hand. I and My Father are one", John 10:29, 30]. You are constantly drawing to yourself that which you are conscious of being. Change your conception of yourself from that of the slave to that of Christ.

Don't be embarrassed to make this claim; only as you claim, "I AM Christ", will you do the works of Christ.

"The works I do ye shall do also, and greater works than these shall ye do, for I go unto my Father" ["Truly, truly, I say to you, he who believes in Me, the works that I do, he will do also; and greater works than these he will do; because I go to the Father", John 14:12]. "He made Himself equal with God and found it not robbery to do the works of God" [Philippians 2:6].

Jesus knew that anyone who dared to claim himself to be Christ would automatically assume the capacities to express the works of his conception of Christ.

Jesus also knew that the exclusive use of this principle of expression was not given to Him alone. He constantly referred to His Father in Heaven.

He stated that His works would not only be equaled but that they would be surpassed by that man who dared to conceive himself to be greater than He (Jesus) had conceived Himself to be.

Jesus, in stating that He and His Father were one but that His Father was greater than He, revealed His awareness (Father) to be one with that which He was aware of being.

He found Himself as Father or awareness to be greater than that which He as Jesus was aware of being.

You and your conception of yourself are one.

You are and always will be greater than any conception you will ever have of yourself.

Man fails to do the works of Jesus Christ because he attempts to accomplish them from his present level of consciousness.

You will never transcend your present accomplishments through sacrifice and struggle.

Your present level of consciousness will only be transcended as you drop the present state and rise to a higher level.

You rise to a higher level of consciousness by taking your attention away from your present limitations and placing it upon that which you desire to be. Do not attempt this in day-dreaming or wishful thinking, but in a positive manner.

Claim yourself to be the thing desired. I AM that; no sacrifice, no diet, no human tricks. All that is asked of you is to accept your desire. If you dare claim it, you will express it.

Meditate on these: "I rejoice not in the sacrifices of men" [probably Malachi 1:10]. "Not by might nor by power, but by my spirit [Zecharian 4:6]. "Ask and you shall receive" [Matthew 7:7, Matthew 21:22, Mark 11:24, Luke 11:9, John 15:7, John 16:24]. "Come eat and drink without price" [probably Isaiah 55:1].

The works are finished. All that is required of you to let these qualities into expression is the claim – I AM that. Claim yourself to be that which you desire to be and that you shall be.

Expressions follow the impressions, they do not precede them. Proof that you are will follow the claim that you are, it will not precede it.

"Leave all and follow Me" [Matthew 8:22; 9:9; Luke 5:27] is a double invitation to you.

First, it invites you to turn completely away from all problems and, then, it calls upon you to continue walking in the claim that you are that which you desire to be.

Do not be a Lot's wife who looks back and becomes salted [Genesis 19] or preserved in the dead past.

Be a Lot who does not look back but who keeps his vision focused upon the promised land, the thing desired.

Do this and you will know that you have found the master, the Master Magician, making the unseen the seen through the command, "I AM THAT".

CHAPTER FIVE - WHO AM I?

"But whom say ye that I AM?" – Matt. 16:15

"I AM the Lord; that is My name; and My glory will I not give to another" [Isaiah 42:8]. "I AM the Lord, the God of all Flesh" [Jeremiah 32:27].

This I AM within you, the reader, this awareness, this consciousness of being, is the Lord, the God of all Flesh.

I AM is He that should come; stop looking for another. As long as you believe in a God apart from yourself, you will continue to transfer the power of your expression to your conceptions, forgetting that you are the conceiver.

The power conceiving and the thing conceived are one but the power to conceive is greater than the conception.

Jesus discovered this glorious truth when He declared, "I and My Father are one, but My Father is greater than I" [John 10:30 & John 14:28].

The power conceiving itself to be man is greater than its conception. All conceptions are limitations of the conceiver.

"Before Abraham was, I AM" [John 8:58]. Before the world was, I AM.

Consciousness precedes all manifestations and is the prop upon which all manifestation rests.

To remove the manifestations, all that is required of you, the conceiver, is to take your attention away from the conception. Instead of "Out of sight, out of mind", it really is "Out of mind, out of sight".

The manifestation will remain in sight only as long as it takes the force with which the conceiver

– I AM – originally endowed it to spend itself. This applies to all creation from the infinitesimally small electron to the infinitely great universe.

"Be still and know that I AM God" [Psalm 46:10].

Yes, this very I AM, your awareness of being, is God, the only God. I AM is the Lord – the God of all Flesh – all manifestation.

This presence, your unconditioned awareness, comprehends neither

[338] NEVILLE GODDARD

beginning nor ending; limitations exist only in the manifestation. When you realize that this awareness is your eternal self, you will know that before Abraham was, I AM.

Begin to understand why you were told, "Go thou and do likewise" [Luke 10:37]. Begin now to identify yourself with this presence, your awareness, as the only reality.

All manifestations but appear to be; you as man have no reality other than that which your eternal self, I AM, believes itself to be.

"Whom do you say that I AM?" [Matthew 16:15, Mark 8:29, Luke 9:20].

This is not a question asked two thousand years ago. It is the eternal question addressed to the manifestation by the conceiver.

It is your true self, your awareness of being, asking you, its present conception of itself, "Who do you believe your awareness to be?"

This answer can be defined only within yourself, regardless of the influence of another. I AM (your true self) is not interested in man's opinion.

All its interest lies in your conviction of yourself.

What do you say of the I AM within you? Can you answer and say, "I AM Christ"? Your answer or degree of understanding will determine the place you will occupy in life.

Do you say or believe yourself to be a man of a certain family race, nation etc.? Do you honestly believe this of yourself?

Then life, your true self will cause these conceptions to appear in your world and you will live with them as though they are real.

"I AM the door" [John 10:9]. "I AM the way" [John 14:6]. "I AM the resurrection and the life" [John 11:25]. "No man (or manifestation) cometh unto My Father save by Me" ["I am the way, the truth, and the life: no man cometh unto the Father, but by Me", John 14:6].

The I AM (your consciousness) is the only door through which anything can pass into your world.

Stop looking for signs. Signs follow; they do not precede. Begin to reverse the statement, "Seeing is believing", to "Believing is seeing". Start now to believe, not with the wavering confidence based on deceptive external evidence but with an undaunted confidence based on the immutable law that you can be that which you desire to be. You will find that you are not a victim of fate but a victim of faith (your own).

Only through one door can that which you seek pass into the world of manifestation. "I AM the door". Your consciousness is the door, so you must become conscious of being and having that which you desire to be and to have. Any attempt to realize your desires in ways other than through the door of consciousness makes you a thief and a robber unto yourself.

Any expression that is not felt is unnatural. Before anything appears, God, I AM, feels itself to be the thing desired; and then the thing felt appears. It is resurrected; lifted out of the nothingness.

I AM wealthy, poor, healthy, sick, free [or] confined were first of all impressions or conditions felt before they became visible expressions.

Your world is your consciousness objectified. Waste no time trying to change the outside; change the within or the impression; and the without or expression will take care of itself.

When the truth of this statement dawns upon you, you will know that you have found the lost word or the key to every door.

I AM (your consciousness) is the magical lost word which was made flesh in the likeness of that which you are conscious of being.

I AM He. Right now, I am overshadowing you, the reader, my living temple, with my presence, urging upon you a new expression. Your desires are my spoken words. My words are spirit and they are true and they shall not return unto me void but shall accomplish where unto they are sent ["So shall my word be that goeth forth out of my mouth: it shall not return unto me void, but it shall accomplish that which I please, and it shall prosper in the thing whereto I sent it", Isaiah 55:11]. They are not something to be worked out.

They are garments that I, your faceless, formless self, wear. Behold! I, clothed in your desire, stand at the door (your consciousness) and knock. If you hear my voice and open unto me (recognize me as your savior), I will come in unto you and sup with you and you with me ["Behold, I stand at the door, and knock: if any man hear my voice, and open the door, I will come in to him, and will sup with him, and he with me", Revelation 3:20].

Just how my words, your desires, will be fulfilled, is not your concern. My words have a way ye know not of [John 4:32]. Their ways are past finding out [Romans 11:33].

All that is required of you is to believe. Believe your desires to be garments your savior wears. Your belief that you are now that which you desire to be is proof of your acceptance of life's gifts. You have opened the door for your Lord, clothed in your desire, to enter the moment you establish this belief.

"When ye pray, believe that ye have received and it shall be so" [Mark 11:24]. "All things are possible to him who believes" [Mark 9:23].

Make the impossible possible through your belief; and the impossible (to others) will embody itself in your world.

All men have had proof of the power of faith. The faith that moves mountains is faith in yourself.

No man has faith in God who lacks confidence in himself. Your faith in God is measured by your confidence in yourself. "I and My Father are one" [John 10:30], man and his God are one, consciousness and manifestation are one.

And God said, "Let there be a firmament in the midst of the waters" [Genesis 1:6]. In the midst of all the doubts and changing opinions of others, let there be a conviction, a firmness of belief, and you shall see the dry land; your belief will appear.

The reward is to him that endureth unto the end ["But he that shall endure unto the end, the same shall be saved", Matthew 24:13]. A conviction is not a conviction if it can be shaken. Your desire will be as clouds without rain unless you believe.

Your unconditioned awareness or I AM is the Virgin Mary who knew not a man [Luke 1:34] and yet, unaided by man, conceived and bore a son. Mary, the unconditioned consciousness, desired and then became conscious of being the conditioned state which she desired to express, and in a way unknown to others, became it. Go and do likewise; assume the consciousness of that which you desire to be and you, too, will give birth to your savior.

When the annunciation is made, when the urge or desire is upon you, believe it to be God's spoken word seeking embodiment through you. Go, tell no man of this holy thing that you have conceived. Lock your secret within you and magnify the Lord [Luke 1:46], magnify or believe your desire to be your savior coming to be with you.

When this belief is so firmly established that you feel confident of results, your desire will embody itself. How it will be done, no man knows. I, your desire, have ways ye know not of [John 4:32]; my ways are past finding out [Romans 11:33]. Your desire can be likened to a seed, and seeds contain within themselves both the power and the plan of self-expression. Your consciousness is the soil. These seeds are successfully planted only if, after you have claimed yourself to be and to have that which you desire, you confidently await results without an anxious thought.

If I be lifted up in consciousness to the naturalness of my desire, I shall automatically draw the manifestation unto me.

Consciousness is the door through which life reveals itself. Consciousness is always objectifying itself.

To be conscious of being or possessing anything is to be or have that which you are conscious of being or possessing. Therefore, lift yourself to the consciousness of your desire and you will see it automatically outpicture itself.

To do this, you must deny your present identity. "Let him deny himself" [Mark 8:34]. You deny a thing by taking your attention away from it. To drop a thing, problem or ego from consciousness, you dwell upon God – God being I AM.

Be still and know that I AM is God [Psalm 46:10].

Believe, feel that I AM; know that this knowing one within you, your awareness of being, is God.

Close your eyes and feel yourself to be faceless, formless and without figure. Approach this stillness as though it were the easiest thing in the world to accomplish. This attitude will assure your success.

When all thought of problem or self is dropped from consciousness because you are now absorbed or lost in the feeling of just being I AM, then begin in this formless state to feel yourself to be that which you desire to be, "I AM that I AM".

The moment you reach a certain degree of intensity so that you actually feel yourself to be a new conception, this new feeling or consciousness is established and in due time will personify itself in the world of form.

This new perception will express itself as naturally as you now express your present identity.

To express the qualities of a consciousness naturally, you must dwell or live within that consciousness. Appropriate it by becoming one with it. To feel a thing intensely, and then rest confidently that it is, makes the thing felt appear within your world.

"I shall stand upon my watch" [Habakkuk 2:1] "and see the salvation of the Lord" [2Chronicles 20:17]. I shall stand firmly upon my feeling, convinced that it is so, and see my desire appear.

"A man can receive nothing (no thing) except it be given him from Heaven" [John 3:27]. Remember, heaven is your consciousness; the Kingdom of Heaven is within you.

This is why you are warned against calling any man Father; your consciousness is the Father of all that you are.

Again you are told, "Salute no man on the highway" [Luke 10:4; 2Kings 4:29]. See no man as an authority. Why should you ask man for permission to express when you realize that your world, in its every detail, originated within you and is sustained by you as the only conceptional center?

Your whole world may be likened to solidified space mirroring the beliefs and acceptances as projected by a formless, faceless presence, namely, I AM. Reduce the whole to its primordial substance and nothing would remain but you, a dimensionless presence, the conceiver.

The conceiver is a law apart. Conceptions under such law are not to be measured by past accomplishments or modified by present capacities for, without taking thought, the conception in a way unknown to man expresses itself.

Go within secretly and appropriate the new consciousness. Feel yourself to be it, and the former limitations shall pass away as completely and as easily as snow on a hot summer's day.

You will not even remember the former limitations; they were never part of this new consciousness.

This rebirth Jesus referred to when he said to Nicodemus, "Ye must be born again" [John 3:7], was nothing more than moving from one state of consciousness to another.

"Whatsoever ye shall ask in My name, that will I do" [John 14:13; similarly, John 15:16; John 16:23]. This certainly does not mean to ask in words, pronouncing with the lips the sounds, God or Christ Jesus, for millions have asked in this manner without results.

To feel yourself to be a thing is to have asked for that thing in His name. I AM is the nameless presence. To feel yourself to be rich is to ask for wealth in His name.

I AM is unconditioned. It is neither rich nor poor, strong nor weak. In other words, in HIM there is neither Greek nor Jew, bond nor free, male nor female. These are all conceptions or limitations of the limitless, and therefore names of the nameless.

To feel yourself to be anything is to ask the nameless, I AM, to express that name or nature".

"Ask whatsoever ye will in My name by appropriating the nature of the thing desired and I will give it unto you".

CHAPTER SIX - I AM HE

For if ye believe not that I AM, ye shall die in your sins. – John 8:24.

"All things were made by Him; and without Him was not anything made that was made" [John 1:3].

This is a hard saying for those trained in the various systems of orthodox religion to accept, but there it stands.

All things, good, bad and indifferent, were made by God. "God made man (manifestation) in His own image; in the likeness of God made He him" [Genesis 1:27]. Apparently adding to this confusion, it is stated, "And God saw that his creation was good" [Genesis 1:31].

What are you going to do about this seeming anomaly? How is man going to correlate all things as good when that which he is taught denies this fact?

Either the understanding of God is erroneous or else there is something radically wrong with man's teaching.

"To the pure all things are pure" [Titus 1:15]. This is another puzzling statement. All the good people, the pure people, the holy people, are the greatest prohibitionists. Couple the foregoing statement with this one, "There is no condemnation in Christ Jesus" ["There is therefore now no condemnation to them which are in Christ Jesus, Who walk not after the flesh, but after the Spirit", Romans 8:1], and you get an impassable barrier to the self-appointed judges of the world. Such statements mean nothing to the self-righteous judges blindly changing and destroying shadows. They continue in the firm belief that they are improving the world.

Man, not knowing that his world is his individual consciousness outpictured, vainly strives to conform to the opinion of others rather than to conform to the one and only opinion existent, namely, his own judgment of himself.

When Jesus discovered His consciousness to be this wonderful law of self-government, He declared, "And now I sanctify Myself that they also might be sanctified through the truth" ["And

for their sakes I sanctify Myself, that they also might be sanctified through the truth", John 17:19].

He knew that consciousness was the only reality, that things objectified were nothing more than different states of consciousness.

Jesus warned His followers to seek first the Kingdom of Heaven (that state of consciousness that would produce the thing desired) and all things would be added to them [Matthew 6:33].

He also stated, "I AM the truth" [John 14:6]. He knew that man's consciousness was the truth or cause of all that man saw his world to be.

Jesus realized that the world was made in the likeness of man. He knew that man saw his world to be what it was because man was what he was.

In short, man's conception of himself determines that which he sees his world to be.

All things are made by God (consciousness) and without him there is nothing made that is made [John 1:3].

Creation is judged good and very good because it is the perfect likeness of that consciousness which produced it.

To be conscious of being one thing and then see yourself expressing something other than that which you are conscious of being is a violation of the law of being; therefore, it would not be good. The law of being is never broken; man ever sees himself expressing that which he is conscious of being.

Be it good, bad or indifferent, it is nevertheless a perfect likeness of his conception of himself; it is good and very good.

Not only are all things made by God, all things are made of God. All are the offspring of God. God is one. Things or divisions are the projections of the one. God being one, He must command Himself to be the seeming other for there is no other.

The absolute cannot contain something within itself that is not itself. If it did, then it would not be absolute, the only one.

Commands, to be effective, must be to oneself. "I AM that I AM" is the only effective command. "I AM the Lord and beside Me there is none else" [Isaiah 45:5; Joel 2:27].

You cannot command that which is not. As there is no other, you must command yourself to be that which you would have appear.

Let me clarify what I mean by effective command. You do not repeat like a parrot the statement, "I AM that I AM"; such vain repetition would be both stupid and fruitless.

It is not the words that make it effective; it is the consciousness of being the thing which makes it effective.

When you say, "I AM", you are declaring yourself to be. The word that in the statement, "I AM that I AM", indicates that which you would be. The second "I AM" in the quotation is the cry of victory.

This whole drama takes place inwardly with or without the use of words. Be still and know that you are.

This stillness is attained by observing the observer.

Repeat quietly but with feeling, "I AM – I AM", until you have lost all consciousness of the world and know yourself just as being.

Awareness, the knowing that you are, is Almighty God; I AM.

After this is accomplished, define yourself as that which you desire to be by feeling yourself to be the thing desired: I AM that. This understanding that you are the thing desired will cause a thrill to course through your entire being. When the conviction is established and you really believe that you are that which you desired to be, then the second "I AM" is uttered as a cry of victory. This mystical revelation of Moses can be seen as three distinct steps: I AM; I AM free; I really AM!

It does not matter what the appearances round about you are like. All things make way for the coming of the Lord. I AM the Lord coming in the appearance of that which I am conscious of being. All the inhabitants of the earth cannot stay my coming or question my authority to be that which I AM conscious that I AM ["All the inhabitants of the earth are as nothing, and He doeth according to His will in the armies of Heaven and among all the inhabitants of the earth; and none can stay His hand, nor say unto Him, ,What doest Thou?"", Daniel 4:35].

"I AM the light of the world" [John 8:12], crystallizing into the form of my conception of myself.

Consciousness is the eternal light, which crystallizes only through the medium of your conception of yourself.

Change your conception of yourself and you will automatically change the world in which you live. Do not try to change people; they are only messengers telling you who you are. Revalue yourself and they will confirm the change.

Now you will realize why Jesus sanctified Himself instead of others

[Ioan 17:19], why to the pure all things are pure [Titus 1:15], why in Christ Jesus (the awakened consciousness) there is no condemnation [Romani 8:1].

Awake from the sleep of condemnation and prove the principle of life. Stop not only your judgment of others but your condemnation of yourself.

Hear the revelation of the enlightened, "I know and am persuaded by the Lord Christ Jesus that there is nothing unclean of itself, but to him that seeth anything to be unclean to him it is unclean" [Romans 14:14], and again, "Happy is the man who condemneth himself not in that which he alloweth" ["Happy is he that condemneth not himself in that thing which he alloweth", Romans 14:22].

Stop asking yourself whether or not you are worthy or unworthy to claim yourself to be that which you desire to be. You will be condemned by the world only as long as you condemn yourself.

You do not need to work out anything. The works are finished.

The principle by which all things are made and without which there is not anything made that is made is eternal.

You are this principle.

Your awareness of being is this everlasting law.

You have never expressed anything that you were not aware of being and you never will. Assume the consciousness of that which you desire to express.

Claim it until it becomes a natural manifestation. Feel it and live within that feeling until you make it your nature.

Here is a simple formula. Take your attention from your present conception of yourself and place it on that ideal of yours, the ideal you had heretofore thought beyond your reach. Claim yourself to be your ideal, not as something that you will be in time, but as that which you are in the immediate present.

Do this, and your present world of limitations will disintegrate as your new claim rises like the phoenix from its ashes.

"Be not afraid nor dismayed by reason of this great multitude; for the battle is not yours, but God's" [2Chronicles 20:15].

You do not fight against your problem; your problem will only live as long as you are conscious of it.

Take your attention away from your problem and the multitude of reasons why you cannot achieve your ideal.

Concentrate your attention entirely upon the thing desired. "Leave all and follow me" [Matthew 8:22; 9:9; Luke 5:27].

In the face of seemingly mountainous obstacles, claim your freedom.

The consciousness of freedom is the Father of freedom. It has a way of expressing itself which no man knows.

"Ye shall not need to fight in this battle. Set yourself, stand still, and see the salvation of the Lord with you" [2Chronicles 20:17].

"I AM the Lord".

I AM (your consciousness) is the Lord. The consciousness that the thing is done, that the work is finished, is the Lord of any situation.

Listen carefully to the promise, "Ye shall not need to fight in this battle: Set yourself, stand still, and see the salvation of the Lord with you" [2Chronicles 20:17].

With you!

That particular consciousness with which you are identified is the Lord of the agreement. He will without assistance establish the thing agreed upon on earth.

Can you, in the face of the army of reasons why a thing cannot be done, quietly enter into an agreement with the Lord that it is done?

Can you, now that you have found the Lord to be your awareness of being, become aware that the battle is won?

Can you, no matter how near and threatening the enemy seems to be, continue in your confidence, standing still, knowing that the victory is yours?

If you can, you will see the salvation of the Lord. Remember, the reward is to the one who endures [Matthew 24:13].

Stand still [Psalm 46:10].

Standing still is the deep conviction that all is well; it is done. No matter what is heard or seen, you remain unmoved, conscious of being victorious in the end.

All things are made by such agreements, and without such an agreement, there is not anything made that is made [John 1:3]. "I AM that I AM" [Exodus 3:14].

In Revelations, it is recorded that a new heaven and new earth shall appear [21:1]. John, shown this vision, was told to write, "It is done" [21:6].

Heaven is your consciousness and earth its solidified state. Therefore, accept as did John – "It is done".

All that is required of you who seek a change is to rise to a level of that which you desire; without dwelling upon the manner of expression, record that it is done by feeling the naturalness of being it.

Here is an analogy that might help you to see this mystery.

Suppose you entered a motion-picture theatre just as the feature picture came to its end. All that you saw of the picture was the happy-ending. Because you wanted to see the entire story, you waited for it to unfold again. With the anti-climactic sequence, the hero is displayed as accused, surrounded by false evidence, and all that goes to wring tears from the audience. But, you, secure in the knowledge of the ending, remain calm with the understanding that, regardless of the seeming direction of the picture, the end has already been defined.

In like manner, go to the end of that which you seek; witness the happy end of it by consciously feeling you express and possess that which you desire to express and possess; and you, through faith, already understanding the end, will have confidence born of this knowledge.

This knowledge will sustain you through the necessary interval of time that it takes the picture to unfold.

Ask no help of man; feel, "It is done", by consciously claiming yourself to be, now, that which as man you hope to be.

CHAPTER SEVEN - THY WILL BE DONE

"Not My will, but Thine, be done." – Luke 22:42.

"Not My will, but Thine, be done" [Luke 22:42; "O My Father, if this cup may not pass away from Me, except I drink it, Thy will be done", Matthew 26:42; "Nevertheless not what I will, but what Thou wilt", Mark 14:36]. This resignation is not one of blind realization that "I can of Myself do nothing, the Father within Me, He doeth the work" ["I can of Mine own Self do nothing: as I hear, I judge: and My judgment is just; because I seek not Mine own will, but the will of the Father which hath sent Me", John 5:30; "Believest thou not that I am in the Father, and the Father in Me? the words that I speak unto you I speak not of Myself: but the Father that dwelleth in Me, He doeth the works", John 14:10].

When man wills, he attempts to make something which does not now exist appear in time and space.

Too often we are not aware of that which we are really doing.

We unconsciously state that we do not possess the capacities to express.

We predicate our desire upon the hope of acquiring the necessary capacities in future time. "I AM not, but I will be".

Man does not realize that consciousness is the Father which does the work, so he attempts to express that which he is not conscious of being.

Such struggles are doomed to failure; only the present expresses itself. Unless I am conscious of being that which I seek, I will not find it.

God (your awareness) is the substance and fullness of all.

God's will is the recognition of that which is, not of that which will be.

Instead of seeing this saying as "Thine will be done", see it as "Thy will is done".

The works are finished.

The principle by which all things are made visible is eternal.

"Eyes have not seen nor ears heard, neither hath it entered into the hearts of men, the things which God hath prepared for those who love the law" ["Eye hath not seen nor ear heard, neither hath entered into the heart of man, the things which God hath prepared for them that love Him", 1Corinthians 2:9-10]

. When a sculptor looks at a formless piece of marble he sees, buried within its formless mass, his finished piece of art. The sculptor, instead of making his masterpiece, merely reveals it by removing that part of the marble which hides his conception.

The same applies to you. In your formless awareness lies buried all that you will ever conceive yourself to be.

The recognition of this truth will transform you from an unskilled laborer who tries to make it so to a great artist who recognizes it to be so.

Your claim that you are now that which you want to be will remove the veil of human darkness and reveal your claim perfectly; I AM that.

God's will was expressed in the words of the Widow, "It is well".

Man's will would have been, "It will be well". To state, "I shall be well", is to say, "I am ill". God, the Eternal Now, is not mocked by words or vain repetition.

God continually personifies that which is.

Thus, the resignation of Jesus (who made Himself equal with God) was turning from the recognition of lack (which the future indicates with "I shall be") to the recognition of supply by claiming, "I AM that; it is done; thank You, Father".

Now you will see the wisdom in the words of the prophet when he states, "Let the weak say, I AM strong", Joel 3:10.

Man in his blindness will not heed the prophet's advice; he continues to claim himself to be weak, poor, wretched and all the other undesirable expressions from which he is trying to free himself by ignorantly claiming that he will be free from these characteristics in the expectancy of the future.

Such thoughts thwart the one law that can ever free him.

There is only one door through which that which you seek can enter your world. "I AM the door" [John 10:9].

When you say, "I AM", you are declaring yourself to be, first person, present tense; there is no future.

[351] THE POWER OF IMAGINATION: THE NEVILLE GODDARD TREASURY

To know that I AM is to be conscious of being. Consciousness is the only door.

Unless you are conscious of being that which you seek, you seek in vain.

If you judge after appearances, you will continue to be enslaved by the evidence of your senses.

To break this hypnotic spell of the senses, you are told, "Go within and shut the door" ["But thou, when thou prayest, enter into thy closet, and when thou hast shut thy door, pray to thy Father which is in secret; and thy Father which seeth in secret shall reward thee openly", Matthew 6:6; "Enter thou into thy chambers, and shut thy doors about thee: hide thyself as it were for a little moment, until the indignation be overpast", Isaiah 26:20; "And when thou art come in, thou shalt shut the door upon thee and upon thy sons", 2Kings 4:4; "He went in therefore, and shut the door upon them twain, and prayed unto the Lord", Kings 4:33].

The door of the senses must be tightly shut before your new claim can be honored. Closing the door of the senses is not as difficult as it appears to be at first.

It is done without effort.

It is impossible to serve two masters at the same time [Matthew 6:24, Luke 16:13].

The master man serves is that which he is conscious of being. I am Lord and Master of that which I am conscious of being.

It is no effort for me to conjure poverty if I am conscious of being poor.

My servant (poverty) is compelled to follow me (conscious of poverty) as long as I AM (the Lord) conscious of being poor.

Instead of fighting against the evidence of the senses, you claim yourself to be that which you desire to be.

As your attention is placed on this claim, the doors of the senses automatically close against your former master (that which you were conscious of being).

As you become lost in the feeling of being (that which you are now claiming to be true of yourself), the doors of the senses once more open, revealing your world to be the perfect expression of that which you are conscious of being.

Let us follow the example of Jesus who realized, as man, He could do nothing to change His present picture of lack.

He closed the door of His senses against His problem and went to His Father, the one to Whom all things are possible [Matthew 19:26; Mark 9:23; 10:27; 14:36; Luke 18:27; Acts 8:37].

Having denied the evidence of His senses, He claimed Himself to be all that, a moment before, His senses told him He was not.

Knowing that consciousness expresses its likeness on earth, He remained in the claimed consciousness until the doors (His senses) opened and confirmed the rulership of the Lord.

Remember, I AM is Lord of all. Never again use the will of man which claims, "I will be". Be as resigned as Jesus and claim, "I AM that".

CHAPTER EIGHT - NO OTHER GOD

"I am the first, and I am the last; and beside Me is no God." – Isaiah 44:6

"I am the Lord thy God, which brought thee out of the land of Egypt, from the house of bondage.

Thou shalt have none other gods before Me." – Deut. 5:6,7

"Thou shalt have no other God beside Me". As long as man entertains a belief in a power apart from himself, so long will he rob himself of the being that he is.

Every belief in powers apart from himself, whether for good or evil, will become the mould of the graven image worshipped.

The beliefs in the potency of drugs to heal, diets to strengthen, moneys to secure, are the values or money changers that must be thrown out of the power [Matthew 21:12; Mark 11:15; Luke 19:45; John 2:14,15] he can then unfailingly manifest that quality.

This understanding throws out the money changers Temple. "Ye are the Temple of the Living God" [1Corinthians 3:16; 6:19 "And what agreement hath the temple of God with idols? for ye are the temple of the living God; as God hath said, I will dwell in them, and walk in them; and I will be their God, and they shall be my people", 2Corinthians 6:16], a Temple made without hands.

It is written, "My house shall be called of all nations a house of prayer, but ye have made it a den of thieves" [Matthew 21:13; "…for Mine house shall be called an house of prayer for all people", Isaiah 56:7].

The thieves who rob you are your own false beliefs. It is your belief in a thing not the thing itself that aids you. There is only one power: I AM He. Because of your belief in external things, you think power into them by transferring the power that you are to the external thing. Realize you yourself are the power you have mistakenly given to outer conditions.

The Bible compares the opinionated man to the camel who could not go through the needle's eye [Matthew 19:24; Mark 10:25; Luke 18:25]. The needle's eye referred to was a small gate in the

walls of Jerusalem, which was so narrow that a camel could not go through it until relieved of its pack.

The rich man, that is the one burdened with false human concepts, cannot enter the Kingdom of Heaven until relieved of his burden [Matthew 19:23] any more than could the camel go through this small gate.

Man feels so secure in his man-made laws, opinions and beliefs that he invests them with an authority they do not possess.

Satisfied that his knowledge is all, he remains unaware that all outward appearances are but states of mind externalized.

When he realizes that the consciousness of a quality externalizes that quality without the aid of any other or many values and establishes the one true value, his own consciousness.

"The Lord is in His holy temple" [Habakkuk 2:20]. Consciousness dwells within that which it is conscious of being. I AM is the Lord and man, his temple.

Knowing that consciousness objectifies itself, man must forgive all men for being that which they are.

He must realize that all are expressing (without the aid of another) that which they are conscious of being.

Peter, the enlightened or disciplined man, knew that a change of consciousness would produce a change of expression.

Instead of sympathizing with the beggars of life at the temple's gate, he declared, "Silver and gold have I none (for thee), but such as I have (the consciousness of freedom), give I unto thee" [Acts 3:6].

"Stir up the gift within you" ["Wherefore I put thee in remembrance that thou stir up the gift of God, which is in thee", 2Timothy 1:6].

Stop begging and claim yourself to be that which you decide to be. Do this and you too will jump from your crippled world into the world of freedom, singing praises to the Lord, I AM.

"Far greater is He that is in you than he that is in the world" ["Ye are of God, little children, and have overcome them: because greater is He that is in you, than he that is in the world", 1John 4:4].

This is the cry of everyone who finds his awareness of being to be God.

Your recognition of this fact will automatically cleanse the temple, your consciousness, of the thieves and robbers, restoring to you that dominion over things, which you lost the moment you forgot the command, "Thou shalt have no other God beside ME".

CHAPTER NINE - THE FOUNDATION STONE

Let every man take heed how he buildeth thereon. For other foundations can no man lay than that is laid, which is Jesus Christ. Now if man build upon this foundation gold, silver, precious stones, wood, hay, stubble; every man"s work shall be made manifest; for the day shall declare it. – 1Cor. 3:10-13

The foundation of all expression is consciousness.

Try as man will, he cannot find a cause of manifestation other than his consciousness of being.

Man thinks he has found the cause of disease in germs, the cause of war in conflicting political ideologies and greed. All such discoveries of man, catalogued as the essence of Wisdom, are foolishness in the eyes of God.

There is only one power and this power is God (consciousness).

It kills; it makes alive; it wounds; it heals; it does all things, good, bad or indifferent. Man moves in a world that is nothing more or less than his consciousness objectified.

Not knowing this, he wars against his reflections while he keeps alive the light and the images which project the reflections.

"I AM the light of the world" [John 8:12]. I AM (consciousness) is the light.

That which I am conscious of being (my conception of myself) – such as "I am rich", "I am healthy", "I am free" – are the images.

The world is the mirror magnifying all that I AM conscious of being.

Stop trying to change the world since it is only the mirror. Man's attempt to change the world by force is as fruitless as breaking a mirror in the hope of changing his face. Leave the mirror and

change your face. Leave the world alone and change your conceptions of yourself. The reflection then will be satisfactory.

Freedom or imprisonment, satisfaction or frustration can only be differentiated by the consciousness of being.

Regardless of your problem, its duration or its magnitude, careful attention to these instructions will in an amazingly short time eliminate even the memory of the problem.

Ask yourself this question: "How would I feel if I were free?" The very moment you sincerely ask this question, the answer comes.

No man can tell another the satisfaction of his desire fulfilled.

It remains for each within himself to experience the feeling and joy of this automatic change of consciousness.

The feeling or thrill that comes to one in response to his self-questioning is the Father state of consciousness or Foundation Stone upon which the conscious change is built.

Just how this feeling will embody itself no one knows, but it will; the Father (consciousness) has ways that no man knows [Romans 11:33]; it is the unalterable law.

All things express their nature. As you wear a feeling, it becomes your nature.

It might take a moment or a year – it is entirely dependent upon the degree of conviction. As doubts vanish and you can feel "I AM this", you begin to develop the fruit or the nature of the thing you are feeling yourself to be.

When a person buys a new hat or pair of shoes, he thinks everyone knows that they are new. He feels unnatural with his newly acquired apparel until it becomes a part of him. The same applies to the wearing of the new states of consciousness.

When you ask yourself the question, "How would I feel if my desire were at this moment realized?" the automatic reply, until it is properly conditioned by time and use, is actually disturbing.

The period of adjustment to realize this potential of consciousness is comparable to the newness of the wearing apparel.

Not knowing that consciousness is ever outpicturing itself in conditions round about you, like Lot's wife, you continually look back upon your problem and again become hypnotized by its seeming naturalness [Genesis 19].

Heed the words of Jesus (salvation): "Leave all and follow Me" [Matthew 4:19; Matthew 8:22; Matthew 16:24; Matthew 19:21; Mark 1:17; Mark 8:34; Mark 10:21; Luke 9:23; Luke 18:22]. "Let the dead bury the dead" [Matthew 8:22; Luke 9:60].

Your problem might have you so hypnotized by its seeming reality and naturalness that you find it difficult to wear the new feeling or consciousness of your savior.

You must assume this garment if you would have results.

The stone (consciousness) which the builders rejected (would not wear) is the chief cornerstone, and other foundations no man can lay.

CHAPTER TEN - TO HIM THAT HATH

Take heed therefore how ye hear; for whosoever hath, to him shall be given; and whosoever hath not, from him shall be taken even that which he seemeth to have. – Luke 8:18

The Bible, which is the greatest psychological book ever written, warns man to be aware of what he hears; then follows this warning with the statement, "To him that hath it shall be given and to him that hath not it shall be taken away".

Though many look upon this statement as one of the most cruel and unjust of the sayings attributed to Jesus, it still remains a just and merciful law based upon life's changeless principle of expression.

Man's ignorance of the working of the law does not excuse him nor save him from the results. Law is impersonal and therefore no respecter of persons [Acts 10:34; Romans 2:11].

Man is warned to be selective in that which he hears and accepts as true.

Everything that man accepts as true leaves an impression on his consciousness and must in time be defined as proof or disproof.

Perceptive hearing is the perfect medium through which man registers impressions.

A man must discipline himself to hear only that which he wants to hear, regardless of rumors or the evidence of his senses to the contrary.

As he conditions his perceptive hearing, he will react only to those impressions which he has decided upon.

This law never fails.

Fully conditioned, man becomes incapable of hearing other than that which contributes to his desire.

God, as you have discovered, is that unconditioned awareness which gives to you all that you are aware of being.

To be aware of being or having anything is to be or have that which you are aware of being. Upon this changeless principle all things rest.

It is impossible for anything to be other than that which it is aware of being.

"To him that hath (that which he is aware of being) it shall be given".

[359] THE POWER OF IMAGINATION: THE NEVILLE GODDARD TREASURY

Good, bad or indifferent – it does not matter – man receives multiplied a hundredfold that which he is aware of being. In keeping with this changeless law, "To him that hath not, it shall be taken from him and added to the one that hath", the rich get richer and the poor get poorer. You can only magnify that which you are conscious of being.

All things gravitate to that consciousness with which they are in tune.

Likewise, all things disentangle themselves from that consciousness with which they are out of tune.

Divide the wealth of the world equally among all men and in a short time, this equal division will be as originally disproportioned. Wealth will find its way back into the pockets of those from whom it was taken.

Instead of joining the chorus of the have-nots who insist on destroying those who have, recognize this changeless law of expression. Consciously define yourself as that which you desire.

Once defined, your conscious claim established, continue in this confidence until the reward is received.

As surely as the day follows the night, any attribute, consciously claimed, will manifest itself.

Thus, that which to the sleeping orthodox world is a cruel and unjust law becomes to the enlightened one of the most merciful and just statements of truth.

"I am come not to destroy but to fulfill" [Matthew 5:17]. Nothing is actually destroyed. Any seeming destruction is a result of a change in consciousness.

Consciousness ever fills full the state in which it dwells.

The state from which consciousness is detached seems to those not familiar with this law to be destructive.

However, this is only preparatory to a new state of consciousness. Claim yourself to be that which you want filled full.

"Nothing is destroyed. All is fulfilled." "To him that hath it shall be given."

CHAPTER ELEVEN - CHRISTMAS

"Behold, a virgin shall be with child and shall bring forth a Son, and they shall call His name Emmanuel, which being interpreted is God with us." – Matthew 1:23

One of the most controversial statements in the New Testament concerns the virgin conception and subsequent birth of Jesus, a conception in which man had no part. It is recorded that a Virgin conceived a Son without the aid of man, then secretly and without effort gave birth to her conception.

This is the foundation upon which all Christendom rests.

The Christian world is asked to believe this story, for man must believe the unbelievable to fully express the greatness that he is.

Scientifically, man might be inclined to discard the whole Bible as untrue because his reason will not permit him to believe that the virgin birth is physiologically possible, but the Bible is a message of the soul and must be interpreted psychologically if man is to discover its true symbology.

Man must see this story as a psychological drama rather than a statement of physical fact. In so doing, he will discover the Bible to be based on a law which, if self-applied, will result in a manifested expression transcending his wildest dreams of accomplishment. To apply this law of self-expression, man must be schooled in the belief and disciplined to stand upon the platform that "all things are possible to God" [Matthew 19:26; Mark 9:23; 10:27; 14:36; Luke 18:27; Acts 8:37].

The outstanding dramatic dates of the New Testament, namely, the birth, death and resurrection of Jesus, were timed and dated to coincide with certain astronomical phenomena.

The mystics who recorded this story noticed that at certain seasons of the year beneficial changes on earth coincided with astronomical changes above.

In writing this psychological drama, they have personified the story of the soul as the biography of man.

Using these cosmic changes, they have marked the Birth and Resurrection of Jesus to convey that the same beneficial changes take place psychologically in the consciousness of man as he follows the law.

Even to those who fail to understand it, the story of Christmas is one of the most beautiful stories ever told.

When unfolded in the light of its mystic symbology, it is revealed as the true birth of every manifestation in the world.

This virgin birth is recorded as having taken place on December 25th or, as certain secret societies celebrate it, on Christmas Eve, at midnight of December 24th.

Mystics established this date to mark the birth of Jesus because it was in keeping with the great earthly benefits this astronomical change signifies.

The astronomical observations which prompted the authors of this drama to use these dates were all made in the northern hemisphere; so from an astronomical point of view, the reverse would be true if seen from the southern latitudes.

However, this story was recorded in the north and therefore was based on northern observation.

Man very early discovered that the sun played a most important part in his life, that without the sun, physical life as he knew it could not be.

So these most important dates in the story of the life of Jesus are based upon the position of the sun as seen from the earth in the northern latitudes.

After the sun reaches its highest point in the heavens in June, it gradually falls southward, taking with it the life of the plant world so that by December almost all of nature has been stilled.

Should the sun continue to fall southward, all nature would be stilled unto death.

However, on December 25th, the sun begins its great move northward, bringing with it the promise of salvation and life anew for the world. Each day, as the sun rises higher in the heavens, man gains confidence in being saved from death by cold and starvation, for he knows

that as it moves northward and crosses the equator all nature will rise again, will be resurrected from its long winter sleep.

Our day is measured from midnight to midnight, and, since the visible day begins in the east and ends in the west, the ancients said the day was born of that constellation which occupied the eastern horizon at midnight. On Christmas Eve, or midnight of December 24th, the constellation Virgo is rising on the eastern horizon.

So it is recorded that this Son and Savior of the world was born of a virgin.

It is also recorded that this virgin mother was traveling through the night, that she stopped at an inn and was given the only available room among the animals and there in a manger, where the animals fed, the shepherds found the Holy Child.

The animals with whom the Holy Virgin was lodged are the holy animals of the zodiac. There in that constantly moving circle of astronomical animals stands the Holy Mother, Virgo, and there you will see her every midnight of December 24th, standing on the eastern horizon as the sun and savior of the world starts his journey northward.

Psychologically, this birth takes place in man on that day when man discovers his consciousness to be the sun and savior of his world. When man knows the significance of this mystical statement, "I am the light of the world" [Matthew 5:14; John 8:12], he will realize that his I AM, or consciousness, is the sun of his life, which sun radiates images upon the screen of space. These images are in the likeness of that which he, as man, is conscious of being. Thus qualities and attributes which appear to move upon the screen of his world are really projections of this light from within himself.

The numberless unrealized hopes and ambitions of man are the seeds which are buried within the consciousness or virgin womb of man. There they remain like the seeds of earth, held in the frozen waste of winter, waiting for the sun to move northward or for man to return to the knowledge of who he is. In returning he moves northward through recognition of his true self by claiming "I AM the light of the world".

When man discovers his consciousness or I AM to be God, the savior of his world, he will be as the sun in its northern passage.

All hidden urges and ambitions will then be warmed and stimulated into birth by this knowledge of his true self.

He will claim that he is that which heretofore he hoped to be.

Without the aid of any man, he will define himself as that which he desires to express.

He will discover that his I AM is the virgin conceiving without the aid of man, that all conceptions of himself, when felt, and fixed in consciousness, will be embodied easily as living realities in his world.

Man will one day realize that this whole drama takes place in his consciousness, that his unconditioned consciousness or I AM is the Virgin Mary desiring to express, that through this law of self-expression he defines himself as that which he desires to express and that without the help or cooperation of anyone he will express that which he has consciously claimed and defined himself as being.

He will then understand: why Christmas is fixed on December 25th, while Easter is a movable date; why upon the virgin conception the whole of Christendom rests; that his consciousness is the virgin womb or bride of the Lord receiving impressions as self-impregnations and then without assistance embodying these impressions as the expressions of his life.

CHAPTER TWELVE - CRUCIFIXION AND RESURRECTION

"I AM the Resurrection and the Life; he that believeth in Me, though he were dead, yet shall he live." – John 11:25

The mystery of the crucifixion and the resurrection is so interwoven that, to be fully understood, the two must be explained together for one determines the other. This mystery is symbolized on earth in the rituals of Good Friday and Easter. You have observed that the anniversary of this cosmic event, announced every year by the church, is not a fixed date as are other anniversaries marking births and deaths, but that this day changes from year to year, falling anywhere from the 22nd day of March to the 25th day of April.

The day of resurrection is determined in this manner. The first Sunday after the full moon in Aries is celebrated as Easter. Aries begins on the 21st day of March and ends approximately on the 19th day of April. The sun's entry into Aries marks the beginning of Spring. The moon in its monthly transit around the earth will form sometime between March 21st and April 25th an opposition to the sun, which opposition is called a full moon. The first Sunday after this phenomenon of the heavens occurs is celebrated as Easter; the Friday preceding this day is observed as Good Friday.

This movable date should tell the observant one to look for some interpretation other than the one commonly accepted. These days do not mark the anniversaries of the death and resurrection of an individual who lived on earth.

Seen from the earth, the sun in its northern passage appears at the Spring season of the year to cross the imaginary line man calls the equator. So it is said by the mystic to be crossified or crucified that man might live. It is significant that soon after this event takes place, all nature begins to arise or resurrect itself from its long Winter's sleep. Therefore, it may be concluded that this disturbance of nature, at this season of the year, is due directly to this crossing. Thus, it is believed that the sun must shed its blood on the Passover.

If these days marked the death and resurrection of a man, they would be fixed so that they would fall on the same date every year as all other historical events are fixed, but obviously this is not the case.

These dates were not intended to mark the anniversaries of the death and resurrection of Jesus, the man.

The scriptures are psychological dramas and will reveal their meaning only as they are interpreted psychologically.

These dates are adjusted to coincide with the cosmic change which occurs at this time of the year, marking the death of the old year and the beginning or resurrecting of the new year or Spring. These dates do symbolize the death and resurrection of the Lord; but this Lord is not a man; it is your awareness of being.

It is recorded that He gave His life that you might live, "I AM come that you might have life and that you might have it more abundantly" [John 10:10]. Consciousness slays itself by detaching itself from that which it is conscious of being so that it may live to that which it desires to be.

Spring is the time of year when the millions of seeds, which all Winter lay buried in the ground, suddenly spring into visibility that man might live; and, because the mystical drama of the crucifixion and resurrection is in the nature of this yearly change, it is celebrated at this Spring season of the year; but, actually, it is taking place every moment of time.

The being who is crucified is your awareness of being. The cross is your conception of yourself. The resurrection is the lifting into visibility of this conception of yourself.

Far from being a day of mourning, Good Friday should be a day of rejoicing, for there can be no resurrection or expression unless there is first a crucifixion or impression.

The thing to be resurrected in your case is that which you desire to be. To do this, you must feel yourself to be the thing desired.

You must feel "I AM the resurrection and the life of the desire".

I AM (your awareness of being) is the power resurrecting and making alive that which in your awareness you desire to be.

"Two shall agree on touching anything and I shall establish it on earth" ["Again I say unto you, That if two of you shall agree on earth as touching any thing that they shall ask, it shall be done for them of my Father which is in heaven, Matthew 18:19].

The two agreeing are you (your awareness – the consciousness desiring) and the thing desired. When this agreement is attained, the crucifixion is completed; two have crossed or crossified each other.

I AM and THAT – consciousness and that which you are conscious of being – have joined and are one; I AM now nailed or fixed in the belief that I AM this fusion.

Jesus or I AM is nailed upon the cross of that.

The nail that binds you upon the cross is the nail of feeling.

The mystical union is now consummated and the result will be the birth of a child or the resurrection of a son bearing witness of his Father.

Consciousness is united to that which it is conscious of being. The world of expression is the child confirming this union.

The day you cease to be conscious of being that which you are now conscious of being, that day your child or expression shall die and return to the bosom of his father, the faceless, formless awareness.

All expressions are the results of such mystical unions.

So the priests are correct when they say that true marriages are made in heaven and can only be dissolved in heaven.

But let me clarify this statement by telling you that heaven is not a locality; it is a state of consciousness.

The Kingdom of Heaven is within you [Luke 17:21].

In heaven (consciousness) God is touched by that which he is aware of being. "Who has touched me? For I perceive virtue has gone out of me" ["Who touched me? And Jesus said, Somebody hath touched me: for I perceive that virtue is gone out of me", Luke 8:45,46; Mark 5:30].

The moment this touching (feeling) takes place, there is an offspring or going-out-of-me into visibility taking place.

The day man feels "I AM free", "I AM wealthy", "I AM strong", God (I AM) is touched or crucified by these qualities or virtues.

The results of such touching or crucifying will be seen in the birth or resurrection of the qualities felt, for man must have visible confirmation of all that he is conscious of being.

Now you will know why man or manifestation is always made in the image of God. Your awareness imag[in]es and outpictures all that you are aware of being.

"I AM the Lord and besides me there is no God" [Isaiah 45:5,6]. "I AM the Resurrection and the Life" [John 11:25].

You shall become fixed in the belief that you are that which you desire to be. Before you have any visible proof that you are, you will, from the deep conviction which you have felt fixed within you, know that you are; and so, without waiting for the confirmation of your senses, you will cry, "It is finished" [John 19:30].

Then, with a faith born of the knowledge of this changeless law, you will be as one dead and entombed; you will be still and unmoved in your conviction and confident that you will resurrect the qualities that you have fixed and are feeling within you.

CHAPTER THIRTEEN
THE I'M-PRESSIONS

"And as we have borne the image of the earthly, we shall also bear the image of the heavenly." – Cor. 15:49

Your consciousness or your I AM is the unlimited potential upon which impressions are made. I'm-pressions are defined states pressed upon your I AM.

Your consciousness or your I AM can be likened to a sensitive film. In the virgin state, it is potentially unlimited.

You can impress or record a message of love or a hymn of hate, a wonderful symphony or discordant jazz. It does not matter what the nature of the impression might be; your I AM will, without a murmur, willingly receive and sustain all impressions.

Your consciousness is the one referred to in Isaiah 53:3-7.

"He is despised and rejected of men; a man of sorrows, and acquainted with grief: and we hid as it were our faces from Him, He was despised, and we esteemed Him not".

"Surely He hath borne our grieves, and carried our sorrows: yet we did esteem Him stricken, smitten of God, and afflicted".

"But He was wounded for our transgressions, He was bruised for our iniquities: the chastisement of our peace was upon him; and with his stripes we are healed".

"All we like sheep have gone astray; we have turned every one to his own way; and the Lord hath laid on Him the iniquity of us all".

"He was oppressed, and He was afflicted, yet He opened not his mouth:

He is brought as a lamb to the slaughter and as a sheep before her shearers is dumb, so He openeth not His mouth.

" Your unconditioned consciousness is impersonal; it is no respecter of persons [Acts 10:34; Romans 2:11].

Without thought or effort, it automatically expresses every impression that is registered upon it. It does not object to any impression that is placed on it for; although it is capable of receiving and expressing any and all defined states, it remains forever an immaculate and an

[369] THE POWER OF IMAGINATION: THE NEVILLE GODDARD TREASURY

unlimited potential.

Your I AM is the foundation upon which the defined state or conception of yourself rests; but it is not defined by, nor is it dependent on, such defined states for its being.

Your I AM neither expands nor contracts; nothing alters or adds to it. Before any defined state was, IT is. When all states cease to be, IT is. All defined states or conceptions of yourself are but ephemeral expressions of your eternal being.

To be impressed is to be I'm-pressed (I AM pressed – first person – present tense). All expressions are the result of I'm-pressions. Only as you claim yourself to be that which you desire to be will you express such desires.

Let all desires become impressions of qualities that are, not of qualities that will be. I'm (your awareness) is God and God is the fullness of all, the Eternal NOW, I AM.

Take no thought of tomorrow; tomorrow's expressions are determined by today's impressions.

"Now is the accepted time" [Cor. 6:2, Isa. 49:8]. "The Kingdom of Heaven is at hand" [Matthew 4:17]. Jesus (salvation) said, "I am with you always" [Matthew 28:20]. Your awareness is the savior that is with you always; but, if you deny Him, He will deny you also [Matei 10:33; Luca 12:9]. You deny Him by claiming that He will appear, as millions today are claiming that salvation is to come; this is the equivalent of saying, "We are not saved".

You must stop looking for your savior to appear and begin claiming that you are already saved, and the signs of your claims will follow.

When the widow was asked what she had in her house, there was recognition of substance; her claim was a few drops of oil [Kings 4:1-6]. A few drops will become a gusher if properly claimed.

Your awareness magnifies all consciousness.

To claim that I shall have oil (joy) is to confess that I have empty measures. Such impressions of lack produce lack.

God, your awareness, is no respecter of persons [Acts 10:34; Romans 2:11]. Purely impersonal, God, this awareness of all existence, receives impressions, qualities and attributes defining consciousness, namely, your impressions.

Your every desire should be determined by need. Needs, whether seeming or real, will automatically be fulfilled when they are welcomed with sufficient intensity of purpose as defined desires.

Knowing that your awareness is God, you should look upon each desire as the spoken word of God, telling you that which is.

"Cease ye from man, whose breath is in his nostrils: for wherein is he to be accounted of?" [Isaiah 2:22].

We are ever that which is defined by our awareness. Never claim, "I shall be that". Let all claims from now on be, "I AM that I AM". Before we ask, we are answered. The solution of any problem associated with desire is obvious. Every problem automatically produces the desire of solution.

Man is schooled in the belief that his desires are things against which he must struggle. In his ignorance, he denies his savior who is constantly knocking at the door of consciousness to be let in (I AM the door).

Would not your desire, if realized, save you from your problem? To let your savior in is the easiest thing in the world.

Things must be, to be let in.

You are conscious of a desire; the desire is something you are aware of now.

Your desire, though invisible, must be affirmed by you to be something that is real.

"God calleth those things which be not (are not seen) as though they were" [Romans 4:17]. Claiming I AM the thing desired, I let the savior in.

"Behold, I stand at the door, and knock: if any man hear My voice, and open the door, I will come in to him, and will sup with him, and he with Me" [Revelation 3:20].

Every desire is the savior's knock at the door. This knock every man hears.

Man opens the door when he claims, "I AM He". See to it that you let your savior in.

Let the thing desired press itself upon you until you are I'm-pressed with nowness of your savior; then you utter the cry of victory, "It is finished" [John 19:30].

CHAPTER FOURTEEN - CIRCUMCISION

"In whom also ye are circumcised with the circumcision made without hands; in putting off the body of the sins of the flesh by circumcision of Christ." – Col. 2:11

Circumcision is the operation which removes the veil that hides the head of creation. The physical act has nothing to do with the spiritual act.

The whole world could be physically circumcised and yet remain unclean and blind leaders of the blind.

The spiritually circumcised have had the veil of darkness removed and know themselves to be Christ, the light of the world.

Let me now perform the spiritual operation on you, the reader.

This act is performed on the eighth day after birth, not because this day has any special significance or in any way differs from other days, but it is performed on this eighth day because eight is the figure which has neither beginning nor end.

Furthermore, the ancients symbolized the eighth numeral or letter as an enclosure or veil within and behind which lay buried the mystery of creation.

Thus, the secret of the operation on the eighth day is in keeping with the nature of the act, which act is to reveal the eternal head of creation, that changeless something in which all things begin and end and yet which remains its eternal self when all things cease to be.

This mysterious something is your awareness of being. At this moment you are aware of being, but you are also aware of being someone.

This someone is the veil that hides the being you really are.

You are first conscious of being, then you are conscious of being man. After the veil of man is placed upon your faceless self, you become conscious of being a member of a certain race, nation, family, creed etc.

The veil to be lifted in spiritual circumcision is the veil of man.

But before this can be done, you must cut away the adhesions of race, nation, family and so on.

"In Christ there is neither Greek nor Jew, bond nor free, male nor female" ["…a renewal in which there is no distinction between Greek and Jew, circumcised and uncircumcised, barbarian, Scythian, slave and freeman, but Christ is all, and in all", Colossians 3:11].

[372] NEVILLE GODDARD

"You must leave father, mother, brother and follow me" ["If anyone comes to Me, and does not hate his own father and mother and wife and children and brothers and sisters, yes, and even his own life, he cannot be My disciple", Luke 14:26].

To accomplish this you stop identifying yourself with these divisions by becoming indifferent to such claims. Indifference is the knife that severs. Feeling is the tie that binds.

When you can look upon man as one grand brotherhood without distinction of race or creed, then you will know that you have severed these adhesions.

With these ties cut, all that now separates you from your true being is your belief that you are man.

To remove this last veil, you drop your conception of yourself as man by knowing yourself just to be.

Instead of the consciousness of "I AM man", let there be just "I AM" – faceless, formless and without figure.

You are spiritually circumcised when the consciousness of man is dropped and your unconditioned awareness of being is revealed to you as the everlasting head of creation, a formless, faceless all-knowing presence.

Then, unveiled and awake, you will declare and know that – I AM is God and beside me, this awareness, there is no God.

This mystery is told symbolically in the Bible story of Jesus washing the feet of his disciples. It is recorded that Jesus laid aside his garments and took a towel and girded himself. Then, after washing his disciples' feet, he wiped them with the towel wherewith he was girded. Peter protested the washing of his feet and was told that unless his feet were washed he would have no part of Jesus. Peter on hearing this replied, "Lord, not my feet only, but also my hands and my head". Jesus answered and said, "He that is washed needeth not save to wash his feet, but is clean every whit" [John 13:1-10].

Common sense would tell the reader that a man is not clean all over just, because his feet are washed. Therefore, he should either discard this story as fantastic or else look for its hidden meaning.

Every story of the Bible is a psychological drama taking place in the consciousness of man, and this one is no exception. This washing of the disciples' feet is the mystical story of spiritual circumcision or the revealing of the secrets of the Lord.

[373] THE POWER OF IMAGINATION: THE NEVILLE GODDARD TREASURY

Jesus is called the Lord. You are told that the Lord's name is I AM – Je Suis. "I AM the Lord that is my name", Isaiah 42:8. The story states that Jesus was naked save for a towel which covered his loins or secrets. Jesus or Lord symbolizes your awareness of being whose secrets are hidden by the towel (consciousness of man). The foot symbolizes the understanding which must be washed of all human beliefs or conceptions of itself by the Lord.

As the towel is removed to dry the feet, the secrets of the Lord are revealed.

In short, the removing of the belief that you are man reveals your awareness as the head of creation. Man is the foreskin hiding the head of creation. I AM the Lord hidden by the veil of man.

CHAPTER FIFTEEN
INTERVAL OF TIME

"Let not your heart be troubled; ye believe in God, believe also in Me. In My Father's house are many mansions; if it were not so, I would have told you. I go to prepare a place for you. And if I go and prepare a place for you, I will come again, and receive you unto Myself; that where I am, there ye may be also." – John 14:1-3

"Let not your heart be troubled; ye believe in God, believe also in me. In my Father's house are many mansions; if it were not so, I would have told you. I go to prepare a place for you. And if I go and prepare a place for you, I will come again, and receive you unto myself; that where I am, there ye may be also".

The ME in whom you must believe is your consciousness, the I AM; it is God.

It is also the Father's house containing within itself all conceivable states of consciousness. Every conditioned state of consciousness is called a mansion.

This conversation takes place within yourself.

Your I AM, the unconditioned consciousness, is the Christ Jesus speaking to the conditioned self or the John Smith consciousness.

"I AM John", from a mystical point of view, is two beings, namely, Christ and John.

So I go to prepare a place for you, moving from your present state of consciousness into that state desired.

It is a promise by your Christ or awareness of being to your present conception of yourself that you will leave your present consciousness and appropriate another.

Man is such a slave to time that, if after he has appropriated a state of consciousness which is not now seen by the world and it, the appropriated state, does not immediately embody itself, he loses faith in his unseen claim; forthwith he drops it and returns to his former static state of being.

Because of this limitation of man, I have found it very helpful to employ a specified interval of time in making this journey into a prepared mansion.

"Wait but a little while" [Job 36:2].

We have all catalogued the different days of the week, months of the year and seasons. By this, I mean you and I have said time and again, "Why, today feels just like Sunday" or "-Monday" or "-Saturday". We have also said in the middle of Summer, "Why, this feels and looks like the Fall of the year".

This is positive proof that you and I have definite feelings associated with these different days, months and seasons of the year. Because of this association, we can at any time consciously dwell in that day or season which we have selected.

Do not selfishly define this interval in days and hours because you are anxious to receive it, but simply remain in the conviction that it is done – time, being purely relative, should be eliminated entirely – and your desire will be fulfilled.

This ability to dwell at any point in time permits us to employ time in our travel into the desired mansion.

Now I (consciousness) go to a point in time and there prepare a place. If I go to such a point in time and prepare a place, I shall return to this point in time where I have left; and I shall pick up and take you with me into that place which I have prepared, that where I AM, there ye may also be.

Let me give you an example of this travel.

Suppose you had an intense desire. Like most men who are enslaved by time, you might feel that you could not possibly realize so large a desire in a limited interval. But admitting that all things are possible to God, believing God to be the ME within you or your consciousness of being, you can say,

"As John, I can do nothing; but since all things are possible to God and God I know to be my consciousness of being, I can realize my desire in a little while.

How my desire will be realized I do not (as John) know, but by the very law of my being I do know that it shall be".

With this belief firmly established, decide what would be a relative, rational interval of time in which such a desire could be realized.

Again, let me remind you not to shorten the interval of time because you are anxious to receive your desire; make it a natural interval. No one can give you the time interval. Only you can say what the natural interval would be to you. The interval of time is relative, that is, no two individuals would give the same measurement of time for the realization of their desire.

Time is ever conditioned by man's conception of himself.

Confidence in yourself as determined by conditioned consciousness always shortens the interval of time.

If you were accustomed to great accomplishments, you would give yourself a much shorter interval in which to accomplish your desire than the man schooled in defeat.

If today were Wednesday and you decided that it would be quite possible for your desire to embody a new realization of yourself by Sunday, then Sunday becomes the point in time that you would visit.

To make this visit, you shut out Wednesday and let in Sunday. This is accomplished by simply feeling that it is Sunday. Begin to hear the church bells; begin to feel the quietness of the day and all that Sunday means to you; actually feel that it is Sunday.

When this is accomplished, feel the joy of having received that which on Wednesday was but a desire. Feel the complete thrill of having received it, and then return to Wednesday, the point in time you left behind you.

In doing this, you created a vacuum in consciousness by moving from Wednesday to Sunday. Nature, abhorring vacuums, rushes in to fill it, thereby fashioning a mould in the likeness of that which you potentially create, namely, the joy of having realized your defined desire.

As you return to Wednesday, you will be filled with a joyful expectancy, because you have established the consciousness of that which must take place the following Sunday.

As you walk through the interval of Thursday, Friday and Saturday, nothing disturbs you regardless of conditions, because you predetermined that which you would be on the Sabbath and that remains an unalterable conviction.

Having gone before and prepared the place, you have returned to John and are now taking him with you through the interval of three days into the prepared place that he might share your joy with you, for where I AM, there ye may also be.

[377] THE POWER OF IMAGINATION: THE NEVILLE GODDARD TREASURY

CHAPTER SIXTEEN
THE TRIUNE GOD

"And God said, Let Us make man in Our image, after Our likeness." – Gen. 1:26

Having discovered God to be our awareness of being and this unconditioned changeless reality (the I AM) to be the only creator, let us see why the Bible records a trinity as the creator of the world.

In the 26th verse of the first chapter of Genesis, it is stated, "And God said, Let Us make man in Our image".

The churches refer to this plurality of Gods as God the Father, God the Son and God the Holy Spirit.

What is meant by "God the Father, God the Son and God the Holy Spirit" they have never attempted to explain for they are in the dark concerning this mystery.

The Father, Son and Holy Spirit are three aspects or conditions of the unconditioned awareness of being called God.

The consciousness of being precedes the consciousness of being something. That unconditioned awareness which preceded all states of awareness is God – I AM.

The three conditioned aspects or divisions of itself can best be told in this manner:

The receptive attitude of mind is that aspect which receives impressions and therefore may be likened to a womb or Mother.

That which makes the impression is the male or pressing aspect and is therefore known as Father.

The impression in time becomes an expression, which expression is ever the likeness and image of the impression; therefore this objectified aspect is said to be the Son bearing witness of his Father-Mother.

An understanding of this mystery of the trinity enables the one who understands it to completely transform his world and fashion it to his own liking.

Here is a practical application of this mystery.

Sit quietly and decide what it is you would like most to express or possess. After you have decided, close your eyes and take your attention completely away from all that would deny the realization of the thing desired; then assume a receptive attitude of mind and play the game of supposing by imagining how you would feel if you were now to realize your desire.

Begin to listen as though space were talking to you and telling you that you are now that which you desire to be.

This receptive attitude is the state of consciousness that you must assume before an impression can be made.

As this pliable and impressive state of mind is attained, then begin to impress upon yourself the fact that you are that which you desired to be by claiming and feeling that you are now expressing and possessing that which you had decided to be and to have.

Continue in this attitude until the impression is made.

As you contemplate, being and possessing that which you have decided to be and to have, you will notice that with every inhalation of breath a joyful thrill courses through your entire being.

This thrill increases in intensity as you feel more and more the joy of being that which you are claiming yourself to be.

Then in one final deep inhalation, your whole being will explode with the joy of accomplishment and you will know by your feeling that you are impregnated by God, the Father.

As soon as the impression is made, open your eyes and return to the world that but a few moments before you had shut out.

In this receptive attitude of yours, while you contemplated being that which you desired to be, you were actually performing the spiritual act of generation so you are now on your return from

this silent meditation a pregnant being bearing a child or impression, which child was immaculately conceived without the aid of man.

Doubt is the only force capable of disturbing the seed or impression; to avoid a miscarriage of so wonderful a child, walk in secrecy through the necessary interval of time that it will take the impression to become an expression.

Tell no man of your spiritual romance. Lock your secret within you in joy, confident and happy that some day you will bear the son of your lover by expressing and possessing the nature of your impression.

Then will you know the mystery of "God said, Let Us make man in

Our image".

You will know that the plurality of Gods referred to is the three aspects of your own consciousness and that you are the trinity, meeting in a spiritual conclave to fashion a world in the image and likeness of that which you are conscious of being.

CHAPTER SEVENTEEN
PRAYER

"When thou prayest, enter into thy closet, and when thou hast shut thy door, pray to thy Father which is in secret; and thy Father which seeth in secret shall reward thee openly." – Matt. 6:6

"What things soever ye desire, when ye pray, believe that ye receive them, and ye shall have them." – Mark 11:24

Prayer is the most wonderful experience man can have.

Unlike the daily murmurings of the vast majority of mankind in all lands who by their vain repetitions hope to gain the ear of God, prayer is the ecstasy of a spiritual wedding taking place in the deep, silent stillness of consciousness.

In its true sense prayer is God's marriage ceremony. Just as a maid on her wedding day relinquishes the name of her family to assume the name of her husband, in like manner, one who prays must relinquish his present name or nature and assume the nature of that for which he prays.

The gospels have clearly instructed man as to the performance of this ceremony in the following manner:

"When ye pray go within in secret and shut the door and your Father who sees in secret will reward you openly" [Matthew 6:6].

The going within is the entering of the bridal chamber. Just as no one but the bride and groom are permitted to enter so holy a room as the bridal suite on the night of the marriage ceremony, likewise no one but the one who prays and that for which he prays are permitted to enter the holy hour of prayer. As the bride and groom on entering the bridal suite securely shut the door against the outside world, so too must the one who enters the holy hour of prayer close the door of the senses and entirely shut out the world round about him.

This is accomplished by taking the attention completely away from all things other than that with which you are now in love (the thing desired).

The second phase of this spiritual ceremony is defined in these words, "When ye pray, believe that ye receive, and ye shall receive".

As you joyfully contemplate being and possessing that which you desire to be and to have, you have taken this second step and are

[381] THE POWER OF IMAGINATION: THE NEVILLE GODDARD TREASURY

therefore spiritually performing the acts of marriage and generation.

Your receptive attitude of mind while praying or contemplating can be likened to a bride or womb for it is that aspect of mind which receives the impressions.

That which you contemplate being is the groom, for it is the name or nature you assume and therefore is that which leaves its impregnation; so one dies to maidenhood or present nature as one assumes the name and nature of the impregnation.

Lost in contemplation and having assumed the name and nature of the thing contemplated, your whole being thrills with the joy of being it. This thrill, which runs through your entire being as you appropriate the consciousness of your desire, is the proof that you are both married and impregnated.

As you return from this silent meditation, the door is once more opened upon the world you had left behind. But this time you return as a pregnant bride.

You enter the world a changed being and, although no one but you knows of this wonderful romance, the world will, in a very short while, see the signs of your pregnancy, for you will begin to express that which you in your hour of silence felt yourself to be.

The mother of the world or bride of the Lord is purposely called Mary, or water, for water loses its identity as it assumes the nature of that with which it is mixed; likewise, Mary, the receptive attitude of mind, must lose its identity as it assumes the nature of the thing desired.

Only as one is willing to give up his present limitations and identity can he become that which he desires to be.

Prayer is the formula by which such divorces and marriages are accomplished. "Two shall agree as touching anything and it shall be established on earth" [Matthew 18:19].

The two agreeing are you, the bride, and the thing desired, the groom.

As this agreement is accomplished, a son bearing witness of this union will be born. You begin to express and possess that which you are conscious of being.

Praying, then, is recognizing yourself to be that which you desire to be rather than begging God for that which you desire.

Millions of prayers are daily unanswered because man prays to a God who does not exist.

Consciousness being God, one must seek in consciousness for the thing desired by assuming the consciousness of the quality desired. Only as one does this will his prayers be answered.

To be conscious of being poor while praying for riches is to be rewarded with that which you are conscious of being, namely, poverty.

Prayers, to be successful, must be claimed and appropriated. Assume the positive consciousness of the thing desired.

With your desire defined, quietly go within and shut the door behind you. Lose yourself in your desire; feel yourself to be one with it; remain in this fixation until you have absorbed the life and name by claiming and feeling yourself to be and to have that which you desired.

When you emerge from the hour of prayer, you must do so conscious of being and possessing that which you heretofore desired.

CHAPTER EIGHTEEN
THE TWELVE DISCIPLES

"And when He had called unto Him His twelve disciples, He gave them power against unclean spirits, to cast them out, and to heal all manner of sickness and all manner of disease." – Matt. 10:1

The twelve disciples represent the twelve qualities of mind which can be controlled and disciplined by man.

If disciplined, they will at all times obey the command of the one who has disciplined them.

These twelve qualities in man are potentials of every mind. Undisciplined, their actions resemble more the actions of a mob than they do of a trained and disciplined army. All the storms and confusions that engulf man can be traced directly to these twelve ill-related characteristics of the human mind in its present slumbering state.

Until they are awakened and disciplined, they will permit every rumor and sensuous emotion to move them.

When these twelve are disciplined and brought under control, the one who accomplishes this control will say to them, "Hereafter I call you not slaves, but friends" ["Henceforth I call you not servants for the servant knoweth not what his lord doeth but I have called you friends, for all things that I have heard of My Father I have made known unto you", John 15:15].

He knows that from that moment on, each acquired disciplined attribute of mind will befriend and protect him.

The names of the twelve qualities reveal their natures. These names are not given to them until they are called to discipleship.

They are: Simon, who was later surnamed Peter, Andrew, James, John, Philip, Bartholomew, Thomas, Matthew, James the son of Alphaeus, Thaddaeus, Simon the Canaanite and Judas [Matthew 10; Mark 1; Mark 3; Luke 6].

The first quality to be called and disciplined is Simon, or the attribute of hearing.

This faculty, when lifted to the level of a disciple, permits only such impressions to reach consciousness as those which his hearing has commanded him to let enter. No matter what the wisdom of

[384] NEVILLE GODDARD

man might suggest or the evidence of his senses convey, if such suggestions and ideas are not in keeping with that which he hears, he remains unmoved. This one has been instructed by his Lord and made to understand that every suggestion he permits to pass his gate will, on reaching his Lord and Master (his consciousness), leave its impression there, which impression must in time become an expression.

The instruction to Simon is that he should permit only dignified and honorable visitors or impressions to enter the house (consciousness) of his Lord. No mistake can be covered up or hidden from his Master, for every expression of life tells his Lord whom he consciously or unconsciously entertained.

When Simon, by his works, proves himself to be a true and faithful disciple, then he receives the surname of Peter, or the rock, the unmoved disciple, the one who cannot be bribed or coerced by any visitor. He is called by his Lord Simon Peter, the one who faithfully hears the commands of his Lord and besides which commands he hears not.

It is this Simon Peter who discovers the I AM to be Christ, and for his discovery is given the keys to heaven, and is made the foundation stone upon which the Temple of God rests.

Buildings must have firm foundations and only the disciplined hearing can, on learning that the I AM is Christ, remain firm and unmoved in the knowledge that I AM Christ and beside ME there is no savior.

The second quality to be called to discipleship is Andrew, or courage.

As the first quality, faith in oneself, is developed, it automatically calls into being its brother, courage.

Faith in oneself, which asks no man's help but quietly and alone appropriates the consciousness of the quality desired and – in spite of reason or the evidence of his senses to the contrary continues faithful-patiently waiting in the knowledge that his unseen claim if sustained must be realized – such faith develops a courage and strength of character that are beyond the wildest dreams of the undisciplined man whose faith is in things seen.

The faith of the undisciplined man cannot really be called faith. For if the armies, medicines or wisdom of man in which his faith is placed be taken from him, his faith and courage go with it. But from the disciplined one the whole world could be taken and yet he would remain faithful in the knowledge that the state of consciousness in which he abides must in due season embody itself. This courage is

Peter's brother Andrew, the disciple, who knows what it is to dare, to do and to be silent.

The next two (third & fourth) who are called are also related.

These are the brothers, James and John, James the just, the righteous judge, and his brother John, the beloved.

Justice to be wise must be administered with love, ever turning the other cheek and at all times returning good for evil, love for hate, non-violence for violence.

The disciple James, symbol of a disciplined judgment, must, when raised to the high office of a supreme judge, be blindfolded that he may not be influenced by the flesh nor judge after the appearances of being. Disciplined judgment is administered by one who is not influenced by appearances.

The one who has called these brothers to discipleship continues faithful to his command to hear only that which he has been commanded to hear, namely, the Good.

The man who has this quality of his mind disciplined is incapable of hearing and accepting as true anything – either of himself or another – which does not on the hearing fill his heart with love.

These two disciples or aspects of the mind are one and inseparable when awakened.

Such a disciplined one forgives all men for being that which they are. He knows as a wise judge that every man perfectly expresses that which he is, as man, conscious of being.

He knows that upon the changeless foundation of consciousness all manifestation rests, that changes of expression can be brought about only through changes of consciousness.

With neither condemnation nor criticism, these disciplined qualities of the mind permit everyone to be that which he is. However, although allowing this perfect freedom of choice to all, they are

nevertheless ever watchful to see that they themselves prophesy and do – both for others and themselves – only such things which when expressed glorify, dignify and give joy to the expresser.

The fifth quality called to discipleship is Philip.

This one asked to be shown the Father. The awakened man knows that the Father is the state of consciousness in which man dwells, and that this state or Father can be seen only as it is expressed.

He knows himself to be the perfect likeness or image of that consciousness with which he is identified.

So He declares, "No man has at any time seen My Father; but I, the Son, who dwelleth in His bosom have revealed Him; ["No one has seen God at any time; the only begotten God who is in the bosom of the Father, He has explained Him", John 1:18]; therefore, when you see Me, the Son, you see My Father, for I come to bear witness of My Father" ["If ye had known Me, ye should have known My Father also: and from henceforth ye know Him, and have seen Him", John 14-7; "Have I been so long time with you, and yet hast thou not known Me, Philip? he that hath seen Me hath seen the Father; and how sayest thou then, Shew us the Father? Believest thou not that I am in the Father, and the Father in Me? the words that I speak unto you I speak not of Myself: but the Father that dwelleth in Me, He doeth the works. Believe Me that I am in the Father, and the Father in Me: or else believe Me for the very works" sake, John 14:9-11].

I and My Father, consciousness and its expression, God and man, are one.

This aspect of the mind, when disciplined, persists until ideas, ambitions and desires become embodied realities. This is the quality which states "Yet in my flesh shall I see God" [Job 19:26].

It knows how to make the word flesh [John 1:14], how to give form to the formless. The sixth disciple is called Bartholomew.

This quality is the imaginative faculty, which quality of the mind when once awake distinguishes one from the masses.

An awakened imagination places the one so awakened head and shoulders above the average man, giving him the appearance of a beacon light in a world of darkness.

No quality so separates man from man as does the disciplined imagination.

This is the separation of the wheat from the chaff. Those who have given most to Society are our artists, scientists, inventors and others with vivid imaginations.

Should a survey be made to determine the reason why so many seemingly educated men and women fail in their after-college years or should it be made to determine the reason for the different earning powers of the masses, there would be no doubt but that imagination played the important part.

Such a survey would show that it is imagination which makes one a leader while the lack of it makes one a follower.

Instead of developing the imagination of man, our educational system oftentimes stifles it by attempting to put into the mind of man the wisdom he seeks. It forces him to memorize a number of textbooks which, all too soon, are disproved by later textbooks.

Education is not accomplished by putting something into man; its purpose is to draw out of man the wisdom which is latent within him. May the reader call Bartholomew to discipleship, for only as this quality is raised to discipleship will you have the capacity to conceive ideas that will lift you beyond the limitations of man.

The seventh is called Thomas.

This disciplined quality doubts or denies every rumor and suggestion that are not in harmony with that which Simon Peter has been commanded to let enter.

The man who is conscious of being healthy (not because of inherited health, diets or climate, but because he is awakened and knows the state of consciousness in which he lives) will, in spite of the conditions of the world, continue to express health.

He could hear, through the press, radio and wise men of the world that a plague was sweeping the earth and yet he would remain unmoved and unimpressed. Thomas, the doubter – when

disciplined – would deny that sickness or anything else which was not in sympathy with the consciousness to which he belonged had any power to affect him.

This quality of denial – when disciplined – protects man from receiving impressions that are not in harmony with his nature. He adopts an attitude of total indifference to all suggestions that are foreign to that which he desires to express. Disciplined denial is not a fight or a struggle but total indifference.

Matthew, the eighth, is the gift of God.

This quality of the mind reveals man's desires as gifts of God.

The man who has called this disciple into being knows that every desire of his heart is a gift from heaven and that it contains both the power and the plan of its self-expression.

Such a man never questions the manner of its expression. He knows that the plan of expression is never revealed to man for God's ways are past finding out [Romans 11:33].

He fully accepts his desires as gifts already received and goes his way in peace confident that they shall appear.

The ninth disciple is called James, the son of Alphaeus.

This is the quality of discernment. A clear and ordered mind is the voice which calls this disciple into being.

This faculty perceives that which is not revealed to the eye of man. This disciple judges not from appearances for it has the capacity to function in the realm of causes and so is never misled by appearances.

Clairvoyance is the faculty which is awakened when this quality is developed and disciplined, not the clairvoyance of the mediumistic séance rooms, but the true clairvoyance or clear seeing of the mystic. That is, this aspect of the mind has the capacity to interpret that which is seen. Discernment or the capacity to diagnose is the quality of James the son of Alphaeus.

Thaddaeus, the tenth, is the disciple of praise, a quality in which the undisciplined man is woefully lacking.

When this quality of praise and thanksgiving is awake within man, he walks with the words, "Thank you, Father", ever on his lips.

He knows that his thanks for things not seen opens the windows of heaven and permits gifts beyond his capacity to receive to be poured upon him.

The man who is not thankful for things received is not likely to be the recipient of many gifts from the same source.

Until this quality of the mind is disciplined, man will not see the desert blossom as the rose. Praise and thanksgiving are to the invisible gifts of God (one's desires) what rain and sun are to the unseen seeds in the bosom of the earth.

The eleventh quality called is Simon of Canaan.

A good key phrase for this disciple is "Hearing good news". Simon of Canaan, or Simon from the land of milk and honey, when called to discipleship, is proof that the one who calls this faculty into being has become conscious of the abundant life. He can say with the Psalmist David, "Thou preparest a table before me in the presence of mine enemies; thou anointest my head with oil; my cup runneth over" [Psalm 23:5]. This disciplined aspect of the mind is incapable of hearing anything other than good news and so is well qualified to preach the Gospel or Good-spell.

The twelfth and last of the disciplined qualities of the mind is called

Judas.

When this quality is awake, man knows that he must die to that which he is before he can become that which he desires to be.

So it is said of this disciple that he committed suicide, which is the mystic's way of telling the initiated that Judas is the disciplined aspect of detachment.

This one knows that his I AM or consciousness is his savior, so he lets all other saviors go. This quality – when disciplined – gives one the strength to let go.

The man who has called Judas into being has learned how to take his attention away from problems or limitations and to place it upon that which is the solution or savior.

"Except ye be born again, you cannot in anywise enter the Kingdom of Heaven" ["Truly, truly, I say to you, unless one is born again, he cannot see the kingdom of God", John 3:3]. "No greater love hath man than this, that he give his life for a friend" ["Greater love hath no man than this, that a man lay down his life for his friends", John 15:13].

When man realizes that the quality desired, if realized, would save and befriend him, he willingly gives up his life (present conception of himself) for his friend by detaching his consciousness from that which he is conscious of being and assuming the consciousness of that which he desires to be.

Judas, the one whom the world in its ignorance has blackened, will, when man awakes from his undisciplined state, be placed on high for God is love and no greater love has a man than this – that he lay down his life for a friend.

Until man lets go of that which he is now conscious of being, he will not become that which he desires to be; and Judas is the one who accomplishes this through suicide or detachment.

These are the twelve qualities which were given to man in the foundation of the world.

Man's duty is to raise them to the level of discipleship. When this is accomplished, man will say, "I have finished the work which thou gavest Me to do. I have glorified Thee on earth and now, o, Father, glorify Thou Me with Thine own Self with the glory which I had with Thee before the world was" [John 17:4, 5].

CHAPTER NINETEEN
LIQUID LIGHT

"In Him we live and move, and have our being." – Acts 17:28

Psychically, this world appears as an ocean of light containing within itself all things, including man, as pulsating bodies enveloped in liquid light.

The Biblical story of the Flood [Genesis 6-8] is the state in which man lives.

Man is actually inundated in an ocean of liquid light in which countless numbers of light-beings move.

The story of the Flood is really being enacted today.

Man is the Ark containing within himself the male-female principles of every living thing.

The dove or idea which is sent out to find dry land is man's attempt to embody his ideas. Man's ideas resemble birds in flight – like the dove in the story, returning to man without finding a place to rest.

If man will not let such fruitless searches discourage him, one day the bird will return with a green sprig. After assuming the consciousness of the thing desired, he will be convinced that it is so; and he will feel and know that he is that which he has consciously appropriated, even though it is not yet confirmed by his senses.

One day man will become so identified with his conception that he will know it to be himself, and he will declare, "I AM; I AM that which I desire to be (I AM that I AM)". He will find that, as he does so, he will begin to embody his desire (the dove or desire will this time find dry land), thereby realizing the mystery of the word made flesh.

Everything in the world is a crystallization of this liquid light. "I AM the light of the world" [John 8:12, John 9:5, John 12:46].

Your awareness of being is the liquid light of the world, which crystallizes into the conceptions you have of yourself.

Your unconditioned awareness of being first conceived itself in liquid light (which is the initial velocity of the universe). All things, from the highest to the lowest vibrations or expressions of life, are nothing more than the different vibrations of velocities of this initial velocity;

gold, silver, iron, wood, flesh etc., are only different expressions or velocities of this one substance-liquid light.

All things are crystallized liquid light; the differentiation or infinity of expression is caused by the conceiver's desire to know himself.

Your conception of yourself automatically determines the velocity necessary to express that which you have conceived yourself to be.

The world is an ocean of liquid light in countless different states of crystallization.

CHAPTER TWENTY
THE BREATH OF LIFE

"Then the LORD God formed man of dust from the ground, and breathed into his nostrils the breath of life; and man became a living being." – Genesis 2:7

"As thou knowest not what is the way of the spirit, nor how the bones do grow in the womb of her that is with child: even so thou knowest not the works of God who maketh all/Just as you don't know how the breath of life enters the limbs of a child within its mother''s womb, you also don't understand how God, who made everything, works." – Ecclesiastes 11:5

"And it came to pass after these things, that the son of the woman, the mistress of the house, fell sick; and his sickness was so sore, that there was no breath left in him." -Kings 17:17

"And he (Elisha) went up, and lay upon the child, and put his mouth upon his mouth, and his eyes upon his eyes, and his hands upon his hands: and stretched himself upon the child; and the flesh of the child waxed warm." -Kings 4:34

But after the three and a half days, the breath of life from God came into them, and they stood on their feet; and great fear fell upon those who were watching them. – Revelation 11:11]

Did the Prophet Elijah [and/or Elisha] really restore to life the dead child of the Widow?

This story, along with all the other stories of the Bible, is a psychological drama which takes place in the consciousness of man.

The Widow symbolizes every man and woman in the world; the dead child represents the frustrated desires and ambitions of man; while the prophet, Elijah [and/or Elisha], symbolizes the God power within man, or man's awareness of being.

The story tells us that the prophet took the dead child from the Widow's bosom and carried him into an upper room. As he entered this upper room he closed the door behind them; placing the child upon a bed, he breathed life into him; returning to the mother, he gave her the child and said, "Woman, thy son liveth" ["See, thy son liveth", Kings 17:23 and Kings 4:36].

Man's desires can be symbolized as the dead child.

The mere fact that he desires is positive proof that the thing desired is not yet a living reality in his world.

He tries in every conceivable way to nurse this desire into reality, to make it live, but finds in the end that all attempts are fruitless.

Most men are not aware of the existence of the infinite power within themselves as the prophet.

They remain indefinitely with a dead child in their arms, not realizing that the desire is the positive indication of limitless capacities for its fulfillment.

Let man once recognize that his consciousness is a prophet who breathes life into all that he is conscious of being, and he will close the door of his senses against his problem and fix his attention – solely on that which he desires, knowing that by so doing, his desires are certain to be realized.

He will discover recognition to be the breath of life, for he will perceive – as he consciously claims himself to be now expressing or possessing all he desires to be or to have – that he will be breathing the breath [sic!] of life into his desire.

The quality claimed for the desire (in a way unknown to him) will begin to move and become a living reality in his world.

Yes, the Prophet Elijah [and/or Elisha] lives forever as man's limitless consciousness of being, the widow as his limited consciousness of being and the child as that which he desires to be.

CHAPTER TWENTY ONE
DANIEL IN THE LIONS' DEN

"Thy God whom thou servest continually; He will deliver thee." – Daniel 6:16

"The story of Daniel is the story of every man. It is recorded that Daniel, while locked in the lions' den, turned his back upon the hungry beasts; and with his vision turned toward the light coming from above, he prayed to the one and only God. The lions, who were purposely starved for the feast, remained powerless to hurt the prophet. Daniel's faith in God was so great that it finally brought about his freedom and his appointment to a high office in the government of his country." -Daniel 6:13-28

This story was written for you to instruct you in the art of freeing yourself from any problem or prison in the world.

Most of us on finding ourselves in the lions' den would be concerned only with the lions, we would not be thinking of any other problem in the whole wide world but that of lions; yet we are told that Daniel turned his back upon them and looked toward the light that was God. If we could follow the example of Daniel while threatened with any dire disaster such as lions, poverty or sickness, if, like Daniel, we could remove our attention to the light that is God, our solutions would be similarly simple.

For example, if you were imprisoned, no man would need to tell you that what you should desire is freedom. Freedom or rather the desire to be free would be automatic.

The same would be true if you found yourself sick or in debt or in any other predicament. Lions represent seemingly unsoluble situations of a threatening nature.

Every problem automatically produces its solution in the form of a desire to be free from the problem.

Therefore, turn your back upon your problem and focus your attention upon the desired solution by already feeling yourself to be that which you desire.

Continue in this belief, and you will find that your prison wall will disappear as you begin to express that which you have become conscious of being.

I have seen people, apparently hopelessly in debt, apply this principle, and, in but a very short time, debts that were mountainous were removed. I have also seen those whom doctors had given up as uncurable apply this principle and, in an incredibly short time, their so-called incurable disease vanished and left no scar.

Look upon your desires as the spoken words of God and every word of prophecy of that which you are capable of being. Do not question whether you are worthy or unworthy to realize these desires. Accept them as they come to you. Give thanks for them as though they were gifts. Feel happy and grateful for having received such wonderful gifts. Then go your way in peace.

Such simple acceptance of your desires is like the dropping of fertile seed into an ever-prepared soil.

When you drop your desire in consciousness as a seed, confident that it shall appear in its full-blown potential, you have done all that is expected of you. To be worried or concerned about the manner of their unfoldment is to hold these fertile seeds in a mental grasp and, therefore, to prevent them from really maturing to full harvest.

Don't be anxious or concerned as to results. Results will follow just as surely as day follows night.

Have faith in this planting until the evidence is manifest to you that it is so. Your confidence in this procedure will pay great rewards. You wait but a little while in the consciousness of the thing desired; then suddenly, and when you least expect it, the thing felt becomes your expression. Life is no respecter of persons [Acts 10:34; Romans 2:11] and destroys nothing; it continues to keep alive that which man is conscious of being.

Things will disappear only as man changes his consciousness. Deny it if you will, it still remains a fact that consciousness is the only reality and things but mirror that which you are conscious of being.

The heavenly state you seek will be found only in consciousness for the Kingdom of Heaven is within you.

Your consciousness is the only living reality, the eternal head of creation. That which you are conscious of being is the temporal body that you wear.

To turn your attention from that which you are aware of being is to decapitate that body; but, just as a chicken or snake continues to jump and throb for a while after its head has been removed, likewise qualities and conditions appear to live for a while after your attention has been taken from them.

Man, not knowing this law of consciousness, constantly gives thought to his previous habitual conditions and, through being attentive to them, places upon these dead bodies the eternal head of creation; thereby he reanimates and re-resurrects them.

You must leave these dead bodies alone and let the dead bury the dead [Matthew 8:22, Luke 9:60].

Man, having put his hand to the plough (that is, after assuming the consciousness of the quality desired), by looking back, can only defeat his fitness for the Kingdom of Heaven [Luke 9:62].

As the will of heaven is ever done on earth, you are today in the heaven that you have established within yourself, for here on this very earth your heaven reveals itself.

The Kingdom of Heaven really is at hand. Now is the accepted time. So create a new heaven, enter into a new state of consciousness and a new earth will appear.

CHAPTER TWENTY TWO
FISHING

"They went forth, and entered into a ship, and that night they caught nothing." – John 21:3

"And He said unto them, Cast the net on the right side of the ship, and ye shall find. They cast therefore, and now they were not able to draw it for the multitude of fishes." – John 21:6

It is recorded that the disciples fished all night and caught nothing. Then Jesus appeared upon the scene and told them to cast their nets again, but, this time, to cast them on the right side. Peter obeyed the voice of Jesus and cast his nets once more into the waters. Where but a moment before the water was completely empty of fish, the nets almost broke with the number of the resulting catch. -John 21:3-6

Man, fishing all through the night of human ignorance, attempts to realize his desires through effort and struggle only to find in the end that his search is fruitless. When man discovers his awareness of being to be Christ Jesus, he will obey its voice and let it direct his fishing. He will cast his hook on the right side; he will apply the law in the right manner and will seek in consciousness for the thing desired. Finding it there, he will know that it will be multiplied in the world of form.

Those who have had the pleasure of fishing know what a thrill it is to feel the fish upon the hook. The bite of the fish is followed by the play of the fish; this play, in turn, is followed by the landing of the fish.

Something similar takes place in the consciousness of man as he fishes for the manifestations of life.

Fishermen know that if they wish to catch big fish, they must fish in deep waters; if you would catch a large measure of life, you must leave behind you the shallow waters with its many reefs and barriers and launch out into the deep blue waters where the big ones play.

To catch the large manifestations of life you must enter into deeper and freer states of consciousness; only in these depths do the big expressions of life live.

Here is a simple formula for successful fishing.

First, decide what it is you want to express or possess. This is essential.

You must definitely know what you want of life before you can fish for it. After your decision is made, turn from the world of sense, remove your attention from the problem and place it on just being, by repeating quietly but with feeling, "I AM".

As your attention is removed from the world round about you and placed upon the I AM, so that you are lost in the feeling of simply being, you will find yourself slipping the anchor that tied you to the shallows of your problem; and effortlessly you will find yourself moving out into the deep.

The sensation which accompanies this act is one of expansion. You will feel yourself rise and expand as though you were actually growing. Do not be afraid of this floating, growing experience for you are not going to die to anything but your limitations.

However, your limitations are going to die as you move away from them for they live only in your consciousness.

In this deep or expanded consciousness, you will feel yourself to be a mighty pulsating power as deep and as rhythmical as the ocean. This expanded feeling is the signal that you are now in the deep blue waters where the big fish swim. Suppose the fish you decided to catch were health and freedom; you begin to fish in this formless pulsating depth of yourself for these qualities or states of consciousness by feeling "I AM healthy" – "I AM free".

You continue claiming and feeling yourself to be healthy and free until the conviction that you are so possesses you.

As the conviction is born within you, so that all doubts pass away and you know and feel that you are free from the limitations of the past, you will know that you have hooked these fish.

The joy which courses through your entire being on feeling that you are that which you desired to be is equal to the thrill of the fisherman as he hooks his fish.

Now comes the play of the fish. This is accomplished by returning to the world of the senses.

As you open your eyes on the world round about you, the conviction and the consciousness that you are healthy and free should be so established within you that your whole being thrills in anticipation.

Then, as you walk through the necessary interval of time that it will take the things felt to embody themselves, you will feel a secret thrill in knowing that in a little while that which no man sees, but that which you feel and know that you are, will be landed.

In a moment when you think not, while you faithfully walk in this consciousness, you will begin to express and possess that which you are conscious of being and possessing; experiencing with the fisherman the joy of landing the big one.

Now, go and fish for the manifestations of life by casting your nets in the right side.

CHAPTER TWENTY THREE
BE EARS THAT HEAR

"Let these sayings sink down into your ears; For the Son of Man shall be delivered into the hands of men." – Luke 9:44

"Let these sayings sink down into your ears, for the Son of Man shall be delivered into the hands of men". Be not as those who have eyes that see not and ears that hear not.

Let these revelations sink deep into your ears, for after the Son (idea) is conceived, man with his false values (reason) will attempt to explain the why and wherefore of the Son's expression, and in so doing, will rend him to pieces.

After men have agreed that a certain thing is humanly impossible and therefore cannot be done, let someone accomplish the impossible thing; the wise ones who said it could not be done will begin to tell you why and how it happened. After they are all through tearing the seamless robe [John 19:23] (cause of manifestation) apart, they will be as far from the truth as they were when they proclaimed it impossible. As long as man looks for the cause of expression in places other than the expresser, he looks in vain.

For thousands of years, man has been told, "I AM the resurrection and the life" [John 11:25]. "No manifestation cometh unto me save I draw it" [John 6:44], but man will not believe it.

He prefers to believe in causes outside of himself.

The moment that which was not seen becomes seen, man is ready to explain the cause and purpose of its appearance.

Thus, the Son of Man (idea desiring manifestation) is constantly being destroyed at the hands of (reasonable explanation or wisdom) man.

Now that your awareness is revealed to you as cause of all expression, do not return to the darkness of Egypt with its many gods. There is but one God. The one and only God is your awareness.

"And all the inhabitants of the earth are reputed as nothing. And He doeth according to His will in the army of Heaven, and among the inhabitants of the earth and none can stay His hand, or say unto him what doest Thou?" ["All the inhabitants of the earth are accounted as nothing, But He does according to His will in the host of heaven And among the inhabitants of earth; And no one can ward off His hand Or say to Him, „What have You done?‟"", Daniel 4:35].

If the whole world should agree that a certain thing could not be expressed and yet you became aware of being that which they had agreed could not be expressed, you would express it.

Your awareness never asks permission to express that which you are aware of being. It does so, naturally and without effort, in spite of the wisdom of man and all opposition.

"Salute no man by the way" ["Carry no money belt, no bag, no shoes; and greet no one on the way", Luke 10:4; 2Kings 4:29].

This is not a command to be insolent or unfriendly, but a reminder not to recognize a superior, not to see in anyone a barrier to your expression.

None can stay your hand or question your ability to express that which you are conscious of being.

Do not judge after the appearances of a thing, "for all are as nothing in the eyes of God" ["All the nations are as nothing before Him, They are regarded by Him as less than nothing and meaningless", Isaiah 40:17].

When the disciples through their judgment of appearances saw the insane child [Mark 9:17-29; Luke 9:37-43], they thought it a more difficult problem to solve than others they had seen; and so they failed to achieve a cure.

In judging after appearances, they forgot that all things were possible to God [Matthew 19:26; Mark 10:27].

Hypnotized as they were by the reality of appearances, they could not feel the naturalness of sanity.

The only way for you to avoid such failures is to constantly bear in mind that your awareness is the Almighty, the all-wise presence; without help, this unknown presence within you effortlessly outpictures that which you are aware of being.

Be perfectly indifferent to the evidence of the senses, so that you may feel the naturalness of your desire, and your desire will be realized.

Turn from appearances and feel the naturalness of that perfect perception within yourself, a quality never to be distrusted or doubted. Its understanding will never lead you astray.

Your desire is the solution of your problem. As the desire is realized, the problem is dissolved.

You cannot force anything outwardly by the mightiest effort of the will. There is only one way you can command the things you want and that is by assuming the consciousness of the things desired.

There is a vast difference between feeling a thing and merely knowing it intellectually.

You must accept without reservation the fact that by possessing (feeling) a thing in consciousness, you have commanded the reality that causes it to come into existence in concrete form.

You must be absolutely convinced of an unbroken connection between the invisible reality and its visible manifestation. Your inner acceptance must become an intense, unalterable conviction which transcends both reason and intellect, renouncing entirely any belief in the reality of the externalization except as a reflection of an inner state of consciousness. When you really understand and believe these things, you will have built up so profound a certainty that nothing can shake you.

Your desires are the invisible realities which respond only to the commands of God. God commands the invisible to appear by claiming himself to be the thing commanded. "He made Himself equal with God and found it not robbery to do the works of God" [Philippians 2:6].

Now let this saying sink deep in your ear: BE CONSCIOUS OF BEING THAT WHICH YOU WANT TO APPEAR.

CHAPTER TWENTY FOUR
CLAIRVOYANCE

"Having eyes, see ye not? and having ears, hear ye not? and do ye not remember?" – Mark 8:18

True clairvoyance rests, not in your ability to see things beyond the range of human vision, but rather in your ability to understand that which you see.

A financial statement can be seen by anyone, but very few can read a financial statement. The capacity to interpret the statement is the mark of clear seeing or clairvoyance.

That every object, both animate and inanimate, is enveloped in a liquid light which moves and pulsates with an energy far more radiant than the objects themselves, no one knows better than the author; but he also knows that the ability to see such auras is not equal to the ability to understand that which one sees in the world around about him.

To illustrate this point, here is a story with which the whole world is familiar, yet only the true mystic or clairvoyant has ever really seen it.

SYNOPSIS

The story of Dumas' "Count of Monte Cristo" is, to the mystic and true clairvoyant, the biography of every man.

I

Edmond Dantés, a young sailor, finds the captain of his ship dead. Taking command of the ship in the midst of a storm-swept sea, he attempts to steer the ship into a safe anchorage.

COMMENTARY Life itself is a storm-swept sea with which man wrestles as he tries to steer himself into a haven of rest.

II

On Dantés is a secret document which must be given to a man he does not know, but who will make himself known to the young sailor in due time. This document is a plan to set the Emperor Napoleon free from his prison on the Isle of Elba.

COMMENTARY

Within every man is the secret plan that will set free the mighty emperor within himself.

III

As Dantés reaches port, three men (who by their flattery and praise have succeeded in worming their way into the good graces of the present king), fearing any change that would alter their positions in the government, have the young mariner arrested and committed to the catacombs.

COMMENTARY

Man in his attempt to find security in this world is misled by the false lights of greed, vanity and power.

Most men believe that fame, great wealth or political power would secure them against the storms of life. So they seek to acquire these as the anchors of their life, only to find that in their search for these they gradually lose the knowledge of their true being. If man places his faith in things other than himself, that in which his faith is placed, will in time destroy him; at which time he will be as one imprisoned in confusion and despair.

IV

Here in this tomb, Dantés is forgotten and left to rot. Many years pass. Then one day, Dantés (who is by this time a living skeleton) hears a knock on his wall. Answering this knock, he hears the voice of one on the other side of the stone. In response to this voice, Dantés removes the stone and discovers an old priest who has been in prison so long that no one knows the reason for his imprisonment or the length of time he has been there.

COMMENTARY

Here behind these walls of mental darkness, man remains in what appears to be a living death. After years of disappointment, man turns from these false friends, and he discovers within himself the ancient one (his awareness of being) who has been buried since the day he first believed himself to be man and forgot that he was God.

V

The old priest had spent many years digging his way out of this living tomb only to discover that he had dug his way into Dantés' tomb. He then resigns himself to his fate and decides to find his joy and freedom by instructing Dantés in all that he knows concerning the mysteries of life and to aid him to escape as well.

Dantés, at first, is impatient to acquire all this information; but the old priest, with infinite patience garnered through his long imprisonment, shows Dantés how unfit he is to receive this knowledge in his present, unprepared, anxious mind. So, with philosophic calm, he slowly reveals to the young man the mysteries of life and time.

COMMENTARY

This revelation is so wonderful that when man first hears it he wants to acquire it all at once; but he finds that, after numberless years spent in the belief of being man, he has so completely forgotten his true identity that he is now incapable of absorbing this memory all at once. He also discovers that he can do so only in proportion to his letting go of all human values and opinions.

VI

As Dantés ripens under the old priest's instructions, the old man finds himself living more and more in the consciousness of Dantés. Finally, he imparts his last bit of wisdom to Dantés, making him competent to handle positions of trust. He then tells him of an inexhaustible treasure buried on the Isle of Monte Cristo.

COMMENTARY

As man drops these cherished human values, he absorbs more and more of the light (the old priest), until finally he becomes the light and knows himself to be the ancient one. I AM the light of the world.

VII

At this revelation, the walls of the catacomb which separated them from the ocean above cave in, crushing the old man to death. The guards, discovering the accident, sew the old priest's body into a sack and prepare to cast it out to sea. As they leave to get a stretcher, Dantés removes the body of the old priest and sews himself into the bag. The guards, unaware of this change of bodies, and believing him to be the old man, throw Dantés into the water.

COMMENTARY

The flowing of both blood and water in the death of the old priest is comparable to the flow of blood and water from the side of Jesus as the Roman soldiers pierced him, the phenomenon which always takes place at birth (here symbolizing the birth of a higher consciousness).

VIII

Dantés frees himself from the sack, goes to the Isle of Monte Cristo and discovers the buried treasure. Then, armed with this fabulous wealth and this superhuman wisdom, he discards his human identity of Edmond Dantés and assumes the title of the Count of Monte Cristo.

COMMENTARY

Man discovers his awareness of being to be the inexhaustible treasure of the universe. In that day, when man makes this discovery, he dies as man and awakes as God.

Yes, Edmond Dantés becomes the Count of Monte Cristo. Man becomes Christ.

CHAPTER TWENTY FIVE
23RD PSALM

I

The Lord is my Shepherd; I shall not want. COMMENTARY

My awareness is my Lord and Shepherd. That which I AM aware of being is the sheep that follow me. So good a shepherd is my awareness of being, it has never lost one sheep or thing that I AM aware of being.

My consciousness is a voice calling in the wilderness of human confusion; calling all that I AM conscious of being to follow me.

So well do my sheep know my voice, they have never failed to respond to my call; nor will there come a time when that which I am convinced that I AM will fail to find me.

I AM an open door for all that I AM to enter.

My awareness of being is Lord and Shepherd of my life. Now I know I shall never be in need of proof or lack the evidence of that which I am aware of being. Knowing this, I shall become aware of being great, loving, wealthy, healthy and all other attributes that I admire.

II

He maketh me to lie down in green pastures. COMMENTARY

My awareness of being magnifies all that I am aware of being, so there is ever an abundance of that which I am conscious of being.

It makes no difference what it is that man is conscious of being, he will find it eternally springing in his world.

The Lord's measure (man's conception of himself) is always pressed down, shaken together and running over.

III

He leadeth me beside the still waters. COMMENTARY

There is no need to fight for that which I am conscious of being, for all that I am conscious of being shall be led to me as effortlessly as a shepherd leads his flock to the still waters of a quiet spring.

IV

He restoreth my soul; He leadeth me in the paths of righteousness for His Name's sake. COMMENTARY

Now that my memory is restored – so that I know I AM the Lord and beside me there is no God

– my kingdom is restored.

My kingdom – which became dismembered in the day that I believed in powers apart from myself – is now fully restored.

Now that I know my awareness of being is God, I shall make the right use of this knowledge by becoming aware of being that which I desire to be.

V

Yea, though I walk through the valley of the shadow of death, I will fear no evil; for Thou art with me; Thy rod and Thy staff, they comfort me.

COMMENTARY

Yes, though I walk through all the confusion and changing opinions of men, I will fear no evil, for I have found consciousness to be that which makes the confusion. Having in my own case restored it to its rightful place and dignity, I shall, in spite of the confusion, outpicture that which I am now conscious of being. And the very confusion will echo and reflect my own dignity.

VI

Thou preparest a table before me in the presence of mine enemies; Thou anointest my head with oil; my cup runneth over.

COMMENTARY

In the face of seeming opposition and conflict, I shall succeed, for I will continue to outpicture the abundance that I am now conscious of being.

My head (consciousness) will continue to overflow with the joy of being God. VII

Surely goodness and mercy shall follow me all the days of my life; and I will dwell in the house of the Lord forever.

COMMENTARY

Because I am now conscious of being good and merciful, signs of goodness and mercy are compelled to follow me all the days of my life, for I will continue to dwell in the house (or consciousness) of being God (good) forever.

CHAPTER TWENTY SIX
GETHSEMANE

"Then cometh Jesus with them unto a place called Gethsemane, and saith unto the disciples, Sit ye here, while I go and pray yonder." – Matt. 26:36

A most wonderful mystical romance is told in the story of Jesus in the Garden of Gethsemane, but man has failed to see the light of its symbology and has mistakenly interpreted this mystical union as an agonizing experience in which Jesus pleaded in vain with His Father to change His destiny.

Gethsemane is, to the mystic, the Garden of Creation – the place in consciousness where man goes to realize his defined objectives. Gethsemane is a compound word meaning to press out an oily substance: Geth, to press out, and Shemen, an oily substance.

The story of Gethsemane reveals to the mystic, in dramatic symbology, the act of creation.

Just as man contains within himself an oily substance which, in the act of creation, is pressed out into a likeness of himself, so he has within himself a divine principle (his consciousness) which conditions itself as a state of consciousness and without assistance presses out or objectifies itself.

A garden is a cultivated piece of ground, a specially prepared field, where seeds of the gardener's own choice are planted and cultivated.

Gethsemane is such a garden, the place in consciousness where the mystic goes with his properly defined objectives. This garden is entered when man takes his attention from the world round about him and places it on his objectives.

Man's clarified desires are seeds containing the power and plans of self-expression and, like the seeds within man, these, too, are buried within an oily substance (a joyful, thankful attitude of mind).

As man contemplates being and possessing that which he desires to be and to possess, he has begun the process of pressing out or the spiritual act of creation.

These seeds are pressed out and planted when man loses himself in a wild, mad state of joy, consciously feeling and claiming himself to be that which he formerly desired to be.

Desires expressed, or pressed out, result in the passing of that particular desire.

Man cannot possess a thing and still desire to possess it at one and the same time. So, as one consciously appropriates the feeling of being the thing desired, this desire to be the thing passes – is realized.

The receptive attitude of mind, feeling and receiving the impression of being the thing desired, is the fertile ground or womb which receives the seed (defined objective).

The seed which is pressed out of a man grows into the likeness of the man from whom it was pressed.

Likewise, the mystical seed, your conscious claim that you are that which you heretofore desired to be, will grow into the likeness of you from whom and into whom it is pressed.

Yes, Gethsemane is the cultivated garden of romance where the disciplined man goes to press seeds of joy (defined desires) out of himself into his receptive attitude of mind, there to care for and nurture them by consciously walking in the joy of being all that formerly he desired to be.

Feel with the Great Gardener the secret thrill of knowing that things and qualities not now seen will be seen as soon as these conscious impressions grow and ripen to maturity.

Your consciousness is Lord and Husband [Isaiah 54:5]; the conscious state in which you dwell is wife or beloved. This state made visible is your son bearing witness of you, his father and mother, for your visible world is made in the image and likeness [Genesis 2:26] of the state of consciousness in which you live; your world and the fullness thereof are nothing more or less than your defined consciousness objectified.

Knowing this to be true, see to it that you choose well the mother of your children – that conscious state in which you live, your conception of yourself.

The wise man chooses his wife with great discretion. He realizes that his children must inherit the qualities of their parents and so he devotes much time and care to the selection of their mother. The mystic knows that the conscious state in which he lives is the choice that he has

made of a wife, the mother of his children, that this state must in time embody itself within his world; so he is ever select in his choice and always claims himself to be his highest ideal.

He consciously defines himself as that which he desires to be.

When man realizes that the conscious state in which he lives is the choice that he has made of a mate, he will be more careful of his moods and feelings. He will not permit himself to react to suggestions of fear, lack or any undesirable impression. Such suggestions of lack could never pass the watch of the disciplined mind of the mystic, for he knows that every conscious claim must in time be expressed as a condition of his world – of his environment.

So, he remains faithful to his beloved, his defined objective, by defining and claiming and feeling himself to be that which he desires to express. Let a man ask himself if his defined objective would be a thing of joy and beauty if it were realized.

If his answer is in the affirmative, then he may know that his choice of a bride is a princess of Israel, a daughter of Judah, for every defined objective which expresses joy when realized is a daughter of Judah, the king of praise.

Jesus took with Him into His hour of prayer His disciples, or disciplined attributes of mind, and commanded them to watch while He prayed, so that no thought or belief that would deny the realization of His desire might enter His consciousness.

Follow the example of Jesus, who, with His desires clearly defined, entered the Garden of Gethsemane (the state of joy) accompanied by His disciples (His disciplined mind) to lose Himself in a wild joy of realization.

The fixing of His attention on His objective was His command to His disciplined mind to watch and remain faithful to that fixation. Contemplating the joy that would be His on realizing His desire, He began the spiritual act of generation, the act of pressing out the mystical seed – His defined desire. In this fixation He remained, claiming and feeling Himself to be that which He (before He entered

Gethsemane) desired to be, until His whole being (consciousness) was bathed in an oily sweat (joy) resembling blood (life), in short, until His whole consciousness was permeated with the living, sustained joy of being His defined objective.

As this fixation is accomplished so that the mystic knows by his feeling of joy that he has passed from his former conscious state into his present consciousness, the Passover or Crucifixion is attained.

This crucifixion or fixation of the new conscious claim is followed by the Sabbath, a time of rest. There is always an interval of time between the impression and its expression, between the conscious claim and its embodiment. This interval is called the Sabbath, the period of rest or non-effort (the day of entombment).

To walk unmoved in the consciousness of being or possessing a certain state is to keep the Sabbath.

The story of the crucifixion beautifully expresses this mystical stillness or rest. We are told that after Jesus cried out, "It is finished!" [John 19:30], He was placed in a tomb. There He remained for the entire Sabbath.

When the new state or consciousness is appropriated so you feel, by this appropriation, fixed and secure in the knowledge that it is finished, then you, too, will cry out, "It is finished!" and will enter the tomb or Sabbath, an interval of time in which you will walk unmoved in the conviction that your new consciousness must be resurrected (made visible).

Easter, the day of resurrection, falls on the first Sunday after the full moon in Aries. The mystical reason for this is simple. A defined area will not precipitate itself in the form of rain until this area reaches the point of saturation; just so the state in which you dwell will not express itself until the whole is permeated with the consciousness that it is so – it is finished.

Your defined objective is the imaginary state, just as the equator is the imaginary line across which the sun must pass to mark the beginning of spring. This state, like the moon, has no light or life of itself; but will reflect the light of consciousness or sun – "I am the light of the world" [Matthew 5:14; John 8:12; John 9:5; John 12:46] – "I am the resurrection and the life" [John 11:25].

As Easter is determined by the full moon in Aries, so, too, is the resurrection of your conscious claim determined by the full consciousness of your claim, by actually living as this new conception.

Most men fail to resurrect their objectives because they fail to remain faithful to their newly defined state until this fullness is attained.

If man would bear in mind the fact that there can be no Easter or day of resurrection until after the full moon, he would realize that the state into which he has consciously passed will be expressed or resurrected only after he has remained within the state of being his defined objective.

Until his whole self thrills with the feeling of actually being his conscious claim, in consciously living in this state of being it, and only in this way, will man ever resurrect or realize his desire.

CHAPTER TWENTY SEVEN - A FORMULA FOR VICTORY

"Every place that the sole of your foot shall tread upon, that have I given unto you." – Joshua 1:3 The majority of people are familiar with the story of Joshua capturing the city of Jericho.

What they do not know is that this story is the perfect formula for Victory, under any circumstances and against all odds.

It is recorded that Joshua was armed only with the knowledge that every place that the sole of his foot should tread upon would be given to him; that he desired to capture or tread upon the city of Jericho but found the walls separating him from the city impassable.

It seemed physically impossible for Joshua to get beyond these massive walls and stand upon the city of Jericho. Yet, he was driven by the knowledge of the promise that, regardless of the barriers and obstacles separating him from his desires, if he could but stand upon the city, it would be given to him.

The Book of Joshua further records that instead of fighting this giant problem of the wall, Joshua employed the services of the harlot, Rahab, and sent her as a spy into the city. As Rahab entered her house, which stood in the midst of the city, Joshua – who was securely barred by the impassable walls of Jericho – blew on his trumpet seven times. At the seventh blast, the walls crumbled and Joshua entered the city victoriously.

To the uninitiated, this story is senseless.

To the one who sees it as a psychological drama, rather than as a historical record, it is most revealing.

If we would follow the example of Joshua, our victory would be similarly simple.

Joshua symbolizes to you, the reader, your present state; the city of Jericho symbolizes your desire, or defined objective.

The walls of Jericho symbolize the obstacles between you and the realization of your objectives. The foot symbolizes the understanding; placing the sole of the foot upon a definite place indicates fixing a definite psychological state.

Rahab, the spy, is your ability to travel secretly or psychologically to any place in space. Consciousness knows no frontier. No one can

[415] THE POWER OF IMAGINATION: THE NEVILLE GODDARD TREASURY

stop you from dwelling psychologically at any point, or in any state in time or space.

Regardless of the physical barriers separating you from your objective, you can, without effort or help of anyone, annihilate time, space and barriers.

Thus, you can dwell, psychologically, in the desired state. So, although you may not be able to tread physically upon a state or city, you can always tread psychologically upon any desired state. By treading psychologically, I mean that you can now, this moment, close your eyes and after visualizing or imagining a place or state other than your present one, actually FEEL that you are now in such a place or state. You can feel this condition to be so real that upon opening your eyes you are amazed to find that you are not physically there.

A harlot, as you know, gives to all men that which they ask of her. Rahab, the harlot, symbolizes your infinite capacity to psychologically assume any desirable state without questioning whether or not you are physically or morally fit to do so.

You can today capture the modern city of Jericho or your defined objective if you will psychologically re-enact this story of Joshua; but to capture the city and realize your desires, you must carefully follow the formula of victory as laid down in this book of Joshua.

This is the application of this victorious formula as a modem mystic reveals it today:

First: define your objective (not the manner of obtaining it) – but your objective, pure and simple; know exactly what it is you desire so that you have a clear mental picture of it.

Secondly: take your attention away from the obstacles which separate you from your objective and place your thought on the objective itself.

Thirdly: close your eyes and FEEL that you are already in the city or state that you would capture. Remain within this psychological state until you get a conscious reaction of complete

satisfaction in this victory. Then, by simply opening your eyes, return to your former conscious state.

This secret journey into the desired state, with its subsequent psychological reaction of complete satisfaction, is all that is necessary to bring about total victory.

This victorious psychical state will embody itself despite all opposition. It has the plan and power of self-expression.

From this point forward, follow the example of Joshua, who, after psychologically dwelling in the desired state until he received a complete conscious reaction of victory, did nothing more to bring about this victory than to blow seven times on his trumpet.

The seventh blast symbolizes the seventh day, a time of stillness or rest, the interval between the subjective and objective states, a period of pregnancy or joyful expectancy.

This stillness is not the stillness of the body but rather the stillness of the mind – a perfect passivity, which is not indolence but a living stillness born of trust in this immutable law of consciousness.

Those not familiar with this law or formula for victory, in attempting to still their minds, succeed only in acquiring a quiet tension, which is nothing more than compressed anxiety.

But you, who know this law, will find that after capturing the psychological state which would be yours if you were already victoriously and actually entrenched in that city, will move forward towards the physical realization of your desires.

You will do this without doubt or fear, in a state of mind fixed in the knowledge of a pre-arranged victory.

You will not be afraid of the enemy, because the outcome has been determined by the psychological state that preceded the physical offensive; and all the forces of heaven and earth cannot stop the victorious fulfillment of that state.

Stand still in the psychological state defined as your objective until you feel the thrill of Victory.

Then, with confidence born of the knowledge of this law, watch the physical realization of your objective.

… Set your self, stand still and watch the salvation of the Law with you…

25.REVERENCE

Never wouldst Thou have made anything if Thou hadst not loved it.
Wisdom 11:24

IN ALL creation, in all eternity, in all the realms of your infinite
being, the most wonderful fact is that which is stressed in the first
chapter of this book. You are God. You are the "I AM that I AM".

You are consciousness. You are the creator. This is the mystery, this is
the great secret known by the seers, prophets, and mystics throughout
the ages.

This is the truth that you can never know intellectually.

Who is this you? That it is you, John Jones or Mary Smith, is absurd.
It is the consciousness which knows that you are John Jones or Mary
Smith. It is your greater self, your deeper self, your infinite being.
Call it what you will. The important thing is that it is within you, it is
you, it is your world.

It is this fact that underlies the immutable law of assumption. It is
upon this fact that your very existence is built. It is this fact that is the
foundation of every chapter of this book. No, you cannot know this
intellectually, you cannot debate it, you cannot substantiate it.

You can only feel it.

You can only be aware of it.

Becoming aware of it, one great emotion permeates your being. You
live with a perpetual feeling of reverence. The knowledge that your
creator is the very self of yourself and never would have made you
had he not loved you must fill your heart with devotion, yes, with
adoration.

One knowing glimpse of the world about you at any single instant
of time is sufficient to fill you with profound awe and a feeling of
worship.

It is when your feeling of reverence is most intense that you are
closest to God, and when you are closest to God, your life is richest.

Our deepest feelings are precisely those we are least able to express,
and even in the act of adoration, silence is our highest praise.

At Your Command

Part 1

Can man decree a thing and have it come to pass? Most decidedly he can! Man has always decreed that which has appeared in his world and is today decreeing that which is appearing in his world and shall continue to do so as long as man is conscious of being man. Not one thing has ever appeared in man's world but what man decreed that it should. This you may deny, but try as you will you cannot disprove it, for this decreeing is based upon a changeless principle. You do not command things to appear by your words or loud affirmations. Such vain repetition is more often than not confirmation of the opposite. Decreeing is ever done in consciousness. That is; everyman is conscious of being that which he has decreed himself to be. The dumb man without using words is conscious of being dumb. Therefore he is decreeing himself to be dumb.

When the Bible is read in this light you will find it to be the greatest scientific book ever written. Instead of looking upon the Bible as the historical record of an ancient civilization or the biography of the unusual life of Jesus, see it as a great psychological drama taking place in the consciousness of man.

Claim it as your own and you will suddenly transform your world from the barren deserts of Egypt to the promised land of Canaan.

Every one will agree with the statement that all things were made by God, and without him there is nothing made that is made, but what man does not agree upon is the identity of God. All the churches and priesthoods of the world disagree as to the identity and true nature of God. The Bible proves beyond the shadow of a doubt that Moses and the prophets were in one hundred per cent accord as to the identity and nature of God. And Jesus' life and teachings are in agreement with the findings of the prophets of old. Moses discovered God to be man's awareness of being, when he declared these little understood words, "I AM hath sent me unto you." David sang in his psalms, "Be still and know that I AM God." Isaiah declared, "I AM the Lord and there is none else. There is no God beside me. I girded thee, though thou hast not known me. I form the light, and create darkness; I make peace, and create evil. I the Lord do all these things."

The awareness of being as God is stated hundreds of times in the New Testament. To name but a few: "I AM the shepherd, I AM the door; I AM the resurrection and the life; I AM the way; I AM the Alpha and Omega; I AM the beginning and the end"; and again, "Whom do you say that I AM?" It is not stated, "I, Jesus, am the door. I, Jesus am the way," nor is it said, "Whom do you say that I, Jesus, am?" It is clearly stated, "I AM the way." The awareness of being is the door through which the manifestations of life pass into the world of form.

Consciousness is the resurrecting power – resurrecting that which man is conscious of being. Man is ever out-picturing that which he is conscious of being. This is the truth that makes man free, for man is always self-imprisoned or self-freed.

If you, the reader, will give up all of your former beliefs in a God apart from yourself, and claim God as your awareness of being – as Jesus and the prophets did – you will transform your world with the realization that, "I and my father are one." This statement, "I and my father are one, but my father is greater than I," seems very confusing – but if interpreted in the light of what we have just said concerning the identity of God, you will find it very revealing. Consciousness, being God, is as 'father.' The thing that you are conscious of being is the 'son' bearing witness of his 'father.' It is like the conceiver and its conceptions. The conceiver is ever greater than his conceptions yet ever remains one with his conception. For instance; before you are conscious of being man, you are first conscious of being. Then you become conscious of being man. Yet you remain as conceiver, greater than your conception – man.

Jesus discovered this glorious truth and declared himself to be one with God – not a God that man had fashioned. For he never recognized such a God. He said, "If any man should ever come, saying, 'Look here or look there,' believe them not, for the kingdom of God is within you." Heaven is within you. Therefore,when it is recorded that "He went unto his father," it is telling you that he rose in consciousness to the point where he was just conscious of being, thus transcending the limitations of his present conception of himself, called 'Jesus.'

Part 2

In the awareness of being all things are possible, he said, "You shall decree a thing and it shall come to pass." This is his decreeing – rising in consciousness to the naturalness of being the thing desired. As he expressed it, "And I, if I be lifted up, I shall draw all men unto me." If I be lifted up in consciousness to the naturalness of the thing desired I will draw the manifestation of that desire unto me. For he states, "No man comes unto me save the father within me draws him, and I and my father are one." Therefore, consciousness is the father that is drawing the manifestations of life unto you.

You are, at this very moment, drawing into your world that which you are now conscious of being. Now you can see what is meant by, "You must be born again." If you are dissatisfied with your present expression in life the only way to change it, is to take your attention away form that which seems so real to you and rise in consciousness to that which you desire to be. You cannot serve two masters, therefore to take your attention from one state of consciousness and place it upon another is to die to one and live to the other.

The question, "Whom do you say that I AM?" is not addressed to a man called 'Peter' by one called 'Jesus.' This is the eternal question addressed to one's self by one's true being. In other words, "Whom do you say that you are?" For your conviction of yourself – your opinion of yourself will determine your expression in life.

He states, "You believe in God – believe also in me." In other words, it is the me within you that is this God. Praying then, is seen to be recognizing yourself to be that which you now desire, rather than its accepting form of petitioning a God that does not exist for that which you now desire.

So can't you see why the millions of prayers are unanswered? Men pray to a God that does not exist. For instance: To be conscious of being poor and to pray to a God for riches is to be rewarded with that which you are conscious of being – which is poverty. Prayers to be successful must be claiming rather than begging – so if you would pray for riches turn from your picture of poverty by denying the very evidence of your senses and assume the nature of being wealthy.

We are told, "When you pray go within in secret and shut the door. And that which your father sees in secret, with that will he reward you openly."We have identified the 'father' to be the awareness of being. We have also identified the 'door' to be the awareness of being. So 'shutting the door' is shutting out that which 'I' am now

[422] NEVILLE GODDARD

aware of being and claiming myself to be that which 'I' desire to be. The very moment my claim is established to the point of conviction, that moment I begin to draw unto myself the evidence of my claim.

Do not question the how of these things appearing, for no man knows that way. That is, no manifestation knows how the things desired will appear.

Consciousness is the way or door through which things appear. He said, "I AM the way" – not 'I,' John Smith, am the way, but "I AM," the awareness of being, is the way through which the thing shall come. The signs always follow. They never precede. Things have no reality other than in consciousness. Therefore, get the consciousness first and the thing is compelled to appear.

You are told, "Seek ye first the kingdom of Heaven and all things shall be added unto you." Get first the consciousness of the things that you are seeking and leave the things alone. This is what is meant by "Ye shall decree a thing and it shall come to pass."

Apply this principle and you will know what it is to 'prove me and see." The story of Mary is the story of every man. Mary was not a woman – giving birth in some miraculous way to one called 'Jesus.' Mary is the awareness of being that ever remains virgin, no matter how many desires it gives birth to. Right now look upon yourself as this virgin Mary – being impregnated by yourself through the medium of desire – becoming one with your desire to the point of embodying or giving birth to your desire.

For instance: It is said of Mary (whom you now know to be yourself) that she know not a man. Yet she conceived. That is, you, John Smith, have no reason to believe that that which you now desire is possible, but having discovered your awareness of being to be God, you make this awareness your husband and conceive a man child (manifestation) of the Lord, "For thy maker is thine husband; the Lord of hosts is his name; the Lord God of the whole earth shall he be called." Your ideal or ambition is this conception – the first command to her, which is now to yourself, is "Go, tell no man." That is, do not discuss your ambitions or desires with another for the other will only echo your present fears. Secrecy is the first law to be observed in realizing your desire.

The second, as we are told in the story of Mary, is to "Magnify the Lord." We have identified the Lord as your awareness of being. Therefore, to 'magnify the Lord' is to revalue or expand one's present conception of one's self to the point where this revaluation becomes natural. When this naturalness is attained you give birth by becoming that which you are one within consciousness.

The story of creation is given us in digest form in the first chapter of John. "In the beginning was the word." Now, this very second, is the 'beginning' spoken of. It is the beginning of an urge – a desire. 'The word' is the desire swimming around in your consciousness – seeking embodiment. The urge of itself has no reality, For, "I AM" or the awareness of being is the only reality. Things live only as long as I AM aware of being them; so to realize one's desire, the second line of this first verse of John must be applied. That is, "And the word was with God." The word, or desire, must be fixed or united with consciousness to give it reality. The awareness becomes aware of being the thing desired, thereby nailing itself upon the form or conception – and giving life unto its conception – or resurrecting that which was heretofore a dead or unfulfilled desire. "Two shall agree as touching anything and it shall be established on earth."

This agreement is never made between two persons. It is between the awareness and the thing desired. You are now conscious of being, so you are actually saying to yourself, without using words, "I AM." Now, if it is a state of health that you are desirous of attaining, before you have any evidence of health in your world, you begin to FEEL yourself to be healthy. And the very second the feeling "I AM healthy" is attained the two have agreed. That is, I AM and health have agreed to be one and this agreement ever results in the birth of a child which is the thing agreed upon – in this case, health. And because I made the agreement I express the thing agreed. So you can see why Moses stated, "I AM hath sent me." For what being, other than I AM could send you into expression? None – for "I AM the way – Beside me there is no other." If you take the wings of the morning and fly into the uttermost parts of the world or if you make your bed in Hell, you will still be aware of being. You are ever sent into expression by your awareness and your expression is ever that which you are aware of being.

Part 3

Again, Moses stated, "I AM that I AM." Now here is something to always bear in mind. You cannot put new wine in old bottles or new patches upon old garments. That is; you cannot take with you into the new consciousness any part of the old man. All of your present beliefs, fears and limitations are weights that bind you to your present level of consciousness. If you would transcend this level you must leave behind all that is now your present self, or conception of yourself. To do this you take your attention away from all that is now your problem or limitation and dwell upon just being. That is; you say silently but feeling to yourself, "I AM. Do not condition this 'awareness' as yet. Just declare yourself to be, and continue to do so, until you are lost in the feeling of just being – faceless and formless. When this expansion of consciousness is attained, then, within this formless deep of yourself give form to the new conception by FEELING yourself to be THAT which you desire to be.

You will find within this deep of yourself all things to be divinely possible. Everything in the world which you can conceive of being, is to you, within this present formless awareness, a most natural attainment.

The invitation given us in the Scriptures is – "to be absent from the body and be present with the Lord." The 'body' being your former conception of yourself and 'the Lord' – your awareness of being. This is what is meant when Jesus said to Nicodemus, "Ye must be born again for except ye be born again ye cannot enter the kingdom of Heaven." That is; except you leave behind you your present conception of yourself and assume the nature of the new birth, you will continue to out-picture your present limitations.

The only way to change your expressions of life is to change your consciousness. For consciousness is the reality that eternally solidifies itself in the things round about you. Man's world in its every detail is his consciousness out-pictured. You can no more change your environment, or world, by destroying things than you can your reflection by destroying the mirror. Your environment, and all within it, reflects that which you are in consciousness. As long as you continue to be that in consciousness so long will you continue to out-picture it in your world.

Knowing this, begin to revalue yourself. Man has placed too little value upon himself. In the Book of Numbers you will read, "In that day there were giants in the land; and we were in our own sight as grasshoppers. And we were in their sight as grasshoppers." This does not mean a time in the dim past when man had the stature of giants. Today is the day, the eternal now when conditions round about you have attained the appearance of giants (such as unemployed, the armies of your enemy, your problems and all things that seem to threaten you) those are the giant that make you feel yourself to be a grasshopper. But, you are told, you were first, in your own sight a grasshopper and because of this you were to the giants – a grasshopper. In other words, you can only be to others what you are first to yourself. Therefore, to revalue yourself and begin to feel yourself to be the giant, a center of power, is to dwarf these former giants and make of them grasshoppers. "All the inhabitants of the earth are as nothing, and he doeth according to his will in the armies of Heaven and among all the inhabitants of the earth; and none can stay his hand, nor say unto him, "What doest thou'?" This being spoken of is not the orthodox God sitting in space but the one and only God – the everlasting father, your awareness of being. So awake to the power that you are, not as man, but as your true self, a faceless, formless awareness, and free yourself from your self imposed prison.

"I am the good shepherd and know my sheep and am known of mine. My sheep hear my voice and I know them and they will follow me." Awareness is the good shepherd. What I am aware of being, is the 'sheep' that follow me. So good a 'shepherd' is your awareness that it has never lost one of the 'sheep' that you are aware of being.

I am a voice calling in the wilderness of human confusion for such as I am aware of being, and never shall there come a time when that which I am convinced that I am shall fail to find me. "I AM" is an open door for all that I am to enter. Your awareness of being is lord and shepherd of your life. So, "The Lord is my shepherd; I shall not want" is seen in its true light now to be your consciousness. You could never be in want of proof or lack the evidence of that which you are aware of being.

This being true, why not become aware of being great; God-loving; wealthy; healthy; and all attributes that you admire?

It is just as easy to possess the consciousness of these qualities as it is to possess their opposites for you have not your present consciousness because of your world. On the contrary, your world is what it is because of your present consciousness. Simple, is it not? Too simple in fact for the wisdom of man that tries to complicate everything.

Paul said of this principle, "It is to the Greeks" (or wisdom of this world) "foolishness." "And to the Jews" (or those who look for signs) "a stumbling block"; with the result, that man continues to walk in darkness rather than awake to the being that he is. Man has so long worshipped the images of his own making that at first he finds this revelation blasphemous, since it spells death to all his previous beliefs in a God apart from himself.

This revelation will bring the knowledge that "I and my father are one but my father is greater than I." You are one with your present conception of yourself. But you are greater than that which you are at present aware of being.

Before man can attempt to transform his world he must first lay the foundation – "I AM the Lord." That is, man's awareness, his consciousness of being is God. Until this is firmly established so that no suggestion or argument put forward by others can shake it, he will find himself returning to the slavery of his former beliefs.

"If ye believe not that I AM he, ye shall die in your sins." That is, you shall continue to be confused and thwarted until you find the cause of your confusion. When you have lifted up the son of man then shall you know that I AM he, that is, that I, John Smith, do nothing of myself, but my father, or that state of consciousness which I am now one with does the works.

When this is realized every urge and desire that springs within you shall find expression in your world.

"Behold I stand at the door and knock. If any man hear my voice and open the door I will come in to him and sup with him and he with me." The "I" knocking at the door is the urge.

The door is your consciousness. To open the door is to become one with that that which is knocking by FEELING oneself to be the thing desired. To feel one's desire as impossible is to shut the door or deny this urge expression. To rise in consciousness to the naturalness of the thing felt is to swing wide the door and invite this one into embodiment.

That is why it is constantly recorded that Jesus left the world of manifestation and ascended unto his father.

Jesus, as you and I, found all things impossible to Jesus, as man. But having discovered his father to be the state of consciousness of the thing desired, he but left behind him the "Jesus consciousness" and rose in consciousness to that state desired and stood upon it until he became one with it. As he made himself one with that, he became that in expression.

This is Jesus simple message to man:Men are but garments that the impersonal being, I AM, the presence that men call God – dwells in. Each garment has certain limitations. In order to transcend these limitations and give expression to that which, as man – John Smith – you find yourself incapable of doing, you take your attention away from your present limitations, or John Smith conception of yourself, and merge yourself in the feeling of being that which you desire. Just how this desire or newly attained consciousness will embody itself, no man knows. For I, or the newly attained consciousness, has ways that ye know not of; its ways are past finding out. Do not speculate as to the HOW of this consciousness embodying itself, for no man is wise enough to know the how. Speculation is proof that you have not attained to the naturalness of being the thing desired and so are filled with doubts.

Part 4

You are told, "He who lacks wisdom let him ask of God, that gives to all liberally, and upbraideth not; and it shall be given unto him. But let him ask not doubting for he who doubts is as a wave of the sea that is tossed and battered by the winds. And let not such a one think that he shall receive anything from the Lord." You can see why this statement is made, for only upon the rock of faith can anything be established. If you have not the consciousness of the thing you have not the cause or foundation upon which thing is erected.

A proof of this established consciousness is given you in the words, "Thank you, father." When you come into the joy of thanksgiving so that you actually feel grateful for having received that which is not yet apparent to the senses, you have definitely become one in consciousness with the thing for which you gave thanks. God (your awareness) is not mocked. You are ever receiving that which you are aware of being and no man gives thanks for something which he has not received. "Thank you father" is not, as it is used by many today a sort of magical formula. You need never utter aloud the words, "Thank you, father." In applying this principle as you rise in consciousness to the point where you are really grateful and happy for having received the thing desired, you automatically rejoice and give thanks inwardly. You have already accepted the gift which was but a desire before you rose in consciousness, and your faith is now the substance that shall clothe your desire.

This rising in consciousness is the spiritual marriage where two shall agree upon being one and their likeness or image is established on earth.

"For whatsoever ye ask in my name the same give I unto you." 'Whatsoever' is quite a large measure. It is the unconditional. It does not state if society deems it right or wrong that you should ask it, it rests with you.

Do you really want it? Do you desire it? That is all that is necessary. Life will give it to you is you ask 'in his name.'

His name is not a name that you pronounce with the lips. You can ask forever in the name of God or Jehovah or Christ Jesus and you will ask in vain. 'Name' means nature; so, when you ask in the nature of a thing, results ever follow. To ask in the name is to rise in consciousness and become one in nature with the thing desired, rise in consciousness to the nature of the thing, and you will become that thing in expression.

[429] THE POWER OF IMAGINATION: THE NEVILLE GODDARD TREASURY

Therefore, "what things soever ye desire, when ye pray, believe that ye receive them and ye shall receive them."

Praying, as we have shown you before, is recognition – the injunction to believe that ye receive is first person, present tense. This means that you must be in the nature of the things asked for before you can receive them.

To get into the nature easily, general amnesty is necessary. We are told, "Forgive if ye have aught against any, that your father also, which is in Heaven, may forgive you. But if ye forgive not, neither will your father forgive you." This may seem to be some personal God who is pleased or displeased with your actions but this is not the case.

Consciousness, being God, if you hold in consciousness anything against man, you are binding that condition in your world. But to release man from all condemnation is to free yourself so that you may rise to any level necessary; there is therefore, no condemnation to those in Christ Jesus.

Therefore, a very good practice before you enter into your meditation is first to free every man in the world from blame. For LAW is never violated and you can rest confidently in the knowledge that every man's conception of himself is going to be his reward. So you do not have to bother yourself about seeing whether or not man gets what you consider he should get. For life makes no mistakes and always gives man that which man first gives himself.

This brings us to that much abused statement of the Bible on tithing. Teachers of all kinds have enslaved man with this affair of tithing, for not themselves understanding the nature of tithing and being themselves fearful of lack, they have led their followers to believe that a tenth part of their income should be given to the Lord.

Meaning, as they make very clear, that, when one gives a tenth part of his income to their particular organization he is giving his "tenth part" to the Lord – (or is tithing). But remember, "I AM" the Lord." Your awareness of being is the God that you give to and you ever give in this manner.

Therefore when you claim yourself to be anything, you have given that claim or quality to God. And your awareness of being, which is no respecter of persons, will return to you pressed down, shaken together, and running over with that quality or attribute which you claim for yourself.

Awareness of being is nothing that you could ever name. To claim

God to be rich; to be great; to be love; to be all wise; is to define that which cannot be defined. For God is nothing that could ever be named.

Tithing is necessary and you do tithe with God. But from now on give to the only God and see to it that you give him the quality that you desire as man to express by claiming yourself to be the great, the wealthy, the loving, the all wise.

Do not speculate as to how you shall express these qualities or claims, for life has a way that you, as man, know not of. Its ways are past finding out. But, I assure you, the day you claim these qualities to the point of conviction, your claims will be honored. There is nothing covered that shall not be uncovered. That which is spoken in secret shall be proclaimed from the housetops. That is, your secret convictions of yourself – these secret claims that no man knows of, when really believed, will be shouted from the housetops in your world.

For your convictions of yourself are the words of the God within you, which words are spirit and cannot return unto you void but must accomplish where unto they are sent.

You are at this moment calling out of the infinite that which you are now conscious of being. And not one word or conviction will fail to find you.

Part 5

"I AM" the vine and ye are the branches." Consciousness is the 'vine,' and those qualities which you are now conscious of being are as 'branches' that you feed and keep alive. Just as a branch has no life except it be rooted in the vine, so likewise things have no life except you be conscious of them. Just as a branch withers and dies if the sap of the vine ceases to flow towards it, so do things in your world pass away if you take your attention from them, because your attention is as the sap of life that keeps alive and sustains the things of your world.

To dissolve a problem that now seems so real to you all that you do is remove your attention from it. In spite of its seeming reality, turn from it in consciousness. Become indifferent and begin to feel yourself to be that which would be the solution of the problem.

For instance; if you were imprisoned no man would have to tell you that you should desire freedom.

Freedom, or rather the desire of freedom would be automatic. So why look behind the four walls of your prison bars? Take your attention from being imprisoned and begin to feel yourself to be free. FEEL it to the point where it is natural – the very second you do so, those prison bars will dissolve. Apply this same principle to any problem.

I have seen people who were in debt up to their ears apply this principle and in the twinkling of an eye debts that were mountainous were removed. I have seen those whom doctors had given up as incurable take their attention away from their problem of disease and begin to feel themselves to be well in spite of the evidence of their sense to the contrary. In no time at all this so called "incurable disease" vanished and left no scar.

Your answer to, "Whom do you say that I AM"? [sic] ever determines your expression. As long as you are conscious of being imprisoned or diseased, or poor, so long will you continue to out-picture or express these conditions.

When man realized that he is now that which he is seeking and begins to claim that he is, he will have the proof of his claim. This cue is given you in words, "Whom seek ye?" And they answered, "Jesus." And the voice said, "I am he." 'Jesus' here means salvation or savior. You are seeking to be salvaged from that which is not your problem.

"I am" is he that will save you. If you are hungry, your savior is food. If you are poor, your savior is riches. If you are imprisoned, your savior is freedom. If you are diseased, it will not be a man called Jesus who will save you, but health will become your savior. Therefore, claim "I am he," in other words, claim yourself to be the thing desired. Claim it in consciousness – not in words – and consciousness will reward you with your claim. You are told, "You shall find me when you FEEL after me." Well, FEEL after that quality in consciousness until you FEEL yourself to be it. When you lose yourself in the feeling of being it, the quality will embody itself in your world.

You are healed from your problem when you touch the solution of it. "Who has touched me? For I perceive virtue is gone out of me." Yes, the day you touch this being within you – FEELING yourself to be cured or healed, virtues will come out of your very self and solidify themselves in your world as healings.

It is said, 'You believe in God. Believe also in me for I am he." Have the faith of God. "He made himself one with God and found it not robbery to do the works of God." Go you and do likewise. Yes, begin to believe your awareness, your consciousness of being to be God. Claim for yourself all the attributes that you have theretofore given an external God and you will begin to express these claims.

"For I am not a God afar off. I am nearer than your hands and feet – nearer than your very breathing." I am your awareness of being. I am that in which all that I shall ever be aware of being shall begin and end. "For before the world was I AM; and when the world shall cease to be, I AM; before Abraham was, I AM." This I AM is your awareness.

"Except the Lord build the house they labor in vain that build it." 'The Lord,' being your consciousness, except that which you seek is first established in your consciousness, you will labor in vain to find it. All things must begin and end in consciousness.

So, blessed indeed is the man that trusteth in himself – for man's faith in God will ever be measured by his confidence in himself. You believe in a God, believe also in ME.

Put not your trust in men for men but reflect the being that you are, and can only bring to you or do unto you that which you have first done unto yourself.

"No man taketh away my life, I lay it down myself." I have the power to lay it down and the power to take it up again.

No matter what happens to man in this world it is never an accident. It occurs under the guidance of an exact and changeless Law.

"No man" (manifestation) "comes unto me except the father within me draw him," and "I and my father are one." Believe this truth and you will be free. Man has always blamed others for that which he is and will continue to do so until he find himself as cause of all. "I AM" comes not to destroy but to fulfill. "I AM," the awareness within you, destroys nothing but ever fill full the molds or conception one has of one's self.

It is impossible for the poor man to find wealth in this world no matter how he is surrounded with it until he first claims himself to be wealthy. For signs follow, they do not precede. To constantly kick and complain against the limitations of poverty while remaining poor in consciousness is to play the fool's game. Changes cannot take place from that level of consciousness for life in constantly out-picturing all levels.

Follow the example of the prodigal son. Realize that you, yourself brought about this condition of waste and lack and make the decision within yourself to rise to a higher level where the fatted calf, the ring, and the robe await your claim.

Part 6

There was no condemnation of the prodigal when he had the courage to claim this inheritance as his own.

Others will condemn us only as long as we continue in that for which we condemn ourselves. So: "Happy is the man that condemneth himself not in that which he alloweth." For to life nothing is condemned. All is expressed.

Life does not care whether you call yourself rich or poor; strong or weak. It will eternally reward you with that which you claim as true of yourself.

The measurements of right and wrong belong to man alone. To life there is nothing right or wrong. As Paul stated in his letters to the Romans: "I know and am persuaded by the Lord Jesus that there is nothing unclean of itself, but to him that esteemeth anything to be unclean, to him it is unclean." Stop asking yourself whether you are worthy or unworthy to receive that which you desire. You, as man, did not create the desire. Your desires are ever fashioned within you because of what you now claim yourself to be.

When a man is hungry, (without thinking) he automatically desires food. When imprisoned, he automatically desires freedom and so forth. Your desires contain within themselves the plan of self-expression.

So leave all judgments out of the picture and rise in consciousness to the level of your desire and make yourself one with it by claiming it to be so now. For: "My grace is sufficient for thee. My strength is made perfect in weakness."

Have faith in this unseen claim until the conviction is born within you that it is so. Your confidence in this claim will pay great rewards. Just a little while and he, the thing desired, will come. But without faith it is impossible to realize anything. Through faith the worlds were framed because "faith is the substance of the thing hoped for – the evidence of the thing not yet seen."

Don't be anxious or concerned as to results. They will follow just as surely as day follows night.

Look upon your desires – all of them – as the spoken words of God, and every word or desire a promise.

The reason most of us fail to realize our desires is because we are constantly conditioning them. Do not condition your desire. Just accept it as it comes to you. Give thanks for it to the point that you are grateful for having already received it – then go about your way in peace.

Such acceptance of your desire is like dropping seed – fertile seed – into prepared soil. For when you can drop the thing desired in consciousness, confident that it shall appear, you have done all that is expected to you. But, to be worried or concerned about the HOW of your desire maturing is to hold these fertile seeds in a mental grasp, and, therefore, never to have dropped them in the soil of confidence.

The reason men condition their desires is because they constantly judge after the appearance of being and see the things as real – forgetting that the only reality is the consciousness back of them.

To see things as real is to deny that all things are possible to God. The man who is imprisoned and sees his four walls as real is automatically denying the urge or promise of God within him of freedom.

A question often asked when this statement is made is; If one's desire is a gift of God how can you say that if one desires to kill a man that such a desire is good and therefore God sent? In answer to this let me say that no man desires to kill another. What he does desire is to be freed from such a one. But because he does not believe that the desire to be free from such a one contains within itself the powers of freedom, he conditions that desire and sees the only way to express such freedom is to destroy the man – forgetting that the life wrapped within the desire has ways that he, as man, knows not of. Its ways are past finding out. Thus man distorts the gifts of God through his lack of faith.

Problems are the mountains spoken of that can be removed if one has but the faith of a grain of a mustard seed. Men approach their problem as did the old lady who, on attending service and hearing the priest say, "If you had but the faith of a grain of a mustard seed you would say unto yonder mountain 'be thou removed' and it shall be removed and nothing is impossible to you."

That night as she said her prayers, she quoted this part of the scriptures and retired to bed in what she thought was faith. On arising in the morning she rushed to the window and exclaimed: "I knew that old mountain would still be there."

For this is how man approaches his problem. He knows that they are still going to confront him. And because life is no respecter of persons and destroys nothing, it continues to keep alive that which he is conscious of being.

[436] NEVILLE GODDARD

Things will disappear only as man changes in consciousness. Deny it if you will, it still remains a fact that consciousness is the only reality and things but mirror that which you are in consciousness. So the heavenly state you are seeking will be found only in consciousness, for the kingdom of heaven is within you. As the will of heaven is ever done on earth you are today living in the heaven that you have established within you. For here on this very earth your heaven reveals itself. The kingdom of heaven really is at hand. NOW is the accepted time. So create a new heaven, enter into a new state of consciousness and a new earth will appear.

"The former things shall pass away. They shall not be remembered not come into mind anymore. For behold, I," (your consciousness) "come quickly and my reward is with me."

I am nameless but will take upon myself every name (nature) that you call me. Remember it is you, yourself, that I speak of as 'me.' So every conception that you have of yourself – that is every deep conviction – you have of yourself is that which you shall appear as being – for I AM not fooled; God is not mocked.

Now let me instruct you in the art of fishing. It is recorded that the disciples fished all night and caught nothing. Then Jesus came upon the scene and told them to cast their nets in once more, into the same waters that only a moment before were barren – and this time their nets were bursting with the catch.

This story is taking place in the world today right within you, the reader. For you have within you all the elements necessary to go fishing. But until you find that Jesus Christ, (your awareness) is Lord, you will fish, as did these disciples, in the night of human darkness. That is, you will fish for THINGS thinking things to be real and will fish with the human bait – which is a struggle and an effort – trying to make contact with this one and that one: trying to coerce this being or the other being; and all such effort will be in vain. But when you discover your awareness of being to be Christ Jesus you will let him direct your fishing. And you will fish in consciousness for the things that you desire. For your desire – will be the fish that you will catch, because your consciousness is the only living reality you will fish in the deep waters of consciousness.

If you would catch that which is beyond your present capacity you must launch out into deeper waters, for, within your present consciousness such fish or desires cannot swim. To launch out into deeper waters, you leave behind you all that is now your present problem, or limitation, by taking your ATTENTION AWAY from it. Turn your back completely upon every problem and limitation that you now possess.

Dwell upon just being by saying, "I AM," "I AM," "I AM," to yourself. Continue to declare to yourself that you just are. Do not condition this declaration, just continue to FEEL yourself to be and without warning you will find yourself slipping the anchor that tied you to the shallow of your problems and moving out into the deep.

This is usually accompanied with the feeling of expansion. You will FEEL yourself expand as though you were actually growing. Don't be afraid, for courage is necessary. You are not going to die to anything by your former limitations, but they are going to die as you move away from them, for they live only in your consciousness. In this deep or expanded consciousness you will find yourself to be a power that you had never dreamt of before.

The things desired before you shoved off from the shores of limitation are the fish you are going to catch in this deep. Because you have lost all consciousness of your problems and barriers, it is now the easiest thing in the world to FEEL yourself to be one with the things desired.

Because I AM (your consciousness) is the resurrection and the life, you must attach this resurrecting power that you are to the thing desired if you would make it appear and live in your world. Now you begin to assume the nature of the thing desired by feeling, "I AM wealthy"; "I AM free"; "I AM strong." When these 'FEELS' are fixed within yourself, your formless being will take upon itself the forms of the things felt. You become 'crucified' upon the feelings of wealth, freedom, and strength. – Remain buried in the stillness of these convictions. Then, as a thief in the night and when you least expect it, theses qualities will be resurrected in your world as living realities.

The world shall touch you and see that you are flesh and blood for you shall begin to bear fruit of the nature of these qualities newly appropriated. This is the art of successful fishing for the manifestations of life.

Successful realization of the thing desired is also told us in the story of Daniel in the lion's den. Here, it is recorded that Daniel, while in the lion's den, turned his back upon the lions and looked towards the light coming from above; that the lions remained powerless and Daniel's faith in his God saved him.

This also is your story and you too must do as Daniel did. If you found yourself in a lion's den you would have no other concern but lions. You would not be thinking of one thing in the world but your problem – which problem would be lions.

Yet, you are told that Daniel turned his back upon them and looked towards the light that was his God. If we would follow the example of Daniel we would, while imprisoned within the den of poverty of sickness, take our attention away from our problems of debts or sickness and dwell upon the thing we seek.

If we do not look back in consciousness to our problems but continue in faith – believing ourselves to be that which we seek, we too will find our prison walls open and the thing sought – yes, "whatsoever things" – realized.

Another story is told us; of the widow and the three drops of oil. The prophet asked the widow, "What have ye in your house?" And she replied, "Three drops of oil." He then said to her, "Go borrow vessels. Close the door after ye have returned into your house and begin to pour." And she poured from three drops of oil into all the borrowed vessels, filling them to capacity with oil remaining. You, the reader, are this widow. You have not a husband to impregnate you or make you fruitful, for a 'widow' is a barren state. Your awareness is now the Lord – or the prophet that has become your husband.

Follow the example of the widow, who instead of recognizing an emptiness or nothingness, recognized the something – three drops of oil.

Then the command to her, "Go within and close the door," that is, shut the door of the senses that tell you of the empty measures, the debts, the problems.

When you have taken your attention away completely by shutting out the evidence of the senses, begin to FEEL the joy, (symbolized by oil) – of having received the things desired. When the agreement is established within you so that all doubts and fears have passed away, then, you too will fill all the empty measures of your life and ill have an abundance running over.

Recognition is the power that conjures in the world. Every state that you have ever recognized, you have embodied. That which you are recognizing as true of yourself today is that which you are experiencing. So be as the widow and recognize joy, no matter how little the beginnings of recognition, and you will be generously rewarded – for the world is a magnified mirror, magnifying everything that you are conscious of being.

"I AM the Lord the God, which has brought thee out of the land of Egypt, out of the house of bondage; thou shalt have no other gods before me." What a glorious revelation, your awareness now revealed as the Lord thy God! Come, awake from your dream of being imprisoned. Realize that the earth is yours, "and the fullness thereof; the world, and all that dwells therein."

You have become so enmeshed in the belief that you are man that you have forgotten the glorious being that you are. Now with your memory restored DECREE the unseen to appear and it SHALL appear, or all things are compelled to respond to the Voice of God, Your awareness of being – the world is AT YOUR COMMAND!

Seedtime & Harvest

THE END OF A GOLDEN STRING

"I Give you the end of a golden string; Only wind it into a ball, It will lead you in at Heaven's gate, Built in Jerusalem's wall." . . . Blake

In the following essays I have tried to indicate certain ways of approach to the understanding of the Bible and the realization of your dreams.

"That ye be not slothful, but followers of them who through faith and patience inherit the promises." . . . Hebrews 6:12

Many who enjoy the old familiar verses of Scripture are discouraged when they themselves try to read the Bible as they would any other book because, quite excusably, they do not understand that the Bible is written in the language of symbolism. Not knowing that all of its characters are personifications of the laws and functions of mind; that the Bible is psychology rather than history, they puzzle their brains over it for awhile and then give up. It is all too mystifying. To understand the significance of its imagery, the reader of the Bible must be imaginatively awake.

According to the Scriptures, we sleep with Adam and wake with Christ. That is, we sleep collectively and wake individually.

"And the Lord God caused a deep sleep to fall upon Adam, and he slept." . . . Genesis 2:21

If Adam, or generic man, is in a deep sleep, then his experiences as recorded in the Scriptures must be a dream. Only he who is awake can tell his dream, and only he would understand the symbolism of dreams can interpret the dream.

"And they said one to another, Did not our heart burn within us, while He talked with us by the way, and while He opened to us the Scriptures?" . . . Luke 24:32

The Bible is a revelation of the laws and functions of Mind expressed in the language of that twilight realm into which we go when we sleep. Because the symbolical language of this twilight realm is much the same for all men, the recent explorers of this realm – human imagination – call it the "collective unconscious."

The purpose of this book, however, is not to give you a complete definition of Biblical symbols or exhaustive interpretations of its stories. All I hope to have done is to have indicated the way in which you are most likely to succeed in realizing your desires. "What things soever ye desire" can be obtained only through the conscious, voluntary exercise of imagination in direct obedience to the laws of Mind. Somewhere within this realm of imagination there is a mood, a feeling of the wish fulfilled which, if appropriated, means success to you. This realm, this Eden – your imagination – is vaster than you know and repays exploration. "I Give you the end of a golden string;" You must wind it into a ball.

THE FOUR MIGHTY ONES

"And a river went out of Eden to water the garden; and from thence it was parted, and became into four heads." . . . Genesis 2:10

"And every one had four faces: . . ." . . . Ezekiel 10:14

"I see four men loose, walking in the midst of the fire, and they have no hurt; and the form of the fourth is like the Son of God." . . . Daniel 3:25

"Four Mighty Ones are in every man." . . . Blake

The "Four Mighty Ones" constitute the selfhood of man, or God in man. There are "Four Mighty Ones" in every man, but these "Four Mighty Ones" are not four separate beings, separated one from the other as are the fingers of his hand. The "Four Mighty Ones" are four different aspects of his mind, and differ from one another in function and character without being four separate selves inhabiting one man's body.

The "Four Mighty Ones" may be equated with the four Hebrew characters: (characters here) which form the four-lettered mystery-name of the Creative Power from and combining within itself the past, present and future forms of the verb "to be." The Tetragrammaton is revered as the symbol of the Creative Power in man – I AM – the creative four functions in man reaching forth to realize in actual material phenomena qualities latent in Itself.

We can best understand the "Four Mighty Ones" by comparing them to the four most important characters in the production of a play.

"All the world's a stage, And all the men and women merely players; They have their exits and their entrances; And one man in his time plays many parts . . ." – As You Like It Act II, Scene VII

The producer, the author, the director and the actor are the four most important characters in the production of a play. In the drama of life, the producer's function is to suggest the theme of a play. This he does in the form of a wish, such as, "I wish I were successful"; "I wish I could take a trip"; "I wish I were married:, and so on. But to appear on the world's stage, these general themes must somehow be specified and worked out in detail. It is not enough to say, "I wish I were successful" – that is too vague. Successful at what? However, the first "Mighty One" only suggests a theme.

The dramatization of the theme is left to the originality of the second "Might One", the author. In dramatizing the theme, the author writes only the last scene of the play – but this scene he writes in detail. The scene must dramatize the wish fulfilled. He mentally constructs as life-like a scene as possible of what he would experience had he realized his wish. When the scene is clearly visualized, the author's work is done.

The third "Mighty One" in the production of life's play is the director. The director's tasks are to see that the actor remains faithful to the script and to rehearse him over and over again until he is natural in the part. This function may be likened to a controlled and consciously directed attention – an attention focused exclusively on the action which implies that the wish is already realized.

"The form of the Fourth is like the Son of God" – human imagination, the actor. This fourth "Mighty One" performs within himself, in imagination, the pre-determined action which implies the fulfill- ment of the wish. This function does not visualize or observe the action. This function actually enacts the drama, and does it over and over again until it takes on the tones of reality. Without the dramatized vision of fulfilled desire, the theme remains a mere theme and sleeps forever in the vast chambers of unborn themes. Nor without the co-operant attention, obedient to the dramatized vision of fulfilled desire, will the vision perceived attain objective reality.

The "Four Mighty Ones" are the four quarters of the human soul. The first is Jehovah's King, who suggests the theme; the second is Jehovah's servant, who faithfully works out the theme in a dramatic vision; the third is Jehovah's man, who was attentive and obedient to the vision of fulfilled desire, who brings the wandering imagination back to the script "seventy times seven". The "Form of the Fourth" is Jehovah himself, who enacts the dramatized theme on the stage of the mind.

"Let this mind be in you, which was also in Christ Jesus: Who, being in the form of God, thought it not robbery to be equal with God: . . ." – Philippians 2:5,6

The drama of life is a joint effort of the four quarters of the human soul.

"All that you behold, tho' it appears without, it is within, in your imagination, of which this world of mortality is but a shadow." – Blake

All that we behold is a visual construction contrived to express a theme – a theme which has been dramatized, rehearsed and performed elsewhere. What we are witnessing on the stage of the world is an optical construction devised to express the themes which have been dramatized, rehearsed and performed in the imagination of men.

The "Four Mighty Ones" constitute the Selfhood of man, or God in man: and all that man beholds, tho' it appears without, are but shadows cast upon the screen of space – optical constructions contrived by Selfhood to inform him in regard to the themes which he has conceived, dramatized, rehearsed and performed within himself.

"The creature was made subject unto vanity" that he may become conscious of Selfhood and its functions, for with consciousness of Selfhood and its functions, he can act to a purpose; he can have a consciously self-determined history. Without consciousness, he acts unconsciously, and cries to an objective God to save him from his own creation.

"O Lord, how long shall I cry, and Thou wilt not hear! Even cry out unto Thee of violence, and Thou wilt not save!" – Habakkuk 1:2

When man discovers that life is a play which he, himself, is consciously or unconsciously writing, he will cease from the blind, self-torture of executing judgment upon others. Instead, he will re- write the play to conform to his ideal, for he will realize that all changes in the play must come from the cooperation of the "Four Mighty Ones" within himself. They alone can alter the script and produce the change.

All the men and women in his world are merely players and are as helpless to change his play as are the players on the screen of the theatre to change the picture. The desired change must be conceived, dramatized, rehearsed and performed in the theatre of his mind. When the fourth function, the imagination, has completed its task of rehearsing the revised version of the play until it is natural, then the curtain will rise upon this so seemingly solid world and the "Mighty Four" will cast a shadow of the real play upon the screen of space. Men and women will automatically play their parts to bring about the fulfillment of the dramatized theme. The players, by reason of their various parts in the world's drama, become relevant to the individual's dramatized theme and, because relevant, are drawn into his drama. They will play their parts, faithfully believing all the while that it was they themselves who initiated the parts they play. This they do because:

"Thou, Father, art in me, and I in thee, . . . I in them, and thou in me." – John 17:21, 23

I am involved in mankind. We are one. We are all playing the four parts of producer, author, director and actor in the drama of life. Some of us are doing it consciously, others unconsciously. It is necessary that we do it consciously. Only in this way can we be certain of a perfect ending to our play. Then we shall understand why we must become conscious of the four functions of the one God within ourselves that w may have the companionship of God as His Sons.

"Man should not stay a man: Hs aim should higher be. For God will only gods Accept as company."
– Angelus Silesius

In January of 1946, I took my wife and little daughter to Barbados in the British West Indies for a holiday. Not knowing there were any difficulties in getting a return passage, I had not booked ours before leaving New York. Upon our arrival in Barbados I discovered that there were only two ships serving the islands, one from Boston and one from New York. I was told there was no available space on either ship before September. As I had commitments in New York for the first week in May, I put my name on the long waiting list for the April sailing.

A few days later, the ship from New York was anchored in the harbor. I observed it very carefully, and decided that this was the ship we should take. I returned to my hotel and determined on an inner action that would be mine were we actually sailing on that ship. I settled down in an easy chair in my bedroom, to lose myself in this imaginative action.

I Barbados, we take a motor launch or rowboat out into the deep harbor when we embark on a large steamer. I knew I must catch the feeling that we were sailing on that ship. I chose the inner action of stepping from the tender and climbing up the gangplank of the steamer. The first time I tried, my attention wandered after I had reached the top of the gangplank. I brought myself back down, and tried again and again. I do not recall how many times I carried out this action in my imagination until I reached the deck and looked back at the port with the feeling of sweet sadness at departing. I was happy to be returning to my home in New York, but nostalgic in saying goodby to the lovely island and our family and friends. I do recall that in one of my many attempts at walk- ing up the gangplank in the feeling that I was sailing, I fell asleep. After I awoke, I went about the usual social activities of the day and evening.

The following morning, I received a call from the steamship company requesting me to come down to their office and pick up our tickets for the April sailing. I was curious to know why Barba- dos had been chosen to receive the cancellation and why I, at the end of the long waiting list, was to have the reservation, but all that the agent could tell me was that a cable had been received that morning from New York, offering passage for three. I was not the first the agent had called, but for reasons she could not explain, those she had called said that now they found it inconvenient to sail in April. We sailed on April 20th and arrived in New York on the morning of May the first.

In the production of my play – the sailing on a boat that would bring me to New York by the first of May – I played the four most important characters in my drama. As the producer, I decided to sail on a specific ship at a certain time. Playing the part of the author, I wrote the script – I visualized the inner action which conformed to the outer action I would take if my desire were realized. As the director, I rehearsed myself, the actor, in that imagined action of climbing the gangplank until that action felt completely natural.

This being done, events and people moved swiftly to conform, in the outer world, to the play I had constructed and enacted in my imagination.

"I saw the mystic vision flow
And live in men and woods and streams. Until I could no longer know
The stream of life from my own dreams."
– George William Russell (AE)

I told this story to an audience of mine in San Francisco, and a lady in the audience told me how she had unconsciously used the same technique, when she was a young girl.

The incident occurred on Christmas Eve. She was feeling very sad and tired and sorry for herself. Her father, whom she adored, had died suddenly. Not only did she feel this loss at the Christmas season, but necessity had forced her to give up her planned college years and go to work. This rainy Christmas Eve she was riding home on a San Diego street car. The car was filled with gay chatter of happy young people home for the holidays. To hide her tears from those round about her, she stood on the open part at the front of the car and turned her face into the skies to mingle her tears with the rain. With her eyes closed, and holding the rail of the car firmly, this is what she said to herself: "This is not the salt of the tears that I taste, but the salt of the sea in the wind. This is not San Diego, this is the South Pacific and I am sailing into the Bay of Samoa". And looking up, in her imagination, she constructed what she imagined to be the Southern Cross. She lost herself in this contemplation so that all faded round about her. Suddenly she was at the end of the line, and home.

Two weeks later, she received word from a lawyer in Chicago that he was holding three thousand dollars in American bonds for her. Several years before, an aunt of hers had gone to Europe, with instructions that these bonds be turned over to her niece if she did not return to the United States. The lawyer had just received word of the aunt's death, and was now carrying out her instructions.

A month later, this girl sailed for the islands in the South Pacific. It was night when she entered the Bay of Samoa. Looking down, she could see the white foam like a "bone in the lady's mouth" as the ship ploughed through the waves, and brought the salt of the sea in the wind. An officer on duty said to her: "There is the Southern Cross", and looking up, she saw the Southern Cross as she had imagined it.

In the intervening years, she had many opportunities to use her imagination constructively, but as she had done this unconsciously, she did not realize there was a Law behind it all. Now that she understands, she, too, is consciously playing her four major roles in the daily drama of her life, producing plays for the good of others as well as herself.

"Then the soldiers, when they had crucified Jesus, took his garments, and made four parts, to every soldier a part; and also his coat; now the coat was without seam, woven from the top throughout." – John 19:23

THE GIFT OF FAITH

"And the Lord had respect unto Abel and in his offerings; But unto Cain and to his offering he had no respect." – Genesis 4:4, 5

If we search the Scriptures, we will become aware of a far deeper meaning in the above quotation than that which a literal reading would give us. The Lord is non other than your own conscious- ness ". . . say unto the children of Israel, I AM hath sent me unto you . . .Exodus 3:14." "I AM" is the self-definition of the Lord.

Cain and Abel, as the grandchildren of the Lord, can be only personifications of two distinct functions of your own consciousness. The author is really concerned to show the "Two Contrary States of the Human Soul," and he has used two brothers to show these states. The two brothers represent two distinct outlooks on the world possessed by everyone. One is the limited perception of the senses, and the other is an imaginative view of the world. Cain – the first view – is a passive surrender to appearances and an acceptance of life on the basis of the world without: a view which inevitably leads to unsatisfied longing or a contentment with disillusion. Abel – the second view – is a vision of fulfilled desire, lifting man above the evidence of the senses to that state of relief where he no longer pines with desire. Ignorance of the second view is a soul on fire. Knowledge of the second view is the wing whereby it flies to the Heaven of fulfilled desire.

"Come, eat my bread and drink of the wind that I have mingled, forsake the foolish and live." – Proverbs 9:56

In the epistle to the Hebrews, the writer tells us that Abel's offering was faith and, states the author, "Without faith it is impossible to please Him . . .Hebrews 11:6."

"Now faith is the substance of things hoped for, the evidence of things not seen. . . Through faith we understand that the worlds were framed by the word of God, so that things which are seen were not made of things which do appear." – Hebrews 11:1, 3

Cain offers the evidence of the senses which consciousness, the Lord, rejects, because acceptance of this gift as a mold of the future would mean the fixation and perpetuation of the present state forever. The sick would be sick, the poor would be poor, the thief would be a thief, the mur- derer a murderer, and so on, without hope of redemption.

The Lord, or consciousness, has no respect for such passive use of imagination – which is the gift of Cain. He delights in the gift of

Abel, the active, voluntary, loving exercise of the imagination on behalf of man for himself and others.

"Let the weak man say, I am strong.: – Joel 3:10

Let man disregard appearances and declare himself to be the man he wants to be. Let him imag- ine beauty where his senses reveal ashes, joy where they testify to mourning, riches where they bear witness to poverty. Only by such active, voluntary use of imagination can man be lifted up and Eden restored.

The ideal is always waiting to be incarnated, but unless we ourselves offer the ideal to the Lord, our consciousness, by assuming that we are already that which we seek to embody, it is incapable of birth. The Lord needs his daily lamb of faith to mold the world in harmony with our dreams.

"By faith Abel offered unto God a more excellent sacrifice than Cain." – Hebrews 11:4

Faith sacrifices the apparent fact for the unapparent truth. Faith holds fast to the fundamental truth that through the medium of an assumption, invisible states become visible facts.

"For what is faith unless it is to believe what you do not see?" – St. Augustine

Just recently, I had the opportunity to observe the wonderful results of one who had the faith to believe what she did not see.

A young woman asked me to meet her sister and her three-year-old nephew. He was a fine, healthy lad with clear blue eyes and an exceptionally fine unblemished skin. Then, she told me her story.

At birth, the boy was perfect in every way save for a large, ugly birthmark covering one side of his face. Their doctor advised them that nothing could be done for this type of scar. Visits to many specialists only confirmed his statement. Hearing the verdict, the aunt set herself the task of proving he faith – that an assumption, though denied by the evidence of the senses, if persisted in, will harden into fact.

Every time she thought of the baby, which was often, she saw, in her imagination, an eight-month-old baby with a perfect face – without any trace of a scar. This was not easy, but she knew that in this case, that was the gift of Abel which pleased God. She persisted in her faith – she believed what was not there to be seen. The result was that she visited her sister on the child's eight-month birthday and found him to have a perfect, unblemished skin with no trace of a birthmark ever having been present. "Luck! Coincidence! Shouts Cain. No. Abel knows that these are names given by those who have no faith, to the works of faith.

"We walk by faith, not by sight." – II Corinthians 5:7

When reason and the facts of life oppose the idea you desire to realize and you accept the evidence of your senses and the dictates of reason as the truth, you have brought the Lord – your consciousness – the gift of Cain. It is obvious that such offerings do not please Him.

Life on earth is a training ground for image making. If you use only the molds which your senses dictate, there will be no change in your life. You are here to live the more abundant life, so you must use the invisible molds of imagination and make results and accomplishments the crucial test of your power to create. Only as you assume the feeling of the wish fulfilled and continue therein are you offering the gift that pleases.

"When Abel's gift is my attire Then I'll realize my desire."

The Prophet Malachi complains that man has robbed God:

"But ye say, Wherein have we robbed thee? In tithes and offerings." – Malachi 3:8

Facts based upon reason and the evidence of the senses which oppose the idea seeking expression, rob you of the belief in the reality of the invisible state. But "faith is the evidence of things not seen", and through it "Good calleth those things which be not as though they were . . . Romans 4:17." Call the thing not seen; assume the feeling of your wish fulfilled.

". . .that there may be meat in mine house, and prove me now herewith, sayeth the Lord of hosts, if I will not open you the windows of heaven, and pour you out a blessing, that there shall not be room enough to receive it." – Malachi 3:10

This is the story of a couple living in Sacramento, California, who refused to accept the evidence of their senses, who refused to be robbed, in spite of a seeming loss. The wife had given her husband a very valuable wristwatch. The gift doubled its value because of the sentiment he attached to it. They had a little ritual with the watch. Every night as he removed the watch he gave it to her and she put it away in a special box in the bureau. Every morning she took the watch and gave it to him to put on.

One morning the watch was missing. They both remembered playing their usual parts the night before, therefore the watch was not lost or misplaced, but stolen. Then and there, they determined not to accept the fact that it was really gone. They said to each other, "This is an opportunity to practice what we believe." They decided that, in their imagination, they would enact their customary ritual as though the watch were actually there. In his imagination, every night the husband took off the watch and gave it to his wife, while in her imagination she accepted the watch and carefully put it away. Every morning she removed the watch from its box and gave it to her husband and he, in turn, put it on. This they did faithfully for two weeks.

After their fourteen-day vigil, a man went into the one and only jewelry store in Sacramento where the watch would be recognized. As he offered a gem for appraisal, the owner of the store noticed the wristwatch he was wearing. Under the pretext of needing a closer examination of the stone, he went into an inner office and called the police. After the police arrested the man, they found in his apartment over ten thousand dollars worth of stolen jewelry. In walking "by faith, not by sight", this couple attained their desire – the watch – and also aided many others in regaining what had seemed to be lost forever.

"If one advances confidently in the direction of his dream, and endeavors to live the life which he has imagined, he will meet with a success unexpected in common hours." – Thoreau

THE SCALE OF BEING

"And he dreamed, and behold a ladder set up on the earth, and the top of it reached to heaven: and behold the angels of God ascending and descending on it. And, behold, the Lord stood above it. . ." – Genesis 28:12, 13

In a dream, in a vision of the night, when deep sleep fell upon Jacob, his inner eye was opened and he beheld the world as a series of ascending and descending levels of awareness. It was a revelation of the deepest insight into the mysteries of the world. Jacob saw a vertical scale of ascending and descending values, or states of consciousness. This gave meaning to everything in the outer world, for without such a scale of values there would be no meaning to life.

At every moment of time, man stands upon the eternal scale of meaning. There is no object or event that has ever taken place or is taking place now that is without significance. The significance of an object or event for the individual is a direct index to the level of his consciousness.

You are holding this book, for example. On one level of consciousness, it is an object in space. On a higher level, it is a series of letters on paper, arranged according to certain rules. On a still higher level, it is an expression of meaning.

Looking outwardly, you see the book first, but actually, the meaning comes first. It occupies a higher grade of significance than the letter arrangement on paper or the book as an object in space. Meaning determined the arrangement of letters; the arrangement of letters only expresses the meaning. The meaning is invisible and above the level of the visible arrangement of letters. If there had been on meaning to be expressed, no book would have been written and published.

"And, behold, the Lord stood above it."

The Lord and meaning are one – the Creator, the cause of the phenomena of life.

"In the beginning was the Word, and the Word was with God, and the Word was God." – John 1:1

In the beginning, was the intention – the meaning – and the intention was with the intender, and the intention was the intender. The objects and events in time and space occupy a lower level of significance than the level of meaning which produced them. All things were made by meaning, and without meaning was not anything made that was

[454] NEVILLE GODDARD

made. The fact that everything seen can be regarded as the effect, on a lower level of significance, of an unseen higher order of significance is a very important one to grasp.

Our usual mode of procedure is to attempt to explain the higher levels of significance – why things happen – in terms of the lower – what and how things happen. For example, let us take an actual accident and try to explain it.

Most of us live on the level of what happened – the accident was an event in space – one automobile struck another and practically demolished it. Some of us live on the higher level of "how" the accident happened – it was a rainy night, the roads were slippery and the second car skidded into the first. On rare occasions, a few of us reach the highest or causal level of "why" such an accident occurs. Then we become aware of the invisible, the state of consciousness which produced the visible event.

In this case, the ruined car was driven by a widow, who, though she felt she could not afford to, greatly desired to change her environment. Having heard that, by the proper use of her imagination, she could do and be all she wished to be, this widow had been imagining herself actually living in the city of her desire. At the same time, she was living in a consciousness of loss, both personal and financial. Therefore, she brought upon herself an event which was seemingly another loss, but the sum of money the insurance company paid her allowed her to make the desired change in her life.

When we see the "why" behind the seeming accident, the state of consciousness that produced the accident, we are led to the conclusion that there is no accident. Everything in life has its in- visible meaning.

The man who learns of an accident, the man who knows "how" it happened, and the man who knows "why" it happened are on three different levels of awareness in regard to that accident. On the ascending scale, each higher level carries us a step in advance towards the truth of the accident.

We should strive constantly to lift ourselves to the higher level of meaning, the meaning that is always invisible and above the physical event. But, remember, the meaning or cause of the phenomena of life can be found only within the consciousness of man.

Man is so engrossed in the visible side of the drama of life – the side of "what" has happened, and "how" it happened – that he rarely rises to the invisible side of "why" it happened. He refuses to accept the Prophet's warning that:

"Things which are seen were not made of things that do appear." – Hebrews 11:3

His descriptions of "what" has happened and "how" it happened are true in terms of his corresponding level of thought, but when he asks "why" it happened, all physical explanations break down and he is forced to seek the "why", or meaning of it, on the invisible and higher level. The mechanical analysis of events deals only with external relationships of things. Such a course will never reach the level which holds the secret of why the events happen. Man must recognize that the lower and visible sides flow from the invisible and higher level of meaning.

Intuition is needed to lift us up to the level of meaning – to the level of why things happen. Let us follow the advice of the Hebrew prophet of old and "lift up our eyes unto the hills" within our- selves, and observe what is taking place there. See what ideas we have accepted as true, what states we have consented to, what dreams, what desires – and, above all, what intentions. It is from these hills that all things come to reveal our stature – our height – on the vertical scale of meaning. If we lift our eyes to "the Thee in Me who works behind the Veil", we will see the meaning of the phenomena of life.

Events appear on the screen of space to express the different levels of consciousness of man. A change in the level of his consciousness automatically results in a change of the phenomena of his life. To attempt to change conditions before he changes the level of consciousness from whence they came, is to struggle in vain. Man redeems the world as he ascends the vertical scale of meaning.

We saw, in the analogy of the book, that as consciousness was lifted up to the level where man could see meaning expressed in the arrangement of its letters, it also included the knowledge that the letters were arranged according to certain rules, and that such arrangements, when printed on paper and bound together, formed a book. What is true of the book is true of every event in the world.

"They shall not hurt or destroy in all my holy mountain: for the earth shall be full of the knowledge of the Lord, as the waters cover the sea." – Isaiah 11:9

Nothing is to be discarded; all is to be redeemed. Our lives, ascending the vertical scale of meaning towards an ever increasing awareness – an awareness of things of higher significance – are the process whereby this redemption is brought to pass. As man arranges letters into words, and words into sentences to express meaning, in like manner, life arranges circumstances, conditions and events to express the unseen meanings or attitudes of men. Nothing is without significance. But man, not knowing the higher level of inner meaning, looks out upon a moving panorama of events and sees no meaning to life. There is always a level of meaning determining events and their essential relationship to our lives.

Here is a story that will enable us to seize the good in things seeming evil; to withhold judgment, and to act aright amid unsolved problems.

Just a few years ago, our country was shocked by a seeming injustice in our midst. The story was told on radio and television, as well as in the newspapers. You may recall the incident. The body of a young American soldier killed in Korea was returned to his home for burial. Just before the service, his wife was asked a routine question: Was her husband a Caucasian? When she replied that he was an Indian, burial was refused. This refusal was in accordance with the laws of that community, but it aroused the entire nation. We felt incensed that anyone who had been killed in the service of his country should be denied burial anywhere in his country. The story reached the attention of the President of the United States, and he offered burial with full military honors in Arlington National Cemetery. After the service, the wife told reporters that her husband had always dreamed of dying a hero, and having a hero's burial service with full military honors.

When, we in America, had to explain why progressive, intelligent people like ourselves, not only enacted but supported such laws in our great land of the free and the brave, we were hard put for an explanation. We, as observers, had seen only "what" happened, and "how" it happened. We failed to see "why" it happened.

That burial had to be refused if that lad was to realize his dream. We tried to explain the drama in terms of the lower level of "how" it happened, which explanation could not satisfy the one who had asked "why" it happened.

The true answer, viewed from the level of higher meaning, would be such a reversal of our com-mon habits of thinking that it would be instantly rejected. The truth is that future states are causa-tive of present facts – the Indian boy dreaming of a hero's death, with full military honors, was like Lady Macbeth transported "beyond this ignorant present", and could "feel now the future in the instant."

". . . and by it he being dead yet speaketh." – Hebrews 11:4

THE GAME OF LIFE

"I can easier teach twenty what were good to be done, than be one of the twenty to follow mine own teaching." – Shakespeare

With this confession off my mind, I will now teach you how to play the game of life. Life is a game and, like all games, it has its aims and its rules.

In the little games that men concoct, such as cricket, tennis, baseball, football, and so on, the rules may be changed from time to time. After the changes are agreed upon, man must learn the new rules and play the game within the framework of the accepted rules.

However, in the game of life, the rules cannot be changed or broken. Only within the framework of its universal and everlastingly fixed rules can the game of life be played.

The game of life is played on the playing field of the mind. In playing a game, the first thing we ask is: "What is its aim and purpose?" and the second, "What are the rules governing the game?" In the game of life, our chief aim is towards increasing awareness – an awareness of things of greater significance; and our second aim is towards achieving our goals, realizing our desires.

As to our desires, the rules reach only so far as to indicate the way in which we should go to realize them, but the desires themselves must be the individual's own concern. The rules governing the game of life are simple, but it takes a lifetime of practice to use them wisely. Here is one of the rules:

"As he thinketh in his heart, so is he." – Proverbs 23:7

Thinking is usually believed to be a function entirely untrammeled and free, without any rules to constrain it. But that is not true. Thinking moves by its own processes in a bounded territory, with definite paths and patterns.

"Thinking follows the tracks laid down in one's own inner conversations."

All of us can realize our objectives by the wise use of mind and speech. Most of us are totally unaware of the mental activity which goes on within us. But to play the game of life successfully, we must become aware of our every mental activity, for this activity, in the form of inner conversations, is the cause of the outer phenomena of our life.

". . . every idle word that man shall speak, they shall give account thereof in the day of judgment. For by thy words thou shall be justified, and by thy words thou shalt be condemned." – Matthew 12:36, 37

The law of the Word cannot be broken.

". . .A bone of him shall not be broken." – John 19:36

The law of the Word never overlooks an inner word nor makes the smallest allowance for our ignorance of its power. It fashions life about us as we, by our inner conversations, fashion life within ourselves. This is done to reveal to us our position on the playing field of life. There is no opponent in the game of life; there is only the goal.

Not long ago, I was discussing this with a successful and philanthropic businessman. He told me a thought-provoking story about himself.

He said, "You know, Neville, I first learned about goals in life when I was fourteen, and it was on

the playing field at school. I was good at track and had a fine day, but there was one more race to run and I had stiff competition in one other boy. I was determined to beat him. I beat him, it is true, but, while I was keeping my eye on him, a third boy, who was considered no competition at all, won the race."

"That experience taught me a lesson I have used throughout my life. When people ask me about my success, I must say, that I believe it is because I have never made 'making money' my goal: 'My goal is the wise, productive use of money'."

This man's inner conversations are based on the premise that he already has money, his constant inner question: the proper use of it. The inner conversations of the man struggling to 'get' money only prove his lack of money. In his ignorance of the power of the word, he is building barriers in the way of the attainment of his goal; he has his eye on the competition rather than on the goal itself.

"The fault, dear Brutus, is not in our stars, But in ourselves, that we are underlings."
– Julius Caesar: Act I, Scene II

As "the worlds were framed by the Word of God", so we as "imitators of God as dear children" create the conditions and circumstances of our lives by our all-powerful human inner words. Without practice, the most profound knowledge of the game would produce no desired results. "To him that knoweth to do good" – that is, knoweth the rules

– and doeth it not, to him it is sin". In other words, he will miss his mark and fail to realize his goal.

In the parable of the Talents, the Master's condemnation of the servant who neglected to use his gift is clear and unmistakable, and having discovered one of the rules of the game of life, we risk failure by ignoring it. The talent not used, like the limb not exercised, slumbers and finally atrophies. We must be "doers of the Word, and not hearers only". Since thinking follows the tracks laid down in one's own inner conversations, not only can we see where we are going on the playing field of life by observing our inner conversations, but also, we can determine where we will go by controlling and directing our inner talking.

What would you think and say and do were you already the one you want to be? Begin to think and say and do this inwardly. You are told that "there is a rod in heaven that revealeth secrets," and, you must always remember that heaven is within you; and to make it crystal clear who God is, where He is, and what His secrets are, Daniel continues, "Thy dream, and the visions of thy head are these". They reveal the tracks to which you are tied, and point the direction in which you are going.

This is what one woman did to turn the tracks to which she had been unhappily tied in the direction in which she wanted to go. For two years, she had kept herself estranged from the three people she loved most. She had had a quarrel with her daughter-in-law, who ordered her from her home. For those two years, she had not seen or heard from her son, her daughter-in-law or her grandson, though she had sent her grandson numerous gifts in the meantime. Every time she thought of her family, which was daily, she carried on a mental conversation with her daughter-in- law, blaming her for the quarrel and accusing her of being selfish.

Upon hearing a lecture of mine one night – it was this very lecture on the game of life and how to play it – she suddenly realized she was the cause of the prolonged silence and that she, and she alone, must do something about it. Recognizing that her goal was to have the former loving relationship, she set herself the task of completely changing her inner talking.

That very night, in her imagination, she constructed two loving, tender letters written to her, one from her daughter-in-law and the other from her grandson. In her imagination, she read them over and over again until she fell asleep in the joyful mood of having received the letters. She repeated this imaginary act each night for eight nights. On the morning of the ninth day, she received one envelope containing two letters, one from her daughter-in-law, one from her grandson. They were loving, tender letters inviting her to visit them, almost replicas of those she had constructed mentally. By using her imagination consciously and lovingly, she had turned the tracks to which she was tied, in the direction she wanted to go, towards a happy family reunion.

A change of attitude is a change of position on the playing field of life. The game of life is not be- ing played out there in what is called space and time; the real moves in the game of life take place within, on the playing field of the mind.

"Losing thy soul, thy soul Again to find; Rendering toward that goal Thy separate mind." – Laurence Housman

"TIME, TIMES, AND AN HALF"

"And one said to the man clothed in linen, which was upon the waters of the river, How long shall it be to the end of these wonders? And I heard the man clothed in linen, which was upon the waters of the river, when he held up his right hand and his left hand unto heaven, and swear by him that liveth forever that it shall be for a time, times, and an half." – Daniel 12:6, 7

At one of my lectures given in Los Angeles on the subject of the hidden meaning behind the stories of the Bible, someone asked me to interpret the above quotation from the Book of Daniel. After I confessed I did not know the meaning of that particular passage, a lady in the audience said to herself, "If the mind behaves according to the assumption with which it starts, then I will find the true answer to that question and tell it to Neville." And this is what she told me.

"Last night the question was asked: 'What is the meaning of "time, times, and an half" as recorded in Daniel 12:7?' Before going to sleep last night I said to myself, 'Now there is a simple answer to this question, so I will assume that I know it and while I am sleeping my greater self will find the answer and reveal it to my lesser self in dream or vision.'"

"Around five A.M. I awakened. It was too early to rise, so remaining in bed I quickly fell into that half dreamy state between waking and sleeping, and while in that state a picture came into my mind of an old lady. She was sitting in a rocking chair and rocking back and forth, back and forth. Then a voice which sounded like your voice said to me: 'Do it over and over and over again until it takes on the tones of reality.'"

"I jumped out of bed and re-read the Twelfth Chapter of Daniel, and this is the intuitive answer I received. Taking the sixth and seventh verses, for they constituted last night's question, I felt that if the garments with which Biblical characters are clothed correspond to their level of consciousness, as you teach, then linen must represent a very high level of consciousness indeed, for the 'man clothed in linen' was standing 'upon the waters of the river' and if, as you teach, water symbolizes a high level of psychological truth, then the individual who could walk upon it must truly represent an exalted state of consciousness. I therefore felt that what he had to say must indeed be very significant. Now the question asked of him was 'How long shall it be to the end of these wonders?' And his answer was, 'A time, times, and an half.' Remembering my vision of the old lady rocking back and forth, and your voice telling me to 'do it over and over and over again until it takes on the tones of reality', and remembering that this vision and your instruction came to me in response to my assumption that I knew the answer, I intuitively felt that the question asked the 'man clothed in linen' meant how long shall it be until the wonderful dreams that I am dreaming become a reality. And his answer is, 'Do it over and over and over again until it takes on the tones of reality'. 'A time' means to perform the imaginary action which implies the fulfillment of the wish;

'Times' mean to repeat the imaginary action over and over again, and 'an half' means the moment of falling asleep while performing the imaginary action, for such a moment usually arrives before the pre-determined action is completed and, therefore, can be said to be a half, or part, of a time."

To get such inner understanding of the Scriptures by the simple assumption that she did know the answer, was a wonderful experience for this woman. However, to know the true meaning of "time, times, and an half" she must apply her understanding in her daily life. We are never at a loss in an opportunity to test this understanding, either for ourselves or for another.

A number of years ago, a widow living in the same apartment house as we, came to see me about her cat. The cat was her constant companion and dear to her heart. He was, however, eight years old, very ill and in great pain. He had not eaten for days and would not move from under her bed. Two veterinarians had seen the cat and advised the woman that the cat could not be cured, and that he should be put to sleep immediately. I suggested that that night, before retiring, she create in her imagination some action that would indicate the cat was its former healthy self. I advised her to do it over and over again until it took on the tones of reality.

This, she promised to do. However, either from lack of faith in my advice or from lack of faith in her own ability to carry out the imaginary action, she asked her niece to spend the night with her. This request was made so that if the cat were not well by morning, the niece could take it to the veterinarian's and she, the owner, would not have to face such a dreaded task herself. That night, she settled herself in an easy chair and began to imagine the cat was romping beside her, scratching at the furniture and doing many things she would not normally have allowed. Each time she found that her mind had wandered from its pre-determined task to see a normal, healthy, frisky cat, she brought her attention back to the room and started her imaginary action over again. This she did over and over again until, finally, in a feeling of relief, she dropped off to sleep, still seated in her chair.

At about four o'clock in the morning, she was awakened by the cry of her cat. He was standing by her chair. After attracting her attention, he led her to the kitchen where he begged for food. She fixed him a little warm milk which he quickly drank, and cried for more.

That cat lived comfortably for five more years, when, without pain or illness, he died naturally in his sleep.

"How long shall it be to the end of these wonders?. . . A time, times, and an half. In a dream in a vision of the night, when deep sleep falleth upon men, in slumberings upon the bed; Then he openeth the ears of men, and sealeth their instructions."
– Job 33:15, 16

BE YE WISE AS SERPENTS

". . .be ye therefore wise as serpents, and harmless as doves." – Matthew 10:16

The serpent's ability to form its skin by ossifying a portion of itself, and its skill in shedding each skin as it outgrew it, caused man to regard this reptile as a symbol of the power of endless growth and self-reproduction. Man is told, therefore, to be "wise as the serpent" and learn how to shed his skin – his environment – which is his solidified self; man must learn how to "loose him, and let him go" . . . how to "put off the old man" . . .how to die to the old and yet know, like the serpent, that he "shall not surely die".

Man has not learned as yet that all that is outside his physical body is also a part of himself, that his world and all the conditions of his life are but the out-picturing of his state of consciousness. When he knows this truth, he will stop the futile struggle of self-contention and, like the serpent,

let the old go and grow a new environment.

"Man is immortal; therefore he must die endlessly. For life is a creative idea; it can only find itself in changing forms." – Tagore

In ancient times, serpents were also associated with the guardianship of treasure or wealth. The injunction to be "wise as serpents" is the advice to man to awaken the power of his subtilized body – his imagination – that he, like the serpent, may grow and outgrow, die and yet not die, for from such deaths and resurrections alone, shedding the old and putting on the new, shall come fulfillment of his dreams and the finding of his treaures. As "the serpent was more subtle than any beast of the field which the Lord God had made" – Genesis 3:1 – even so, imagination is more subtle than any creature of the heavens which the Lord God had created. Imagination is the creature that:

". . .was made subject to vanity, not willingly, but by reason of him who hath subjected the same in hope. . .For we are saved by hope: but hope that is seen is not hope: for what a man seeth, why doth he yet hope for it? But if we hope for that we see not, then do we have patience wait for it." – Romans 8:20, 24, 25

Although the outer, or "natural", man of the senses is interlocked with his environment, the inner, or spiritual, man of imagination is not thus interlocked. If the interlocking were complete, the charge to be "wise as serpents" would be in vain. Were we completely interlocked with our environment, we could not withdraw our attention from the evidence of the senses and feel ourselves into the situation of our fulfilled desire, in hope that that unseen state would solidify as our new environment. But:

"There is a natural body, and there is a spiritual body." – I Corinthians 15:44

The spiritual body of imagination is not interlocked with man's environment. The spiritual body can withdraw from the outer man of sense and environment and imagine itself to be what it wants to be. And if it remains faithful to the vision, imagination will build for man a new environment in which to live. This is what is meant by the statement:

". . .I go to prepare a place for you. And if I go and prepare a place for you, I will come again, and receive you unto myself; that where I am, there ye may be also." – John 14:2, 3

The place that is prepared for you need not be a place in space. It can be health, wealth, companionship, anything that you desire in this world. Now, how is the place prepared?

You must first construct as life-like a representation as possible of what you would see and hear and do if you were physically present and physically moving about in that "place." Then, with your physical body immobilized, you must imagine that you are actually in that "place" and are seeing and hearing and doing all that you would see and hear and do if you were there physically. This you must do over and over again until it takes on the tones of reality. When it feels natural, the "place" has been prepared as the new environment for your outer or physical self. Now you may open your physical eyes and return to your former state. The "place" is prepared, and where you have been in imagination, there you shall be in the body also.

How this imagined state is realized physically is not the concern of you, the natural or outer man. The spiritual body, on its return from the imagined state to its former physical state, created an invisible bridge of incident to link the two states. Although the curious feeling that you were actually there and that the state was real is gone, as soon as you open your eyes upon the old familiar environment, nevertheless, you are haunted with the sense of a double identity – with the knowledge that "there is a natural body, and there is a spiritual body." When you, the natural man, have had this experience you will go automatically across the bridge of events which leads to the physical realization of your invisibly prepared place.

This concept – that man is dual and that the inner man of imagination can dwell in future states and return to the present moment with a bridge of events to link the two – clashes violently with the widely accepted view about the human personality and the cause and nature of phenomena. Such a concept demands a revolution in current ideas about the human personality, and about space, time and matter. The concept that man, consciously or unconsciously, determines the conditions of life by imagining himself into these mental states, leads to the conclusion that this supposedly solid world is a construction of Mind – a concept which, at first, common sense rejects. However, we should remember that most of the concepts which common sense at first rejected, man was afterward forced to accept. These never-ending reversals of judgment which experience has forced upon man led Professor Whitehead to write: "Heaven knows what seem- ing nonsense may not tomorrow be demonstrated truth."

The creative power in man sleeps and needs to be awakened. "Awake thou that sleepest, and arise from the dead." – Ephesians 5:14 Wake from the sleep that tells you the outer world is the cause of the conditions of your life. Rise from the dead past and create a new environment.

"Know ye not that ye are the temple of God, and that the Spirit of God dwelleth in you?" – I Corinthians 3:16

The Spirit of God in you is your imagination, but it sleeps and needs to be awakened, in order to lift you off the bar of the senses where you have so long lain stranded.

The boundless possibilities open to you as you become "wise as serpents" is beyond measure. You will select the ideal conditions you want to experience and the ideal environment you want to live in. Experiencing these states in imagination until they have sensory vividness, you will externalize them as surely as the serpent now externalizes its skin.

After you have outgrown them, then, you will cast them off as easily as "the snake throws her enamelled skin". The more abundant life – the whole purpose of Creation – cannot be saved through death and resurrection.

God desired form, so He became man: and it is not enough for us to recognize His spirit at work in creation, we must see His work in form and say that it is good, even though we outgrow the form, forever and ever.

"He   leads
Through widening chambers of delight to where Throbs rapture

near an end that aye recedes, Because His touch is Infinite and lends A yonder to all ends."

"And, I, if I be lifted up from the earth, will draw all men unto me." – John 12:32

If I be lifted up from the evidence of the senses to the state of consciousness I desire to realize and remain in that state until it feels natural. I will form that state around me and all men will see it. But how to persuade man this is true – that imaginative life is the only living; that assuming the feeling of the wish fulfilled is the way to the more abundant life and not the compensation of the escapist – that is the problem. To see as "though widening chambers of delight" what living in the realms of imagination means, to appreciate and enjoy the world, one must live imaginatively; one

must dream and occupy his dream, then grow and outgrow the dream, forever and ever. The unimaginative man, who will not lose his life on one level that he may find it on a higher level, is nothing but a Lot's wife – a pillar of self-satisfied salt. On the other hand, those who refuse form as being unspiritual and who reject incarnation as separate from God are ignorant of the great mystery: "Great is the mystery, God was manifest in the flesh."

Your life expresses one thing, and one thing only, your state of consciousness. Everything is dependent upon that. As you, through the medium of imagination, assume a state of consciousness, that state begins to clothe itself in form, It solidifies around you as the serpent's skin ossifies around it. But you must be faithful to the state. You must not go from state to state, but, rather, wait patiently in the one invisible state until it takes on form and becomes an objective fact. Patience is necessary, but patience will be easy after your first success in shedding the old and growing the new, for we are able to wait according as we have been rewarded by understanding in the past. Understanding is the secret of patience. What natural joy and spontaneous delight lie in seeing the world – not with, but as Blake says – through the eye! Imagine that you are seeing what you want to see, and remain faithful to your vision. Your imagination will make for itself a corresponding form in which to live.

All things are made by imagination's power. Nothing begins except in the imagination of man. "From within out" is the law of the universe. "As within, so without." Man turns outward in his search for truth, but the essential thing is to look within.

"Truth is within ourselves; it takes no rise
From outward things, what e'er you may believe. There is an inmost center in us all,

Where truth abides in fullness .. . and to know, Rather consist in
opening out a way
Whence the imprisoned splendor may escape, Than in effecting
entry for a light
Supposed to be without."
– Browning: "Paracelsus"

I think you will be interested in an instance of how a young woman
shed the skin of resentment and put on a far different kind of skin.
The parents of this woman had separated when she was six years old
and she had lived with her mother. She rarely saw her father. But once
a year he sent her a five dollar check for Christmas. Following her
marriage, he did increase the Christmas gift to ten dollars.

After one of my lectures, she was dwelling on my statement that man's
suspicion of another is only a measure of his own deceitfulness, and
she recognized that she had been harboring a resentment towards her
father for years. That night she resolved to let go her resentment and
put a fond reaction in its place. In her imagination, she felt she was
embracing her father in the warm- est way. She did it over and over
again until she caught the spirit of her imaginary act, and then she fell
asleep in a very contented mood.

The following day she happened to pass through the fur department
of one of our large stores in California. For some time she had been
toying with the idea of having a new fur scarf, but felt she could not
afford it. This time her eye was caught by a stone marten scarf, and
she picked it up and tired it on. After feeling it and seeing herself in
it, reluctantly she took off the scarf and returned it to the salesman,
telling herself she really could not afford it. As she was leaving the
department, she stopped and thought, "Neville tells we can have
whatever we desire if we will only capture the feeling of already
having it." In her imagination, she put the scarf back on, felt the
reality of it, and went about her shopping, all the while enjoying the
imagined wearing of it.

This young woman never associated these two imaginary acts. In
fact, she had almost forgotten what she had done until, a few weeks
later, on Mother's Day, the doorbell rang unexpectedly.

There was her father. As she embraced him, she remembered her first
imaginary action. As she opened the package he had brought her – the
first gift in these many years – she remembered her second imaginary
action, for the box contained a beautiful stone marten scarf.

"Ye are gods; and all of you are children of the most High." – Psalms
82:6

". . .be ye therefore wise as serpents, and harmless as doves." –
Matthew 10:16

THE WATER AND THE BLOOD

"…Except a man be born again he cannot
see the kingdom of God."
– John 3:3

"But one of the soldiers with a spear pierced
his side, and forthwith came there out blood
and water."
– John 19:34

"This is he that came by water and
blood, even Jesus Christ; not by water
only, but by water and blood."
– I. John 5:6

According to the gospel and the Epistle of John, not only must man
be "born again" but he must be born again of water and blood. These
two inward experiences are linked with two outward rites – baptism
and communion. But the two outward rites – baptism to symbolize
birth by water, and the wine of communion to symbolize acceptance
of the blood of the Savoir, cannot produce the real birth or radical
transformation of the individual, which is promised to man. The
outward use of water and wine cannot bring about the desired change
of mind. We must, therefore, look for the hidden meaning behind the
symbols of water and blood.

The Bible uses many images to symbolize Truth, but the images used
symbolize Truth on different levels of meaning. On the lowest level,
the image used is stone. For example:

"… a great stone was upon
The well's mouth. And thither
were all the flocks gathered:
and they rolled the stone from
the well's mouth, and watered
the sheep…"
…Genesis 29:2, 3

"…They sank into the bottom
as a stone."
…Exodus 15:5

When a stone blocks the well, it means that people have taken these
great symbolical revelations of truth literally. When someone rolls
the stone away, it means that an individual has discovered beneath
the allegory or parable its psychological life germ, or meaning. This

hidden meaning which lies behind the literal words is symbolized by water. It is this water. In the form of psychological Truth, that he then offers to humanity.

"The flock of my pasture are men." … Ezekiel 34:31

The literal-minded man who refuses the "cup of water" – psychological Truth – offered him, "sinks into the bottom as a stone." He remains on the level where he sees everything in pure objectivity, without any subjective relationship he may keep all the commandments – written on stone – literally, and yet break them psychologically all day long.

He may, for example not literally steal the property of another, and yet see the other in want. To see another in want, is to rob him of his birthright as a child of God. For we are all "children of the most high."

"And if children, then heirs; heirs of God, and joint-heirs with Christ…" …Romans 8:17

To know what to do about a seeming misfortune is to have the "cup of water" – the psychological Truth – that could save the situation. But such knowledge is not enough. Man must not only "fill the water pots of stone with water" – that is, discover the psychological truth – into wine.

This he does by living a life according to the truth which he has discovered.

Only by such use of the truth can he "taste the water that was made wine…" – John 2:9

A mans birthright is to be Jesus. He is born to "save his people from their sins"… Matthew 1 : 21.

But the salvation of a man is "not by water only, but by water and blood".

To know what to do to save yourself or another is not enough; you must do it.

Knowledge of what to do is water; doing it is blood.

This is he that came not by water only, but by water and blood." The whole of this mystery is in the conscious, active use of imagination to appropriate that particular state of consciousness that would save you or another from the present limitation. Outward ceremonies cannot accomplish this.

"…   there   shall   meet   you   a   man
bearing   a   pitcher   of   water;   follow
h   i   m   .
And   wheresoever   he   shall   go   in,
say   ye   to   the   goodman   of   the
house,   The   Master   saith,   Where   is   the   guest-chamber,
where   I   shall   eat   the   Passover   with   my   disciples?
And he will show you a large upper room furnished and prepared:
there make ready for us."

Whatever you desire is already "furnished and prepared".

Your imagination can put you in touch inwardly with that state of consciousness. If you imagine that you are already the one you want to be, you are following the "man bearing a pitcher of water". If you remain in that state, you have entered the guest-chamber – Passover – and committed your spirit into the hands of God – your consciousness.

A man's state of consciousness is his demand on the Infinite Store House of God, and, like the law of commerce, a demand creates a supply.

To change the supply, you change the demand – your state of consciousness.

What you desire to be, that you must feel you already are. Your state of consciousness creates the conditions of your life, rather than the conditions create your state of consciousness. To know this Truth, is to have the "water of life".

But your savior – the solution of your problem – cannot be manifested by such knowledge only.

It can be realized only as such knowledge is applied.

Only as you assume the feeling of your wish fulfilled, and continue therein, is your side pierced; from whence cometh blood and water". In this manner only is Jesus – the solution of your problem – realized.

"for thou must know that in the
government of the mind thou art
thine own lord and master, that
there will rise up no fire in the
circle or whole circumference of
thy body and spirit, unless thou
awakes it thyself."

[473] THE POWER OF IMAGINATION: THE NEVILLE GODDARD TREASURY

God is your consciousness.

His promises are conditional. Unless the demand – your state of consciousness – is changed, the supply – the present conditions of your life remain as they are. "As we forgive" – as we change our mind – the law is automatic.

Your state of consciousness is the spring of action, the directing force, and that which creates the supply.

"if that nation, against whom I have pronounced, turn from their evil, I will repent of the evil that I thought to do unto them. And at what instant I shall speak concerning a nation, and concerning a kingdom, to build and to plant it; If it do evil in my sight, that it obey not my voice, then I will repent of the good, wherewith I said I would benefit them." ... Jeremiah 18:8, 9, 10

This statement of Jeremiah suggests that a commitment is involved if the individual or nation would realize the goal – a commitment to certain fixed attitudes of mind. The feeling of the wish fulfilled is a necessary condition in mans search for the goal.

The story I am about to tell you shows that man is what the observer has the capacity to see in him; that what he is seen to be is a direct index to the observer's state of consciousness.

This story is, also, a challenge to us all to shed our blood" – use our imagination lovingly on behalf of another.

There is no day that passes that does not afford us the opportunity to transform a life by the shedding of our blood".

"Without the shedding of blood there is no remission." ... Hebrews 9:22

One night in New York City I was able to unveil the mystery of the "water and the blood" to a school teacher. I had quoted the above statement from Hebrews 9:22, and went on to explain that the realization that we have no hope save in ourselves is the discovery that God is within us – that this discovery causes the dark caverns of the skull to grow luminous, and we know that: "The spirit of man is the candle of the lord"... Proverbs 20:27 – and that this realization is the light to guide us safely over the earth.

"His Candle shined upon my head and by his light I walked through darkness"

... Job 29:3

However, we must not look upon this radiant light of the head as God, for man is the image of God.

"God appears, and God is light,
To those poor souls who dwell in Night;

But does a Human Form display To those who dwell in realms of Day."
Blake

But this must be experienced to be known. There is no other way, and no other man's experience can be a substitute for our own.

I told the teacher that her change of attitude in regard to another would produce a corresponding change in the other; that such knowledge was the true meaning of the water mentioned in I. John 5:6, but that such knowledge alone was not enough to produce the re-birth desired; that such re-birth could only come to pass by "water and blood", or the application of this truth.

Knowledge of what to do is the water of life, but doing it is the blood of the savior.

In other words, a little knowledge, if carried out in action is more profitable than much knowledge which we neglect to carry out in action.

As I talked, one student kept impinging upon the teachers mind. But this, thought she, would be a too difficult case on which to test the truth of what I was telling her concerning the mystery of re-birth. All knew, teachers and students alike, that this particular student was incorrigible.

The outer facts of her case were these: The teachers, including the principal and school psychiatrist, had sat in judgment on the student just a few days before. They had come to a unanimous decision that the girl, for the good of the school, must be expelled upon reaching her sixteenth birthday. She was rude, crude, unethical and used most vile language. The date for dismissal was but a month away.

As she rode home that night, the teacher kept wondering if she could really change her mind about the girls, and if so, would the student undergo a change of behavior because she herself had undergone a change of attitude?

The only way to find out would be to try. This would be quite an undertaking for it meant assuming full responsibility for the incarnation of the new values in the student. Did she dare to assume so great a power – such creative, God-like power? This meant a complete reversal of man's normal attitude towards life from "I will love him if he first loves me", to "He loves me, because I first loved him." This was too much like playing God.

"We love him, because he first Loved us."
… I. John 4:19

But no matter how she tried to argue against it, the feeling persisted that my interpretation gave meaning to the mystery of re-birth by "water and blood." The teacher decided to accept the challenge. And this is what she did.

She brought the child's face before her mind's eye and saw her smile. She listened and imagined she heard the girl say "Good morning". This was something the student had never done since coming to that school. The teacher imagined the very best about the girl, and then listened and looked as though she heard and saw all that she would hear and see after these things should be. The teacher did this over and over again until she persuaded herself it was true, and fell asleep.

The very next morning, the student entered her classroom and smilingly said "Good morning". The teacher was so surprised she almost did not respond, and, by her own confession, all through the day she looked for signs of the girl's returning to her former behavior. However, the girl continued in the transformed state. By the end of the week, the change was noted by all; a second staff meeting was called and a decision of expulsion was revoked. As the child remained friendly and gracious, the teacher has had to ask herself, "Where was the bad child in the first place?"

"For Mercy, Pity, Peace, and Love Is God, Our father dear, And Mercy, Pity, Peace and Love Is man, His child and care."
(The Divine Image) – Blake

Transformation is in principle always possible, for the transformed being lives in us, and it is only a question of becoming conscious of it.

The teacher had to experience this transformation to know the mystery of "blood and water"; there was no other way, and no mans experience could have been a substitute for her own.

"We have redemption through his blood."
… Ephesians 1:7

Without the decision to change her mind in regard to the child, and the imaginative power to carry it out, the teacher could never have redeemed the student. None can know the redemptive power of the imagination who has not "shed his blood", and tasted the cup of experience.

"Once read thy own breast right, And thou hast done with fears! Man gets no other light, Search he a thousand years."
… Matthew Arnold

A MYSTICAL VIEW

"And with many such parables spake he the word unto them, as they were able to hear it.
But without a parable spake he not unto them: and when they were alone, he expounded all things to his disciples."
… Mark 4:33, 34

This collection of parables which is called the bible is a revelation of Truth expressed in symbolism to reveal the Laws and purposes of the mind of man. As we become aware of deeper meanings in the parables than those which are usually assigned to them, we are apprehending them mystically.

For example, let us take a mystical view of the advice given to the disciples in Matthew 10:10. We read that as the disciples were ready to teach and practice the great laws of mind which had been revealed to them, they were told not to provide shoes for the journey. A disciple is one who disciplines his mind that he may consciously function and act on higher and higher levels of of consciousness. The shoe was chosen as a symbol of vicarious atonement or the spirit of "let-me-do-it-for-you", because the shoe protects the wearer and shields him from impurities by taking them upon himself. The aim of the disciple is always to lead himself and others from the bondage of dependency into the liberty of the Sons of God. Hence the advice, take no shoes. Accept no intermediary between yourself and God. Turn from all who would offer to do for you what you should do, and could, do far better yourself.

"Earth's crammed with Heaven, And every common bush afire with God, But only he who sees takes off his shoes."
… Elizabeth Barrett Browning

"Verily I say unto you, inasmuch as ye have done it unto one of the least of these my breathren,
Ye have done it unto me."
… Matthew 25:40

Every time you exercise your imagination on behalf of another, be it good, bad or indifferent, you have literally done that to Christ, for Christ is awakened Human Imagination. Through the wise and loving use of imagination, man clothes and feeds Christ, and through ignorant and fearful misuse of imagination, man disrobes and scourges Christ.

"let none of you imagine evil in your hearts against your neighbor"
… Zechariah 8:17, is sound but negative advice. A man may stop

[478] NEVILLE GODDARD

misusing his imagination on the advice of a friend; he may be negatively served by the experience of others and learn not to imagine, but that is not enough. Such lack of use of the creative power of imagination could never clothe and feed Christ. The purple robe of the Son of God is woven, not by not imagining evil, but by imaging the good; by the active, voluntary and loving use of imagination.

"Whatsoever things are of good report; if there be any virtue, and if there be any praise, think on these things."
…Philippians 4:8

"King Solomon made himself a chariot of the wood of Lebanon.
He made the pillars thereof of silver, the bottom thereof of gold, the covering of it of
purple, the midst thereof being
paved with love…"
… Song of Solomon 3: 9, 10

The first thing we notice is "King Solomon made himself". That is what every man must eventually do – make himself a chariot of the wood of Lebanon. By chariot, the writer of this allegory means Mind, in which stands the spirit of Wisdom – Solomon – controlling the four functions of Mind that he may build a world of Love and Truth.

"And Joseph made ready his chariot and went up to meet Israel his father." "What tributaries follow him to Rome to grace in captive bonds his chariot wheels?" If man does not make himself a chariot of the wood of Lebanon, then his will be like Queen Mab's: "She is the fairies' midwife; … her chariot is an empty hazelnut."

The wood of Lebanon was the mystic's symbol of incorruptibility. To a mystic, It is obvious what King Solomon made himself. Silver typified knowledge, gold symbolized wisdom, and purple – clothed or covered the incorruptible Mind with the red of Love and the blue of Truth.

"And   they   clothed   him   with   purple."
… Mark 15:17

Incarnate, incorruptible four-fold wisdom, clothed in purple – Love and Truth – the purpose of man's experience on earth.

Love is the sage's stone;
It takes gold from the clod;
It turns naught into aught,
Transforms me into God."
… Angelus Silesius

Prayer: The Art of Believing

Chapter I
Law of Reversibility

"Pray for my soul, more things are wrought by prayer than this world dreams of" (Tennyson).

Prayer is an art and requires practice. The first requirement is a controlled imagination. Parade and vain repetitions are foreign to prayer. Its exercise requires tranquility and peace of mind, "Use not vain repetitions," for prayer is done in secret and "thy Father which seeth in secret shall reward thee openly." The ceremonies that are customarily used in prayer are mere superstitions and have been invented to give prayer an air of solemnity. Those who do practice the art of prayer are often ignorant of the laws that control it. They attribute the results obtained to the ceremonies and mistake the letter for the spirit. The essence of prayer is faith; but faith must be permeated with understanding to be given that active quality which it does not possess when standing alone. "Therefore, get wisdom; and with all thy getting get understanding."

This book is an attempt to reduce the unknown to the known, by pointing out conditions on which prayers are answered, and without which they cannot be answered. It defines the conditions governing prayer in laws that are simply a generalization of our observations The universal law of reversibility is the foundation on which its claims are based.

Mechanical motion caused by speech was known for a long time before anyone dreamed of the possibility of an inverse transformation, that is, the reproduction of speech by mechanical motion (the phonograph). For a long time electricity was produced by friction without ever a thought that friction, in turn, could be produced by electricity. Whether or not man succeeds in reversing the transformation of a force, he knows, nevertheless, that all transformations of force are reversible. If heat can produce mechanical motion, so mechanical motion can produce heat. If electricity produces magnetism, magnetism too can develop electric currents. If the voice can cause undulatory currents, so can such currents reproduce the voice, and so on. Cause and effect, energy and matter, action and reaction are the same and inter-convertible.

This law is of the highest importance, because it enables you to foresee the inverse transformation once the direct transformation is verified. If you knew how you would feel were you to realize your objective, then, inversely, you would know what state you could realize were you to awaken in yourself such feeling. The injunction, to pray believing that you already possess what you pray for, is based upon a knowledge of the law of inverse transformation. If your realized prayer produces in you a definite feeling or state of consciousness, then, inversely, that particular feeling or state of consciousness must produce your realized prayer. Because all transformations of force are reversible, you should always assume the feeling of your fulfilled wish. You should awaken within you the feeling that you are and have that which heretofore you desired to be and possess. This is easily done by contemplating the joy that would be yours were your objective an accomplished fact, so that you live and move and have your being in the feeling that your wish is realized.

The feeling of the wish fulfilled, if assumed and sustained, must objectify the state that would have created it. This law explains why "Faith is the substance of things hoped for, the evidence of things not seen" and why "He calleth things that are not seen as though they were and things that were not seen become seen." Assume the feeling of your wish fulfilled and continue feeling that it is fulfilled until that which you feel objectifies itself.

If a physical fact can produce a psychological state, a psychological state can produce a physical fact. If the effect (a) can be produced by the cause (b), then inversely, the effect (b) can be produced by the cause (a). Therefore I say unto you, "What things soever ye desire, when ye pray, believe that ye have received them, and ye shall have them" (Mark 11:24).

Chapter II
Dual Nature of Consciousness

A clear concept of the dual nature of man's consciousness must be the basis of all true prayer. Consciousness includes a subconscious as well as a conscious part. The infinitely greater part of consciousness lies below the sphere of objective consciousness. The subconscious is the most important part of consciousness. It is the cause of voluntary action. The subconscious is what a man is. The conscious is what a man knows. "I and my Father are one but my Father is greater than I." The conscious and subconscious are one, but the subconscious is greater than the conscious.

"I of myself can do nothing, the Father within me He doeth the work." I, objective consciousness, of myself can do nothing; the Father, the subconscious, He doeth the work. The subconscious is that in which everything is known, in which everything is possible, to which everything goes, from which everything comes, which belongs to all, to which all have access.

What we are conscious of is constructed out of what we are not conscious of. Not only do our subconscious assumptions influence our behavior but they also fashion the pattern of our objective existence. They alone have the power to say, "Let us make man— objective manifestations—in our image, after our likeness." The whole of creation is asleep within the deep of man and is awakened to objective existence by his subconscious assumptions. Within that blankness we call sleep there is a consciousness in unsleeping vigilance, and while the body sleeps this unsleeping being releases from the treasure house of eternity the subconscious assumptions of man.

Prayer is the key which unlocks the infinite storehouse. "Prove me now herewith, saith the Lord of hosts, if I will not open you the windows of heaven, and pour you out a blessing, that there shall not be room enough to receive it." Prayer modifies or completely changes our subconscious assumptions, and a change of assumption is a change of expression.

The conscious mind reasons inductively from observation, experience and education. It therefore finds it difficult to believe what the five senses and inductive reason deny. The subconscious reasons deductively and is never concerned with the truth or falsity of the premise, but proceeds on the assumption of the correctness of the premise and objectifies results which are consistent with the premise.

This distinction must be clearly seen by all who would master the art of praying. No true grasp of the science of prayer can be really obtained until the laws governing the dual nature of consciousness are understood and the importance of the subconscious realized.

Prayer—the art of believing what is denied by the senses — deals almost entirely with the subconscious. Through prayer, the subconscious is suggested into acceptance of the wish fulfilled, and, reasoning deductively, logically unfolds it to its legitimate end. "Far greater is He that is in you than he that is in the world."

The subjective mind is the diffused consciousness that animates the world; it is the spirit that giveth life. In all substance is a single soul — subjective mind.

Through all creation runs this one unbroken subjective mind. Thought and feel- ing fused into beliefs impress modifications upon it, charge it with a mission, which mission it faithfully executes.

The conscious mind originates premises. The subjective mind unfolds them to their logical ends. Were the subjective mind not so limited in its initiative power of reasoning, objective man could not be held responsible for his actions in the world. Man transmits ideas to the subconscious through his feelings. The subconscious transmits ideas from mind to mind through telepathy. Your unexpressed convictions of others are transmitted to them without their conscious knowledge or consent, and if subconsciously accepted by them will influence their behavior.

The only ideas they subconsciously reject are your ideas of them which they could not wish to be true of anyone. Whatever they could wish for others can be believed of them, and by the law of belief which governs subjective reasoning they are compelled to subjectively accept, and therefore objectively express, accordingly.

The subjective mind is completely controlled by suggestion. Ideas are best suggested when the objective mind is partly subjective, that is, when the objective senses are diminished or held in abeyance. This partly subjective state can best be described as controlled reverie, wherein the mind is passive but capable of functioning with absorption. It is a concentration of attention. There must be no conflict in your mind when you are praying. Turn from what is to what ought to be. Assume the mood of fulfilled desire, and by the universal law of reversibility you will realize your desire.

Chapter III
Imagination & Faith

Prayers are not successfully made unless there is a rapport between the conscious and subconscious mind of the operator. This is done through imagination and faith.

By the power of imagination all men, certainly imaginative men, are forever casting forth enchantments, and all men, especially unimaginative men, are continually passing under their power. Can we ever be certain that it was not our mother while darning our socks who began that subtle change in our minds? If I can unintentionally cast an enchantment over persons, there is no reason to doubt that I am able to cast intentionally a far stronger enchantment.

Everything, that can be seen, touched, explained, argued over, is to the imaginative man nothing more than a means, for he functions, by reason of his controlled imagination, in the deep of him-self where every idea exists in itself and not in relation to something else. In him there is no need for the restraints of reason. For the only restraint he can obey is the mysterious instinct that teaches him to eliminate all moods other than the mood of the fulfilled desire.

Imagination and faith are the only faculties of the mind needed to create objective conditions. The faith required for the successful operation of the law of consciousness is a purely subjective faith and is attainable upon the cessation of active opposition on the part of the objective mind of the operator. It depends on your ability to feel and accept as true what your objective senses deny. Neither the passivity of the subject nor his conscious agreement with your suggestion is necessary, for without his consent or knowledge he can be given a subjective order which he must objectively express. It is a fundamental law of consciousness that by telepathy we can have immediate communion with another.

To establish rapport you call the subject mentally. Focus your attention on him and mentally shout his name just as you would to attract the attention of anyone. Imagine that he answered, and mentally hear his voice. Represent him to yourself inwardly in the state you want him to obtain. Then imagine that he is telling you in the tones of ordinary conversation what you want to hear. Men- tally answer him. Tell him of your joy in witnessing his good fortune. Having mentally heard with all the distinctness of reality that which you wanted to hear and having thrilled to the news heard, return to objective consciousness. Your subjective conversation must awaken what it affirmed.

"Thou shalt decree a thing and it shall be established unto thee." It is not a strong will that sends the subjective word on its mission so much as it is clear thinking and feeling the truth of the state affirmed. When belief and will are in conflict, belief invariably wins. "Not by might, nor by power, but by my spirit, saith the Lord of hosts." It is not what you want that you attract; you attract what you believe to be true. Therefore, get into the spirit of these mental conversations and give them the same degree of reality that you would a telephone conversation. "If thou canst believe, all things are possible to him that believeth. Therefore, I say unto you, what things soever you desire, when you pray, believe that ye received them, and ye shall have them." The acceptance of the end wills the means. And the wisest reflection could not devise more effective means than those which are willed by the acceptance of the end. Men- tally talk to your friends as though your desires for them were already realized.

Imagination is the beginning of the growth of all forms, and faith is the substance out of which they are formed. By imagination, that which exists in latency or is asleep within the deep of consciousness is awakened and is given form. The cures attributed to the influence of certain medicines, relics and places are the effects of imagination and faith. The curative power is not in the spirit that is in them, it is in the spirit in which they are accepted. "The letter killeth, but the spirit giveth life."

The subjective mind is completely controlled by suggestion, so, whether the object of your faith be true or false, you will get the same results. There is nothing unsound in the theory of medicine or in the claims of priesthood for their relics and holy places. The subjective mind of the patient accepts the suggestion of health conditioned on such states, and as soon as these conditions are met proceeds to realize health. "According to your faith be it done unto you for all things are possible to him that believeth." Confident expectation of a state is the most potent means of bringing it about. The confident expectation of a cure does that which no medical treatment can accomplish.

Failure is always due to an antagonistic auto-suggestion by the patient, arising from objective doubt of the power of medicine or relic, or from doubt of the truth of the theory. Many of us, either from too little emotion or too much intellect, both of which are stumbling blocks in the way or prayer, cannot believe that which our sense deny. To force ourselves to believe will end in greater doubt. To avoid such counter-suggestions the patient should be unaware, objectively, of the suggestions which are made to him. The most effective method of healing or influencing the behavior of others consists in what is known as "the silent or absent treatment." When the subject is unaware, objectively, of the suggestion given him there is no possibility of him setting up an antagonistic belief. It is not necessary that the patient know, objectively, that anything is being done for him. From what is known of the subjective and objective processes of reasoning, it is better that he should not know objectively of that which is being done for him. The more completely the objective mind is kept in ignorance of the suggestion, the better will the subjective mind perform its functions. The subject subconsciously accepts the suggestion and thinks he originates it, proving the truth of Spinoza's dictum that we know not the causes that determine our actions.

The subconscious mind is the universal conductor which the operator modifies with his thoughts and feelings. Visible states are either the vibratory effects of subconscious vibrations within you or they are vibratory causes of the corresponding vibrations within you. A disciplined man never permits them to be causes unless they awaken in him the desirable states of consciousness. With a knowledge of the law of reversibility, the disciplined man transforms his world by imagining and feeling only what is lovely and of good report. The beautiful idea he awakens within himself shall not fail to arouse its affinity in others. He knows the savior of the world is not a man but the manifestation that would save. The sick man's savior is health, the hungry man's is food, the thirsty man's savior is water. He walks in the company of the savior by assuming the feeling of his wish fulfilled. By the law of reversibility, that all transformations of force are reversible, the energy or feeling awakened transforms itself into the state imagined. He never waits four months for the harvest. If in four months the harvest will awaken in him a state of joy, then, inversely, the joy of harvest now will awaken the harvest now. "Now is the acceptable time to give beauty for ashes, joy for mourning, praise for the spirit of heaviness; that they might be called trees of righteousness, the planting of the Lord that he might be glorified."

Chapter IV
Energy & Power

Everyone is amenable to the same psychological laws which govern the ordinary hypnotic subject. He is amenable to control by suggestion. In hypnosis, the objective senses are partly or totally suspended. However, no matter how profoundly the objective senses are locked in hypnosis, the subjective faculties are alert, and the subject recognizes everything that goes on around him. The activity and power of the subjective mind are proportionate to the sleep of the objective mind. Suggestions which appear powerless when presented directly to the objective consciousness are highly efficacious when the subject is in a hypnotic state. The hypnotic state is simply being unaware, objectively. In hypnotism, the conscious mind is put to sleep and the subconscious powers are exposed as to be directly reached by suggestion. It is easy to see from this, providing you accept the truth of mental suggestions, that anyone not objectively aware of you is in a profound hypnotic state relative to you. Therefore "Curse not the king, no not in thy thought; and curse not the rich in the bed-chamber; for a bird of the air shall carry the voice, and that which hath wings shall tell the matter" (Ecc. 10:20). What you sincerely believe as true of another you will awaken within him.

No one need be entranced, in the ordinary manner, to be helped. If the subject is consciously unaware of the suggestion, and if the suggestion is given with conviction and confidently accepted by the operator as true, then you have the ideal setting for a successful prayer. Represent the subject to yourself mentally as though he had already done that which you desire him to do. Mentally speak to him and congratulate him on having done what you want him to do.

Mentally see him in the state you want him to obtain. Within the circle of its action, every word subjectively spoken awakens objectively, what it affirms. Incredulity on the part of the subject is no hindrance when you are in control of your reverie.

Bold assertion by you, while you are in a partly subjective state, awakens what you affirm. Self-confidence on your part and the thorough belief in the truth of your mental assertion are all that is needed to produce results. Visualize the subject and imagine that you hear his voice. This establishes contact with his subjective mind. Then imagine that he is telling you what you want to hear. If you want to send him words of health and wealth, then imagine that he is telling you "I have never felt better and I have never had more," and mentally tell him of your joy in witnessing his good fortune. Imagine that you see and hear his joy.

A mental conversation with the subjective image of another must be in a manner which does not express the slightest doubt as to the truth of what you hear and say. If you have the least idea that you do not believe what you have imagined you have heard and seen, the subject will not comply, for your subjective mind will transmit only your fixed ideas. Only fixed ideas can awaken their vibratory correlates in those toward whom they are directed. In the controlled reverie, ideas must be suggested with the utmost care. If you do not control your imagination in the reverie, your imagination will control you. Whatever you suggest with confidence is law to the subjective mind; it is under obligation to objectify that which you mentally affirm. Not only does the subject ex- ecute the state affirmed but he does it as though the decision had come of itself, or the idea or the idea had originated by him.

Control of the subconscious is dominion over all. Each state obeys one mind's control. Control of the subconscious is accomplished through control of your beliefs, which in turn is the all-potent factor in the visible states. Imagination and faith are the secrets of creation.

Chapter V
Law of Thought Transmission

"He sent his word and healed them, and delivered them from their destructions." He transmitted the consciousness of health and awoke its vibratory correlate in the one toward whom it was directed. He mentally represented the subject to himself in a state of health and imagined he heard the subject confirm it. "For no word of God shall be void of power; therefore hold fast the pattern of healthful words which thou has heard."

To pray successfully you must have clearly defined objectives. You must know what you want before you can ask for it. You must know what you want before you can feel that you have it, and prayer is the feeling of the fulfilled desire. It does not matter what it is you seek in prayer, or where it is, or whom it concerns. You have nothing to do but convince yourself of the truth of that which you desire to see manifested. When you emerge from prayer you no longer seek, for you have—if you have prayed correctly—subconsciously assumed the reality of the state sought, and by the law of reversibility your subconscious must objectify that which it affirms.

You must have a conductor to transmit a force. You may employ a wire, a jet of water, a current of air, a ray of light or any intermediary whatsoever. The principle of the photophone or the transmission of the voice by light will help you to understand thought transmission, or the sending of a word to heal another. There is a strong analogy between a spoken voice and a mental voice. To think is to speak low, to speak is to think aloud. The principle of the photophone is this: A ray of light is reflected by a mirror and projected to a receiver at a distant point. Back of the mirror is a mouthpiece. By speaking into the mouthpiece you cause the mirror to vibrate. A vibrating mirror modifies the light reflected on it. The modified light has your speech to carry, not as speech, but as represented in its mechanical correlate. It reaches the distant station and impinges on a disc within the receiver; it causes the disc to vibrate according to the modification it undergoes — and it reproduces your voice.

"I am the light of the world." I am, the knowledge that I exist, is a light by means of which what passes in my mind is rendered visible. Memory, or my ability to mentally see what is objectively present, proves that my mind is a mirror, so sensitive a mirror that it can reflect a thought. The re-perception of an image in memory in no way differs as a visual act from the perception of my image in a mirror. The same principle of seeing is involved in both.

Your consciousness is the light reflected on the mirror of your mind and projected in space to the one of whom you think. By mentally speaking to the subjective image in your mind you cause the mirror of your mind to vibrate. Your vibrating mind modifies the light of consciousness reflected on it. The modified light of consciousness reaches the one toward whom it is directed and impinges on the mirror of his mind; it causes his mind to vibrate according to the modification it undergoes. Thus, it reproduces in him what was mentally affirmed by you.

Your beliefs, your fixed attitudes of mind, constantly modify your consciousness as it is reflected on the mirror of your mind. Your consciousness, modified by your beliefs, objectifies itself in the conditions of your world. To change your world, you must first change your conception of it. To change a man, you must change your conception of him. You must first believe him to be the man you want him to be and mentally talk to him as though he were. All men are sufficiently sensitive to reproduce your beliefs of them. Therefore, if your word is not reproduced visibly in him toward whom it is sent, the cause is to be found in you, not in the subject. As soon as you believe in the truth of the state affirmed, results follow. Everyone can be transformed; every thought can be transmitted; every thought can be visibly embodied.

Subjective words—subconscious assumptions—awaken what they affirm. "They are living and active and shall not return unto me void, but shall accomplish that which I please, and shall prosper in the thing whereto I sent them." They are endowed with the intelligence pertaining to their mission and will persist until the object of their existence is realized; they persist until they awaken the vibratory correlates of themselves within the one toward whom they are directed, but the moment the object of their creation is accomplished they cease to be. The word spoken subjectively in quiet confidence will always awaken a corresponding state in the one in whom it was spoken; but the moment its task is accomplished it ceases to be, permitting the one in whom the state is realized to remain in the consciousness of the state affirmed or to return to his former state.

Whatever state has your attention holds your life. Therefore, to become attentive to a former state is to return to that condition. "Remember not the former things, neither consider things of old."

Nothing can be added to man, for the whole of creation is already perfected in him. "The kingdom of heaven is within you." "Man can receive nothing, except it be given him from heaven." Heaven is your subconsciousness. Not even a sunburn is given from without. The rays without only awaken corresponding rays within. Were the burning rays not contained within man, all the concentrated rays in the universe could not burn him. Were the tones of health not contained within the consciousness of the one whom they are affirmed, they could not be vibrated by the word which is sent. You do not really give to another—you resurrect that which is asleep within him. "The damsel is not dead, but sleepeth." Death is merely a sleeping and forgetting. Age and decay are the sleep—not death— of youth and health. Recognition of a state vibrates or awakens it.

Distance, as it is cognized by your objective senses, does not exist for the subjective mind. "If I take the wings of the morning, and dwell in the uttermost parts of the sea; even there shall they hand lead me." Time and space are conditions of thought; the imagination can transcend them and move in a psychological time and space. Although physically separated from a place by thou- sands of miles, you can mentally live in the distant place as though it were here. Your imagination can easily transform winter into summer, New York into Florida, and so on. Whether the object of your desire be near or far, results will be the same. Subjectively, the object of your desire is never far off; its intense nearness makes it remote from observation of the senses. It dwells in consciousness, and consciousness is closer than breathing and nearer than hands and feet.

Consciousness is the one and only reality. All phenomena are formed of the same substance vibrating at different rates. Out of consciousness I as man came, and to consciousness I as man return. In consciousness all states exist subjectively, and are awakened to their objective existence by belief. The only thing that prevents us from making a successful subjective impression on one at a great distance, or transforming there into here, is our habit of regarding space as an obstacle.

A friend a thousand miles away is rooted in your consciousness through your fixed ideas of him. To think of him and represent him to yourself inwardly in the state you desire him to be, confident that this subjective image is as true as it were already objectified, awakens in him a corresponding state which he must objectify. The results will be as obvious as the cause was hidden. The subject will express the awakened state within him and remain unaware of the true cause of his action. Your illusion of free will is but ignorance of the causes which make you act. Prayers depend upon your attitude of mind for their success and not upon the attitude of the subject. The subject has no power to resist your controlled subjective ideas of him unless the state affirmed by you to be true of him is a state he is incapable of wishing as true of another. In that case it returns to you, the sender, and will realize itself in you. Provided the idea is acceptable, success depends entirely on the operator not upon the subject who, like compass needles on their pivots, are quite indifferent as to what direction you choose to give them. If your fixed idea is not subjectively accepted by the one toward whom it is directed, it rebounds to you from whom it came. "Who is he that will harm you, if ye be followers of that which is good? I have been young, and now am old; yet have I not seen the righteous forsaken, nor his seed begging bread." "There shall no evil happen to the just." Nothing befalls us that is not of the nature of ourselves.

A person who directs a malicious thought to another will be injured by its rebound if he fails to get subconscious acceptance of the other. "As ye sow, so shall ye reap." Furthermore, what you can wish and believe of another can be wished and believed of you, and you have no power to reject it if the one who desires it for you accepts it as true of you. The only power to reject a subjective word is to be incapable of wishing a similar state of another—to give presupposes the ability to receive. The possibility to impress an idea upon another mind presupposes the ability of that mind to receive that impression. Fools exploit the world; the wise transfigure it. It is the highest wisdom to know that in the living universe there is no destiny other than that created out of imagination of man. There is no influence outside of the mind of man.

"Whatsoever things are lovely, whatsoever are of good report; if there be any virtue and if there be any praise, think on these things." Never accept as true of others what you would not want to be true of you. To awaken a state within another it must first be awake within you. The state you would transmit to another can only be transmitted if it is believed by you. Therefore to give is to receive. You cannot give what you do not have and you have only what you believe. So to believe a state as true of another not only awakens that state within the other but it makes it alive within you. You are what you believe.

"Give and ye shall receive, full measure, pressed down and running over." Giving is simply believing, for what you truly believe of others you will awaken within them. The vibratory state transmitted by your belief persists until it awakens its corresponding vibration in him of whom it is believed. But before it can be transmitted it must first be awake within the transmitter. Whatever is awake within your consciousness, you are. Whether the belief pertains to self or another does not matter, for the believer is defined by the sum total of his beliefs or subconscious assumptions.

"As a man thinketh in his heart"— in the deep subconscious of himself— "so is he." Disregard appearances and subjectively affirm as true that which you wish to be true. This awakens in you the tone of the state affirmed which in turn realizes itself in you and in the one of whom it is affirmed. Give and ye shall receive. Beliefs invariably awaken what they affirm. The world is a mirror wherein everyone sees himself reflected. The objective world reflects the beliefs of the subjective mind.

Some people are self-impressed best by visual images, others by mental sounds and still others by mental actions. The form of mental activity which allows the whole power of your attention to be focused in one chosen direction is the one to cultivate, until you can bring all to play on your objective at the same time.

Should you have difficulty in understanding the terms, "visual images," "mental sounds" and "mental actions," here is an illustration that should make their meanings clear: A imagines he sees a piece of music, knowing nothing at all about musical notations. The impression in his mind is purely visual image. B imagines he sees the same piece, but he can read music and can imagine how it would sound when played on the piano; that imagination is mental sound. C also reads music and is a pianist; as he reads, he imagines himself playing the piece. The imaginary action is mental action.

The visual images, mental sounds and mental actions are creations of your imagination, and though they appear to come from without, they actually come from within yourself. They move as if moved by another but are really launched by your own spirit from the magical store-house of imagination. They are projected into space by the same vibratory law that governs the sending of a voice or picture. Speech and images are projected not as speech or images but as vibratory correlates. Subjective mind vibrates according to the modifications it undergoes by the thought and feelings of the operator. The visible state created is the effect of the subjective vibrations. A feeling is always accompanied by a corresponding vibration, that is, a change in expression or sensation in the operator.

There is no thought or feeling without expression. No matter how emotionless you appear to be if you reflect with any degree of intensity, there is always an execution of slight muscular movements. The eye, though shut, follows the movements of the imaginary objects and the pupil is dilated or contracted according to the brightness or the remoteness of those objects; respiration is accelerated or slowed, according to the course of your thoughts; the muscles contract correspondingly to your mental movements.

This change of vibration persists until it awakens a corresponding vibration in the subject, which vibration then expresses itself in a physical fact. "And the word was made flesh." Energy, as you see in the case of radio, is transmitted and received in a "field," a place where changes in space occur. The field and energy are one and inseparable. The field or subject becomes the embodiment of the word or energy received. The thinker and the thought, the operator and the subject, the energy and the field are one. Were you still enough to hear the sound of your beliefs you would know what is meant by "the music of the spheres." The mental sound you hear in prayer as coming from without is really produced by yourself. Self-observation will reveal this fact. As the music of the spheres is defined as the harmony heard by the gods alone, and is supposed to be produced by the movements of the celestial spheres , so, too, is the harmony you subjectively hear for others heard by you alone is produced by the movements of your thoughts and feelings in the true kingdom or "heaven within you."

Chapter VI
Good Tidings

"How beautiful upon the mountains are the feet of him that bringeth good tidings, that publisheth peace, that bringeth good tidings of good, that pubisheth salvation."

A very effective way to bring good tidings to another is to call before your minds eyes the subjective image of the person you wish to help and have him affirm that which you desired him to do. Mentally hear him tell you he has done it. This awakens within him the vibratory correlate of the state affirmed, which vibration persists until its mission is accomplished. It does not matter what it is you desire to have done, or whom you select to do it. As soon as you subjectively affirm that it is done, results follow. Failure can result only if you fail to accept the truth of your assertion or if the state affirmed would not be desired by the subject for himself or another. In the latter event, the state would realize itself in you, the operator.

The seemingly harmless habit of "talking to yourself" is the most fruitful form of prayer. A mental argument with the subjective image of another is the surest way to pray for an argument. You are asking to be offended by the other when you objectively meet. He is compelled to act in a manner displeasing to you, unless before the meeting you countermand or modify your order by subjectively affirming a change.

Unfortunately, man forgets his subjective arguments, his daily mental conversations with others, and so is at a loss for an explanation of the conflicts and misfortunes of his life. As mental arguments produce conflicts, so happy mental conversations produce corresponding visible states of good tidings. Man creates himself out of his own imagination.

If the state desired is for yourself and you find it difficult to accept as true what your senses deny, call before your mind's eye the subjective image of a friend and have him mentally affirm that you are already that which you desire to be. This establishes in him, without his conscious consent or knowledge, the subconscious assumption that you are that which he mentally affirmed, which assumption, because it is unconsciously assumed, will persist until it fulfills its mission. Its mission is to awaken in you its vibratory correlate, which vibration when awakened in you realizes itself as an objective fact.

Another very effective way to pray for oneself is to use the formula of Job who found that his own captivity was removed as he prayed for his friends. Fix your attention on a friend and have the imaginary voice of your friend tell you that he is, or has that which is comparable to that which you desire to be or have. As you mentally hear and see him, feel the thrill of his good fortune and sincerely wish him well. This awakens in him the corresponding vibration of the state affirmed, which vibration must then objectify itself as a physical fact. You will discover the truth of the statement, "Blessed are the merciful for they shall receive mercy." "The quality of mercy is twice blessed— it blesses him who taketh and him who giveth." The good you subjectively accept as true of others will not only be expressed by them, but a full share will be realized by you.

Transformations are never total. Force A is always transformed into more than a force B. A blow with a hammer produces not only a mechanical concussion, but also heat, electricity, a sound, a magnetic change and so on. The vibratory correlate in the subject is not the entire transformation of the sentiment communicated. The gift transmitted to another is the like the divine measure, pressed down, shaken together and running over, so that after five thousand are fed from the five loaves and two fish, twelve baskets full are left over.

Chapter VII
The Greatest Prayer

Imagination is the beginning of creation. You imagine what you desire, and then you believe it to be true. Every dream could be realized by those self-disciplined enough to believe it. People are what you choose to make them; a man is according to the manner in which you look at him. You must look at him with different eyes before he will objectively change. "Two men looked from prison bars, one saw the mud and the other saw the stars." Centuries ago, Isaiah asked the question; "Who is blind, but my servant, or deaf, as my messenger that I sent?" "Who is blind as he that is perfect, as blind as the Lord's servant?" The perfect man judges not after appearances, but judges righteously. He sees others as he desires them to be; he hears only what he wants to hear. He sees only good in others. In him is no condemnation for he transforms the world with his seeing and hearing.

"The king that sitteth on the throne scattereth the evil with his eye." Sympathy for living things—agreement with human limitations—is not in the consciousness of the king because he has learned to separate their false concepts from their true being. To him poverty is but the sleep of wealth. He does not see caterpillars, but painted butterflies to be; not winter, but summer sleeping; not man in want, but Jesus sleeping. Jesus of Nazareth, who scattered the evil with his eye, is asleep in the imagination of every man, and out of his own imagination must man awaken him by subjectively affirming "I AM Jesus" Then and only then will he see Jesus, for man can only see what is awake in himself. The holy womb is man's imagination. The holy child is that conception of himself which fits Isaiah's definition of perfection. Heed the words of St. Augustine, "Too late have I loved thee, for behold thou were within and it was without that I did seek thee." It is your own consciousness that you must turn as to the only reality. There, and there alone, you awaken that which is asleep. "Though Christ a thousand times in Bethlehem be born, if He is not born of in thee thy soul is still forlorn."

Creation is finished. You call your creation into being by feeling the reality of the state you would call. A mood attracts its affinities but it does not create what it attracts. As sleep is called by feeling "I am sleepy," so, too, is Jesus Christ called by the feeling, "I am Jesus Christ." Man sees only himself. Nothing befalls man that is not the nature of himself. People emerge out of the mass betraying their close affinity to your moods as they are engendered. You meet them seemingly by accident but find they are intimates of your moods. Because your moods continually externalize themselves you could prophesy from your moods, that you, without search, would soon meet certain characters and encounter certain conditions. Therefore call the perfect one into being by living in the feeling, "I am Christ," for Christ is the one concept of self through which can be seen the unveiled realities of eternity.

Our behavior is influenced by our subconscious assumption respecting our own social and intellectual rank and that of the one we are addressing. Let us seek for and evoke the greatest rank, and the noblest of all is that which disrobes man of his morality and clothes him with uncurbed immortal glory. Let us assume the feeling "I am Christ," and our whole behavior will subtly and unconsciously change in accordance with the assumption.

Our subconscious assumptions continually externalize themselves that others may consciously see us as we subconsciously see ourselves, and tell us by their actions what we have subconsciously assumed of ourselves to be. Therefore let us assume the feeling "I AM Christ," until our conscious claim becomes our subconscious assumption that "We all with open face beholding as in a glass the glory of the Lord are changed into the same image from glory to glory." Let God Awake and his enemies be destroyed. There is no greater prayer for man.

CPSIA information can be obtained
at www.ICGtesting.com
Printed in the USA
LVHW032014200223
739963LV00026B/385